# A Critical History and Filmography of Toho's Godzilla Series

SECOND EDITION

# A Critical History and Filmography of Toho's Godzilla Series

## Second Editon

## DAVID KALAT

McFarland & Company, Inc., Publishers
*Jefferson, North Carolina, and London*

LIBRARY OF CONGRESS CATALOGUING-IN-PUBLICATION DATA

Kalat, David, 1970–
A critical history and filmography of
Toho's Godzilla series / David Kalat.—2nd ed.
p.    cm.
Includes bibliographical references and index.

ISBN 978-0-7864-4749-7
illustrated case binding : 50# alkaline paper ∞

1. Godzilla films—History and criticism.    I. Title.
PN1995.9.G63K36    2010        791.43'651—dc22        2010017748

British Library cataloguing data are available

Cover image ©2010 Photodisc

Manufactured in the United States of America

*McFarland & Company, Inc., Publishers
Box 611, Jefferson, North Carolina 28640
www.mcfarlandpub.com*

For Haven and Spencer Lisek,
for reminding me that monsters
can be at least half real.

# Contents

# Preface to the New Edition

When I first started to try to make my way in the world as a professional film historian, I was frustrated and discouraged that—at that moment in time—Godzilla had never received any serious consideration from anyone. The best one could find in terms of critical discussion of this phenomenon of popular culture was dismissive or contemptuous, and often riddled with factual errors and misunderstandings.

I stepped into that breach to try to correct the record. I was not the first in this mission nor was I ever alone—I was consciously following in the footsteps of Stuart Galbraith IV, and reliant on the research published by J.D. Lees in the magazine *G-Fan*. Ed Godzizewski, Steve Ryfle, Guy Mariner Tucker, Robert Biondi, David Milner, Jörg Buttgereit ... these are just some of the names of the researchers and fans from whom I ... stole, I guess you could say.

This underground community of scholars and fans connected the dots to tell a story that otherwise went largely unreported in the Western press, unknown to all but the true believers. They chronicled a pop cultural institution of global reach—one that, at the time I was writing in the mid–1990s, was still treated with ignorance and contempt by the American critical establishment.

In the original 1997 edition of this book I set out to explore the evolving relationship between the United States and Japan, using the world of giant monster movies as a lens through which to filter a larger set of cultural questions. I still stand by that analysis, and I hope this new, expanded 2010 edition improves upon it.

However, that first edition was written at a specific moment in time, both in the life of its author and in the world of Godzillology. I wrote it at a time when few of the movies I covered were commercially available in this country, and so I felt obliged to describe in maddening detail their plots, so as to provide common ground for further discussion. Now all but a very few are readily available on DVD in forms that often pair the unexpurgated Japanese original with the bowlderized American cuts; the few stragglers may well have come out by the time you read this. In any event, I no longer feel that exhaustive plot synopses serve anyone's interests.

By the same token, many films previously unavailable have come my way in the twelve years since the publication of the first edition. Important, seminal works like *Agon the Atomic Dragon*, *Varan the Unbelievable*, *The Invisible Avenger*, *The Submersion of Japan* and others now play a more vital role in the story, thanks quite simply to my ability, at last, to sit down and watch them. Add to that a comprehensive set of Godzilla films as released in Germany, Spain, Italy, and other countries providing new perspectives I was obliged to omit in 1997.

These have bubbled to the surface in the years since, as part of a growing interest in Godzilla that has come out of the closet, as it were. The cadre of fans and researchers who once toiled for personal pleasure on fanzines and websites have become recognized authorities in the field, with actual trade publications in ordinary bookstores and contributions to mainstream journals.

In short, the attitude of the original text had become dated. The impetus for revising the original was not simply to provide coverage for the films made since 1997. The larger goal of this revision has been to reorient the conversation.

Over the years, as the fan press gradually started to grow and cohere into a movement, something of a fan ideology evolved, with its own dogmas about what was and was not acceptable. In the interest of promoting a serious consideration of Godzilla, only a serious Godzilla would do, and so notions of camp comedy were mightily resisted. And since it was the Americanization of the films that represented the most in-your-face lack of respect for the Japanese originals, these too were rejected.

I grew up with the campy Godzilla. I love him. I do not accept that the only way to honor the artistry of the people who made these movies, or to appreciate their role in popular culture, is to reject such an enormous chunk of their appeal. There is silly Godzilla, and serious, and this reinvigorated, revamped, reimagined book celebrates both.

# Introduction

Together, we are about to embark on a sincere and serious analysis of some of the looniest movies ever made. We will bring a scholarly attention to detail to movies in which stunt men wearing rubber monster suits stomp on toy tanks and model trains. We will care, very deeply, about a fire-breathing radioactive mutant dinosaur and his relationship to a moth with a wingspan of a city block. But before we do any of this, I must ask you to understand why—and to do that, I must ask you to accompany me on a brief thought experiment.

First, cast your mind back to the terrorist attacks on New York City and Washington, D.C., on September 11, 2001. Remember the outpouring of anger, hatred, and patriotism that followed those tragedies. Remember the flags, the window signs proclaiming "These colors never run," "God bless America," and "We will never forget." Remember when you first heard of Osama bin Laden, and the way in which he and his Al-Qaeda organization quickly became universal icons of evil and villainy. Think of the myriad ways in which that pivotal moment altered popular culture, and how television programs like *Lost*, *Battlestar Galactica*, and *24* sampled aspects of that real-life horror to explore in richly nuanced fictional contexts.

Now, imagine the same events but with one small but critical difference. Imagine that the attacks of 9/11 did not just wound America, but crippled it.

Imagine the United States was unable to respond militarily, unable even to rebuild itself without outside help—and that such help came from only one source: Al-Qaeda. Imagine that as the dust settled on Ground Zero in New York City, Osama bin Laden came forward and offered to help rebuild, to help care for the injured, to not only make peace but to become America's brother, ally, friend. There would be

but one price for such seeming generosity: The United States would need to admit that it had deserved to be attacked. America had to realize that by its misbehavior it had left Al-Qaeda with no choice, and would now have to redesign its society to be more like them.

If this were to have happened, where would all of that anger, hatred, and patriotism go? All those flags and "God bless America" banners would be impermissibly provocative. The explicit mission of popular culture would be to reorient American society into a newly pro–Al-Qaeda worldview. All the powerful emotions that gushed out in the wake of the 9/11 attacks would not cease to exist if the surrounding political circumstance were changed. Those emotions would still need to be vented, but they could not be vented openly or honestly. In such a case, they would have to emerge in some twisted, mutated form. They would emerge in some kind of disguise.

I do not wish to draw any deeper moral parallels between Japan's experience at the end of World War II and America's experience on 9/11; the differences far outweigh the facile similarities. Nevertheless, I hope that by drawing a purely superficial analogy between them, I can help illustrate what lies at the root of the Godzilla phenomenon.

All citizens, no matter to which country they may belong, go about their daily lives on the assumption that their culture is generally in the right. When conflicts arise with other countries—whether polite diplomatic disagreements or full-blown wars—it is the default position to conclude your homeland is in the right, and the other side is in the wrong. This perspective is of course largely an accident of birth. If my grandfather had been born in Japan, perhaps he would have been a kamikaze pilot; and the Japanese bomber who dropped a bomb (a dud, thank goodness) on his destroyer in the Pacific, had he been born in South Carolina, may have grown up to join the United States Navy. I am not arguing that there is no objective arbiter of morality, or that right and wrong are entirely relative concepts. I merely note that most people's instincts about right and wrong are driven more by national interest than by the loftier principles under which those national self-interests often masquerade.

Japan's condition after World War II thrust its citizens into the painful position of having to reconcile their patriotic beliefs with a new world order that condemned their nation. Throughout the war, military leaders had strafed Japan with propaganda insisting that divine providence guaranteed their triumph; it was now necessary to publicly admit that, no, Hirohito was not actually a god. In order to put the ruined nation back together again, American soldiers and money came to the rescue— meaning that Japan was now accepting help from the very people it had demonized, the very people who had turned its cities into ash. And that help came with a price tag: The new Japan would embrace principles of democracy, capitalism, and equality. Where those American values clashed with traditionally Japanese traditions, the traditions had to be rejected.

In a land where pride and honor were the primary currency of all interactions, everyday life suddenly became a constant exercise in humiliation. Although principles of a free press were now formally enshrined in the constitution (which, it must be noted, was not written by an elected Japanese parliament, but by General Douglas MacArthur, the conqueror himself), openly critiquing this new world was both explicitly and implicitly forbidden. The public needed to process memories of the war, but to do so in ways that did not flagrantly promote the now-discredited ideals of Japanese militarism nor linger on painful thoughts of defeat.

There was also the issue of the nuclear arms race, and how to articulate a principled stance on that.

From the American perspective, the Soviet Union was undeniably an inscrutable and seemingly unstable foe, which had nuclear weapons technology and an avowed intention to destroy everything America valued. Opposing such an enemy through traditional diplomacy was unlikely at best, and opposing it with traditional military force was certainly impossible. The only thing that remained was an ever-escalating nuclear arms program intended to keep the Soviet Union locked in a stalemate. Paradoxically, to preserve peace, America felt it had no choice but to prepare for war—to design machinery capable of destroying the world as a necessary precondition for saving the world from that very fate. And we need not be shy about admitting the additional fact that a growing military-industrial complex was deeply invested in nuclear arms, and stood to gain financially by a booming defense budget. In summary, American policy was firmly committed to nuclear weaponry, and as such was primed to view all opposition to nuclear technology as being, by definition, anti–American.

In Japan, opposition to nuclear proliferation was seen as fundamentally humanistic in principle, a reflexive position any right-thinking person would affirm. The MacArthur-authored constitution did away with the Japanese military, so the country had no significant defense industry of its own. Yet Japan had been on the receiving end of the only atomic bombs ever used on humans. As a growing quorum of Japanese voices organized to protest nuclear testing, the American response was typical: Those ungrateful Japanese are being anti–American! The result was to turn those protesters into genuinely anti–American groups. In 1954, anti–American sentiment was starting to break through openly in the press and in public, in ways that threatened the still-fragile relationship between former enemies.

It was into this context that the first Godzilla movie appeared. Images designed to mimic newsreel footage of the war gave audiences a cathartic thrill but painted Japan as an innocent victim of forces outside its control. Nuclear horror rains down on Tokyo, but without America playing any role in the proceedings or even being mentioned once. Godzilla, as a symbol of the Bomb, gave audiences a mechanism by which to rage against the damage done to their country, to decry the arms race, to see their nation as both victim and savior, without transgressing the many taboos that postwar life had imposed on such discussions.

It strains no one's credulity to claim that the original 1954 Godzilla movie is an allegory about Japan's experience with nuclear horror. It is not subtext, it is plainly text, with nothing sub- about it. Thinly disguised images of and openly direct references to the firebombings of Tokyo, the atomic bombings of Hiroshima and Nagasaki, and the Lucky Dragon incident are spread liberally throughout the film. Even the first Godzilla sequel, hastily made and with no ambition higher than to quickly cash in, displays enough seriousness of purpose to merit equally serious consideration as another postwar allegory.

But these are not Godzilla, not as we know him today. They are but the birth of a pop cultural figure that shed his darkly serious pallor in favor of family-friendly thrills. Godzilla may have originated in austere political metaphor, but he was popularized as a superhero. He dances happy jigs, imitates rock stars, acts like a wrestler, talks with his pals, sometimes even flies—all while saving the Earth from such menaces as a monster made of living pollution, a ginormous bionic cockroach, and even a giant killer rose.

To pretend that Godzilla movies did not veer into absurdity and rampant silliness is futile. The filmmakers admitted it themselves; special effects master Eiji Tsuburaya and screenwriter Shinichi Sekizawa were the chief architects of this change in direction. That it happened is not in doubt. What it means, however, is a matter of debate. It is the purpose of this book to engage this debate. In order to explore the root causes and cultural significance of Godzilla absurdity, it is necessary to take these movies seriously. All of them.

During the middle stretch of the 20th century, when these movies were at their creative and commercial peak, American attitudes towards Japan were still tainted by wartime prejudices. To the extent that Japan had been transformed from an enemy into a friend, Americans still viewed their culture with suspicion, or disrespect. Japanese consumer goods were often cheaply made and unreliable—why would cultural products like movies exhibit any greater care than, say, clothes that fell apart when washed, or electronics that broke easily? As American critics reviewed the special effects extravaganzas from Toho and other Japanese studios in the 1960s, it was from a foregone conclusion that such movies represented the worst aspects of commercial filmmaking, and the worst in technical quality as well.

Many of the things American audiences laughed at in Godzilla movies, however, were not the work of the Japanese producers, but were alterations added by American distributors. Americans recut the films, adding new footage in some cases and scratchy stock footage in others. Sometimes they replaced the original music, changed the stories and altered character motivations, resulting in confusing and illogical plots unlike the Japanese originals. Little wonder, then, American reviewers deride the results.

One of the most obvious points of ridicule for American audiences is the dubbing. This is a catch-22, since few Americans go see subtitled movies. Although subtitled versions of the Godzilla films are preferred among aficionados, for mainstream distribution there was no option but that distributors dub the dialogue.

For dubbing to be reasonably unobtrusive, it is important that the spoken words match as closely as possible the onscreen actors' mouths. The extreme differences between English and Japanese makes this, at best, an extreme challenge. The lip movements involved in speaking Japanese are so different from the typical sounds and speech patterns of English, creating a script that captures the meaning of the original dialogue and also manages to stay in synch with the actors asks the impossible. Imagine a ventriloquist who is trying gamely to maintain his act and keep his comedy banter in synch with a dummy whose lip movements are being generated by a heckler in the audience. No matter how good a job he does, it will never be perfect, and rarely be satisfactory.

For Hollywood's great stars, such as Clint

Eastwood, Bela Lugosi, John Wayne, Marilyn Monroe, and Kathleen Turner, their voices are among their most distinctive characteristics. Would *Casablanca* be as satisfying if Humphrey Bogart, Ingrid Bergman, and Peter Lorre's voices were dubbed by unknown, possibly amateur, actors? Would *Star Wars* be as spectacular a blockbuster if the music were replaced, the special effects re-edited, the story changed to remove subplots, and if the characters spoke with squeaky cartoon-like voices? Would it then be fair to evaluate George Lucas' skill by viewing only this bastardized version? Given that the dubbing was not supervised by the original filmmakers, using that attribute as a target for scorn is a bit like making fun of a movie because the theater you saw it in was in decrepit condition. It might be true, but it is irrelevant.

As the sixties gave way to the seventies, changes in the film industry on both sides of the ocean could be seen in the way these films were made and distributed. Where American distributors once marketed science fiction and fantasy films to all-ages crowds at all venues, the 1970s found such fare increasingly relegated to teenage crowds at drive-ins. Instead of the relatively expensive investment in extensive Americanization of Japanese imports, the often fly-by-night outfits that brought over Godzilla's latter films opted to dump them into drive-ins and late-night TV with nothing but cheapjack English dubbing inexpertly executed. The economic pressure that led American distributors to curtail their filtering efforts hit Japanese producers even harder: The 1970s were for Japanese cinema a time of great hardship and frugality from which few emerged unscathed. Inevitably, Godzilla movies made during that period declined in quality. Where the filmmakers at Toho had launched their flagship series as a cutting edge work, it wound down the decade merely cutting corners.

It is true that over the course of many years and many sequels, the meat of that 1954 allegory was greatly diminished, but never altogether abandoned. Even in the silliest and most childish of the Godzilla sequels, there remains an irreducible element whose presence became increasingly conspicuous. Time and again, Godzilla and his monstrous foes would wade into Japan and tear its cities apart—time and again, the imagery of World War II–era devastation would be invoked for a generation increasingly removed from the original context. On into the 21st century, Japanese audiences continued to derive some perverse kick out of watching their country destroyed. Even diluted, some part of that original allegory continued to serve a meaningful social function.

When I wrote the first edition of this book, it was all but impossible to find a serious film critic willing to accord any of these movies even the most grudging respect. Reviewers routinely approached the Godzilla movies expecting to find little of value. In fact, I have many books on science fiction films that perpetuate inaccurate plot summaries of Godzilla movies, showing how often writers merely quote one another without even viewing the films for themselves.

On closer examination, many of these books were wrong on basic facts. If the facts themselves are untrustworthy, why trust the author's opinions? For that matter, how far are those opinions influenced by cultural biases? Why make jokes about how alien invaders in *Destroy All Monsters* happen to look Japanese when only one chapter earlier the same author praises *The Day the Earth Stood Still*, in which an alien visitor just happens to look and talk like an American? Why ridicule the Japanese use of actors in rubber suits to depict monsters when the same technique receives compliments in the British-made film *Gorgo*? Why argue that modern audiences need to allow for the sense of fantasy and whimsy that underscores the original *King Kong* but not make the same justification for the lightheartedness of *Mothra*?

At the heart of this attitude is the belief, the ingrained prejudice, that films can be either art or commerce, but rarely both. In other words, an art film is made by artists whose only motivation is to express something meaningful and/or beautiful, while popular movies reflect only base commercial concerns.

Although this prejudice pervades much of film criticism, both in America and in Japan, it does not reflect the reality of the film industry. In practice, "art films" are made with commercial expectations, even if the intended audience is smaller than that for mass-marketed releases. By the same token, the makers of popular movies feel the same creative motivations as their art-house peers.

Nonetheless, critics employ different words to maintain this arbitrary distinction: *Kagemusha* is a film, *Godzilla* is only a movie. It is no small irony that one man played a prominent role in both, and that the Kurosawa films and Godzilla movies shared the same studio, cast, and technicians.

In 1980, Kurosawa sought financing for his comeback film *Kagemusha*. Francis Ford Coppola and George Lucas, both longtime fans of the Master's, talked 20th Century–Fox into coproducing the picture. With Fox's financial involvement secured, Toho Studios, Japan's largest and most powerful movie company, agreed to invest $5 million in the project, the largest sum ever spent on a Japanese movie at the time. Kurosawa found a natural partner in Toho, as the studio had previously produced most of his best-known works. Tomoyuki Tanaka oversaw the project as producer.[1]

Kurosawa received considerable help from a longtime friend, Ishiro Honda, who served as Kurosawa's "creative consultant" for many of his later films, until Honda's death in 1993. As creative consultant and assistant director, Honda co-wrote Kurosawa's last five films (*Kagemusha* through *Madadayo*), directed most or all of the location footage, and co-directed in the studio.[2]

Honda's work with Kurosawa, however, was eclipsed by the international fame and recognition he earned on his own as a director. Some of Honda's better known works include: *Godzilla, Half Human, Rodan, The Mysterians, The H-Man, Varan the Unbelievable, Battle in Outer Space, The Human Vapor, Mothra, Gorath, King Kong vs. Godzilla, Matango: Attack of the Mushroom People, Mothra vs. Godzilla, Dogora the Space Monster, Ghidrah, The Three-Headed Monster, Frankenstein Conquers the World, Invasion of Astro-Monster, War of the Gargantuas, King Kong Escapes, Destroy*

*All Monsters, Latitude Zero, Space Amoeba*, and *Terror of Mechagodzilla*, all produced by *Kagemusha*'s producer Tomoyuki Tanaka.

That Honda would play a prominent role in Japan's two most famous film exports, the prestigious Kurosawa films and the notorious Godzilla movies, might at first glance seem an odd contradiction. For many in the American press, the contradiction could not be reconciled. One book on Japanese cinema split Honda into two men: Since Japanese names are written in kanji characters and can be translated in a variety of ways, the author translated the name as "Ichiro Honda" for Kurosawa's films and "Inoshiro Honda" for the Godzilla movies. Evidently the author could not believe that the same man could have done both.

Ishiro Honda defined the genre of Japanese monster movies (the Japanese term is *kaiju eiga*, literally *monster movies*). He was an artist, and his friend Akira Kurosawa respected that. Starring in such pictures over the years were Takashi Shimura, Minoru Chiaki, Akira Kubo, and Yoshio Tsuchiya—actors who also worked for Kurosawa. When these actors appeared in a Kurosawa film, they received international acclaim. When the same cast appeared in a monster movie, critics dismissed them with snide remarks, or ignored them altogether. When Yoshio Tsuchiya got a starring role in *The Human Vapor*, the actor who had played in *The Seven Samurai* and *Yojimbo* rated nothing better than an advertisement blandly crediting, "A cast of international players," while the American edition of that film deleted cast and crew credits altogether.

Most of Toho's *kaiju eiga* boast musical scores by Akira Ifukube, one of Japan's most respected classical composers. Others were scored by the internationally renowned Masaru Sato, who was also responsible for most of Kurosawa's scores. The special effects came from Eiji Tsuburaya, a gifted special effects artist who, working with vastly smaller budgets and fewer resources than his American counterparts, created effective and impressive images that earned the Godzilla series fans around the world.

It is an article of faith among American reviewers that the guy-in-a-rubber-suit technique cannot produce impressive visuals (though it didn't stop Rick Baker from winning the 1976 Academy Award for his suitmation effects in Dino De Laurentiis' *King Kong*). Although less expensive than stop-motion animation or digital effects, the suitmation process is neither easy nor cheap. When done well, as it often is in the Godzilla series, the results can be quite breathtaking.

That is not to say the effects look "realistic," but realism was not the point. American audiences conditioned to expect realism conclude that anything short of that goal must be a mistake. By contrast, Japanese art often values beauty, poetry, or fantasy above realism.

The director of special effects for the Godzilla movies of the 1990s, Koichi Kawakita, noted how Americans view the Godzilla movies differently than Japanese audiences: "I'm sure there are a lot of Americans who don't even know Godzilla films are Japanese."[3] In the course of researching this book, I discovered that Mr. Kawakita is wrong. I have read many film critics and film historians passing harsh judgment on both the state of Japanese filmmaking *and* the overall quality of Japanese culture. Their stinging criticism seems borne not just from a dislike of Godzilla and Company, but also from a larger prejudice.

I do not wish to accuse anyone of racism, certainly not over something as trivial as a monster movie. Nevertheless, I am left speechless by reviewers who spend one page deriding Japanese productions for man-in-a-suit-monsters but then on the next page express admiration for Western films using the same technique. I have read countless apologists for some of the worst science fiction films ever made (by such *auteurs* as Jerry Warren and Bert I. Gordon) that just happen to be American productions, while Japanese imports of extremely high quality receive ridicule and contempt. The sheer volume of anti–Japanese sentiment I have found while researching this topic proves that Mr. Kawakita is sadly mistaken.

On a different level, however, he is right on target. While Americans may be aware that Godzilla is a Japanese creation, many do not fully understand what this means. Popular culture is an expression of the values, attitudes, and heritage of a country. As a part of Japanese pop culture, Godzilla movies can give Westerners a look into Japanese culture. American viewers who watch Godzilla movies from an American perspective, however, miss or misunderstand elements that are uniquely Japanese. While Godzilla has become an internationally popular icon, his roots are Japanese, and he must be understood within that context.

The enduring success of Godzilla was an accident, not a deliberate calculation on the part of Honda, Tsuburaya, and the rest. Godzilla lovers to this day still wonder precisely what attracts them. Part of the appeal is the surprising sophistication in what seems at first glance to be simple-minded Saturday matinee fare. In the wreckage left in the wake of this awesome beast lies the tattered remains of human hubris, a moral lesson left smoldering in the ruins. As series producer Tomoyuki Tanaka put it, "As long as the arrogance of human beings exists, Godzilla will survive."

# A Note on the Text

This book is divided into five parts, each of which discusses a distinct era in the history of Godzilla movies. Real life, though, does not break up into narratives quite so neatly. To discuss how the series evolved over the course of a half-century, I had to confront the fact that these films appeared in America in a different order than in Japan, forcing me to choose between two competing chronologies. I elected to cover the films in the order of their Japanese releases, since that corresponded best with the historical development I hoped to address.

Choosing which titles by which to refer to the films, however, posed a stickier dilemma. Many are known by multiple titles. *Ebirah, Horror of the Deep* and *Godzilla vs. the Sea Monster* are the same picture, but there are three different films bearing the title *Godzilla vs. Mechagodzilla*. Using the Japanese language titles did not improve matters, as the casual reader would find it a challenge to remember the difference between *All Kaiju Daishingeki* and *Kaiju Shoshingeki*, although in content those two films are as different from one another as possible. Furthermore, many of the movies were reissued in Japan in edited forms in the late sixties and early seventies under very different Japanese titles.

In the original edition of this book, I used the original American release titles. At the time of that publication, the majority of the films in discussion were unavailable through legitimate commercial sources, and the American release titles seemed the most likely ones by which access to the films would come for the average reader. In the years since that publication, this situation has changed. Not only are nearly all of the films now readily available in a variety of home video formats and media, but Toho Studios has demanded that U.S. licensors standardize the titles of all of its monster films. In several cases, these newly standardized titles differ from the ones I used in the original text. For the purposes of clarity, I have changed these references to be in accord with Toho's standards. Alternate titles are listed in the credits and discussed in the body of the text where relevant.

On a related subject, Japanese names are written in characters that have multiple possible pronunciations and lack standard English spellings. Most of the American versions of the movies discussed in this book credit "Inoshiro Honda" as director. It has been well documented that Honda preferred the pronunciation "Ishiro," and so that spelling has been used here. In the case of many of the lesser known individuals, their names have rarely been printed at all in English language prints and there is no documentation as to their preferred renderings. For example, the cinematographer credited in this book as "Motoyoshi Tomioka" is known in other sources as Mototake, Mototaka, and Motonari Tomioka. Which of these names he would be preferred to be known as, I simply do not know. To further complicate matters, one of the actors who has played Godzilla, Kenpachiro Satsuma, used to work under the name Kengo Nakayama, while writer Takashi Kimura also used the pen name Kaoru Mabuchi. I have attempted to standardize the spellings of these names, but I cannot promise that errors or discrepancies have been fully expunged.

For any errors in the credit lists or elsewhere, I take full responsibility. For anything accurate, however, I cannot give enough praise to the research done by Stuart Galbraith IV, Steve Ryfle, Guy Mariner Tucker, R. M. Hayes, David Milner, Horacio Higuchi, and Ed Godziszewski from whom I have borrowed extensively.

# Part One

# King Kong vs. Godzilla
# (1954–1963)

As Japan confronted the real-life consequences of nuclear bombings, a team of young and ambitious filmmakers came together in the service of an unprecedented project: the creation of a Japanese monster movie. Producer Tomoyuki Tanaka, director Ishiro Honda, and special effects director Eiji Tsuburaya, buttressed by a brilliant composer and a roster of talented and respected actors, inaugurated a cycle of films that would perpetuate itself to this day. While the full artistic merits of these movies would often go unacknowledged by American audiences, obscured by cultural prejudices and a different set of expectations for genre pictures, Godzilla films would become increasingly spectacular in their native home. The arrival of a satirically minded and inventive storyteller named Shinichi Sekizawa gave new fire to the enterprise, and helped turn Japanese monster movies into their own genre, *kaiju eiga*.

# Chapter 1

# G for Giant

*The thesis was very simple. What if a dinosaur sleeping in the Southern Hemisphere had been awakened and transformed into a giant by the bomb? What if it attacked Tokyo?*
— Tomoyuki Tanaka[1]

There are some films that are so explosively original and groundbreaking that they unleash a torrent of progeny and imitators, and in so doing lay claim to starting a new genre, or sub-genre. *King Kong* was such a film, but it did this only at a considerable remove. A good twenty years elapsed before imitators started to appear, and another ten years after that before *Kong*-like pictures became common.

In hindsight it is easy to locate why *King Kong* did not sire a host of successors right off the pitch. The extraordinarily specialized skill set of the technicians responsible for creating Kong and executing the stop-motion animation process required a staggering investment of time and money. The thinking behind bandwagon-jumpers and knock-offs is to reduce the inherent risk of film production. That logic is incompatible with increasing one's risk by investing vast sums in painstakingly meticulous special effects work.

Not right away, but eventually, the audience that sat enthralled in theaters watching *King Kong* in 1933 would grow up, and some of the youths inspired by that experience would take their places in the film industry, ready to pay homage with their own contributions. In 1952, just twenty years shy of its original run, *King Kong* was reissued to theaters by RKO. Television had not yet established itself as a serious force in people's lives, and it was long before any thing like the video industry existed to allow individual audience members to access movies at will. In those days, if you wanted to see a movie, you had to see it in a theater. If the film was not playing, there was no other option. The owners of *King Kong* were sitting on a property that had grown in value. Those once-awestruck kids had now grown up and harbored an intense nostalgic urge to revisit this beloved film, while a new generation of viewers had grown up hearing tales of this legendary film but had never seen it for themselves.

The reissued *Kong* not only bested the returns of its original pass, but finished as one of the biggest box office draws of 1952. If it had been painful for producers to pass up the opportunity to exploit such success in 1933, it was nigh impossible to do so now — and a new generation of *Kong*-inspired filmmakers was now available as a ready talent pool.

Consider for example Ray Harryhausen. He had studied the stop-motion technique under Willis O'Brien and in 1953 established himself in the field with *The Beast from 20,000 Fathoms*. In the film, a nuclear test at the North Pole revives a long-dormant prehistoric creature, a fictional dinosaur called a rhedosaurus, which then attacks New York. Eventually, the scientists and the military manage to kill the marauder by firing a radioactive isotope into a wound in its neck. Adapted from a short story by renowned science fiction author Ray Bradbury (himself a "*Kong* baby" come of age), *Beast* was a platform for spectacular effects that demonstrated how the field had matured in just twenty years.[2] *The Beast from 20,000 Fathoms* was one of the biggest moneymakers of 1953, earning back nearly five million dollars for Warner Brothers' investment of $400,000.[3]

It was the first of numerous new monster-on-the-loose thrillers, many with Cold War nuclear themes. With the exception of the usually prestigious Harryhausen films, most of the monster movies that started to flood into American theaters were low-budget and low ambition, with crude special effects, lazy scripting, and rushed filmmaking the rules of the game.[4]

On the other side of the world, *King Kong*'s reach extended even there and triggered a Japanese trend of monster movies. The cruel irony is how these lavishly appointed and genuinely well-made Japanese films came to be viewed in the West with such a prejudiced eye. But even if it did not get critical respect, the Japanese monster boom was big business. Toho Studios worked hard, paid its staff modestly, operated like a production line, and made popular products that dominated the market.

Eiji Tsuburaya, like Ray Bradbury and Ray Harryhausen, was enthralled as a young man when *King Kong* hit screens in the thirties, and it drove him into the career of special effects. Like so many of the individuals associated with Godzilla over the years, he started off training for a completely different career. Tsuburaya went to flight school, and then studied electrical engineering. And he put that training to use, oddly enough, as a screenwriter at what would become Kokatsu studios. It was there, during the silent movie era, that he started to learn the craft of special effects.

Before that career blossomed, he was drafted into the Imperial Army and served from 1921 to 1923. Returning to civilian life, Tsuburaya joined Shochiku in their art department in the late 1920s. There he befriended Akira Watanabe, the designer with whom he would work on Toho's special effects extravaganzas four decades later. Tsuburaya soon became one of Nikkatsu Studio's more acclaimed cinematographers. With his background in engineering, he was wont to fashion his own equipment and jerry-rig devices to achieve special pictorial effects impossible otherwise. His colleagues nicknamed him "Smoke," but smoke-pots and atmospheric effects were but tools in a wider arsenal, and he aspired to improve upon the still-primitive art of special effects, when he saw a film that shattered him. He acquired a print of *King Kong* for his own personal use,

and spent his nights examining it frame by frame, to reverse-engineer its secrets. He approached his employers at the studio and implored them to authorize a full-scale attempt to develop the same techniques. In the rigid hierarchy of the Japanese film industry, Tsuburaya was but a lowly cameraman, despite his considerable skills, and the executives could not imagine he had any business advice worth their attention. Conventional wisdom in the Japanese industry held that trick effects were just that — tricks, cheating, something dishonest. So, his dreams of a Japanese *King Kong* would remain a hobby.[5]

Toho Studios came into being in 1937 when a railroad magnate with a desire to be in the picture business orchestrated a merger of several smaller firms that, once fused, formed a formidable movie outfit. With an official mandate of modernization and progress, the Toho board sought out Tsuburaya to head up their technical division.[6] During the war years, Tsuburaya's special talents came into demand on propaganda films, and after the war ended he was so closely associated with wartime propaganda that he was virtually blacklisted. His skill at recreating battles with miniatures was such that his miniatures depicting the attack on Pearl Harbor convinced the American occupying forces that they were watching documentary films shot by Zero pilots.[7]

In 1952, Tsuburaya was seconded to producer Tomoyuki Tanaka on a seminal drama called *Farewell Rabaul*—"seminal" because although the movie itself is not well-remembered, it united in one production Tanaka, Tsuburaya, director Ishiro Honda, and actor Akihiko Hirata. In other words, the production team that two years later would launch Godzilla.

Tanaka would go on to become the most prolific producer of fantasy entertainment in cinema history. A business major who served a stint as a theater director, he joined the newborn Toho movie studio in 1940. Like Tsuburaya, he was another figure in the tale whose life took some unexpected turns along the way. Promoted to producer, Tanaka oversaw films by the internationally acclaimed director Akira

Kurosawa, including such classics as *Yojimbo* (1961) and *Sanjuro* (1962).[8] In 1954, Tanaka was put in charge of an intended Japanese-Indonesian co-production, *Beyond the Glory*, planned as Toho's premier big-budget release for the year. However, the Indonesian government, as part of a larger diplomatic squabble against their former occupier, denied visas to the Japanese stars Ryo Ikebe and Toshiko Yamaguchi. Tanaka had to shelve *Beyond the Glory* and confront a significant gap in Toho's release schedule. He needed a blockbuster film, and fast.[9]

According to the stories Tanaka would tell over the next several decades, it was on the plane ride back to Tokyo that he began thinking about combining modern fears about radiation with a giant monster movie along the lines of *King Kong*.[10]

Many science fiction films in the fifties revolved around the fear of radiation. Among American releases, one can find monsters mutated by radiation in *Monster from the Ocean Floor*, *Them!*, *It Came from Beneath the Sea*, *Bride of the Monster*, *The Amazing Colossal Man*, *Attack of the Crab Monsters*, *The Monster that Challenged the World*, *Attack of the 50 Foot Woman*, *Monster From Green Hell*, *Monster on the Campus*, *The Alligator People*, *The Giant Behemoth*, *The Hideous Sun Demon* ... the list goes on and on. Surely the use of atomic radiation in these and other films reflects some of the society's concern with this dangerous new age and the terrors science could unleash upon the world.

However, as Bill Warren points out in his two-volume set *Keep Watching the Skies!*, the use of radiation in fifties science fiction films was primarily a gimmick.[11] Electricity, radar, satellites and gland transplants were similar gimmicks in other eras. A 1930s mad doctor flick with a monster created by electricity strongly resembles a 1950s radiation monster flick with a giant creature spawned by radiation exposure. There is a danger in reading too much into the frequent use of atomic science in such films; instead of reflecting a pervasive social fear, it may simply reflect lazy scripting.

In Japan, though, the case was different.

Only the Japanese have directly experienced the horrors of nuclear war, and their perspective as victims of the atomic age carries a deeper significance. The Japanese did not develop or test nuclear weapons, and therefore hold no responsibility for this act of hubris. Even with radioactivity as a mere gimmick, American movie monsters can be seen as some kind of reaction to the bomb. In a Japanese context, the monster is less a reaction *to* the bomb than a symbol *of* the bomb.

Tanaka sought out science fiction author Shigeru Kayama, a novelist whose recent publications included tales about mutant sea creatures, and as such the ideal person to develop Tanaka's notion into a workable scenario. In just three weeks, Kayama crafted an outline which was, perhaps unsurprisingly, closely modeled after *The Beast from 20,000 Fathoms*, even using a similar title, *Daikaiju No Kaitei Niman Maru* ("Big Monster from 20,000 Miles Beneath the Sea"). Storyboards for the film even mimicked the design of Ray Harryhausen's "rhedosaurus" monster.[12] The similarities to *The Beast from 20,000 Fathoms* led Harryhausen to harbor a personal grudge against Toho's Godzilla series for decades thereafter, thinking that they had won commercial success only by stealing from his film.[13]

Kayama's story outline, using a monster octopus proposed by Eiji Tsuburaya as the menace, won approval from Toho's impressed executives. By the summer of 1954, production on the film began in earnest. The title *Daikaiju No Kaitei Niman Maru* had been abandoned by this point, replaced by a generic *G* for "Giant." Exactly how the name for the monster was decided is a matter of some dispute. Tomoyuki Tanaka claims that he borrowed the nickname of a burly Toho stagehand.[14] Although a TV news crew claimed to have found this very technician in 2000, Tanaka's story has the strong whiff of apocryphal legend-making about it. Most of the surviving personnel on the film instead recall a studio-wide contest for thinking up a monster name.[15]

By all accounts, however, the name was a fusion of the English word "gorilla" with the Japanese word *kujira*, for whale. The name is comprised of three Japanese characters, which when transliterated into English letters by today's standards would produce *go-ji-ra*. Pronouncing that word in English, though, is a whole different problem from writing it — and since the "ji" syllable would actually sound like "dzi," and Japanese makes no differentiation between "l" and "r" sounds, the word written as *gojira* would end up sounding like go-dzi-la.

While both Tanaka and Tsuburaya were looking forward to making a monster movie in the American mold, director Honda approached the project from a different perspective. Honda, born in 1911, studied art at Nihon University. In 1933, he joined Photo Chemical Laboratory (PCL) studios, which would later become the Toho Studio, one of Japan's five foremost movie companies.[16] Honda left PCL temporarily when he was called away to war in China in 1938, the first of three times he was drafted to the Imperial Army.[17]

Returning in 1946, he found his close friend and neighbor Akira Kurosawa recently promoted to director.[18] Honda began his film career as an assistant director to Kurosawa on such films as *Stray Dog* (1949).[19] In his book *Something Like An Autobiography*, Kurosawa acknowledges Honda's role:

> I had Honda do mainly second-unit shooting. Every day I told him what I wanted and he would go out into the ruins of postwar Tokyo to film it. There are few men as honest and reliable as Honda. He faithfully brought back exactly the footage I requested, so almost everything he shot was used in the final cut of the film. I'm often told that I captured the atmosphere of postwar Japan very well in *Stray Dog*, and if so I owe a great deal of that success to Honda.[20]

Honda's wartime experiences left an enduring psychological scar and a lasting pacifist streak, which would later inform his directorial style. While on furlough from the army, he survived the firebombings of Tokyo. Later, as a prisoner of war in China, he heard about the atomic bombings of Hiroshima and Nagasaki. Visiting Hiroshima in 1946, he became particularly fascinated with nuclear energy, a force so profoundly powerful yet also invisible.[21] Honda felt compelled to translate the horrors of

modern war into a film. "The number one question concerning [*Gojira*] was the fear connected to what was then known as the atomic bomb, in the original film," Honda explained in an interview in 1991. "At the time, I think there was an ability to grasp 'a thing of absolute terror,' as Shigeru Kayama himself called it. When I directed that film, in terms of society at the time, it was a surprising movie with all its special effects but, actually, when I returned from the war and passed through Hiroshima, there was a heavy atmosphere — a fear the Earth was already coming to an end. That became my basis."[22]

Shigeru Kayama had only provided a story outline; it would be up to Honda and his co-writer Takeo Murata to turn that scenario into an actual screenplay.[23] They improved the characterization of the humans and decreased the obvious animalism of Godzilla, making the creature more of a true monster. Also dropped from Kayama's story were obvious "lifts" from *The Beast from 20,000 Fathoms*, such as Godzilla's assault on a lighthouse, and other overly familiar horror-movie conventions. In all, Honda and Murata gave the script its emotional intensity, which greatly helped to elevate the film above the standard monster-on-the-loose scenario.[24]

One of Honda's script embellishments was to give the monster the ability to emit radiation from its mouth, like a fire-breathing dragon. It was a simple idea, born of the desire to make radiation visible, yet became a defining trademark for Toho's monster icon.

While American monster films used radiation as a narrative device to get the monster up and running around, Honda saw his monster as a narrative device to directly confront the terror of the nuclear age. This intelligent, sensitive approach gave Toho's *Gojira* an uncommon depth. Honda's wartime experiences influenced his filmmaking on many levels. One of his associates once said of Honda that "when he shot scenes of people being threatened by Godzilla, he would have recalled the air attacks he had experienced."[25]

In the spirit of this deadly-serious approach to the film, Honda cast his key roles very carefully. In Kayama's original story, there was no love triangle. The character of Dr. Yamane was an enigmatic recluse, something of a mad scientist, whose eccentric dress and gothic castle seemed ideas on loan from old Universal horror pictures. Honda did not like how Yamane was portrayed, as if his scientific brilliance naturally made him a suspicious character of uncertain allegiance. For Honda, scientists were the true heroes, whose values of rational thought trumped petty nationalism. He rewrote the Yamane role, and as a marker of the importance he placed in the role, cast Takashi Shimura in the part.[26]

Shimura was at the time one of Japan's finest actors and part of Kurosawa's repertory. His presence in the film was a clear signal of artistic ambition and serious intent. Shimura starred in many of Kurosawa's films, including *Rashomon* (1950), *The Seven Samurai* (1954) and *Throne of Blood* (1957). *The New York Times*, reviewing Kurosawa's *Ikiru* (1952), called Shimura "the best actor in the world." But when reviewing the eventual American release of *Gojira* (as *Godzilla, King of the Monsters!*), the very same paper declared, "[N]ot one of [them] can act."[27]

Across the globe, "the best actor in the world" would reprise his role in the next installment, as well as return in other roles in other Godzilla films—one of many Kurosawa players to appear in the series. Toho's monster films were flashy, big-budget spectacles, and Japan's top actors gladly took roles in them. American science fiction films, by stark contrast, were frequently looked down upon as second-class, and rarely attracted high profile stars.[28]

Some of Toho's A-list performers cut their teeth on monster pictures. The ostensible leading man of *Gojira*, and one of Toho's matinee idols of the coming decade, was Akira Takarada. He had by that point been working in movies for only a year, with just two movies under his belt. He would ascend quickly to star status, a sort of Japanese Cary Grant, with a specialty in light comedy. In later years he would also perform on stage in theatrical productions of *Annie Get Your Gun* and a Japanese-

language version of *Gone With the Wind* (he played Rhett).[29] Another of Toho's soon-to-be stars, Kenji Sahara, made his film debut in *Gojira* in a brief wordless cameo. He was a former model who had joined Toho as a lowly extra and worked his way into star roles, appearing in thirty classic science fiction films of the era, and more than a hundred movies in all.[30]

Akihiko Hirata, veteran of Honda's war melodrama *Farewell Rabaul* earlier that year, was a trained lawyer who had joined Toho as an assistant director before moving to a more successful career as an actor. Honda asked Hirata to screen test for the role of Ogata, the romantic lead in *Gojira*. Shortly before filming was to begin, Honda decided on the basis of their respective screen tests to switch Hirata with Akira Takarada, originally cast as the reclusive scientist Dr. Serizawa. Both men would continue to star in the Godzilla series and other special effects–based pictures for Toho over the decades to come. Takarada returned frequently to the series, and even appeared in 2004's *Godzilla: Final Wars*. Hirata intended to return in *Godzilla 1985*, but died of cancer in July 1984.[31]

The true star of the film, of course, was Godzilla himself, portrayed by both Haruo Nakajima and Katsumi Tezuka. Nakajima, a veteran stuntman with such auspicious credits as *Seven Samurai* to his name, would continue alone in the part through 1972.[32] Tezuka, a senior member of the studio's stunt staff, leveraged his seniority to get onto the exciting assignment. In the end, he found his older body no match for the rigors of the job, and few of Tezuka's scenes were deemed usable in the final cut.[33]

In order to prepare himself to play the role of a giant monster, Nakajima was invited to review Eiji Tsuburaya's personal copy of *King Kong*.[34] Then, lacking real-life monsters to use as role models, Nakajima visited Ueno Zoo to study the behavior of bears.[35] While neither man received screen credit for playing Godzilla, they do both appear outside the monster suit in cameos during the course of the film: Nakajima appears as the technician pulling the switch on the high tension wires intended to stop Godzilla's advance, and Tezuka plays the editor who sends a reporter to interview the reclusive Dr. Serizawa.[36]

Nakajima and Tezuka suffered considerably inside the Godzilla suit. To enhance the illusion of watching a giant beast in action, Tsuburaya shot most of the footage at a higher frame rate than the normal 24 frames per second. When projected at normal speed, Godzilla lumbered realistically. In order to properly expose the scenes at this high frame rate, special effects lighting director Kuichiro Kishida had to light the stage more brightly than usual. Under the hot lights, and without ventilation inside the costume, the actor inside could scarcely withstand three minutes of filming. Nakajima fainted several times during the shoot; when studio technicians removed his bulky rubber suit, they usually drained out a cup of his sweat, too. Nakajima also suffered blisters (from rubbing against the costume) and painful muscle cramps, and ultimately lost twenty pounds.[37]

Ryosaku Takayama and Iwao Mori designed the costume. Tsuburaya's original concept of a giant octopus having been rejected by producer Tanaka, the design combined features of a dinosaur with the look of a Chinese dragon. Sculptor Sadami Toshimitsu prepared a clay model of a Tyrannosaurus-looking creature with scaly skin and the back plates of a Stegosaurus. Tanaka disliked the scales, so a second model was built with a bumpy, warty skin texture and a smaller head. A third model kept the basic body design but changed the skin texture again to that of an alligator.

From this model, Toshimitsu and Kanzi Yagi began work on a full-size suit molded to fit the two actors. The first version, hand-crafted from latex rubber, was made from a crude grade material that hardened into 220 pounds of stiff, inflexible uselessness. That suit could be used for isolated effects shots where motion was less important than sturdiness, but for the rigors of filming, Toshimitsu and Yagi had to try all over again.[38]

The latex skin was stuffed with bamboo and urethane foam to provide sturdiness and bulk. Although a popular misconception exists that Godzilla is green, the two-piece suit was painted a deep charcoal gray, and subsequent screen appearances maintained that charcoal coloring. The actor's head fit in the neck of the suit, with Godzilla's head serving as a sort of hat. Inside the suit, Nakajima and Tezuka could open and close the monster's mouth. The tail was manipulated by wires like a marionette. A Godzilla hand puppet was used for close-ups involving more detailed facial expressions.[39]

While Iwao Mori developed hundreds of storyboards from the finished screenplay to assist Tsuburaya in planning the many complex and demanding effects sequences, Tsuburaya and Honda discussed the task ahead of them. Honda, who had once been a documentary filmmaker, desired a semi-documentary feel for *Gojira*. The two stood atop the Matsuzakaya department store in the Ginza district of Tokyo, discussing Godzilla starting a fire in Tokyo's Shinbashi district that would spread to the Ginza shopping district. Worried, the store's security guards stopped them for investigation.[40]

The 1/25th scale model of downtown Tokyo taxed the abilities of Tsuburaya's crew. Each building destroyed by Godzilla needed a complete interior in order to crumble realistically. The first Tokyo model set did not meet Tsuburaya's standards, and had to be rebuilt. The miniature vehicles Godzilla tramples were constructed from cast iron so as not to appear unnaturally flimsy.

In fact, every aspect of the special effects work was unusually taxing. The scale and scope of the project was unprecedented, which meant that there was no body of skilled technicians upon whose expertise and experience *Gojira* would rest. Tsuburaya was obliged to hire many new aides, most of whom had never worked in movies at all previously. They invented their techniques, and perfected them on the fly as they went.[41]

*Gojira*'s budget of 62 million yen made it one of the most expensive Japanese films ever made. Three times the budget of the average Japanese movie, *Gojira* cost approximately $175,000 to make — yet even as a record-breaker, it came in well under the $200,000 budget of its most obvious Western analog, *The Beast from 20,000 Fathoms.*[42] With the cost of theatrical prints and advertising included, *Gojira* required an investment of over 100 million yen from Toho.[43]

With so much at stake, Toho marketed their intended blockbuster with extreme care. Toho prepared a radio play based on the shooting script and broadcast it in serialized form over Japan Broadcasting from July 17 through September 25, 1954. Audiences heard the monster, and became anxious to see it, too.[44]

On November 3, 1954, with elaborate and enticing artwork gracing the theaters, *Gojira* opened at last. After one hundred twenty-two days of shooting and months of pre- and post-production, the biggest Japanese movie event of the year exploded. Audiences waited hours in line for tickets.[45] Opening day ticket sales were the highest in Japanese history, and yet were only the tip of the iceberg. *Gojira* went on to pull in 152 million yen from 9.6 million viewers. The film placed twelfth on the list of Japan's box office successes for the year, after seven Japanese features (including *The Seven Samurai*) and four foreign ones.[46] Tsuburaya won the Japanese Film Technique award for his effects, one of many times he would be so honored.[47] The film would come to be considered one of Japan's twenty best feature films by an elite group of film critics writing for *Kinema Junpo* (Cinema Journal).[48]

Toho's gamble paid off. Although they did not know it yet, the reign of the king of the monsters was only just beginning.

# Chapter 2

# *Gojira*
## (GODZILLA)

*Godzilla was irradiated by the H-Bomb and still managed to survive. Why do you insist on killing him? Instead, the study of the mysterious force that keeps him alive should be our top priority.*

— Dr. Yamane

Japanese version: 98 minutes, Released November 3, 1954, Released in U.S. in subtitled form as *Gojira* to Japanese language theaters in 1955 and to selected theaters in 1982 and 2004
Black and White, Academy Aspect Ratio
Produced by Tomoyuki Tanaka; directed by Ishiro Honda; screenplay by Takeo Murata and Ishiro Honda; story by Shigeru Kayama; music by Akira Ifukube; cinematography by Masao Tamai; art direction by Satoshi Chuko; special effects by Eiji Tsuburaya; special effects art direction by Akira Watanabe; optical effects by Hiroshi Mukoyama
Starring Takashi Shimura (Dr. Yamane), Akihiko Hirata (Dr. Daisuke Serizawa), Akira Takarada (Hideto Ogata), Momoko Kochi (Emiko Yamane), Sachio Sakai (Hagiwara), Fuyuki Murakami (Dr. Tanabe), Toranosuke Ogawa (President of Nankai Shipping Co.), Ren Yamamoto (Masaji), Toyoaki Suzuki (Shinkichi), Miki Hayashi (Diet Chairman), Seijiro Onda and Kin Sugai (Parliamentarians), Ren Imaaizumi (Nankai Radio Chief), Kuninori Kodo, Keiji Sakakida, Shizuko Higashi, Kiyoshi Kamoto, Takeo Oikawa
GODZILLA portrayed by Haruo Nakajima and Katsumi Tezuka

*A series of unexplained maritime disasters occurs around Odo Island, a fishing community, whose natives believe the mysterious events herald the return of their god, Godzilla. Paleontologist Dr. Yamane discovers evidence that a prehistoric creature has been awakened from millions of years of underground hibernation by recent hydrogen bomb tests, and that the creature is now itself radioactive. As the creature attacks Tokyo without reason or pity, the Japanese Self-Defense Force finds itself unable to prevent catastrophic destruction. Meanwhile, a reclusive scientist named Serizawa struggles privately with his conscience: He has invented a device that could stop Godzilla, but in so doing might trigger a new arms race.*
*Which is the worse threat to humanity: allowing Godzilla to rampage, or to unleash a new weapon of mass destruction?*

Although frequently compared to *King Kong*, *Gojira* has more notable differences than similarities. There is a surface similarity, of course: This is a movie about a giant monster on a rampage in a major metropolis. Under that surface, though, lies a very different movie.

*King Kong* is a fantasy action movie with a relatively light tone. *Gojira* is a harsh, dark movie suffused with a sense of dread and doom, a horror movie about the end of the world. No other giant monster movie of the era dwells so on pain and suffering.

There is a love triangle at the core of the story that implicates the fate of the world. Emiko, daughter of Dr. Yamane, is in love with sailor Ogata, whose shipping line is one of the first hit by Godzilla. Their affair could produce a scandal, however, as she is supposedly betrothed to Dr. Serizawa, the enigmatic scientist who has invented the Oxygen Destroyer, the only weapon capable of combating the monster. The details of these people's private lives have global consequences. When a jealous Serizawa takes his angry fists to Ogata, it is not only partly about who will win Emiko's hand, but moreover whose philosophy about defense research will triumph.

There is a distinct operatic quality to this dark tragedy. Even the Americanized version of the film emphasizes the momentous aspects of this love triangle, as reporter Steve Martin (played by Raymond Burr) says, "It was the usual triangle, only this time it was to play an important part in the lives of millions of people."

Akihiko Hirata's brooding portrayal of Dr. Serizawa anchors the drama. Yet the creator of the ultimate weapon is not alone in suffering inner turmoil. Emiko (played by an inexperienced actress named Momoko Kochi) is torn between her betrothal to her father's colleague and her true love, Ogata. She sees no way to resolve this conflict with honor. Although she intends to tell Serizawa about her feelings for Ogata, she never manages to do so. Serizawa ultimately deduces the truth from her silence. Ogata fares no better in asking Dr. Yamane for permission to marry Emiko, enraging the old scientist before he gets to the point.

Dr. Yamane, too, broods—over Godzilla. He sees the creature as an unparalleled opportunity for paleontological research, yet the future of his people depends on destroying the monster.

The admittedly rather weird love triangle in *King Kong* has Ann Darrow (played by Fay Wray) as the object of the affections of both Jack Driscoll (Bruce Cabot) and the titular monster. This love triangle reflects the central conflict of the monster-on-the-loose plot: Civilized society must confront a destructive force of nature, and the struggle between those elemental forces plays itself out in the struggle for the attentions of the female lead. King Kong is a noble savage, at once terrifyingly brutal and sympathetically heroic. The resolution of this love triangle, the death of the great ape, also resolves the conflict between the monster and society. Society wins and the savage is tamed, if only in death.

In *Gojira*, too, the resolution of the love triangle involves the death of one of the suitors. Unlike *King Kong*'s tension between a man and a monster for the attention of a woman, both of Emiko's suitors are human. Dr. Serizawa, though, plays a narrative role similar to the monster's. Godzilla was mutated by nuclear weapons; Serizawa was disfigured during the war. Only Serizawa holds the power to destroy this incredible monster, which in turn holds the power to destroy the world. Serizawa's

death and Godzilla's death are linked: To destroy Godzilla, Serizawa must destroy himself. However, by having Dr. Serizawa displace the monster as one of the vertices of the love triangle, the love story's relationship to the main conflict has been substantially altered.

*King Kong*'s archetypal conflict between man and nature resolves cleanly, with man the victor. In *Gojira*, the monster cannot be interpreted simply as a symbol for nature. Godzilla, described by Dr. Yamane as "child of the H-Bomb," symbolizes modern technological society as much as anything else. The monster is defeated by *even more* technology, and so the central conflict of the story is not so much society against nature as society against itself. The resolution of this conflict does not really identify a victor, nor can it: The end is a draw. In both cases, the resolution of the love story also resolves the monster plot. However, *Gojira*'s more complicated narrative structure offers only ambiguous interpretations, quite unlike the straightforward storytelling of *King Kong*.

Notably, Shigeru Kayama's original story for *Gojira* did not include this love triangle. Ishiro Honda and Takeo Murata added it as a way to improve the emotional content of the human plot and to better motivate the characters.[1]

This emotional emphasis distinguishes *Gojira* from its numerous imitators—and indeed from most of its sequels. Of the four primary characters, only one really wants to kill off the menace. Dr. Yamane wants to keep Godzilla alive for study, Dr. Serizawa wants to have nothing to do with Godzilla, and Emiko is sworn to keep silent about the only weapon that might have an effect on Godzilla. This conflicted loyalty divides the sympathies of the viewer. Despite the terror of Godzilla, two of the characters with whom we identify refuse to fight the monster. In one scene, Dr. Yamane ruminates in the darkness of his room, driven almost to tears at the thought that Godzilla is to be killed. In a later scene, at a hospital overrun with the victims of Godzilla's onslaught, a doctor waves a Geiger counter over a small child, confirming that this beautiful young girl has no hope of survival. We are torn between incompatible viewpoints, an effect that the

Godzilla series would not achieve again until nearly four decades later.

Enhancing the sensation of watching a monster opera is the stirring and memorable score by Akira Ifukube. Then a professor of musical composition at Tokyo University, Ifukube was one of Japan's foremost classical composers.[2] Associated with the Godzilla series until his retirement in 1995, Ifukube stood as one of Japan's most respected classical composers. Ironically, his classical works have gone largely unnoticed abroad, and his reputation is in many ways maintained by his soundtracks for Toho's science fiction and fantasy films.

Raised in the village of Kushiro in Hokkaido, Ifukube grew up with the folk music of the Ainu tribe, the indigenous people of Hokkaido. His subsequent compositions have a quality to them distinct from traditional Japanese music, and many ascribe this to the "pagan" influence of the Ainu folk music. By contrast, most of Ifukube's peers drew their influence from European classical music.[3] Originally trained as a forestry engineer, Ifukube became inspired by a recording of Jean Francaix's *Concertino for Piano and Orchestra*. "The expression of classical music is going in this way?" Ifukube marveled. "I have to do something, not in the forest, but in the civilized world."[4]

Hindered by his father's opposition, Ifukube never studied music formally, but as a self-taught musician quickly became a protégé of composer-pianist Alexandre Tcherepnine. In 1935, Ifukube became the first to receive the Tcherepnine Award, making him the first Japanese composer ever to win the attention and respect of the Western world. Ifukube earned the distinction of being the only Japanese composer mentioned in Nicholas Slominsky's book *Music Since 1900*.[5]

Ifukube's compositional style is one of emotional extremes, operatic values on an epic scale. During World War II, the Japanese military commissioned him to compose nationalistic hymns for the Pacific islands the Japanese "liberated" from the white people. Ironically, when General Douglas MacArthur arrived at Atsugi Air Force Base in August 1945 at the end of the war, the band performed Ifukube's brass band march for the Filipino people, much to Ifukube's surprise. His skill at creating music with epic dimensions and distinctly Asian qualities while using the instrumentals of traditional European classical music also found favor at the Chinese court during World War II, when Captain Amakasu commissioned Ifukube to compose music for Manchuria.[6]

In addition to composing nationalistic themes, Ifukube spent the war years cultivating an interest in film music. The Japanese military confiscated a print of Walt Disney's *Fantasia* (1940) and asked Ifukube and others to review the film to determine its suitability for viewing by the Japanese public. The reviewers decided *Fantasia* should not be exhibited. Ifukube later explained the panel's thinking: "They thought that if the public saw it and realized that the Americans had created such a wonderful film, it would adversely affect the morale of the Japanese people."[7]

After the end of the war, Ifukube's close friend Fumio Hayasaka left Hokkaido to begin a career as a film composer in Tokyo, soon becoming Akira Kurosawa's primary composer. Although the Japanese public held musicians in low esteem, and the composing community saw film composers as even lower, Ifukube ignored the advice of those around him and joined his friend in Tokyo.[8] Ifukube's first film composition was for *Snow Trail* (1947), Toshiro Mifune's first film as well. Ifukube later scored *The Quiet Duel* (1949) for Kurosawa.[9] During these years, Ifukube sought inspiration not from other film scores, but from opera.[10]

When Ishiro Honda offered *Gojira* to him in 1954, Ifukube saw an opportunity to address his own experiences with radiation. Wartime radiation exposure killed his brother Isao and made Ifukube himself very ill.[11]

His grand, epic scores would bless a dozen Godzilla films. Even after his retirement, his memorable Godzilla theme would be re-recorded by other musicians on successive films, an indelible and inviolate ingredient in the Godzilla formula. In addition to scoring Godzilla movies, Ifukube wrote music for the

Daiei Company's Giant Majin series* as well as such dramas as *Children of Hiroshima* (1952), *The Burmese Harp* (1956), *The Birth of Japan* (1959) and *Night Drum* (1958).[12] At the peak of his career, Ifukube scored as many as fifteen films per year, eventually scoring over 200 features.[13] Although Ifukube's themes would make a lasting mark on listeners, ironically he composed the *Gojira* soundtrack in under a week without having seen any of the footage. Ifukube simply relied on Honda's assertion that Godzilla would be "one of the biggest things ever on the screen."[14]

Drawing from his knowledge of Ainu folk music, Ifukube incorporated elements of that primitivist musical tradition into his Godzilla themes. As Ifukube scored subsequent Godzilla films, he developed distinctive leitmotifs for the various monsters, and in scenes where monsters fought one another, his music brought the separate themes together in musical confrontation as well.

Ifukube also created the sound of Godzilla's roar, among many sound effects that he tackled as extensions of the musical score. Concerned that the roar should be organic and natural without sounding like any living animal, he created the sound by rubbing a leather glove across a contrabass and applying an echo to that recording. At the time, there was only one contrabass in all of Japan, held at the Tokyo Music Conservatory. When Ifukube requested access to the instrument for use in creating his monster roar, he had not previously had any opportunity to practice this sound effect. His finely tuned sensitivity to the sounds of objects and instruments allowed him to deduce in advance what lesser musicians could only learn by trial and error.[15]

The historical dimension of this monster movie "opera" is most often interpreted as the nuclear bomb. Toshio Takahashi, professor of modern literature at Tokyo's Waseda University, says, "Godzilla was and is a powerful antiwar statement. Besides that, he is a mirror into the Japanese soul."[16] Several Japanese commentators towards the end of the 20th century offered an alternative interpretation. Film historian Tomoyasu Kobayashi, writing in 1992, saw significance in the fact that the United States never assists Japan against the various monsters in the cycle. Even during the era of the 1954 Mutual Security Act promising American military support, the Japanese must face Godzilla alone. Kobayashi concludes, "The Japanese can only count on themselves to defend Japan."[17] It should be added that the American navy does fight Godzilla on Japan's behalf in the 1964 film *Mothra vs. Godzilla*. This sequence, however, was requested by the distributor, American International Pictures, for inclusion in the English language version only.[18] Japanese viewers such as Tomoyasu Kobayashi have therefore never seen the U.S. lend a helping hand.

Writer Norio Akasaka interprets Godzilla as a "representation of the spirits of soldiers who died in the South Pacific during the Second World War ... After coming from the South Pacific to destroy most of the Ginza and the Diet building, [Godzilla] stops suddenly in front of the Imperial Palace, then turns right and heads back out to sea with this look of painful sadness on his face." Akasaka compares this scene to a story by Yukio Mishima, "The Voice of the Hero Spirits," in which ghosts of fallen kamikaze pilots accuse the emperor of allowing Japan to decay spiritually. For Akasaka, both Mishima's story and *Gojira* are critiques of the moral decline of postwar Japan.[19]

Interestingly, this idea also occurred to Akira Ifukube during his work on the film. In a later

---

*Daiei (which means "Big Picture") Studios attempted to compete with Toho's kaiju eiga with two series of their own. Gamera, a fire-breathing monster turtle, appeared in nine movies between 1965 and 1995. The Giant Majin series, with only three films, all of which appeared in Japan in 1966, told the story of a warrior-god living in a giant statue. When the tyranny of the local lords becomes intolerable, the Majin returns to life to wreak holy vengeance. Although the Majin films sported higher production values than the Gamera series, its odd blend of Japanese folklore and monster movie chaos did not lend itself well to international exploitation. AIP released the three features to American television in 1968. Although they still claim some Western fans, the films have by and large fallen into obscurity. Toho planned to include a monster inspired by the Majin in 1972's Godzilla vs. Gigan, but later abandoned that plan. By contrast, Gamera's influence on the Godzilla series in the 1970s was far more overt and direct.*

interview, he remarked that for his generation, Godzilla was "like the souls of the Japanese soldiers who died in the Pacific Ocean during the war."*[20]

Current-affairs commentator Yasuo Nagayama sees Godzilla as a symbol of Takamori Saigo, who led a nationalist revolutionary movement in the late 19th century. "Like Godzilla, Saigo was famed for his imposing physique," writes reporter Jim Bailey, "conquered in a path that ran from south to north, was ultimately defeated and underwent a transformation in his reputation from villain to hero." Nagayama himself notes, "Saigo and Godzilla were not enemies of the people, but enemies of mistaken government policies."[21]

Nonetheless, the most common critical interpretation sees Godzilla as a living symbol of the nuclear bomb. This interpretation, however, invokes the tense postwar relationship between Japan and the United States. As Godzilla was exported as a pop cultural creation to North America, these political undercurrents would begin to pose problems. Godzilla in the United States, then, would be a rather different beast.

---

*This idea was directly adapted into the 2002 sequel Godzilla, Mothra, King Ghidorah: Giant Monsters All-Out Attack, and will be discussed again in that chapter.

*Chapter 3*

# Godzilla Conquers America

## (GODZILLA IN AMERICA, PART ONE)

*Recently I was told by an American magazine writer who came to Japan to do research that what was done to my film was rude. He was concerned that I might be infuriated by it.*
— Ishiro Honda[1]

Joseph E. Levine was one of the quintessential movie moguls of mid-century Hollywood. He founded Embassy Pictures in 1934 and began distributing independent motion pictures. His innate talent for understanding and exploiting mass public tastes enabled him to achieve commercial success with "art films" at a time when Hollywood's conventional wisdom believed such pictures to be unmarketable. Levine established the careers of such stars as Sophia Loren, Dustin Hoffman, Michael Caine, Marcel Mastroianni, and Mel Brooks.

Levine's earliest releases were Italian art films, including *Open City* (1945), *Paisan* (1946), and *The Bicycle Thief* (1948). These would be hailed then and now as landmarks of European art film, and Levine began seeking foreign films with an even larger potential audience.

Several years later, Edmund Goldman, of the small film distribution outfit Manson International, paid Toho $25,000 for the U.S. rights to *Gojira*. With the dollar at 360 yen, the offer made Toho's president Kazumi Kobayashi ecstatic. Goldman recognized he had a prize worth potentially more in exploitation markets than he could work out of it on his own, so he brought in Harold Ross and Richard Kay of Jewell Pictures to provide some additional funding. They in turn showed the film to Levine, who felt his heart quicken as he saw what they had. Done right, this could be something big. Together, these men formed Trans-World Releasing to handle the distribution, and Levine put up another $100,000 of his own to underwrite the project.[2]

Levine, an experienced exhibitor and distributor, was now about to take his first major step into production. In the years to come he would help create such classics as *The Graduate* (1967), *The Lion in Winter* (1968), and *A Bridge Too Far* (1977). That *Gojira* would in any way be a step towards such a future may seem nonsensical — not just because of some perceived misfit between giant monsters and respected film dramas, but because of the simple fact that when Levine showed up, *Gojira* had already been made. However, the fact is that Levine did commission a writer, engage a director, and supervise the production of new footage, by which *Gojira* was transformed into *Godzilla, King of the Monsters!*

To a greater or a lesser extent, most of Toho Studio's special effects pictures released in the United States endured some form of "Americanization." American audiences have never shown a predilection for supporting foreign features. In order to make these Japanese features marketable to a largely teenage audience in the United States, changes had to be made. Dubbing the Japanese language dialogue into English was the first among many steps, and one that has drawn criticism, contempt, and sarcasm ever since. For generations of filmgoers, the dubbing of Godzilla movies has been a standing joke.

The very practice of dubbing in itself poses severe problems. Different languages, by definition, employ different grammatical forms and different sounds to express ideas. In dubbing a line of dialogue from one language into another, the underlying content of the line must be more or less maintained, but a direct translation might produce an English-language line that is either too long or too short for the amount of lip-moving the speaking character does. So, instead of straight translations, the dialogue must be adapted to fit both the length of the actor's lip movements and the general distribution of vowels and consonants. Dubbing Japanese language dialogue into English often produces strange results, particularly disconcerting pauses in the English where pauses appropriate to Japanese speech occurred. This can be a damned-if-you-do, damned-if-you-don't problem, because if the voice-over artist does not stop speaking when the on-screen actor does, that can lead viewers to criticize the asynchronous quality of the dubbing.

Since the dubbed speech must be an *adaptation* of the original rather than a direct translation, the opportunity arises for the English-language version to adjust the dialogue to match the expectations of American audiences at the expense of ideas inherent in the original language.

Only a handful of voice performers handled the dubbing, each voice performer speaking for several characters. One of the most common voice artists was Paul Frees. Frees's voice ranks among the most familiar voices in American film history, although few recognize his name. Frees lent his considerable voice talents to countless feature films and cartoons, and later to Japanese fantasy films. Frees was so prolific in this respect that he even directed the dubbing of *King Kong Escapes* (1967). Although his skill is beyond dispute, he was often called upon to voice many of the characters in a given film, leading to a deplorable lack of distinction between major characters.

Assisting Frees over the years was Marvin Miller, better known as the voice of Robby the Robot. George Takei, who would go on to stardom as Mr. Sulu on *Star Trek*, got his first break in Hollywood as the only Japanese American on the dubbing roster.[3] While many Japanese American actors struggled and looked for work, white voice performers affected fake Japanese accents for most of the films discussed

in this book.[4] This approach sometimes resulted in racial caricatures.

In all fairness to Frees, Miller, Takei, and their colleagues, the practice of dubbing simply does not allow for perfect results. To a certain extent, dubbing equals bad dubbing. Frees and the others deserve some credit for, in such films as *Mothra vs. Godzilla* and *Ghidrah, The Three-Headed Monster*, producing excellent results within the limits of the form.

There exists today a conventionally understood dichotomy between serious arthouse fare, aimed at high-brow audiences and which uses subtitles to preserve the original filmmakers' intents, versus mass-market movies whose audience is expected to be impatient with subtitles. To this viewpoint, it must seem quite natural that *Godzilla* was dubbed into English, because its distributors would have had a hard time recognizing a monster movie as serious art, and therefore unlikely to accord it the respect implied by subtitles. This is a historical distortion, however, that should be corrected if a proper appreciation of the revisions to *Godzilla, King of the Monsters* is to be achieved.

The first point worth realizing is that the question of whether to subtitle or dub a picture comes into play only when one is dealing with a foreign-language import. This may seem obvious, but consider that prior to World War II, exceedingly few foreign language pictures made it to American screens at all, and of that pitifully few number nearly all came from Western Europe. When war consumed the European continent, naturally enough the flow of movies stopped. Even when the war ended, almost no foreign-language pictures even appeared in the United States to trigger the question of how best to translate them. In 1946, only ten out of the over 400 movies screened in America came from abroad, and all were from England and therefore already in English.

The 1950s saw a larger trickle of foreign imports, especially from Italy and France, and during that period the most common solution was subtitling. This was by far the cheapest method. The subtitling of a feature could generally be done for less than a thousand dollars. It was also cheap-looking, as the process invariably degraded the picture quality substantially. The most important voice in foreign film promotion at the time was Bosley Crowther, film critic for the *New York Times*. Crowther's review could make or break a movie. He made it his *cause celebre* to adamantly *promote* dubbing as preferable to subtitles— and spent the decade beating that drum. It was his contention that subtitles distracted the eye from the rest of the screen and damaged the visual experience of a foreign film.

Dubbing, however, was an outrageous expense. Compared to the mere hundreds that could be spent on subtitles, it could cost between $10,000 and $20,000 to properly dub a movie into English (the lower end if the work was done overseas; the higher cost was for an American post-production house to handle the work). Foreign film producers took to advocating for their pictures to be dubbed, as a way of hooking U.S. distributors into taking their promotion more seriously; many foreign film companies began to dub their pictures themselves to overcome American distributor resistance to the idea. In the 1950s, to get a foreign film dubbed into English was a sign of prestige. Considering that many foreign films were licensed for an average of just $3,000, and that a box office take of $200,000 was considered a huge success for an imported film, the enormous cost of dubbing was widely regarded as a waste of money for all but the most commercial prospects.

The first time in history that a foreign film made a million dollars at the American box office, it was Roberto Rossellini's *Open City*, which had been distributed dubbed in English.[5] Edmund Goldman paid Toho nearly ten times as much as was customary because he believed *Godzilla* had the ability to follow in the footsteps of *Open City*, *Paisan*, and *The Bicycle Thief* as the next big import. He and his partners turned to Levine because of Levine's experience in dubbing those pictures— and because they needed him to help finance the Americanization. The decision to dub *Godzilla* into English should never be characterized as a mark of disrespect; it was actually an uncommon show of faith.

However, the aesthetic debate over subtitles versus dubbing remained an unsettled issue. Just as Bosley Crowther constantly wrote editorials pushing for dubbing, the arthouse audiences in major markets like New York voted with their feet to show their support for subtitles instead. Some distributors tried a compromise, splicing explanatory intertitles into movies like in the days of silent film, but leaving the spoken dialogue otherwise untranslated.[6] It was in this environment that Levine concocted a clever and novel solution. Using an ingenious narrative device, they managed to translate *Godzilla* into English yet also leave its Japanese dialogue somewhat intact.

The American version added footage of an American character witnessing the events while his translator summarizes the content of the undubbed Japanese dialogue for him and the audience. Although this version runs about 10 minutes shorter than the Japanese original, changes the chronology of the events, and deletes a few subplots here and there, it nevertheless retains most of the spirit of the original. As film critic Tim Lucas noted, "Much has been done to Americanize the Godzilla series over the decades, much of it inane and destructive, but the craft and cleverness that went into *Godzilla, King of the Monsters* is immediately apparent."[7]

Goldman's associate Paul Schreibman (who will return in a larger capacity in Chapter 5) hired actor Raymond Burr to star in new footage designed to Americanize the proceedings. Burr, born in 1917, had yet to make his splash as TV's Perry Mason, but was still familiar to American audiences for roles such as the wife-murderer in Alfred Hitchcock's *Rear Window* (1954). Terry Morse, most commonly employed as an editor, was contracted to direct the new footage.[8]

Burr plays Steve Martin, a reporter on assignment in Japan who becomes caught up in Godzilla's onslaught. Scenes with other characters talking to one another were re-edited to make it look like they were talking with Steve Martin, who never appears in the same shot with the movie's other stars. In so doing, Morse and his team also created a Japanese security official (played by Frank Iwanaga) to escort the reporter through the events of the film. Although in the original version, the government is anxious to keep all news of Godzilla under wraps to avoid a panic, the American version shows the government itself providing unlimited access to a foreign press agent.

This new footage replaces some valuable scenes of character development for the Japanese cast. Hastily filmed in a mere handful of days on a soundstage at Visual Drama Inc. in Los Angeles, the new footage is also pictorially inferior to the original's crisp cinematography by Masao Tamai. However, *Godzilla, King of the Monsters* is the only Godzilla feature released in the U.S. with original Japanese-language dialogue. Akihiko Hirata, Akira Takarada, and Momoko Kochi are dubbed in the scenes where they appear alone, but when Burr is on-screen, the original dialogue is run without alteration. Instead, Burr gets lines like, "My Japanese is a little rusty," prompting his sidekick Iwanaga to do some on-the-fly translations.[9]

However, in the very scene in which Burr makes that statement, Iwanaga translates the Japanese conversation as Dr. Yamane suggests that the authorities question the inhabitants of Odo Island because it is so close to the mysterious accident site. One does not need to know Japanese to recognize the name "Gojira" spoken repeatedly throughout the scene. "Godzilla" would not be officially mentioned until later in the film, and no one had yet even proffered the theory that a giant monster might have anything to do with the accidents. This scene has been moved in the course of reshuffling the footage around Burr's character, and Levine apparently expected American viewers to pay no attention to the Japanese words. The Japanese dialogue in *Godzilla, King of the Monsters* serves much the same function as the nonsense sounds uttered by the adult characters in Charles Schulz's *Peanuts* television specials: a sound that merely acknowledges a character is saying something.

Another condescending attitude surfaces when Godzilla first attacks Odo Island. A survivor of one of the wrecked ships washes ashore, and Burr's narration clearly implies that

the man dies of shock on arrival, just like all previous survivors. In the Japanese version, that character does not die, and so appears in later scenes set on Odo. Some of these scenes remain intact in the American version, so a supposedly dead character resurfaces in later scenes with no explanation for his miraculous return from the grave. Again, the editors of the Embassy Pictures version evidently do not expect American viewers to be able to recognize Japanese faces with ease, an assumption that justifies the sloppy editing.

In the course of Americanization, the story changed somewhat. The original had the feel of a mystery unfolding, with a gradual build-up of tension. Morse's version begins with the aftermath of Godzilla's attack on Tokyo, and then goes into flashback mode to explain the events leading to this catastrophe. The gradual horrifying realization that a terrible monster has been loosed on the world is replaced by the given fact that a terrible monster is loose. As a monster movie, the structure of the American version is by far the more dramatically satisfying, but what it gains in cinematic effectiveness it loses in historical allegory.

The original contains repeated references to the Second World War and explicitly links Godzilla with nuclear war; all of this was cut. Among the lines American viewers never heard was a politician saying, "Godzilla is some kind of illegitimate child of the H-Bomb." Instead, the American version merely includes Dr. Yamane theorizing that H-bomb tests have *awakened* a prehistoric creature. Yamane's theories about the bomb also mutating that creature, however, did not survive translation. Most of the original version's references to the Second World War have been either excised from Embassy's edition, or remain in Japanese without translation. The Japanese *Gojira* shows people on a commuter train pondering their plight. One woman says it's a miracle she survived Nagasaki, but now she has to face Godzilla. A man moans, "Back to the shelters again!" When Godzilla does attack the mainland, the Japanese edition shows a mother gathering her children around her, seconds from being incinerated. She tells them, "We're going to join

Daddy in a moment!" Her haunting last words, though, go untranslated in the English version.

One war reference removed from the American cut has interesting implications. A reporter interviews Dr. Serizawa, saying that he has learned from one of Serizawa's German colleagues that his current line of research might be of use against Godzilla. Serizawa curtly denies knowing any Germans and ends the interview. Serizawa seems as anxious to hide any connections to Germany as he is to hide his Oxygen Destroyer. It is doubtful that this passing moment carries any genuine political significance, and to posit that Serizawa has any Nazi ties would be a considerable stretch unfounded in any other aspect of the film.

In all likelihood, the removal of this scene from the American cut is not so much an act of censorship as it is a necessary rejiggering of elements: The reporter in the scene, Hagiwara, is a minor character in *Gojira* used by Honda as a narrative device to explain certain aspects of the plot. In the American version, Steve Martin largely substitutes for that role, and indeed is often cut into scenes in Hagiwara's place. While it would have been possible to cut shots of Raymond Burr into this scene and let it play out as is, in order to keep the American "star" from seeming too much like a bystander in his own movie, Steve Martin is presented as an old "college buddy" of the mysterious Dr. Serizawa, no longer a man of mystery with something to hide. In the Japanese version, Serizawa's eyepatch stood as a constant reminder of his wartime experiences, and as such an ominous symbol of his darker side. The eyepatch goes unexplained in the American version, now little more than a handy way to help distinguish one Japanese face from another.

The American version also alters Serizawa's reluctance to use the Oxygen Destroyer. In the original, he feared his discovery being used by the military, and notes with disgust the existing arms race ("A-bomb against A-bomb, H-bomb against H-bomb"). In the American version, he articulates his dread as a fear of the Oxygen Destroyer falling "into the wrong hands." The difference is subtle but telling; in the original, Serizawa did not think *any* hands were the right

hands, and therefore there were not any specific "wrong" hands. This Japanese attitude differed too much from the American perspective on the arms race, which did distinguish between "right" and "wrong" hands.

*Godzilla, King of the Monsters* opened on April 26, 1956, across the United States. Interestingly, the Americanized version was subsequently released in Japan as *Kaiju O Gojira* ("Monster King Godzilla"), with Burr's dialogue subtitled into Japanese.[10] Japanese audiences liked the Americanized version, and Toho began using the "King of the Monsters" moniker in their own publicity materials. Perhaps Toho also found the new reporter hero to be an influential American addition: Reporter characters populated the series throughout the sixties and seventies, and these reporter heroes may owe their prominence to the legacy of Raymond Burr's Steve Martin.

For decades, Godzilla fans in America had no viable access to any version of the film other than Embassy's revised edition. Word of a longer, darker "director's cut" circulated, but few were able to see it. In 1982, in honor of the recent passing of Takashi Shimura, the original *Gojira*, *sans* Raymond Burr and with all the politically sensitive undercurrents intact, appeared in subtitled form in art-movie theaters across the U.S. Ironically, in subtitled form, *Gojira* earned praise from the same critics who lambasted it in dubbed form. Without the inherently unsatisfying effects of dubbing, the movie now seemed more serious and legitimate.[11]

In writing about this schism between the two versions of the movie, many commentators have said that the American recut was for long the only version generally available *in the West*. This is largely, but not entirely, true. Embassy's version was distributed in Italy and Spain, with the opening title sequence translated for local audiences and the soundtrack dubbed all over again into Italian, and Spanish, respectively. But there was one major European country that embraced Godzilla, and fell hard for his charms, that went another route.

In West Germany on August 10, 1956, Atrium Film-Verlieh released a film called

*Godzilla*. It was the first time the spelling Godzilla was used — prior to Joe Levine's having anything to do with it. Clocking in at 84 minutes, this version is substantially shorter than the Japanese cut yet longer than the American one, consists exclusively of footage filmed by Honda (no Raymond Burr here), and has not been reorganized in structure. It is especially interesting to note that almost without exception, the cuts to the German version track those that Levine and Morse would re-do on their cut: Gone is the scene of the Japanese Parliament arguing over whether to admit the crisis publicly, gone is the frank acknowledgment that Godzilla is a "child of the H-bomb," gone are the references to Hiroshima and Nagasaki. And while the German cut retains the shot of the mother huddling her terrified children as Godzilla tears a building down around them, her provocative line implying her husband died in the war has been changed to something that (in German) says, "Don't worry, the mean

Godzilla won't get you, your mother will protect you." The one significant cut to the American version not duplicated in the German cut is the scene in which Hagiwara mentions Serizawa's alleged German colleague. This scene remains in the German cut, and thus refutes the suggestion that its removal had censors worried about Nazi-era references.[12]

Many years later, a film historian asked Ishiro Honda if he was offended by the way in which his film had been reworked without his permission in other countries. Honda merely laughed, too amused by the changes to be infuriated. He openly acknowledged that *Gojira* was trying to imitate American monster movies.[13] In that, he succeeded all too well. Ultimately Toho would corner the market on monster movies. In the years to come, Toho's regular output of *kaiju eiga* would come to be distributed on American shores with only minimal changes.

# Chapter 4

# *Godzilla, King of the Monsters!*
## GOJIRA (GODZILLA)

*Then you have a responsibility no man has ever faced. You have your fears, which might become reality, and you have Godzilla, which is reality.*

— Ogata

U.S. version (Embassy Pictures): 81 minutes, Released April 27, 1956, double-billed with *Prehistoric Women*, released theatrically in Japan as *Kaiju O Gojira* (Monster King Godzilla)
Black and white, Academy Aspect Ratio
Produced by Richard Kay, Harry Rybnick, and Edward B. Barison; directed by and screenplay by Terrell O. Morse; cinematography by Guy Roe
Starring Raymond Burr (Steve Martin), Frank Iwanaga (Security Officer Iwanaga) in addition to Japanese cast already listed

*Steve Martin, a foreign correspondent for United World News, awakes in the ruins of Tokyo. Rescue workers take him to an overcrowded hospital, teeming with injured and irradiated survivors of a terrible catastrophe. In flashbacks, he remembers reporting on a bizarre story alleging the discovery of an ancient reptile, irradiated and enraged by nuclear testing. His friend Dr. Serizawa holds the key to their survival: an experimental weapon called the Oxygen Destroyer. Using that defense, though, may be worse than enduring Godzilla's wrath...*

Some reviewers criticized *Godzilla, King of the Monsters* for being too derivative of American monster movies. They argued that American monster movies were superior, partly on the basis of their special effects, but also for being more intelligent. Godzilla's attack on Tokyo is unmotivated by logic, they said, unlike the clear motivations given King Kong or the Beast from 20,000 Fathoms. King Kong was lost in a confusing, alien environment, trying his best to adapt, and the Beast is headed for its ancestral breeding ground. By contrast, Godzilla lacks any recognizable animalistic motivation for his assault. He is not hungry, nor lost, nor looking to breed; he is attacking just its own sake.

What these critics have overlooked is that Godzilla's apparent lack of motivation is the whole point: Godzilla is not an animal, but an angry god. The natives of Skull Island in *King Kong* believe their monster to be a god, which is a natural conclusion to reach. Since they live daily with first-hand knowledge of a giant ape, to worship the powerful beast is a logical reaction. The natives of Odo Island recognize Godzilla as their god, too, but they have never before had first-hand experience with Godzilla. Until the start of the movie, the thing was dormant under the sea. There is a fundamental difference between seeing a giant creature and saying, "I think I'll worship it as a god," and worshiping a giant creature as a god that later turns out to be real. The natives of Skull Island could well be wrong about Kong being a god; there is no reason to take their word for it. The natives of Odo Island have supposedly never seen Godzilla before, which makes their legend frighteningly prescient. If Godzilla is not a real god, then the legend is something of a disturbing coincidence.

In American monster-on-the-loose movies, a scientist is usually the agent for bringing the monster into the world, through some experiment gone awry. The monster then is punishment for toying in God's realm. Although Godzilla is the result of man's nuclear experiments, none of the researchers responsible for the Bikini Island H-Bomb tests ever appear in the film. Nuclear testing is clearly the villain of the movie, even in the sanitized American version, but responsibility for nuclear testing is displaced to some anonymous off-screen party. Whether the viewer concludes that all humanity shares responsibility or that the Americans hold sole responsibility, the fact remains that none of the characters in this film have any direct, specific responsibility. Imagine a Frankenstein movie in which Dr. Frankenstein is not among the cast. (Toho made such a film, but that is another story.)

The senselessness of Godzilla's attack is central to the effectiveness of the movie. It adds to the ominous doom-laden atmosphere, and it enhances the awesomeness of Godzilla. The animalistic motivations of King Kong and the Beast from 20,000 Fathoms make them easier to understand and therefore reduce them, if only a little bit. Ishiro Honda and Takeo Murata carefully removed the animalism of Shigeru Kayama's Godzilla when they translated his story into a screenplay. Godzilla is beyond human understanding and that makes him all the more frightening.

The Japanese have never willingly acknowledged much responsibility for the Second World War.[1] The bombings of Hiroshima and Nagasaki may or may not have resulted in less loss of life than had the war continued with conventional weapons. Irrespective of the arguments as to the bombings' necessity (which far exceed the scope of this book), the Japanese have traditionally viewed the two events as unprecedented attacks on innocent civilians. In other words, Japanese popular culture views the victims of Hiroshima and Nagasaki as the targets of outside aggression, not as casualties resulting from their own government's aggression. Godzilla serves as a convenient metaphor for the Japanese view of these tragic and traumatic events. Godzilla's violence is directed at innocent parties who carry no responsibility for the punishments they suffer.

The entire fabric of *Godzilla* is woven from the threads of real horror, human suffering, and apocalypse on a global scale.

After the development of the atomic bomb, the researchers at Los Alamos were appalled at what they had done. Robert Oppenheimer voiced his profound feelings of regret, saying he had become "the destroyer of worlds." Al-

though the World War had ended, the Cold War had begun. The new mission of the Los Alamos laboratories was the development of the "Super," now known as the hydrogen bomb.

Oppenheimer refused to participate. When he left, he took the entire scientific A-list with him. The departure of so many top researchers left Edward Teller, head of the Super Project, with the second-best minds of the free world. Teller feared Oppenheimer was trying to dissuade even them.

By 1954, after many years of vicious in-fighting and an FBI investigation of Oppenheimer's political beliefs, Teller was at last ready to test the Super. On March 1, 1954, in the Marshall Islands, the very first hydrogen bomb was exploded, releasing a force a thousand times more powerful than the bomb dropped on Hiroshima. The Atomic Energy Commission declared the first hydrogen bomb a complete success. However, in a small but significant wrinkle, the resulting fallout spread in the wrong direction. American sailors in the area had been notified and took the necessary precautions, but the Japanese population affected had received virtually no prior notice. For obvious reasons, the United States did not want to have publicized the test if it then proved a dud. In the early days of the Cold War, national security usually meant "mum's the word."

Meanwhile, off the coast of the Marshall Islands, a small Japanese fishing boat called *Daigo Fukuryo Maru* (The Lucky Dragon) was struggling to make a good day's catch. The crew saw the explosion and became nervous. Before they made it back to shore, they were hit by the fallout cloud and fell seriously ill. Aikichi Kuboyama, the *Fukuryo Maru*'s radioman, died of radiation sickness on September 23, 1954, the first victim of the hydrogen bomb. His last words, widely reported in Japan: "Please make sure that I am the last victim of the nuclear bomb."

The American officials supervising his treatment at the hospital had given misleading information to his doctors in an effort to keep the details of their new weapon secret. Kuboyama's pitifully drawn-out death made front-page news in Japan for months. One headline declared it "The Second Atomic Bombing of Mankind."

The Japanese government asked the United States for reparations of $13,850 on behalf of Kuboyama's family. Atomic Energy Commission Chairman Lewis Strauss publicly protested, claiming that he, not the fishermen, was the true victim in all this. Eisenhower refused to make the payment. A spokesperson explained that in these tense modern times, unfortunate accidents will happen, but all for the common good. Intense anti–American fervor broke out in Japan, and the Anti Bomb Test Group was formed in early August 1954.[2]

While the Americans tried to spin the situation as a reasonable technological test that had some minor unfortunate casualties caused by the victims not having followed clear instructions, the Japanese island struggled with an ever-widening spiral of problems. Fish caught by the *Lucky Dragon*—and indeed the other fishing vessels that had followed the direc-

tives—had to be destroyed due to lethal amounts of radiation. Radioactive rain fell on mainland Japan for days on end. All crops had to be tested with Geiger counters, and entire harvests were ruined.[3]

*Gojira* hit Japanese screens scarcely more than a month after Kuboyama's death. Honda originally planned to make the connection to the *Lucky Dragon* even more explicit, and expected to start *Gojira* with the irradiated fishing vessel floating, completely uninhabited, back to its port like the death ship of the famed silent horror film *Nosferatu*. Fearing that the issue of the *Lucky Dragon* was simply too acute to address so directly, Honda abandoned the sequence, opting instead to let his monster movie merely suggest such recent horrors.[4] He knew that these headlines would be stingingly fresh in the minds of the audience when Godzilla came out of the sea, attacking fishermen, and a renowned scientist pondered the ethical questions of an "ultimate weapon."

# Chapter 5

# *Godzilla Raids Again*

## GOJIRA NO GYAKUSHU (GODZILLA'S COUNTERATTACK)

*Every lesson we've ever learned has told us this: Horrors in the world of science are part of nature's plan.*

— Dr. Tadokoro

Japanese version: 82 minutes, Released April 24, 1955; released in the U.S. in 1956 to Japanese-language theaters as *Godzilla Raids Again*

U.S. version (Warner Brothers): 78 minutes, Released May 21, 1959, double-billed with *Teenagers from Outer Space,* Original U.S. release title: *Gigantis the Fire Monster*

Black and white, Academy Aspect Ratio

Produced by Tomoyuki Tanaka; U.S. version produced by Paul Schreibman, Harry B. Swerdlon, and Edmund Goldman; directed by Motoyoshi Oda; U.S. version re-edited and dubbed by Hugo Grimaldi; screenplay by Takeo Murata and Shigeaki Hidaka; story by Shigeru Kayama; music by Masaru Sato (not used in U.S. release); U.S. version music editor Rex Lipton with music by Paul Sawtell and Bert Shefter; cinematography by Seiichi Endo; art direction by Takeo Kita; special effects by Eiji Tsuburaya; special effects art direction by Akira Watanabe; optical effects by Kiroshi Mukoyama; U.S. version includes footage from *Unknown Island, One Million B.C.,* and the Mexican feature *Adventuras en la Centro del la Tiera,* and unused animation from *Lost Continent*

Starring Hiroshi Koizumi (Tsukioka), Minoru Chiaki (Kobayashi), Setsuko Wakayama (Hidemi), Takashi Shimura (Dr. Yamane), Masao Shimizu (Dr. Tadokoro), Yukio Kasama (Owner of Cannery), Mayuri Mokusho (Radio Operator), Sonosuke Sawamura (Hokkaido Branch Manager), Takeo Oikawa (Police Chief), Seijiro Onda (Captain of Defense Corps), Yoshio Tsuchiya (Tajima), Minosuke Yamada (Commander of Defense Corps), Ren Yamamoto (Commander of Landing Craft)

GODZILLA portrayed by Haruo Nakajima, ANGUIRUS portrayed by Katsumi Tezuka

*Tsukioka and Kobayashi, pilots for a cannery in a small fishing community near Osaka, are terrified to discover two prehistoric monsters locked in battle on* Iwato Island. *Reluctantly, Japan is forced to admit that the terror of Godzilla is not over — that in fact there is a second Godzilla, and another irradiated dinosaur, an ankylosaurus they take to calling "Anguirus."*

*Without Serizawa and the secret of the Oxygen Destroyer, the residents of Osaka are helpless in the face of the monsters' attacks. Godzilla defeats Anguirus and leaves Osaka in flames.*

*Tsukioka and Kobayashi relocate to Hokkaido in the grim aftermath, only to find that Godzilla's rampage is spreading even to there. The Japanese Air Defense Force launches an all-out offensive, with Tsukioka and Kobayashi bravely taking their crude prop planes into battle. Trapping Godzilla on an ice-covered island, the Air Force bombards the monster relentlessly. In kamikaze fashion, Kobayashi crashes his plane into an icy mountain, sending an avalanche crashing down on the giant monster. As the creature digs its way out, the military focuses its efforts on sealing Godzilla in ice, finally entombing him for good.*

According to Ishiro Honda, Toho never expected to bring Godzilla back; he said, "Believe it or not, we had no plans for a sequel and naively hoped that the end of *Godzilla* was going to coincide with the end of nuclear testing."[1] The original monster died at the hands of Dr. Serizawa, but in the final moments of the movie Dr. Yamane speculated that other members of the same family might appear in the future. Indeed, the star of *Godzilla Raids Again* is a second Godzilla, and it is this new creature that has carried the series ever since.

With the phenomenal success of the first film, there was no question but to bring the monster back, one way or another. Just as the producers of *King Kong* followed up their smash hit with the hastily made sequel *The Son of Kong,* the makers of *Godzilla* wasted precious little time. *Godzilla Raids Again* arrived on Japanese screens within six months of the original.[2] It shows some signs of being a rush job, too. The script rehashes the plot of the previous film, but with twice as many monsters and a diminished emotional core. While the production values of the special effects sequences remain high, the human portion of the movie is filmed without atmosphere or imagination.

The film also suffers from not having Ishiro Honda at the helm. In fact, this and 1970's *Godzilla vs. Hedorah* are the only two first series Godzilla films directed by neither Honda nor his successor, Jun Fukuda. The director here, Motoyoshi Oda, does a competent job, but never achieves the sense of terror in Honda's original.

Oda, inexplicably credited as "Motoyoshi Qdq" in the American print (how is that supposed to be pronounced?), was a colleague and contemporary of Honda's. Oda, Honda, and Akira Kurosawa all learned the craft of directing as apprentices to revered Japanese filmmaker Kajiro Yamamoto. Any similarities between the styles of Honda, Oda and Kurosawa, then, should be credited to the influence of Yamamoto.[3]

Oda was a journeyman director for Toho, happily accepting B-picture level assignments in all genres and cranking out acceptable results as if they were widgets. Putting such a man in charge of the Godzilla sequel then was a clear signal of intent: This was to be a quickie profit center, not an artistic indulgence. To the extent anyone besides Honda could be said to be qualified for the post, Oda seemed the one. Oda had served as special effects supervisor on Honda's *Eagle of the Pacific* (1953), and just after Honda wrapped *Gojira*, Oda was put in charge of a science fiction film called *Tomei Ningen*— literally, "The Invisible Man," but best known in English as *The Invisible Avenger*, a fun mix of horror and yakuza-style gangster thrills. The invisibility effects by Eiji Tsuburaya were clever but sparingly used, and allowed him to develop techniques he had pioneered in

1949 for *Tomei Ningen Arawaru* (*Enter the Invisible Man*). That earlier picture had the distinction of being Japan's first significant science fiction film, and set a tone for the development of the genre.[4]

*Enter the Invisible Man* initiated a minigenre of "insubstantial man" films, and provided a template of crazy, mismatched ingredients: mad scientists, criminal thugs, nightclub dancers, circus clowns, and people who fade away.* In 1958, Ishiro Honda joined the party with *Bijo to Ekitainingen* (*The H-Man*), which revamped many of Oda's *Invisible Avenger* ideas into lurid color and high pulpy style. Honda also directed the 1960 *Gasu Ningen Dai Ichigo*, "Gas Human #1" or *The Human Vapor*. It was so popular a sequel was mooted, to pit the Human Vapor against Frankenstein(!). Even rival studio Daiei contributed, with 1957's *Tomei Ningen to Hae Otoko*, known in English as *Vapor Man Meets the Human Fly*—and advertised with a terrific poster depicting a transparent assassin beside a beautiful woman, while a miniature man scales her cleavage. *Denso Ningen* (*The Secret of the Telegian*) in 1960 was arguably the last of the informal cycle, and allowed a young director named Jun Fukuda to try his hand on Toho's special-effects extravaganzas before being promoted to the Godzilla series. Fukuda even considered a sequel, *The Telegraphed Man vs. the Flame Man*. (Fukuda described the plot of the unfilmed sequel thusly: "I just remember that the transparent man was pitted against a flame man."[5])

Aside from mixing gaseous or invisible people with film noir-style histrionics, these various movies— made and unmade — share only vague, superficial aspects in common, and were not a franchise *per se*. They were however popular and influential in their own right, and represented one of the myriad manifestations of Toho's increasing confidence with special effects–oriented filmmaking, of which the Godzilla films were merely the most internationally prominent.

---

*Sometime in 1954, Motoyoshi Oda also made* Yurei Otoko, *"The Ghost Man." Eiji Tsuburaya was not involved in this production. I have been unable to find a copy and cannot say how it fits into the "insubstantial man" cycle, although the title does imply something along those lines.*

The creative team from *The Invisible Avenger* was ported over to the Godzilla sequel largely intact. Screenwriter Shigeaki Hidaka, director Oda, and special effects master Tsuburaya barely had a couple of months of rest between the two projects, and it would not be surprising to learn that they planned some of the work specifically to recycle techniques and props already at hand: The climax of *The Invisible Avenger* is staged at an oil refinery and closely prefigures one of the most exciting sequences in *Godzilla Raids Again*.

Despite having a fraction of the time in which to work, Tsuburaya's effects for *Godzilla Raids Again* largely measure up to the standard of the first film. Several sequences are breathtakingly good. Nevertheless, the man who famously made his team tear apart one model set because it did not meet his perfectionist standards was in this film obliged by budgetary constraints to include footage that ought to have been reshot: During Godzilla's climactic battle with Anguirus in downtown Osaka, one of the camera operators became confused about the proper way to adjust the frame rate. Instead of overcranking the film to produce slightly slowed-down action, he ran the film slowly and thereby produced speeded-up, Keystone Cops–style action. Tsuburaya was not pleased, but let the error in anyway.[6]

Because the rubber used for the monster costumes tended to decompose in storage, and the rigors of filming took a considerable toll on the suit, the technicians frequently had to rebuild the Godzilla costume. Until 1984 each suit was made from scratch, so with each reconstruction the design changed slightly. Inevitably, Godzilla's appearance differs from suit to suit — and sometimes even within each film. Tsuburaya's team redesigned the Godzilla suit to be slimmer and more flexible, to accommodate combat with another rubber-suited stunt actor. The head featured pronounced ears and, for shots that employed a smaller-scale hand puppet, jagged and misshapen teeth.[7]

The story is familiar in its outline. Again, the monster is first spotted in a fishing community. Paleontologists brief the authorities, a plan for defense is made and the nervous wait for the monster's attack begins. The city's defenses fail, and the metropolis is destroyed. *Godzilla Raids Again* operates on a much smaller scale, however. In the original, the smallest details of the heroes' personal lives took on global implications, but in the sequel the global problems are trivialized by the emphasis on the heroes' personal lives. In one infuriatingly inappropriate scene, smack in the middle of the climactic final confrontation between the army and Godzilla, Kobayashi interrupts the drama to ask Hidemi what kind of gift to give his sweetheart.

The American version makes much of the lead character's self-doubt. Over and over again, Tsukioka questions his courage. Ultimately, his comical sidekick Kobayashi proves to be the braver man, sacrificing himself gallantly. The original Japanese edition does not include this running theme, but instead focuses on the characters' love lives. The various attacks by Godzilla and Anguirus interrupt Tsukioka and Hidemi's wedding plans; all romantic moments conclude with something monstrous occurring.

Kobayashi's self-sacrifice in battle against Godzilla assumes slightly different significances in the two versions. In the English-language *Gigantis the Fire Monster*, his kamikaze attack on Godzilla demonstrates the kind of bravery foreshadowed by the obsessive self-doubt of his friend. By contrast, the Japanese version has foreshadowed no such thing, and his sad fate merely leaves behind his girlfriend and those who loved him. Despite the attempts by the American cut to imply he has summed up his resolve to live up to a heroic role, all that really happens is that Kobayashi gives up his life and love to defend his home from a monster.

The emphasis is on the effect of the monsters' rampage on a sector of society almost unable to defend itself. As the opening narration of the English version intones, "This then is the story of the price of progress to a little nation of people." As with *Godzilla*, the story focuses on innocent people caught in a terrible circumstance for which they hold no responsibility. In the 1954 film, although Ogata, Emiko and Serizawa were blameless for Godzilla's creation, they were nevertheless ready to face the menace and defeat it. The sequel takes us down a notch, to ordinary people without any special knowledge or abilities. No one in this little cannery operation is going to invent a super-weapon. These people do their best in this darkest hour, but it is not easy for them. Unfortunately, this daring approach misfires. After the destruction of Osaka, the characters simply move up north to Hokkaido. The disaster seems to be more of an inconvenience to them than a tragedy. The characters in *Godzilla* were eaten up by personal demons, but these folks seem infernally cheery.

The strange optimism of the sequel points to a change in the allegory. While *Godzilla* symbolized the horrors of war, *Godzilla Raids Again* depicts the postwar process of rebuilding. After their cities are destroyed by enemy nuclear forces, the Japanese pick themselves up and put their world back together again. In this story of survival, war references also appear in non-allegorical forms. The only strategy against Godzilla and Anguirus the Japanese authorities can formulate is to lure the monsters away with flares, requiring Osaka to remain in blackout. There is no small coincidence in the fact that such a blackout is also the defense against aerial bombing raids.

In the end, it is a kamikaze flight by Kobayashi that saves the day. The story takes some of the shame off the kamikaze pilots and shows how their bravery and self-sacrifice can have positive benefits to their society, which (in the film if not in real life) emerges intact from the nightmare of a nuclear attack. Ironically, the kamikaze references are stronger in the American version, which shows Tsukioka reunited with his Air Force regiment, who are happy to put their skills to use in battle against the monster. In the Japanese version, Tsukioka is reunited with *former college buddies*. Strangely, this change achieves the opposite effect of a similar change in the Americanization of *Godzilla*, in which the wartime experiences of Dr. Serizawa were deleted from the American version and replaced with a reference to Serizawa being reporter Steve Martin's former college buddy.

The rights to the North American distribution for *Gojira No Gyakushu* were initially purchased by the American Broadcasting-Paramount Theaters Pictures Corporation (AB-PT), for release through Republic Pictures. Inspired by what Embassy Pictures had done to *Godzilla, King of the Monsters!*, they intended to strip away everything but the special effects sequences, and build a new, American movie around those shots. Producers Harry Rybnick, Ed Barison, and Richard Kay announced in the May 7, 1957, issue of *Variety* that production would begin on *The Volcano Monsters* on June 17. AB-PT planned *The Volcano Monsters* as a total remake, with only the special effects footage of the Japanese original to be used.

It was not an unprecedented idea. Not only did Embassy's retooling of *Godzilla, King of the Monsters* serve as an inspirational model, but other Toho special effects pictures had endured even more radical revisions for the American market. The Distributors Corporation of America (DCA) took Ishiro Honda's 1955 *Jujin Yukiotoko* ("The Abominable Snowman") and turned into the John Carradine–starring *Half Human* (1958), even going so far as having Toho ship them the monster suit so they could film new footage tailored for the American edition.[8]

This was in fact the same plan Rybnick, Barison and Kay had in mind for *The Volcano Monsters*. The Godzilla and Anguirus suits were crated up and shipped off to Hollywood for new filming. The producers hired screenwriters Ed Watson and Ib Melchior to pen a new storyline to be filmed stateside using an all–American cast. Melchior would later write such science fiction movies as *The Angry Red Planet* (1959), *Journey to the Seventh Planet* (1961), *Reptilicus* (1962), and *Robinson Crusoe on Mars* (1964). Step one was for Melchior to exhaustively catalogue the Japanese cut of the film to ascertain which shots he could recycle, and from that to devise a workable storyline in which a Tyrannosaurus Rex and an Ankylosaurus are discovered hibernating in a volcano. Brought back to San Francisco for further study, the creatures break free and begin to battle, leveling San Francisco in the process (so that shots of Asian-looking buildings and signs in the footage could be passed off as "Chinatown").

Melchior drew up a list of new effects shots that he would need, including images of the "volcano monsters" being transported into San Francisco by boat, but before filming could begin, AB-PT went out of business.[9] As their assets were liquidated, the distribution rights to *Godzilla Raids Again* were acquired by entertainment attorney Paul Schreibman along with a small cadre of fellow venture capitalists. Looking to get a swift profit on their investment, they financed a quick Americanization of the film that did not entail any new photography, and paired the result on a double bill with another low-budget acquisition, *Teenagers from Outer Space*.[10]

Warner Brothers distributed the revised, dubbed *Gojira No Gyakushu* in the United States under the title *Gigantis the Fire Monster*. Some have speculated that the title switch was required because the distributors of the sequel had not acquired the rights to the name Godzilla, still held by the distributors of the original — but this is nonsense. Schreibman had been part of the team that worked on the Americanization of *Godzilla*, and he had come to the bizarre conclusion that he would be better off if this picture were not treated as a sequel, but was sold as a new and unrelated monster movie.[11]

*Gigantis the Fire Monster* could have been much more than it is, aiming for a greater goal than it achieves. The poorly executed Americanization all but ruins the virtues of the original film. The U.S. version begins with an irrelevant prologue featuring stock footage of nuclear test explosions and rockets. A somber narrator warns us that as Man "attempts to unlock the mystery of the universe in which he dwells, are there not darker and more sinister secrets on this planet Earth still unanswered, still baffling and defying men?" The pomposity of this narration sets the stage for what will be a mind-numbingly over-narrated 78 minutes. Every event and character motivation is described in such detail by the main character, Tsukioka, one could recommend this film to the blind. By contrast, the original version uses silence frequently to very powerful effect, creating eerie and haunting moods the English version merely tells the audience about.

Hugo Grimaldi, supervisor of the Americanization process, appended the entirely unrelated opening montage in an attempt to cash in on the space age craze. The endless and unnecessary narration by Tsukioka was an American alteration, as was the decision to delete almost all of Masaru Sato's original score. While Akira Ifukube's classic scores are the most iconic in the series, Masaru Sato was a towering figure in Japanese film soundtracks, likened by some to being Japan's Ennio Morricone. Sato took over as Kurosawa's primary film composer following the death of Fumio Hayasaka. In addition to scoring eight of Kurosawa's features, from 1957's *Throne of Blood* through 1965's *Red Beard*, Sato composed scores for four of the original series of Godzilla films.[12] Unfortunately, his moody and ominous soundtrack was removed from the American cut of *Gigantis*, replaced by less-effective music culled from American B-movies, making *Gigantis* sound more like a B-movie itself.

Keye Luke, a Chinese-born actor known for playing Charlie Chan's "Number One Son," talks himself hoarse as the voice of Tsukioka. George Takei of *Star Trek* fame got his Hollywood start dubbing Japanese fantasy films, and he can be heard throughout *Gigantis* in various supporting roles. Kobayashi was voiced by Daws Butler, who later supplied the voice for Hanna-Barbera's Yogi Bear. Since Butler speaks in essentially his Yogi Bear voice, with a fake Japanese accent, the character of Kobayashi assumes an even greater comic quality. Kobayashi's comic characterization is intended, however. The great Japanese actor Minoru Chiaki, one of Akira Kurosawa's repertory players, plays Kobayashi. Chiaki appears in *Seven Samurai* (1954) and *Throne of Blood*, among others. Chiaki's role in *The Hidden Fortress* (1958) provided the inspiration for C3PO in George Lucas' *Star Wars* (1977).[13]

What the characters have to say makes precious little sense. The dialogue has been badly mangled in translation, with some Japanese idioms apparently being translated literally. During a discussion about Hidemi's love life between her and another woman, the other woman inexplicably comments, "Kiss me again, I'm all yours." Later, stranded on Iwato Island, Tsukioka tells Kobayashi that "trying to please a woman is like swimming the ocean." Not all of the mysterious talk revolves around love, either. Tsukioka tries to tell Hidemi that he is not nearly as brave as she thinks he is, saying, "Ah, banana oil," a bizarre remark that had even the dubbing cast laughing at their own work.[14]

The most egregious example of this dubbing disaster occurs in the briefing scene, as the Osakan authorities discover they face a second Godzilla and another prehistoric monster to boot. Characters contradict themselves, confuse the monsters with one another, and assert spurious nonsense that any child would recognize as preposterous. The scene, heavy with non sequiturs, is worthy of the theater of the absurd. A section is quoted below, and while it may help to know that the English dubbed release calls Godzilla "Gigantis," and Anguirus "Angilas," such a fact will only help so far.

> TADOKORO: One of these animals is a Gigantis, born millions of years ago.
> MILITARY OFFICIAL: So, wouldn't that open worlds new to you?
> TADOKORO: So, a new book came out and we learn so much. And it is called Ankylosaurus, killer of the living.
> MILITARY OFFICIAL: Ankylosaurus?
> TADOKORO: True. Take a look at this — it's a picture. Ankylosaurus, a monster commonly known as the Angilas, a specimen of giant reptile roamed the Earth millions of years ago. Murderers, original plundering murderers who killed everything in their way. These creatures ruled the Earth at one time, and disappeared suddenly. I'll read you what it says: "Enormous in its size, tremendous in its strength. Somewhere, although it is not known when, these creatures may come alive after years of hibernation due to radioactive fallout. He has brains in several parts of his body, including the head, abdomen and the chest. He is a member of the Angilas family of fire monsters and can wipe out the human race." These boys saw both Gigantis and Angilas.
> MILITARY OFFICIAL: Gentlemen, Dr. Yamane has flown in from Tokyo. Perhaps he can show us the way to destroy the Gigantis monster of Angilas family. Dr. Yamane.
> YAMANE: Gentlemen, who is there among us who knows the way to destroy Gigantis? There is no way. None that I happen to know of, not one. I'm afraid there is no weapon to kill the monster. I brought with me a film. It shows what such a monster did to Tokyo. I remember the terrible sight in the city of Tokyo. You shall see what the monster did. All right, run the film please. (*Narrating the film:*) What you are looking at, gentlemen, is the formation of the world, millions of years ago, as science has been able to reconstruct it for you. Out of the boiling atmospheric gases of our planet Earth, nature evolved a world much hotter than the one we know of today. Out of these boiling Earth pools came a primitive form of life, which, normally enough, required oxygen and nitrogen. These creatures were born out of fiery matter, their very existence was based upon the element of fire. They breathed fire, they survived in fire, fire was a part of their organic makeup.

The original Japanese dialogue for this scene is dignified and perfectly sensible. In the American version, though, the very premise becomes laughable. This is supposedly being quoted from a paleontological textbook. A textbook that calls an extinct animal "killer of the living"? A textbook that says prehistoric animals will be revived by hydrogen bomb tests to destroy the human race? Evidently, producer Paul Schreibman did not expect his audience to care about scientific plausibility. American science fiction films of this period share this attitude of condescension, and modern audiences have a right to feel insulted.

The dialogue does not distinguish between Gigantis and Angilas, each one being called by the other's name at times. For that matter, the English version dubs both monsters with the same roar, further blurring any distinction between them.

With its clumsy dubbing, the sequel to *Godzilla, King of the Monsters!* feels like an amateurish effort. Although the screenplay of the Japanese version and Motoyoshi Oda's leisurely pacing is partly to blame, most of the fault lies with the Americanization. *Gojira No Gyakushu* is a movie about people, and the havoc giant monsters wreak on their lives. It is about the terror of living during wartime, about the struggle to find courage during a crisis, about love, about putting normal life back together again. American producers, conditioned to the formulaic plots of monster-on-the-loose films, expected a movie about monsters, and misplaced the emphasis.

*Chapter 6*

# Rodan

## SORA NO DAIKAIJU RADON
## (GIANT MONSTER OF THE SKY RODAN)

*And when, still calling to each other, one of them fell at last into the molten lava stream, the other still refused to save itself. Last of its kind, blasters of the air and earth, strongest, swiftest creatures that ever breathed, now they sank against the earth like weary children. Each had refused to live without the other, and so they were dying together. I wondered whether I, a twentieth century man, could ever hope to die as well.*

— Shigeru

Japanese version: 82 minutes, Released December 26, 1956
U.S. version (King Brothers-DCA): 79 minutes, Released in August 1957, advertised as *Rodan the Flying Monster*
Color, Academy Aspect Ratio
Produced by Tomoyuki Tanaka; U.S. version produced by Frank and Maurice King; directed by Ishiro Honda; assistant director Jun Fukuda; screenplay by Takeshi Kimura and Takeo Murata; story by Takashi Kuronomura; U.S. version narration written by David Duncan; music by Akira Ifukube; cinematography by Isamu Ashida; art direction by Takeo Kita; special effects by Eiji Tsuburaya; special effects art direction by Akira Watanabe; optical effects by Hiroshi Mukoyama
Starring Kenji Sahara (Shigeru), Yumi Shirakawa (Kyo), Akihiko Hirata (Dr. Kashiwagi), Akio Kobori (Nishimura), Yasuko Nakata (Young Woman), Monosuke Yamada (Ohsaki), Yoshifumi Tajima (Izeki), Kiyoharu Ohnaka
RODANS portrayed by Haruo Nakajima and Katsumi Tezuka

*A series of senseless killings has rocked the mining community of Kitamatsu. Circumstantial evidence and bald prejudice points to a disgruntled miner as the culprit, but the shocking truth soon reveals itself: The mine has opened up a long-buried cave of prehistoric creatures. Meganuron, giant dragonfly larva the size of cows, are loose and preying on people. Worse, a pair of pteranodons emerge from the mine, wreaking havoc as they fly around Japan. Unable to stop the monsters with conventional military might, the Japanese Self-Defense Forces lure the creatures to a volcano and cause an artificial eruption, burning them alive in the lava.*

Heroes in the Godzilla movies tend to be figures of authority, members of elite groups, people such as reporters, scientists, detectives, or leaders of the Self-Defense Forces. These are brave, intelligent, resourceful individuals capable of coping with giant monsters, space alien invaders, terrorists, gangsters, or criminally ruthless businessmen. However, on occasion the series presents protagonists from lower down the socio-economic ladder. For example, *Godzilla Raids Again* followed a small community of fishermen, figures out of Japan's pre-industrial heritage, as they faced horrors unleashed by the modern world. *Rodan* also tells its story from the point of view of the working class.

Shigeru (played by newly ascendant movie star Kenji Sahara) and his fellow miners in Kitamatsu face one monster after another. While being devoured alive by giant insects is a strictly science-fictional problem, the Meganuron larva make handy monster-movie metaphors for the various life-threatening dangers confronted by miners in the real world. Some of these dangers are depicted early in the film, from the "creeping floor" phenomenon to the sudden flood. Even without giant monsters to contend with, Shigeru notes that the mine "was becoming dangerous."

Miners are a literal underclass, forced to work in treacherous conditions underground to provide fuel for the prosperous world above. Although the job involves deadly occupational hazards, miners are notoriously underpaid. To tell a story about miners being killed by a mysterious underground force is on its face a form of social criticism.

However, the underworld workers face more than just the giant insects. Shigeru discovers a monster that literally eats the Meganuron for breakfast; the mere sight of it almost renders the poor fellow insane.

Notably, the monsters Rodan have no direct ties to nuclear tests. The American distributors tacked on an irrelevant prologue, similar to that of *Gigantis*, comprised of stock footage of nuclear bomb tests. This sequence concludes with a narrator intoning, "But what have these tests done to Mother Earth? Can the human race continue to deliver these staggering blows without arousing, somewhere in the depths of Earth, a reaction? A counterattack? A horror still undreamed of?" Outside of the American prologue, though, the only other reference to nuclear testing occurs when Dr. Kashiwagi offers his theory that the eggs were buried in lava during the Cretaceous period and held in suspended animation for millions of years. The recent nuclear tests then fractured the Earth's crust and released the eggs into air and warm water, reviving them.

Kashiwagi's theory, however, also comes with the doctor's own admission that he is merely making a guess. To put his theory into proper perspective, it is worth looking at another film made shortly after *Rodan*. In 1958, Toho released *The H-Man*, an "insubstantial man" film from the same creative team of Tomoyuki Tanaka, Ishiro Honda, and Eiji Tsuburaya, and starring the same cast of Kenji Sahara, Akihiko Hirata, and Yumi Shirakawa. Even more significantly, Takashi Kimura wrote the screenplays for both *The H-Man* and *Rodan*. Honda once said that Kimura's scripts were those that were most pointedly political and serious, unlike the more satirical work done by Shinichi Sekizawa.[1] In *The H-Man*, Kimura makes the link between nuclear testing and the movie's monsters explicit. Throughout *The H-Man*, the scientist played

by Sahara describes in detail how radioactive fallout turns animals and people into bloodthirsty liquid monstrosities, demonstrates his theory in various laboratory experiments, and goes to great lengths to prove that the various victims were indeed exposed to fallout. In short, although the science in question remains fictional and even absurd, Kimura treats it seriously and misses no details.

In the year between *The H-Man* and *Rodan*, the same creative team and again the same cast made *The Mysterians* (1957). Here, Kimura presented a race of genetically damaged aliens from a planet rendered uninhabitable by nuclear weapons. Although less serious and detailed in its approach than *The H-Man*, *The Mysterians* does take pains to highlight the terrible consequences of radiation.

By contrast, *Rodan* merely depicts a minor character making the link between radiation and the monsters *in passing*, while cautioning that he can only speculate on what has really happened. Had the filmmakers intended *Rodan* to indict nuclear testing, they could surely have employed some of the methods used in other concurrent productions to make that point. *Rodan*'s best-developed argument instead points to the mining operation as the cause of the monsters' appearance. Shigeru remarks at one point, "How could prehistoric monsters stir from their long death to move about on the Earth again? The only answer to that could be that they never really died, they only slept. We had dug too deeply for our coal and awakened them to destroy us all."

Movies like *Godzilla Raids Again* and *Rodan* depict a modern civilization that has invaded nature to fuel its expansion across the globe. Old cultures, like the fishermen of *Godzilla Raids Again*, are swept aside by progress. In response, the Earth sends out a force to exact its revenge. Rodan comes both from the Earth's prehistoric past and out of the planet's depths. In fact, many of Toho's monsters come out of the Earth itself: Both Godzilla and Anguirus crawl out of the ground after nuclear tests loosen the way and Mothra's egg tumbles out of a mountainside. These monsters represent an ancient, primal, and utterly natural force. Some critics have also noted that the tendency for giant monsters to emerge from the ground in the *kaiju eiga* symbolizes the nation's fears about the fragile nature of their world. After the many traumatic natural disasters visited on Japan in the twentieth century, not to mention the man-made disasters associated with the war, along come a breed of giant monsters to remind the country that the ground on which they build their society could give way at any moment. The monsters Rodan generate a flood, contribute to the eruption of a volcano, and cause two earthquakes. It has been said that "if Japan has a national nightmare, it is not the atomic bomb which fell from above, but the earthquake which comes from below."[2]

This serious, somber film marks the monster-movie debut of writer Takeshi Kimura, who co-authored the screenplay with *Godzilla* stalwart Takeo Murata. Kimura, a prominent and prolific member of Toho's screenwriting department, would also write *Destroy All Monsters* (1968) and *Godzilla vs. Hedorah* (1971). Along with his Godzilla credits, Kimura also penned the aforementioned *The Mysterians* and *The H-Man* plus *The Human Vapor* (1960), *The Last War* (1961), *Gorath* (1962), *Matango* (1963), *Frankenstein Conquers the World* (1965), *War of the Gargantuas* (1966) and *King Kong Escapes* (1966).

Kimura's script for *Rodan* includes a number of harrowing glimpses of human pain and suffering. The wailing of a distraught widow punctuates an early scene. The death by Rodan's first victim, a JSDF jet pilot, leads to a disturbing scene in which the dead man's bloodied helmet sits in the center of the screen as his JSDF superiors ponder what could have killed him. Later, a young couple meet their tragic end, eaten alive by one of the Rodans. The Japanese cut features several gory moments, in lurid color, trimmed from the American release. Such scenes would become increasingly rare over subsequent years.

Kimura modeled his script somewhat on the American film *Them!* (1954), even recreating a few scenes. Not only do the giant insects recall the mutated ants of *Them!*, but Kimura's story also follows the same structure, as both films gradually unfold a mystery. The script breaks evenly into two parts. The first half concerns the gradual discovery of the Meganuron, which turn out to be an easily disposed of menace. Only then are there hints of the real monster. However, the first sighting of Rodan occurs more than a half-hour in, and the identification of it as a prehistoric pteranodon occurs 45 minutes into the movie. Rodan does not appear on-screen in full adult glory until quite late. By the time Rodan's identity is established, the film is already nearing its completion. There is precious little time for any depth to the story; the mystery exists for its own sake.

Rodan's Japanese name is Radon, a shortening of Pteranodon. Pteranodons, however, most likely could not fly, certainly not at supersonic speeds. Although Kimura should not be expected to know that, he could have looked up the Cretaceous period. Had he done so, he might not have placed it only twenty million years ago when sixty-five million would have been a better guess.

Kenji Sahara's starring role here more or less began his long-lasting career in *kaiju eiga*. (He had previously appeared in *The Abominable Snowman*, but his role was all but removed from the mangled version released in America well after *Rodan*, and as such did not serve as a meaningful introduction for him to American audiences.) Sahara would perform in *The Mysterians*, *The H-Man*, *Atragon* (1963), *War of the Gargantuas* (1966), *Space Amoeba* (1970), and an astonishing total of ten Godzilla films, all the way into the 21st century.[3]

Haruo Nakajima, this time playing Rodan, continued to face hardship as a suitmation performer. The wire that allowed him to fly through the air (at less than supersonic speed, of course) snapped, dropping him three and a half feet to the stage below.[4]

Notably unlike the flat, gray, faux *cinema-verite* style of *Them!*, *Rodan* is a splashy spectacle in full color. In the wake of Warner Brothers' influential film, American monster-moviemakers took to shooting their pictures in a similarly undistinguished gray style — inexpensive and forgiving to special effects technicians. Toho's brashly colorful movies stand out by contrast. Eiji Tsuburaya manages his effects very well in color. The miniatures are superbly detailed, and the monsters' rampage in Tokyo makes a stunning centerpiece. Scenes from *Rodan* were even recycled for use in the American film *Valley of the Dragons* (1961).[5]

In their relentless (and dispassionately unmotivated) assault on downtown Sasebo, the Rodans wreak havoc in a novel fashion. Whereas Godzilla smashed buildings by physically tearing into them or by incinerating them with his atomic ray, the Rodans cause destruction without contact. They merely fly around, and the gale force winds created in their wake rip the city apart. The spectacular orgy of destruction features some astonishing effects in which invisible forces demolish entire cityscapes. Buildings implode, glass shatters, buses and terrified policemen fly helplessly into the air. With the Rodans offscreen, such images show a city destroying itself. Evidently proud of his achievements, Tsuburaya included an in-joke for the eagle-eyed viewer: During the attack on Sasebo, the Rodans destroy a camera shop bearing the name Tsubumaya (sic).

Just over six months after Rodan appeared on Japanese screens, Distributors Corporation of America (DCA) released a slightly shortened, dubbed version to the American market. Ironically, the American version of *Rodan* was produced by Frank and Maurice King, who would just a few years later produce their very own monster movie, *Gorgo* (1961) in Ireland and England.[6] DCA had been involved with TransWorld in the distribution of *Godzilla, King of the Monsters!*, and in a few years would deconstruct *The Abominable Snowman* into *Half Human*. *Rodan*'s Americanization process was comparatively minor. Aside from a stock-footage prologue implying that nuclear testing had triggered the release of the monsters, no new footage was added, and little was cut. Unfortunately, the haunting and subtle soundtrack by Akira Ifukube was one of the casualties, almost completely deleted from the U.S. print in favor of unmemorable B-movie cues.

The most significant addition was a layer of near-constant narration. Whereas the smothering voice-over of *Gigantis* needlessly summarized onscreen events that were plainly visible to the viewer, here the narration explores the unseen. Character motivations, expressed subtly and ambiguously by the tensely underplayed original, are given voice.

In the conclusion, humankind has trapped the two Rodans in a volcanic eruption. In the finale of the Japanese version, various characters exchange silent glances, pregnant with conflict: fear that the volcanic eruption will fail to stop the monsters, fear that it will go too far and destroy more than just the monsters, regret at the death of such awesome creatures, disgust at their pain.... The viewer is left to fill in the details. In the American version, the narration makes everything quite clear — yet infinitely more poignant. As recut by editor Robert S. Eisen, one of the Rodans is caught in the fiery lava, unable to escape and burning to death. The other, in a gesture of love, tries first to save the other, then realizes the futility of it and joins its mate (or sibling?) in the lava. Unwilling to go on alone, the second Rodan commits suicide — something not suggested by the Japanese version.

The human emotions exhibited by the monsters in this tragic scene mirror an earlier moment between human heroes Kyo and Shigeru. Fearing the volcanic eruption, the authorities evacuate the area. Kyo violates the evacuation orders to join Shigeru at the most dangerous spot of all. She explains her reasons for risking her life: "I love you." He holds her tight: "I love you too." They will face the danger together. When one Rodan joins the other in death rather than separate from its loved one, Kyo buries her head in Shigeru's shoulder, as if she has recognized something of herself in the creature that now burns to death. With Ifukube's elegiac music underscoring the tragic dimensions of the scene, and Shigeru's narration honoring the monster's sacrifice, *Rodan* concludes with monster movie pathos.

The humans have not simply defeated the monsters, they have tortured them to death. In this presentation, this scene audaciously asks for, and receives, audience sympathy for giant monsters that have murdered thousands and destroyed an entire city.

In its recut form, *Rodan*'s touching and tragic conclusion leaves an indelible impression on the viewer and makes the film one of Toho's strongest entries. *The Monthly Film Bulletin* commented in its review that "the [R]odans die horribly, but nobly," a sentiment harder to summon up for the more austere original cut.[7]

The notion of a sympathetic monster protagonist had not yet echoed back to the filmmakers at Toho, but when it did, the consequences would redefine the genre.

# Chapter 7

# *Varan the Unbelievable*

## DAIKAIJU VARAN (GIANT MONSTER VARAN)

*We requested logical reinforcements here but their army went overboard in order to appease public opinion. They sent us tanks, bazookas, full battle equipment. Not so much to intimidate a few natives into leaving their village, but ostensibly to protect them from some prehistoric animal rumored to be at the bottom of the lake. This whole thing's gotten out of hand.*
— Commander Bradley

Japanese version: 87 minutes, Released October 14, 1958

U.S. version (Crown International): 70 minutes, Released December 12, 1962, double-billed with *First Spaceship on Venus*

Black and white, Widescreen

Produced by Tomoyuki Tanaka; U.S. version produced by Jerry A. Baerwitz; directed by Ishiro Honda; assistant director Koji Kajita; U.S. version directed by Jerry A. Baerwitz; screenplay by Shinichi Sekizawa; story by Takashi Kuronomura; U.S. version written by Sid Harris; music by Akira Ifukube; U.S. version music by Albert Glasser; cinematography by Hajime Koizumi; U.S. version photographed by Jack Marquette; art direction by Kiyoshi Suzuki; special effects by Eiji Tsuburaya; special effects art direction by Akira Watanabe; optical effects by Hiroshi Mukoyama

Starring Kozo Nomura (Dr. Kenji Uozaki), Ayumi Sonoda (Yuriko), Fumito Matsuo (Motohiko Horiguchi), Koreya Senda (Dr. Sugimoto), Akihiko Hirata (Dr. Fujimura), Fuyuki Murakami (Dr. Umajima), Akira Sera (Village Priest), Akio Kusama (Officer Kusama), Yoshio Tsuchiya (Office Katsumoto), Minosuke Yamada (Secretary of Defense), Hisaya Ito (Ichiro Shinjo), Yoshifumi Tajima (Captain), Takashi Ito (Village Boy)

U.S. version stars Myron Healey (Commander Bradley), Tsuruko Kobayashi (Anna Bradley), Clifford Kawada (Captain Kishi), Derick Shimatsu (Matsu)

RODANS portrayed by Haruo Nakajima and Katsumi Tezuka

*Yuriko Shinjo, an intrepid reporter from Tokyo, joins Dr. Kenji Uozaki and a group of biological researchers as they head into a primitive village for clues regarding the mysterious disappearance of a previous expedition. The locals blame their angry god Baradaki — and despite all reason, there indeed is an enormous creature deep in the wilderness that proceeds to attack the mainland. The military is outmatched, until Dr. Fujimura steps forward with an experimental explosive that may offer a solution ... if only they can get the substance inside the creature somehow.*

Encouraged by the strong television revenues for the American broadcast of *Godzilla, King of the Monsters*, AB-PT Pictures, the motion picture division of ABC Television, approached Toho in 1957 to produce a monster flick expressly for the occasion. It was a bold move. Made-for-TV movies were still largely unprecedented, not to mention ones commissioned from Japanese filmmakers.[1]

Tomoyuki Tanaka had no illusions about the nature of the assignment. By this point he had fashioned a flourishing franchise all his own of increasingly spectacular and wildly popular science fiction movies, few of which had ever been screened in America at all. Going from strength to strength, he had produced *Godzilla, Godzilla Raids Again, The Abominable Snowman, Rodan, The Mysterians,* and *The H-Man* — of which only *Godzilla* and *Rodan* had been granted export visas, and then only in substantially altered form.

Most importantly, Tanaka already had a relationship with AB-PT for *The Volcano Monsters,* a project that was intended to strip away all but the special effects scenes of *Godzilla Raids Again* (see Chapter 5). Tanaka knew there was no reason to approach this new assignment with any undue ambition. It would be as generic as possible, a routine programmer. It would be custom-fit to TV expectations—shot in black and white and in the standard dimensions of a television frame. His other pictures were now full color and widescreen — but no Japanese theatrical release was even planned for *Varan*, which would be made on the cheap to ensure a profit from the ABC sale alone.[2]

*Varan* was conceived as an amalgam of the least distinctive characteristics of *Godzilla* and *Rodan*, with a monster that fuses attributes of both previous monsters. Varan, a reptilian sea creature, improbably flies (although footage of the lumbering critter taking to the air was removed from the American version, about which more anon). This ancient beast emerges from the depths of Japan's primitive past, and is swiftly identified so as to move quickly onto the scenes of destruction. That monsters crawled out of poor fishing and mining communities in these films is no accident: The formula allowed Japanese audiences to vicariously work through cultural fears of the conflict between their old traditional past and the brave new world of modern Westernized cities— and the calamities that result from that culture clash. Here, the filmmakers found their giant monster living amongst the Ainu, an indigenous people similar to Australian's aborigines. Anti-Ainu prejudice had always been a problem for Japan, and what once came thoughtlessly as a result of those prejudices would later become sources of embarrassment, as the mainstream Japanese culture matured. Individual shots depicting the Ainu as not just backward but deformed would be snipped from later reissues of *Varan*. *The Abominable Snowman* (the original film from which *Half Human* was created) featured such extensive condescending portrayals of Ainu culture that it could not be similarly rescued with some judicious editing, and would in later years be completely suppressed — much as Disney has buried *The Song of the South*, to avoid having to rationalize its now outdated racial stereotypes.[3]

In a clear sign of the film's reduced status, its leading man is Kozo Nomura. This would be Nomura's one and only starring credit in a career spent on the sidelines as a supporting player. He shows up in small roles in a multitude of more ambitious features, like *Battle in Outer Space*, *The Human Vapor*, *Gorath*, *Frankenstein Conquers the World*, *Mothra vs. Godzilla*, and *Ghidrah, The Three-Headed Monster*. His charm-deprived performance here as Dr. Kenji Uozaki demonstrates why he was not typically allowed to take center stage. His costar is Ayumi Sonoda, last seen in a brief part in *The H-Man* as a nightclub dancer liquefied by the titular monster. Far more capable performers like Akihiko Hirata and Yoshio Tsuchiya pop up in supporting roles, but their time and attention were considered more valuable elsewhere.[4]

Eiji Tsuburaya took the budget-conscious approach to heart as well. Knowing his work was destined for a low-resolution TV screen, he cut corners and recycled snippets of footage from the Godzilla films. During production, AB-PT collapsed, taking both the *Volcano Monsters* and *Varan* deals with them into oblivion. Tanaka was now obliged either to abandon it and lose what had been thus far invested, or retool it for a Japanese release after all. In opting for that latter choice, though, some of their previous decisions would now create problems. As a sizable chunk of footage had already been completed, the rest of the film would be produced, anachronistically, in black and white. Widescreen was a non-negotiable standard for theatrical release, however, so the completed footage would be zoomed in and cropped during printing to artificially conform it to the wider dimensions of the movie screen — and greatly enhancing the flaws inherent in the material, which Tsuburaya had assumed would be concealed by the small screen.[5]

Ishiro Honda more or less sleepwalked through the endeavor, which lacked even a cursory attempt to express a deeper message or hidden significance. The script lacked any coherent explanation for the monster menace; there was no logical explanation of where it came from or what it wants. *Godzilla* and *Rodan* also conspicuously lacked such explanations, but they made up for it with heady metaphorical suggestion. No such hidden significance is attached to Varan's marauding. This is merely garden-variety monster-on-the-loose shenanigans for their own sake.

None of the filmmakers had any reason to regard the resulting picture with pride, but it did its job and made money. Four years afterwards, it did come to American screens, in a radically altered form. The American print lists an entirely different slate of credits, not once mentioning any of the Toho cast or crew, appropriate since the American print, while bearing the same title, includes less than 15 minutes of footage from the original. Akira Ifukube's score had been one of the highlights of the original cut; his subtle soundtrack played with Ainu folk melodies and anticipated the masterwork that was to come with Ifukube's compositions for *King Kong vs. Godzilla*. The American cut disposed of nearly all of this music in favor of cues from Albert Glasser's *The Amazing Colossal Man* soundtrack.[6]

Producer Jerry A. Baerwitz, who also directed the new footage, supervised a wholescale overhaul of the film into an entirely new creation. The new script by Sid Harris revolves around Commander James Bradley (played by Myron Healey), an American military scientist stationed in Japan. He plans to test an experimental de-salinization procedure on a large lake. It is an inconvenience to him that the lake he has selected happens to be home to an entire village whose inhabitants do not especially want to evacuate. Pressured by the press (which dogs him as a "cruel-hearted tyrant who drives poor homeless natives from their home and pollutes their sacred lake") and his distressed Japanese wife (Tsuruko Kobayashi), Bradley finally relents and allows the villagers to stay in their homes. When he puts the chemical into the lake, though, it enrages a giant monster which proceeds to lay waste to all of Japan.

The American version provides no better explanation for the proceedings than the Japanese original, and seems content to let things happen just because the audience expects them to. Curiously, the American cut is also uncertain what to call the monster; despite the title, no one ever refers to the thing as Varan. The villagers worship a god they call Obachi, from the

Japanese for "goblin." In the Japanese version, the villagers call their god "Baradaki" (or "Varadaki," because Japanese mixes "b" with "v" as freely as it does "r" with "l"). Scientists eventually identify the thing as an extinct "Varanopode," and "Varan" would seem a natural shortening of that name. The filmmakers had started with the Latin phrase "Varanus Pater" for "Father of Lizards" and let that devolve into something more monster-sounding.[7]

Baerwitz's *Varan* is 17 minutes shorter than Honda's cut, and includes almost an hour's worth of Myron Healey complaining. Interestingly, Healey's character sees himself as a misunderstood figure who has offered his time and expertise to help a foreign country improve its lot, and his sincere efforts are attacked and protested by the very people he hopes to aid. The tense relationship between postwar Japan and its former occupier does not get so overt an airing in any of the original Japanese versions of these films, and was largely taboo from Japanese cinema of all genres. This low-budget exploitation picture is too insubstantial a confection to warrant a deep analysis of this theme; nevertheless the American version of *Varan* deserves a passing nod for its unusually politicized content.

The combination of Honda's material with Baerwitz's is as clumsy as possible. What little Japanese language footage was retained from Honda's was left without either subtitles or dubbing, and these clips are printed such that the American material literally shoves them off the screen. Like its Japanese source, the American *Varan* was a programmer, judged by box office receipts rather than artistic aims, and is forgotten today in almost all respects. While the attitude expressed by this Americanization shows rude disrespect to the source, Baerwitz effectively took a film that had no viable U.S. market and made it into a profitable B-picture suitable for exploitation use.

Although the original Japanese version of *Varan* remains a fairly unimpressive outing for all concerned, it has been included here for consideration for one outstanding contribution. Seen in its unaltered form, *Varan* may be a low-rent retread of increasingly well-worn tropes, but one salted liberally with irreverent dialogue and sly humor. The overall plot structure remains traditional in its stodgy familiarity, but the characters that populate it have quirky, sparkling personalities that come across through *Mad* magazine–worthy wisecracks.

Screenwriter Shinichi Sekizawa was a late addition to the Toho team, but a vital one. Tomoyuki Tanaka, Ishiro Honda, Eiju Tsuburaya, and Akira Ifukube had proven that they could make great monster movies; with Shinichi Sekizawa writing, they were set to make *kaiju eiga*. It took Sekizawa's unique mind to bring the right flavor of craziness to the proceedings, to embrace the inherent absurdity of the enterprise without undermining any of it.

He started out as an animator, studying at the Kyoto Animation Studio alongside Osamu Tezuka, arguably Japan's most influential manga artist. It is easy to see in hindsight the critical role it would later play in Sekizawa's profession that he began his creative life so intimately connected to visual storytelling and trick photography — but before that came to any fruition, there was a painful lacuna in the man's life. World War II came along and Sekizawa found himself drafted into service in the South Pacific. From 1941 until 1946 he was stuck in bug-infested muggy islands with little to eat.

Sekizawa hated the war, he was hungry, and he wanted to go home.

When the war ended and he finally did get to go home, he set his mind to eating, and living life to its joyful fullest. Ishiro Honda once said that Sekizawa was never political. To put that remark into proper context, Sekizawa's colleague on the Toho lot writing these science fiction spectacles was Takashi Kimura, a dour, dark man. Kimura was most explicitly political, and his status as a card-carrying member of the Communist Party was something of an issue for him. Obviously, compared to Kimura, Sekizawa was certain to be seen as apolitical. Seen aside from this relief and taking Sekizawa only in his own context, his *joie de vivre*, his lust for life, was itself a private political response to the ascetic authoritarianism behind Imperial Japan's wartime ambitions.

Once back home from the war, Sekizawa rebooted his film career, initially at the marvelously named Beehive Studios. He started off as an assistant director, but was recommended for a writing gig as well. Sekizawa managed to turn in a finished script for *Profile of the City* in just four days — a record so astonishing he cemented a career there and then. In 1956, over at Shintoho, he wrote and directed a now-forgotten sci-fi bauble called *Fearful Attack of the Flying Saucers* (only a rough translation: it has never received distribution outside Japan). Following that, Sekizawa was asked to develop a TV series about a giant monster.

Thus was born *Agon: The Atomic Dragon*, in which atomic testing unleashes a maninasuitasaurus, which just happens to look and act like the low-rent Godzilla knock-off he was, even down to the fiery breath. Rightfully unhappy at such blatant plagiarism, Toho shut the thing down.

To keep Sekizawa from developing any further viable competition, they put him to work on their own projects, first with *Varan*. Sekizawa had found a niche, and would specialize in monster movie scenarios until his retirement in 1974, with *Godzilla vs. Mechagodzilla*.[8]

It is often cited that Toho assigned Kimura to the darker, more adult, more politically charged stories while Sekizawa got all the so-called "childish" gigs. Guy Tucker, in his book *Age of the Gods*, cites an exchange between Kimura and Sekizawa. Kimura asked Sekizawa, "Do you really enjoy writing this?" to which Sekizawa replied, "Of course, I think it's a lot of fun." Kimura brooded, "Not for me."[9]

Sekizawa loved monster movies. After the deprivation and suffering of the war years, he found a job where he could without question enjoy himself, and that enthusiasm spilled over to the audience as well. Sekizawa's passion worked to make the genre his own, and his contributions made Toho's science fiction spectacles into unique cultural expressions.

All the elaborate effects and spectacle in the world means little without a good script. With a dry wit, a flair for characterization, and a boyish embrace of the absurd, Sekizawa wrote great scripts, more often than not. In place of the stalwart heroes and frail heroines who populated the earlier expressions of the genre, Sekizawa wrote for flawed, funny, personable characters. The leading roles in such films had often been little more than utilitarian ciphers, bland figures serving functional narrative roles. Sekizawa's characters bubble with life.

*Varan* served as a testing ground for ideas that Sekizawa would revamp and improve upon over the coming years. Its basic plot structure would prove useful for *Mothra* and *King Kong vs. Godzilla*: An excursion to a remote area turns up strange discoveries that prompt a second, better outfitted expedition that finds a giant monster worshipped by primitive locals. Sekizawa also signaled his lack of interest in the shrinking violets and mousy love interests of the previous films: His heroines would be fully engaged in the action. Ayumi Sonada's Yuriko character was also a reliable template for brassy reporter heroes to come. A Japanese Lois Lane investigating "The Mysteries of the 20th Century," Yuriko would return in both name and characterization (but with a different actress in the role) a few years later for one of the strongest (and strangest) Godzilla entries, *Ghidrah, The Three-Headed Monster*.

After *Varan*, Sekizawa admitted he was bored by the typical monster-on-the-loose scenario. He wanted to change the formula. His ambition, something no other screenwriter involved in giant monster movies anywhere else in the world was even considering, now seems elegantly simple and obvious: to interconnect the human dramas with the monster action. In other words, the human characters didn't have to be reacting to the monster mayhem; it could work the other way around. You could build a coherent narrative that continued to develop equally well when the actors were stunt men in rubber suits as when they were trained thespians, as long as you treated *all* of the characters as characters.[10]

*Varan*, like its predecessors in Japan and the West, involves humans in conflict with monsters. What happens to the main characters, how they comport themselves and what they do, will settle the monster problem — by killing or vanquishing the giant animal and its threat. Sekizawa added quirky humor to those human scenes, but the overall pattern stayed intact. But he started to think turning that pattern on its head.

In the old paradigm, monsters threaten people and people resolve it. But what if people threaten people, and monsters resolve it?

# Chapter 8

# *Mothra*
## Mosura (Mothra)

*Oh no, these weren't children. They were two fully grown women a foot high.*

— Chujo

Japanese version: 101 minutes, Released July 30, 1961 (Champion Festival Release: 62 minutes), double-billed with *Latitude Zero*

U.S. version (Columbia Pictures): 88 minutes, Released May 10, 1962, double-billed with *The Three Stooges in Orbit*

Color, Widescreen

Produced by Tomoyuki Tanaka; U.S. version produced by David Horne; directed by Ishiro Honda; assistant director Masaji Nanagase; U.S. version dubbing directed by Lee Kressel; screenplay by Shinichi Sekizawa; story by Shinichiro Nakamura, Takehido Fukunaga and Yoshi Hotta; U.S. version written by Robert Myerson; music by Yuji Koseki; cinematography by Hajime Koizumi; art direction by Takeo Kita and Teruaki Abe; edited by Echiji Taira; special effects by Eiji Tsuburaya; special effects cinematography by Sadamasa Arikawa; special effects art direction by Akira Watanabe; optical effects by Hiroshi Mukoyama and Yukio Manoda

Starring Frankie Sakai (Tsinchan "Bulldog" Fukuda), Hiroshi Koizumi (Dr. Chujo Nakazo), Ken Uehara (Dr. Haradawa), Kyoko Kagawa (Photographer Michi Hanamura), Jerry Ito (Clark Nelson), Emi and Yumi Ito (The Shobijin), Takashi Shimura (News Editor), Akihiko Hirata (Doctor), Yoshifumi Tajima (Military Advisor), Akihiro Tayama (Shiro, Chujo's son), Andrew Hughes (Rolisican Official), Kenji Sahara (Helicopter Pilot), Robert Dunham (Rolisican), Tetsu Nakamura (Nelson's Henchman), Seizaburo Kawazu, Yoshio Kosugi, Yasushi Yamamoto, Haruya Kato, Ko Mishima, Shoichi Hirose, Koro Sakurai, Hiroshi Iwamoto, Mitzuo Tsuda, Masamitsu Tayma, Toshio Miura, Tadashi Okabe, Akira Wakamatsu, Johnny Yuseph, Obel Wyatt, Harold Conway, Akira Yamada, Koji Uno, Wataru Ohmae, Toshihiko Furuta, Keisuke Matsumaya, Yoshiyuki Kamimura, Takeo Nagashima, Mitsuo Matsumoto, Shinpei Mitsu, Kazuo Higata, Shideo Kato, Rinsaku Ogata, Yutaka Oka, Arai Hayamizu, Hiroyuki Satake, Kazuo Imai, Yoshio Hatton, Hiroshi Akitsu, Akio Kusama

MOTHRA portrayed by Haruo Nakajima and Katsumi Tezuka

*A vicious typhoon crashes a ship in the middle of an atomic test site. Inexplicably, the survivors show no signs of radiation exposure. Reporter Tsinchan "Bulldog" Fukuda and his photographer Kyoko Kagawa learn that the men credit their survival to the natives of Infant Island, who fed them a mysterious juice that apparently protected them from fallout.*

*Rolisica, the country responsible for the Infant Island atomic tests, sends an exploratory expedition, led by businessman Clark Nelson. The team, including "Bulldog" and anthropologist Dr. Chujo Nakazo, discovers an ancient civilization presided over by two miniature women. Nelson kidnaps the girls and exhibits them in "The Secret Fairies Show," a tawdry spectacle in which the captured priestesses pray to their god Mothra.*

*"We'll return to our island and that's good. The part that makes us unhappy is you could be...." They trail off ominously, adding, "And there isn't anything you can do to stop her."*

*A giant larva hatches and heads for Tokyo, destroying everything in its path. Nelson refuses to relent and denies responsibility for the carnage — and has the diplomatic backing of his country's government to hide behind. As Japan faces down the wrath of Mothra, it seems the law cannot protect the innocent...*

Three writers collaborated on the basic scenario of *Mothra*. When they had finished, Shinichiro Nakamura, Takehido Fukunaga and Yoshi Hotta had prepared a draft with a fairly preposterous premise about an enormous monster moth. From that outline, Shinichi Sekizawa created his masterpiece and permanently rewrote the rules of the genre. The character Mothra would remain his brainchild; Sekizawa would pen all of Mothra's subsequent

51

first-series appearances except for *Destroy All Monsters* (1968). In addition to his Godzilla series credits, Sekizawa also wrote *Varan the Unbelievable* (1958), *Battle in Outer Space* (1959), *Secret of the Telegian* (1960), *Atragon* (1963), *Dogora the Space Monster* (1964), and *Latitude Zero* (1969).

Sekizawa, like Honda, had served in the Japanese Imperial Army during World War II. His wartime experiences, however, largely consisted of starving on isolated islands in the South Pacific. His war years influenced his writing, and many of his scripts are set on South Pacific islands where weird things take place.

It has been said of Sekizawa that he most resembled the character of "Bulldog." Like his fictional alter ego, Sekizawa was a large, ebullient man; one of Toho's producers, Fumio Tanaka, called him "childish, but in the most positive way."[1]

*Mothra* makes no pretense at sophistication. This is a family picture with entertainment as its primary goal. James Cameron's *Aliens* (1986) covers much of the same territory, but in a film that is self-consciously arty and quite grim. *Mothra* never takes itself too seriously, and therefore is more surprising for its subtextual depth. One of Toho's greatest achievements, *Mothra* stands as a unique monster movie event. In a standard monster-on-the-loose plot, the heroes ultimately discover the monster's Achilles heel and destroy it in the final reel. In the audacious conclusion to *Mothra*, the humans stop fighting her altogether. In fact, they give the monster exactly what she wants, and let her return home, waving goodbye and saying, "Sayonara." They even invite Mothra's priestesses to return when they wish. Mothra may be a force to reckon with, but she is not a menace to be destroyed. Mothra is a monster with distinct intelligence and noble motivations.

"Monsters are tragic beings," said Ishiro Honda. "They are not evil by choice. They're born too tall, too strong, too heavy: That is their tragedy. They do not attack humanity intentionally, but because of their size, they cause damage and suffering. Therefore, man defends himself against them. After several stories of this type, the public finds sympathy for the monsters. In reality, they *favor* the monsters."[2]

The actual villain of the movie is not the giant monster, but the greedy capitalist Clark Nelson — a template for selfish businessmen who terrorize many of Sekizawa's scripts to come. Nelson's egotism costs thousands of people their lives and leaves two cities in ruin. At first, the Rolisican government backs him, asserting their obligation to protect the rights and property of their citizens abroad. (*Mothra* does not directly indict America or its policies, but the name "Rolisica" fools no one watching the film.) This attitude gives way as the giant creature advances unabated, and by the time Mothra heads for New Kirk City, public opinion finally turns against Nelson. It may be possible to countenance a monster destroying a foreign land in the name of one man's profits, but Not In My Backyard.

The priestesses are identified in the Japanese dialogue as "Shobijin," a word coined by Sekizawa for "little beauties." The original scenario provided for four of them, but Sekizawa collapsed them into two to take advantage of a new relationship his studio had forged with Columbia Pictures.[3] The Peanuts, also known as Emi and Yumi Ito — and for that matter, originally born Hideyo and Tsukiko Ito — were a singing sensation who had hit number one on the Japanese pop music charts with their debut single, "Kuroi Hanabera," released by King Records in 1959. Known for their covers of American pop songs, the Peanuts released an album in the United States through Columbia Records, called "The Peanuts Around the World." They also made American television appearances on *The Danny Kaye Show* and *The Ed Sullivan Show*.[4] Twins are, for some reason, especially rare in Japan, which lent an extra-special hook along with their innate charm and talent. Toho had signed the Peanuts to a recording deal with a mind to fitting the pop idols somewhere into their fast-growing world of giant monsters. At this point, the studio was working out a co-production deal with Columbia for several pictures, including *Mothra*. Seeing as how the Peanuts' American albums were on Columbia's label, it was a perfect synergy to cast the girls in *Mothra* so that Columbia could use the movie to publicize their first American album, and vice versa.[5]

The Peanuts appeared in ten movies in all before their retirement in 1975. Three of which featured them as Mothra's priestesses—which means 30 percent of their entire movie career was spent singing to a giant moth. In addition to playing miniature women in science fiction thrillers, they were also adept at comedy; their first comedy feature was distributed on the lower half of the double bill with *King Kong vs. Godzilla*.

Exposure to the Peanuts' Shobijin inspires moral maturity in the various players of the film. While most of the characters initially exhibit a guarded quality, looking to protect themselves and their interests, all but Nelson become aware of a greater good. "Bulldog"'s editor angrily confronts his star reporter for keeping quiet about the tiny twins. "Bulldog" justifies his secrecy by pointing out that the world would have been better off if Mothra's people were simply left alone. "Are you a reporter or a social worker?" demands his editor, to which "Bulldog" replies, "In this case I don't know." "Bulldog"'s attitude mellows from the gung ho approach with which he began. He earned his nickname by relentless dogging every story, yet now he wants nothing more than to let this particular story go unreported.

Clark Nelson does not mature from his exposure to Mothra's people, however. He not only callously responds to news of Mothra's onslaught with a snide, "How am I concerned?" but his only property rights in question involve two girls he kidnapped and holds against their will. When "Bulldog" accuses him of slavery, he files a libel suit against the newspaper. The Rolisicans support him, despite the controversy over whether the Shobijin can be rightfully called "his." Jerry Ito's portrayal of Nelson, dubbed with a Bela Lugosi–esque voice, oozes villainy in every scene. Ito could not speak Japanese, and spoke his Japanese dialogue phonetically. Toho frequently employed Westerners living in Japan to play such roles, the primary requirement being a Caucasian look, not necessarily acting ability.[6] Ito, a bright and talented man, has both. His Nelson is wonderfully smarmy, and his final shootout with the Rolisican police provides a very satisfying death scene for one of the series' most memorable bad guys.

Of course, Clark Nelson is not the first evil capitalist in a monster movie, but *Mothra* was made and released during the period of Japan's economic rebuilding. Including a critique of capitalism, however limited, was daring simply by being there at all. In many ways, this critique is an attack on Western values and the Americanization of Japan. Even today, Japanese businesses value social good over pure profit. Americans are often surprised and befuddled by the fact that the Japanese companies with which they do business sometimes sacrifice obvious or immediate profits. Maintaining long-term social goals carries a greater importance than simply turning a profit on every transaction.[7] *Mothra*'s social criticism reflects the tension between the individual-orientation of American-style capitalism and Japanese communal values.

In a tellingly ironic touch, Nelson overlooks an excellent opportunity for profitmaking. The Infant Island juice evidently has the power to protect humans from radiation poisoning. Nelson makes no effort to cultivate or sell this juice, his Secret Fairies Show having seduced him with show biz glamour. He overlooks a miracle drug in his search for a blockbuster show, choosing style over substance. Perhaps this, too, reflects the image of Americans abroad.

Mothra is beautiful, colorful, and elegant, simultaneously delicate and powerful. She is a distinctively Japanese monster; no American would have created such a character. In fact, the American toy company Trendmasters discontinued the Mothra figure from their line of Godzilla action figures in the mid–1990s. Sales for the toy were low, and Trendmasters market research revealed that American children had difficulty recognizing Mothra as a monster.[8]

Unusually for films of this genre, *Mothra* has a considerable number of religious overtones.

As Mothra destroys New Kirk City, Chujo sees a cross atop a nearby church framed with a halo of sunlight. He realizes that the symbol he saw on Mothra's island had similarly iconic religious significance and, by treating Mothra with the respect due such a god, manages to defuse the situation. The tiny twins prayed for relief in their hour of need, and their god came through for them. The notion of Toho's *kaiju* as monster-gods recurs in many of the films. Deeply rooted in a Japanese folklore replete with images of demon-gods, the concept distinguishes Toho's output from American films.

These giant monster-gods are also like super-weapons, called into action when competing interest groups cannot solve their differences peacefully. Like real-life super-weapons, monster-gods attack indiscriminately. In the defense of her priestesses, Mothra injures and kills many innocent civilians. A frequently recurring theme throughout the series is a desire for international cooperation and peace, the only hope for a monster-free world. The army is always powerless against the monsters, who appear immortal or at least virtually so. Continued hostilities never resolve the problems. Only when the humans peaceably resolve their problems do the monsters go away — another departure from the American pattern, in which military action nearly always triumphs over monsters.

The screenplay never makes clear where Mothra's civilization on Infant Island came from, or how long they have lived there. It is certainly possible the Rolisicans are lying when they claim to have investigated the island before running their atomic tests. Possibly Mothra and her people lived underground until after the tests, or perhaps they migrated there only recently. The script raises many questions it never answers, but that is not a mistake. As mentioned earlier, Japanese art does not adhere to the values of "realism" in the way Westerners expect. *Cinderella*, for example, wastes none of the audience's time arguing whether fairy princesses exist; the storyteller simply takes the premise as given and moves on. *Mothra* asks its audience that they take as given the existence of a lost civilization, a giant moth, and miniature people. From where these weird, fantastic elements came is not the issue, just the interaction between them and the normal world.

The first two Godzilla films and *Rodan* were somber affairs whose sometimes clumsy English dubbing produced occasional moments of unintentional humor. *Mothra*, by contrast, included significant amounts of deliberate humor, one of Sekizawa's notable contributions to the genre. Most of the comedy comes from the slapstick antics of "Bulldog," played by Frankie Sakai, a very popular Japanese comedian. Funny without being a laughingstock, Sakai allows the film to maintain a light touch without ruining the tension necessary for a monster movie.

Several elements from *Mothra* would be swiftly recycled. In *King Kong vs. Godzilla*, Sekizawa again created a monster god with intelligence, who tramples cities without becoming unsympathetic. Again, a greedy capitalist's pursuit of profit threatens the lives of others. Even the mysterious berry juice made a return appearance (in fact, strange juice would crop up in numerous Sekizawa screenplays, including *Mothra vs. Godzilla*, *Godzilla vs. the Sea Monster*, and *Son of Godzilla*). *King Kong vs. Godzilla* would continue the lightly comic approach, which would permanently replace the humorless approach of the first few films.

## Chapter 9

# *King Kong vs. Godzilla*

## *KINGU KONGU TAI GOJIRA*
## (KING KONG AGAINST GODZILLA)

*I'm sick of Godzilla! I want my own monster!*

— Mr. Tako

Japanese version: 98 minutes, Released August 11, 1962 (Champion Festival Release: 74 minutes) U.S. version (Universal-International): 91 minutes, Released June 3, 1963, double-billed with *The Traitors*
Color, Widescreen
Produced by Tomoyuki Tanaka; U.S. version produced by John Beck; directed by Ishiro Honda; U.S. version directed by Thomas Montgomery; screenplay by Shinichi Sekizawa from the screenplay by George Yates; story by Willis O'Brien; characters created by Merian Cooper and Shigeru Kayama; U.S. version screenplay by Paul Mason and Bruce Howard; music by Akira Ifukube (not used in U.S. release); U.S. version music editor Paul Zinner with music by Henry Mancini, Herman Stein, Milton Rosen, and Robert Emmet Dolan; cinematography by Hajime Koizumi; art direction by Takeo Kita; edited by Echiji Taira; special effects by Eiji Tsuburaya; special effects assistant director Teruyoshi Nakano; special effects cinematography by Sadamasa Arikawa and Motoyoshi Tomioka; special effects assistant camera operator Koichi Kawakita; special effects art direction by Akira Watanabe; optical effects by Hiroshi Mukoyama, Taka Yuki and Yukio Manoda; U.S. version includes footage from *The Mysterians*
Starring Tadeo Takashimi (Sakurai), Mie Hama (Fumiko), Kenji Sahara (Fujita), Yu Fujiki (Kinsaburo), Ichiro Arishima (Mr. Tako), Tatsuo Matsumura (Dr. Markino), Jun Tazaki (General Shinzo), Akihiko Hirata (Premier Shigezawa), Yoshio Kosugi (Faro Island Native Chief), Akiko Wakabayshi (Tamiye), Senkichi Omura (Translator), Ikio Sawamura (Witch Doctor), Akemi Negishi (Dancing Girl)
U.S. version also stars Michael Keith (Eric Carter), Harry Holcombe (Dr. Johnson), James Yagi (Yataka Omura), Les Tremayne (Narrator)
GODZILLA portrayed by Haruo Nakajima and Katsumi Tezuka, KING KONG portrayed by Shoichi Hirose

*Mr. Tako, head of Pacific Pharmaceuticals, hopes that the legendary monster god of Faro Island can be used in an advertising campaign to boost the ratings for a television program he sponsors. "Find me a genuine monster," he orders his associates Sakurai and Kinsaburo, "if he exists or not!"*

*Meanwhile, the U.N. sub Sea Hawk approaches a glowing iceberg. One of the scientists aboard recognizes the glow as light radiated from a nuclear furnace. Godzilla breaks free from the ice, destroys the sub and begins a relentless advance on Tokyo.*

*Sakurai and Kinsaburo use a naturally occurring narcotic berry juice indigenous to Faro Island to capture King Kong. But the giant ape easily escapes his bondage, and instinctively seeks out his rival Godzilla.*

*Tokyo's last line of defense, a blockade of high tension wires carrying a million volts, is all that stands between the monsters and ten million people. Godzilla and Kong are going to fight — and the fate of Japan lies with the winner.*

The thought of King Kong, an icon of Americana, becoming a Japanese monster met with disapproval among many American critics. These reviewers failed to realize, however, that King Kong's bout with Godzilla was the work of American producers, and the project began with Willis O'Brien himself.

Anyone who admires *King Kong*, and by extension those who admire *Godzilla*, must pay their respects to Willis O'Brien, a true cinematic legend. To fully understand O'Brien's legacy, however, one must acknowledge the tragic disappointments that marked his career. Despite his many successes, he repeatedly failed to get his films made. His protégé, Ray Harryhausen, marveled that "he had so many projects fall through before they reached the screen. How he survived all these disappointments I'll never know."[1]

Following his success with the seminal 1925 silent adventure *The Lost World*, O'Brien spent seven years trying to find a producer for his proposed film *Creation*. Eventually Merian C. Cooper at RKO was interested, but only so far as it showed him how to produce *King Kong*. After the success of *King Kong*, O'Brien was forced into working on *The Son of Kong*, reluctantly. He then spent six months working on his *War Eagles*, only to have that project cancelled by the RKO top brass. O'Brien's next project was *Valley of Mist*, but Paramount stopped production when the full cost of stop-motion animation became apparent to them. *Valley of Mist* was eventually made, without O'Brien, as *The Beast of Hollow Mountain* (1956), and was animated with the stop-motion models Marcel Delgado had built for O'Brien's version. *The Beast of Hollow Mountain* was later semi-remade as *The Valley of Gwangi*, with animation by Ray Harryhausen.

Harryhausen and O'Brien worked together for Irwin Allen on the 1956 *The Animal World*, but Allen balked at the costs of animation. When Allen hired O'Brien to remake *The Lost World* in 1960, he forbade O'Brien from using his own pioneering technique. When O'Brien's trademark technique finally won an Academy Award, it was for *Mighty Joe Young*, which had been animated by Harryhausen under O'Brien's supervision.[2]

Disgruntled with his treatment in Hollywood, O'Brien tried to take control of his career. He wrote a treatment for a *King Kong* sequel, called alternately *King Kong vs. Frankenstein*, *King Kong vs. the Ginko* and *King Kong vs. Prometheus*. In the proposed sequel, Carl Denham brings the giant ape to San Francisco, where Kong squares off against a giant monster built by Dr. Frankenstein's grandson. The Ginko monster, a pastiche of elephants, bulls, and other jungle animal parts, fought the great Kong at the Golden Gate Bridge, with both monsters falling into the bay at the end.

O'Brien presented his treatment to John Beck, who bought the project and removed O'Brien from any further involvement. Beck hired screenwriter George Yates (author of *Them!*) to revise O'Brien's treatment. Unable to get financing in the States, Beck took the project to Toho. Tomoyuki Tanaka asked for the script to be changed again, to replace the Ginko with Godzilla, and agreed to finance production. RKO supplied the rights to the King Kong character, and Universal co-produced the film, now called *King Kong vs. Godzilla*, in return for the North American distribution rights.[3]

The year 1962 was to be Toho's thirtieth anniversary (counting from the firm's founding in 1932 as a theater company, five years before they stated making movies), and Tomoyuki Tanaka prepared *King Kong vs. Godzilla* as a celebration. It would have a go-for-broke budget and extensive promotion — and would need to be a softer, more friendly movie than the dark allegory of the 1954 original. Toho's bread and butter was comedies, comprising roughly thirty percent of the company's output, and so *King Kong vs. Godzilla* would naturally be seen as an extension of that filmic philosophy.[4]

For the first time, Godzilla would be shown in the glory of color and "Tohoscope" widescreen — which would expose some imperfections in the effects previously concealed by monochromatic film.

The new Godzilla suit designed by Akira Watanabe and constructed by Teizo Toshimitsu is strikingly effective, a distinctly reptilian Godzilla. Watanabe's King Kong design, however, is appalling, and a far cry from the otherwise high quality monster suits Toho had been making. The giant ape has a ratty, moldy look with misshapen arms and an inexpressive rubber face. The contrast with the very expressive and effective Godzilla costume is depressingly stark.

As in *Varan*, Kong is discovered living in a remote and primitive enclave within the Japanese islands, where natives worship the enormous thing as a god. No surprises here, as the same setup was used in the 1933 *King Kong*, long before Shinichi Sekizawa put pen to paper for the first time. Although Akira Ifukube digs into his Ainu-inspired *Varan* themes to create the islanders' chant, the visualization of the natives is markedly different this time. As if to avoid offending the Ainu again, the natives are now just Japanese actors in blackface(!). In one jaw-dropping scene, an actress coated in black makeup and wearing only a bikini made from coconuts does a suggestive dance in honor of Kong.

The American cut assumes that the two great beasts come into battle due to ancient, prehistoric rivalries between dinosaurs and apes—much as Godzilla and Anguirus went to war in *Godzilla Raids Again* as a mindless instinctual conflict over turf. However, not even the substantial alterations to the American version can completely get around the fact that, in Sekizawa and Honda's original rendition, the monsters have been brought together by human agency.

In Sekizawa's world, human conflicts come first, and the monsters cope with that: Mr. Tako's greed and narrow attention on his own publicity needs brings Kong to the mainland, and the humans consciously recruit Kong as a defense against Godzilla. Mr. Tako even says it in dialogue: "King Kong vs. Godzilla!" They will fight, because he says so. Employing the monsters as agents of human conflict, Sekizawa cannot afford to let his human characters slip into the poorly defined cipher roles of past films. He writes every character with style, and gives the cast a chance to shine.

Akihiko Hirata appears briefly as a government minister rejecting the use of nuclear weapons against the monsters (in dialogue only heard in the American version; in the Japanese version, Hirata's character, like everyone else, takes for granted that Japan will have nothing to do with nuclear weapons under any circumstances). Kenji Sahara plays the heroic inventor Fujita. Sahara, last seen in *Rodan*, would become a familiar face in the series along with Hirata. Appearing in the 2004 Godzilla anniversary *Godzilla Final Wars*, Sahara had become the most seen of Toho's stock players.[5] As Kenji Shara's love interest Fumiko, Mie Hama makes her series debut; she would later play Kissy Suzuki in 1967's James Bond thriller *You Only Live Twice*. Tadeo Takashima, the dashing leading man of the picture, returned to the series in *Son of Godzilla*, and Takashima's sons Masanobu and Masahiro starred in 1989's *Godzilla vs. Biollante* and 1993's *Godzilla vs. Mechagodzilla*, respectively.[6]

Another name in the credits would not find notice for many years to come. Tsuburaya's assistant camera operator, Koichi Kawakita, ultimately took Tsuburaya's place at the helm of the special effects department in 1989.

Incidentally, it cannot be said that no animals were injured in the production of this film. For the gooey and disturbingly realistic fight between Kong and the giant octopus, Tsuburaya in fact used a real octopus. According to then-assistant director of special effects Teruyoshi Nakano, Tsuburaya cooked and ate the octopus after filming.[7]

Tsuburaya and his team took special care to stage Godzilla's onslaught with flair. The sight of a giant monster stomping around in a miniature city can be a very abstract image, lacking the visceral horror of a smaller monster menacing a single individual. Toho's filmmakers avoid this problem by frequently including scenes in which the terror of Godzilla is shown through the eyes of a single person's experience. The original *Godzilla* featured a harrowing sequence set in a hospital, depicting the pain and suffering wrought by the monster's rampage. The plot of *Godzilla Raids Again* attempted to revolve around the consequences of the monsters' attack. With the post–*Mothra* shift to a more light-hearted presentation of Godzilla, these kinds of scenes would no longer be included (with the notable exception of *Godzilla vs. Hedorah* in 1971). From *King Kong vs. Godzilla* onwards, Godzilla's battles would largely result only in property damage, not death. To compensate, Shinichi Sekizawa's screenplay shows us the effect of Godzilla's march on one person, Fumiko. She goes to Hokkaido to search for her lover, whom she believes to be dead. He races after her, knowing she headed into the juggernaut's path. The sequence takes poor Fumiko on a *Perils of Pauline*–style series of near-misses as she has to face Godzilla alone. The terrifying and memorable sequence is mirrored later, when she is attacked on a train, this time by King Kong.

Such effective horror scenes stand out even further in the original Japanese version, because the original cut of *King Kong vs. Godzilla* is primarily a wry satire that cleverly skewers commercial exploitation and even makes self-referential jabs at itself. Mr. Tako, desperate to prop up the flagging viewership of the "boring" science program his company sponsors, wants to find a monster to use in his commercials. The entire expedition to find Kong rests on Tako's intent to use Kong as his company's spokesperson. The subsequent destruction wrought on Japan can then be plainly blamed on the selfishness of a man who was willing to let people die if it would bring him better TV ratings.

Later, one of Tako's subordinates notes Godzilla's popularity: "There's even a movie." The office workers at Pacific Pharmaceuticals then start wondering aloud which is the stronger of the two monsters. One level-headed employee tries to restore some sense of gravity: "This isn't a wrestling match!" Throughout the film, various characters continue to treat the situation as if it were indeed a wrestling match. In one acidly written scene, the Self-Defense Forces and government representatives sheepishly admit they have wagers placed on the outcome of the monsters' bout.

Tsuburaya took a cue from Sekizawa's emphasis on the commercial exploitation of the battle between King Kong and Godzilla, and staged the monster fights much like the wrestling matches referenced by the dialogue. However, the Americanized version deletes all references to wrestling and gambling, so the monsters' comic anthropomorphism seems silly and inappropriate.

The 1970 Champion Festival was a sort of summer camp for couch potatoes, a massive children's festival oriented around marathon screenings of monster movies and cartoons. Ishiro Honda recut eight of his classic Godzilla features from the 1960s for use in the festival. Honda's revised *King Kong vs. Godzilla* was slashed to a mere 74 minutes. With the other Champion Festival reissues, Honda often used the American cuts as a guide, trimming his own films to keep the essentials but lose extraneous garnishes. The 74-minute version of *King Kong vs. Godzilla* carefully preserves all of the funniest scenes, and is inarguably played as a comedy. This was that rare time when the Champion cut ignored the American version, for the sad fact is, Shinichi Sekizawa's satire did not survive translation. Although Hollywood had been instrumental in generating and financing *King Kong vs. Godzilla*, Toho's finished film was deemed too foreign for American audiences. The American edition is also played for laughs, but in a far less sophisticated manner.

Producer Jerry Beck hired director Thomas Montgomery to adapt the film for American audiences. He jettisoned all scenes of character development, reshuffled scenes, altered the pacing, re-edited the special effects footage, and changed the meaning of the remaining dialogue by replacing Sekizawa's social satire with broad comedy. Montgomery's version created continuity errors and logical problems where there had been none. Perhaps embittered at seeing America's classic movie monster appropriated by the Japanese, American critics generally attack *King Kong vs. Godzilla* as an example of what was wrong with the genre. In fact, many of their criticisms apply only to Universal's version.

Akira Ifukube's thunderous score for the Japanese original is widely regarded as his best. This powerful music, in stereophonic sound, complemented Tsuburaya's visuals excellently: Different themes for Godzilla and King Kong play on opposing channels, battling musically as the monsters struggle on screen, with the musical themes mixing into and out of each other. For some reason, though, Montgomery discarded Ifukube's score and replaced it with music borrowed from the existing soundtracks of American films like *Creature from the Black Lagoon* (1954). Only Ifukube's song for the Faro Island ritual dance remains.

Further, all-new scenes were shot at a "United Nations news center" where an American newscaster explained the events in a way that made otherwise sensible ideas seem ridiculous. The newscast badly slows down the pacing, adds little, and at no point does it sound like an authentic broadcast. Far from getting the movie off to a dramatic start, the newscast opens the film with a totally irrelevant report of an earthquake in Chile. Carter's reporting includes details he cannot possibly know, such as when he announces that the Pacific Pharmaceutical expedition has heard Kong's roar, or that Kong draws strength from electricity.

A supposed expert called Dr. Johnson is brought on the broadcast to explain Godzilla origins, using a child's picture book of dinosaurs as his reference. Dr. Johnson's half-baked explanations show a bald-faced disregard for plausibility. In the Japanese version, Godzilla is clearly breaking free from the same icy tomb in which he was trapped back in 1955, yet Dr. Johnson tells American audiences that Godzilla has been trapped in that iceberg since the Jurassic Age. This is absurd. Unless this monster is the same one that was seen seven years ago, how do the frightened U.N. helicopter pilots know to call the thing "Godzilla"?

Scenes removed in order to make room for the leaden newscast were almost always comic ones. During the battle between the giant monsters, the Japanese version depicts both titans as somewhat buffoonish. The American cut removes many of Kong's humorous scenes, leaving Godzilla comparatively sillier. Perhaps someone involved wanted to preserve at least some of King Kong's dignity.

This desire to protect the image of America's monster icon may have contributed to a persistent but untrue rumor that *King Kong vs. Godzilla* has two endings; in the American version, Kong wins and in the Japanese version, Godzilla wins. Although false, the story has its intuitive appeal, especially in light of the many ways the Godzilla films were indeed altered for their U.S. release. However, in 1962 Godzilla was still a villainous menace. Americans more familiar with Godzilla's yet-to-come role as Protector of the Earth find it odd, but Godzilla would not ultimately prevail until he faced Ghidorah in 1964, in Godzilla's fifth feature film. Apparently, the rumor first surfaced in the late 1970s in an issue of *Famous Monster of Filmland*, at a time when Godzilla was indeed the victor in each of his films.[8] The rumor may have originated in a press release by Henry Saperstein. The story spread to the mainstream press. It has become so entrenched in the U.S. that no less respected an authority than *The New York Times* repeated the legend in 1995.

Tsuburaya's cinematographer Sadamasa Arikawa, who briefly took over the department after Tsuburaya's death, reports a story that sheds more light on the possible source of the dual-ending rumor. According to Arikawa, Honda viewed King Kong as a symbol of the United States and Godzilla as a symbol of Japan: "The fighting between the two monsters was to represent conflict between the two countries."[9] With an overtly symbolic battle, it may come as a surprise to find that the American monster trounces the Japanese one even in the Japanese edition. However, one could all too easily take this line of interpretation too far: As a symbol of America, King Kong is depicted as a drug addict controlled by callous and greedy capitalists, while the symbol of Japan is a tiny-brained creature engaging in unmotivated and relentless violence. In the end, the battle between Kong and Godzilla has less political significance than entertainment value.

*King Kong vs. Godzilla* is indeed an enjoyable movie, even in the compromised American edition. The audience voted with its pocketbook: *King Kong vs. Godzilla* set attendance records that stand to this day, and was the fourth highest grossing film released in Japan that year. Tomoyuki Tanaka saw the future: family-oriented movies pitting Godzilla against another (famous) monster. In the years since the first *Godzilla*, Toho's crew had perfected their art. Tanaka, Honda, Tsuburaya, Sekizawa, Ifukube, and their colleagues were ready to corner the market on *kaiju eiga*.

# Chapter 10

# Tsuburaya Enterprises

*Naturally, growing up, I was frequently offended by those who didn't understand. "Those Jap flicks are so cheap!" "Godzilla is only a man in a costume!" My reply: "So is Dracula. So is Clint Eastwood, only it's a cowboy suit." I similarly knocked flat those ... who stated Godzilla doesn't look realistic. My answer: "How do you know? ... You ever seen a real monster?" [Go] to a zoo and look at an alligator. They don't look realistic, they're rubbery in appearance and have no facial expression.*

— Damon Foster[1]

Nothing about Toho's monster movies have galled American critics quite so much as the sight of America's beloved King Kong being played by a man in a suit (one critic described Toho's *King Kong Escapes* as a "disgustingly vulgar abortion"[2]). In all, no single aspect of the Godzilla movies has received more derision than "suitmation."

Certainly, Willis O'Brien's animation in the original *King Kong* ranks among the finest moments in filmmaking. No doubt the enduring popularity of *King Kong* depends on the fact that producer Merian C. Cooper had the good sense to abandon his plan to realize the giant ape with a stunt man in a gorilla suit.[3] Inarguably, Toho's two Kong films, *King Kong vs. Godzilla* and *King Kong Escapes*, feature special effects below Eiji Tsuburaya's usual standards. Nevertheless, it is high time to put Tsuburaya's suitmation Kong in its proper perspective.

The men in gorilla suits of American B-movies fail as effective special effects largely because of the low quality costumes and the poor miming of the actors inside. When Dino De Laurentiis remade *King Kong* in 1976, special effects director Rick Baker chose to use suitmation techniques instead of stop-motion. The result won the 1976 Academy Award for special effects. American special effects technicians are not fundamentally averse to suitmation techniques, and success or failure depends on the skill of the effects directors and the actors in the costumes.

Willis O'Brien was a pioneer. He and his successors Ray Harryhausen and Jim Danforth deserve their renown as the greats of American special effects artists. O'Brien, Harryhausen and Danforth worked their magic with small staffs and small production budgets. That it now takes vast teams of highly paid effects technicians to surpass what was once done by individual artists is a true testament to those artists' abilities.

Although O'Brien and Harryhausen's cost of services seems meager by modern standards, few movie producers could afford their expensive expertise. *Monster from Green Hell* (1958), *Dinosaurus!* (1960), and *Journey to the Seventh Planet* (1961) were among the films that opted for cut-rate stop-motion animation, with appalling results.

Even securing the services of Willis O'Brien himself was no guarantee of quality. Producer Jack Dietz felt that the effects work Ray Harryhausen provided for *The Beast from 20,000 Fathoms* was unacceptably expensive. In 1959, Dietz contracted Harryhausen's mentor instead for *The Giant Behemoth*, O'Brien being willing to settle for less money. With insufficient funds to do his job properly, O'Brien's effects for *The Giant Behemoth* are only mediocre.[4]

In 1956, Irwin Allen hired both Harryhausen and O'Brien to animate a dinosaur sequence for the film *The Animal World*. Like many in Hollywood, Allen balked at the huge budgets his special effects artists demanded. When

Allen began work on a remake of *The Lost World*, the film that catapulted O'Brien to stardom in the first place, he turned to O'Brien to update his classic effects work. However, Allen forbade O'Brien from using stop-motion. So the pioneer of stop-motion animation suffered the indignity of presiding over a cast of lizards dressed up with plastic fins. In effect, Allen paid O'Brien to eviscerate his own work.[5]

If there is one effects technique critics like less than suitmation, it is dressed-up lizards. While lizards irritate paleontologists and audiences, they are by far the cheapest way to create giant monster effects. Ironically, the dressed-up lizards of the 1940 Hal Roach film *One Million B.C.* have been reused as stock footage in countless other features (including *Gigantis the Fire Monster*), making it the most widely seen American special effects footage of all time.[6]

While critics lambaste suitmation in Japanese films, it generally escapes criticism when used in American or British films, such as *Gorgo* (1961) or the 1976 remake of *King Kong*. Toho's special effects under Eiji Tsuburaya, while not up to the standards of the best American productions, were superior to the majority of them. The work of greats like Harryhausen were exceptions to the rule, and it does no harm to their reputation to acknowledge the perfectionism and skill of Eiji Tsuburaya.

Tsuburaya began his career in filmmaking as a cinematographer before taking over Toho's special effects department.[7] A consummate professional, he came to work each day in a suit and tie. He kept his soundstage meticulously tidy.[8] Concerned with keeping his special effects magical, he refused to let photos of him at work be used for publicity purposes.[9]

Tsuburaya's remarkable images, produced on a limited budget in an age when special effects technology was still embryonic, led George Lucas and Steven Spielberg to publicly acknowledge their debt of inspiration.[10] In the book *The Making of Jurassic Park*, Spielberg is quoted as saying, "*Godzilla*, of course, was the most masterful of all the dinosaur movies because it made you believe it was really happening."[11]

Henry G. Saperstein, American co-producer of several Godzilla movies, visited Tsuburaya on his special effects soundstage and said he felt like Paul Bunyan walking around the elaborate miniatures. "I watched Tsuburaya at work and he was a genius, " said Saperstein. "Consider what he worked with in his day: There were no electronics, no computers or anything like that."[12]

Tsuburaya enjoyed his work tremendously. As the series evolved into a more family-oriented one, Tsuburaya camped up the monster scenes. Honda occasionally bristled at the level of comedy Tsuburaya injected into the special effects sequences.[13] In a sequence for the film *Frankenstein Conquers the World* (1965), the giant monster Baragon was supposed to eat a horse. Tsuburaya objected to using footage of a real horse matted into the suitmation scenes, although he could easily have achieved it. Instead, he insisted on using a much less convincing puppet horse, because, "It's funny."[14]

When Tsuburaya began planning the effects for *Godzilla*, he knew stop-motion would be prohibitively expensive. His first estimate was that it would take up to *seven years*, if he copied O'Brien's techniques. Some wrong-headed and ill-informed sources assert that Tsuburaya did not understand how O'Brien brought King Kong to life, and therefore was unable to duplicate it. This is disproven by the two (brief) stop-motion shots Tsuburaya animated for *Godzilla*: a speeding truck careening onto its side and a swipe of Godzilla's tail. (Stop-motion scenes appear in Tsuburaya's work on other films as well.) Nevertheless, Tsuburaya needed to find an affordable alternative.

Although economic considerations precluded the use of stop-motion on *Godzilla*, that is no reason to conclude that Tsuburaya would have produced his effects any differently if he had a larger budget. Stop-motion was snubbed because for all its benefits, it also has some inherent limitations.

In addition to cost, there is the issue of scale. The smaller a model's scale, the less detailed it can be. The use of a man-sized monster supposedly 50 meters tall allowed Tsuburaya's team to construct their miniature Tokyo at 1/25th scale[15], which was small enough to somewhat hamper detailing but vastly larger and more detailed than would have been possible with a stop-motion miniature. King Kong was a fraction of Godzilla's size, allowing O'Brien's New York miniature to be built at a larger scale. Harryhausen's rhedosaurus, while closer to Godzilla's size, had only a limited rampage through New York compared to Godzilla's decimating of Tokyo. For the kinds of effects demanded by the *Godzilla* screenplay, a man in a suit allowed for better, more convincing miniature cities to be used.

The other, and more significant, drawback to traditional stop-motion is a phenomenon called "strobing." To understand strobing, consider what happens when a speeding train is filmed. The film runs through the camera at 24 frames per second, so for every second there are 24 separate pictures. During that second the train was in constant motion, so each of the 24 pictures of the train is somewhat blurred. This blur may not be noticeable when the sequence is projected, because human eyes interpret the series of blurred pictures as an image of a well-focused, moving train. Now consider a train animated by stop-motion. Again, there are 24 pictures per second, but the train is never actually moving while the pictures are taken, and hence no motion blur. When projected, the train moves smoothly but also appears unnaturally sharp and crisp. It looks hyper-real. The term "strobing" refers to the fact that a high-frequency strobe light can interrupt the perception of continuous motion to produce this unnatural-looking effect in real life.

Stop-motion animators have tried various techniques for applying a motion blur to each frame to eliminate the strobe effect. One such technique, called "go-motion," was unveiled in the 1981 movie *Dragonslayer*. Famed animator Jim Danforth remains convinced that a realistic motion blur technique can be found, but it has not been developed yet.[16]

One thing American audiences often misunderstand about Japanese fantasy films is that Western notions of realism are a cultural value not necessarily held by other peoples. Japanese art does not value "realism" as single-mindedly as Western art does. Japanese filmmakers recognize other values as well: beauty, interesting images, and spectacle. To criticize Japanese fantasy films for not being "realistic" is both to miss the point and miss the fun.

Movies should not be judged against the entirety of cinema history. Athletic events always place competitors in their proper category; high school basketball players do not compete against NBA superstars. By the same logic, films need to be viewed within the context of their league. For example, movies made during the early–1930s heyday of Hollywood's Production Code deal with sexual issues much differently than those made today, but that does not mean that audiences cannot enjoy romantic comedies from the 1930s.

Knowing what is the fault of the original filmmaker, what is the fault of the Americanization, and what is merely reflecting the attitudes and tastes of the reviewer is crucial to being a Godzilla film critic. Comparing Toho's monster pictures against other science fiction films of the age, against other monster-on-the-loose pictures especially, reveals that the Godzilla movies are among the very best in their league. To fully appreciate them, however, American viewers need to overcome some cultural biases.

"Realism" is a style of fiction. American audiences know the difference between true reality and realism, and do not find documentaries as emotionally compelling or entertaining as realistic fiction films. Americans are accustomed to seeing realism, and assume that it is one of the fundamental aims of art and storytelling. Certainly, not all Western art aims to be realistic. Audiences that fail to enjoy *The Muppet Movie* because Kermit is not a realistic frog cheat themselves. Japanese monster movies share some of the appeal of the Muppets, and Godzilla should not be taken as a true representation of a dinosaur any more than Fozzie represents a true bear.

Bill Warren reports a telling incident in his two-volume set *Keep Watching the Skies!* The producers of the expensive 1980 Japanese American co-production *Virus*, starring Glenn

Ford and Chuck Connors, hired American special effects technicians, expecting the best. However, the resulting effects were cut from the film and redone by Japanese technicians, adding to the film's already bloated budget. The American artists were surprised, as they had rendered very realistic images. But the Japanese producers did not want realism; they wanted evocative, poetic images.[17]

In the same vein, the director of Toho's special effects department in the 1990s, Koichi Kawakita, was once asked his opinion of *Jurassic Park*. "I enjoyed the film, but it was too realistic," he replied. "It would have been much more enjoyable if some fantasy elements had been incorporated into it."[18]

Eiji Tsuburaya delivered evocative and poetic images. That the majority of his effects work is not "realistic" by Western standards does not reflect on his abilities, merely his priorities. For the original *Godzilla*, Ishiro Honda specifically strove for an almost documentary-style mood, and Tsuburaya's effects were very realistic indeed.

His work in the 1950s and early 1960s won the acclaim of American critics, who recognized that his effects were at least as good as those of the majority of that era's American films, many of which were far more expensive. Unfortunately, the lower quality of Toho's effects in the 1970s, supervised by Teruyoshi Nakano with drastically reduced budgets and an overall changed set of expectations, damaged the series' reputation, leading modern viewers to expect poor effects from the older Godzilla films. Until his untimely death in 1970, however, Eiji Tsuburaya ruled as Japan's maestro of special effects.

# *Part Two*

# Monsterland (1964–1969)

After the success of *King Kong vs. Godzilla*, Toho knew they had a star. Each subsequent sequel was patterned after *King Kong vs. Godzilla*; a franchise developed. As Toho added new monsters to its roster, a gradual transformation took place: Godzilla slowly metamorphosed from a villainous destroyer into a superhero. His onetime opponents became allies, and his new opponents became explicitly evil. With the introduction of the three-headed space dragon Ghidorah, the Godzilla series found its glory days.

# Chapter 11

# *Mothra vs. Godzilla*

## Mosura Tai Gojira (Mothra Against Godzilla)

*Just as you distrust us, so we distrust others as well. It's wrong. We're all human. As humans we are responsible to each other. We are related. Refuse us and you abandon your brothers. We must learn to help each other.*

— Sakai

Japanese version: 89 minutes, Released April 29, 1964 (Champion Festival Release: *Godzilla tai Mosura*, 74 minutes)

U.S. version (American International Pictures): 88 minutes, Released September 17, 1964, double-billed with *Voyage to the End of the Universe*, Original U.S. release title: *Godzilla vs. the Thing* Color, Widescreen

Produced by Tomoyuki Tanaka and Sanezumi Fujimoto; U.S. version produced by James H. Nicholson and Samuel Z. Arkoff; directed by Ishiro Honda; screenplay by Shinichi Sekizawa; music by Akira Ifukube; cinematography by Hajime Koizumi; art direction by Takeo Kita; edited by Ryohei Fujii; special effects by Eiji Tsuburaya; special effects assistant director Teruyoshi Nakano; special effects cinematography by Sadamasa Arikawa and Motoyoshi Tomioka; special effects art direction by Akira Watanabe; optical effects by Hiroshi Mukoyama, Yukio Manoda, Sokei Tomioka, Yoshiyuki Tokumasa; optical animation by Minoru Nakano

Starring Akira Takarada (Sakai), Yuriko Hoshi (Junko), Hiroshi Koizumi (Professor Miura), Yu Fujiki (Jiro), Emi and Yumi Ito (The Shobijin), Yoshifumi Tajima (Kumoyama), Kenji Sahara (Torahata), Jun Tazaki (Editor), Ikio Sawamura (Priest), Kenzo Tadake (Mayor), Susumu Fumita (Public Relations Officer), Yutaka Sada and Yoshio Kosugi (Old Men), Yasuhisa Tsutsumi (Longshoreman), Ren Yamamoto (Sailor)

GODZILLA portrayed by Haruo Nakajima; MOTHRA portrayed by Katsumi Tezuka

*Reporter Sakai, photographer Junko, and Professor Miura investigate a giant monster egg that has washed ashore. Kumoyama, an entrepreneur representing business tycoon Torahatta of Happy Enterprises, announces he has purchased the egg from the fishermen who found it and plans to set it up as a tourist attraction. Even scientists wishing to examine the amazing* find will have to pay for the privilege. Not even Mothra's miniature priestesses can convince Kumoyama and Torahatta to return the egg to Infant Island.

*When Godzilla appears and begins to lay waste to the Japanese mainland, Sakai, Junko and Miura realize they must beg Mothra for help. Unsurprisingly, the usually good-natured Shobijin refuse to listen: "You didn't help us. Because of that, no one here will help you." Sakai argues in passionate terms and with deep humility that all of humanity are brothers, and this brotherhood of man needs to look past these petty differences and work together for the common good. The giant monster Mothra agrees and offers to help against Godzilla. But Mothra is old and weak, and in combat with Godzilla she dies. The fate of Japan now lies inside the giant egg, sitting in Torahatta's incubator, waiting to hatch...*

Toho's monster makers had learned their lessons well. *Mothra vs. Godzilla* breaks little new ground, but does what it does by refining and perfecting what had gone before.

As with *Mothra*, the story begins with a storm, after which a reporter and a female photographer investigate a mysterious phenomenon, befriend a scientist and encounter a villainous capitalist whose mad pursuit of profits endangers the lives of others. Of course, the story also brings back Mothra and her tiny priestesses. Repeated from *King Kong vs. Godzilla* is the notion of pitting a famous movie monster against Godzilla, who falls into the sea after his defeat while the victorious "good" monster swims away.

These surface parallels belie a deeper sophistication to *Mothra vs. Godzilla*, widely regarded today as the greatest of the Godzilla movies. By 1964, the artists and craftspeople under Tomoyuki Tanaka's supervision were working at their creative peak, with ten years' experience fine-tuning the genre. From Tsuburaya's astounding visuals to Ifukube's grand score to the fine performances by familiar faces such as Kenji Sahara, Akira Takarada, and Hiroshi Koizumi, everything shines. Honda maintains a high level of suspense and tension without abandoning the comic elements now a part of the formula. *Mothra vs. Godzilla* marks the perfect union of the dark horror of the early Godzilla series and the new directions the series was taking. This would be the final time Godzilla would be depicted as a marauding menace. The humorous approach to Godzilla's character in *King Kong vs. Godzilla* was set aside this time, and the giant monster was played straight.

Even the costume exuded evil. Monster costumes were ephemeral creations. During filming on a stage that burned at 170 degrees under blazing studio lamps, as the actors smashed into model buildings, pummeled each other, and endured various trick explosions, the suits were destined to suffer some damage. Whenever they were used in the water tank, the damage was only compounded. And the rubber could not survive long in storage without rotting. The team was obliged to manufacture a new suit every year or two.

Teizo Toshimitsu, the hands-on supervisor of this process, started by sketching the Godzilla suit at full-size scale on a sheet of plywood. From that life-size design, the body was constructed — a wire frame to hold the contours of the shape, then a fabric skin stuffed with foam. On top of that understructure, an outer skin of latex rubber, with an alligator-like bumpy texture, was applied. Throughout this process, the actor Haruo Nakajima was often obliged to wear the unfinished thing so that it could be form-fitted to his body. Feeling personally invested in the enterprise, Nakajima went above and beyond the call of duty: He would routinely put on the unfinished suit and wrestle around in it to identify problem areas and weak points before it was finalized. That

way, the suit builders could be confident it would endure the stresses of filming.

Stresses like these: Inside all the layers of rubber and foam, the suit would reach temperatures of 130 degrees. The total weight of the costume was somewhere above 200 pounds. Nakajima could only bear wearing it for short bursts, and required frequent breaks. Moving under the weight of all that caused Nakajima severe muscle cramps, and on average he would shed 20 pounds per film. The head was built like a sort of hat. He could see, if that's the word, through tiny holes puncturing the suit's neck. A hard plastic head was braced on top of his own. He entered the suit through an opening in the back, which would be hidden by the application of the spiky dorsal fins. In the end, the whole deal was painted black. In crafting this new 1964 variant, Teizo Toshimitsu perfected the process first devised in 1954, and all subsequent Godzilla suits were variations on this one.[1]

In place of a virtually mindless Godzilla attacking Japan, the new approach aimed at a broader family audience, with sympathetic monster stars with recognizable personalities. Against the villainous Godzilla, Honda and Sekizawa brought back the courageous and compassionate monster hero Mothra. The proposal that Mothra be asked to combat Godzilla on Japan's behalf rests on the assumption that Mothra is intelligent and trustworthy, two characteristics not normally assigned to giant monsters. Mothra is not merely a giant monster, she is a monster-god. In her second screen appearance, Mothra sacrifices herself to save humans from certain death, and is then resurrected. Such overtly religious symbolism tops that seen in *Mothra*.

As a godlike figure, Mothra exhibits a moral superiority to the human characters, an audacious innovation for a monster-on-the-loose movie. In the original *Mothra*, human society had good reason to feel ashamed. The capitalist values of the "civilized" world had not only cruelly exploited the people of Infant Island, but virtually prohibited anyone from righting the obvious wrongs. Mothra's high priestesses had nowhere to turn to free them from slavery, but the most powerful government in the world came quickly to Clark Nelson's defense when anyone tried to interfere with his profitmaking. *Mothra vs. Godzilla* brings this sense of shame to the forefront. After their people have done nothing but take from the inhabitants of Infant Island, Sakai and friends have to go there and *ask for more.* The heroes must beg charity from people they themselves did not help. In a society where saving face and maintaining a harmonious atmosphere are prized above all else, this represents a profoundly humiliating and emotionally painful moment.

Interestingly, Mothra chirps her agreement with Sakai's "brotherhood of man" argument before any of her people can respond. Sakai's stirring speech may or may not have had any effect on the natives of Mothra Island. Perhaps Mothra possesses a more developed faculty of forgiveness than her subjects. In every way, Mothra appears morally and spiritually superior.

The combination of Shinichi Sekizawa's humane creation Mothra and the brutish Godzilla inherited from Shigeru Kayama and Takeo Murata gives the film a moral depth missing from *King Kong vs. Godzilla.* That Sekizawa's monster wins is telling; his approach wins, too. Future installments in the series would see Sekizawa humanize Godzilla to match Mothra.

It must be said, however, that the "brotherhood of man" theme was not present in Sekizawa's screenplay, but was added to the film by Honda during production, along with other embellishments. Honda often revised the screenplays himself, and in this case he used the situation created by Sekizawa as a platform for his own deeply felt humanist principles.[2] *Mothra vs. Godzilla* is an auteurist message picture, and Honda's commitment to it shines in every frame.

Sekizawa's script bristles with the same flair for comedy that made both *Mothra* and *King Kong vs. Godzilla* into hits. The elements of social satire were enhanced by Honda's contributions, however, as Sekizawa had not included a greedy capitalist villain this time around. Honda wisely felt that one was needed, and cleverly cast Kenji Sahara against type in the

role of Torahatta.[3] In one scene, Sakai confronts Torahatta, arguing that the egg rightfully belongs to "The Thing." Torahatta scoffs, "If that's the case, let's see power of attorney given to you by the Thing."

To properly understand the way Japanese audiences would have approached such material, it is helpful to put it into a larger perspective. From the end of the war to 1952, the Japanese economy grew by 11.5 percent, which at the time seemed like a miracle. In 1956, the Economic Planning Agency issued a report confidently declaring the "postwar period" over — but if that was true, then what was next? As the 1950s drew to a close, most economists agreed that the era of sustained economic growth was over.

Then came Prime Minister Hyaoto Ikeda, who took office on July 18, 1960. He had not gotten the memo about the end of postwar economic growth, because he boldly announced that he was going to see the incomes of the Japanese people double by the end of the decade![4] He might as well have promised to change the color of the sky, so absurd was the idea. And indeed Ikeda was wrong. He did not double the Japanese income in ten years.

He did it in more like eight.

At the point when the guys in the propeller beanies announced that the Japanese economy had peaked, it was ranked fifteenth in the world — which was not bad for a nation soundly ruined by war, and which had only started engaging with other countries a century earlier. But by 1968, the Japanese economy was second in the world, surpassing all comers save the United States. If analysts had marveled that Japan's economy grew at 11.5 percent between 1947 and 1952, what could they say when it was growing at ten percent or more *every single year*?[5]

This was the fabled Economic Miracle. Ikeda had pushed the fast-forward button on life itself, and a century's worth of gradual progress and development was compressed into one crazy decade. Progress is never without cost, and the transformation of Japan into one of the world's most formidable financial powers meant the razing of ancient traditions and societal conventions. Average Japanese citizens were torn, between the glories and benefits that this miracle provided, and the sense of loss that came with it. Ambivalence was the only sane response.

The ritualized property destruction that characterizes Japanese monster movies—focused on shopping malls and power plants, modern skyscrapers and tourist landmarks—obsesses over the Economic Miracle in reverse: All this wealth and prosperity, created so suddenly, can disappear just as fast. Perhaps this also explains the recurring emphasis on objects out of scale—ordinary people scrunched down to miniature size, dwarfed by the surroundings, or other things once small, suddenly giants.

It is also worth noting that pop cultural anthropologists who study such things say that when societies undergo a rapid economic growth, generating vast pools of disposable wealth quickly without providing enough time for the overall culture to mature, the result is a camp sensibility. The boom years of the 1960s were good to all capitalist economies, which found once-grim characters in pop culture reimagined as campy figures. *Batman*, once a brooding crime fighter forged in the Depression, became a standard bearer for camp. In England, the James Bond tropes were turned into pop art comedy in *The Avengers*. France's Fantomas, a ghastly terrorist in the age of silent serials, returned in absurdist films cut from the *Pink Panther* mold. In Japan, the economic boom was faster and bigger than anywhere else, and the trend towards camp was that much stronger as a result.[6]

Honda said in an interview that he felt the movies should first and foremost be enjoyable.[7] The comic aspects of *Mothra vs. Godzilla* do not extend to the monsters; their battle displays utmost seriousness. The comedy nestles within an earnest atmosphere not matched since the days of black and white.

Neither Yoshifumi Tajima nor Kenji Sahara in their roles as Kumoyama and Torahatta indulge in the campy villainy of Jerry Ito's Clark Nelson. In fact, the only comic *character* is the egg-obsessed Jiro, played by Yu Fujiki, who

plays much the same comic foil as he first performed in *King Kong vs. Godzilla*.

Akira Takarada returns to the Godzilla series as the hero. However, as he plays a character named Sakai, perhaps Toho originally hoped Frankie Sakai would return for *Mothra*'s sequel, and Takarada was the second choice. In any event, Takarada gives one of his best performances. When Mothra's egg hatches two giant larvae, the look on his face simultaneously conveys relief and horrified apprehension. In one facial expression, Takarada sums up the ambivalent usage of the film's monster characters.

This was the first Godzilla film released in the United States by AIP, a distribution company that would, along with Henry Saperstein's United Productions of America (UPA), bring the vast majority of Toho's special effects films to North America in the sixties and seventies. In the mid–1950s, James H. Nicholson and Samuel Z. Arkoff recognized that the decline in audiences for theatrical features was primarily a decline in adult audiences. The trend towards suburban neighborhoods and the growth of television as a leisure activity kept adults at home. However, Nicholson and Arkoff believed that teenagers were compelled to get out of the house and seek entertainment. The two men formed the American Releasing Corporation in 1954 to cater to that teenage movie-going audience. At the time, Hollywood movies targeted either an adult audience or a family audience. American Releasing, which eventually became American International Pictures, was the first company to actively court a youth market outside the context of the whole family.

AIP released mostly B-movies that catered to the largely unsophisticated tastes of its intended viewers, an approach that found phenomenal commercial success. By the early sixties, Nicholson and Arkoff recognized the strong storytelling and production values Toho put into their work, and saw the appeal Godzilla had with the youth market they were courting. AIP had many years of financial success distributing Godzilla movies.

In Americanizing the film, AIP decided to build its promotional campaign around a sense of suspense regarding Godzilla's opponent. The title was therefore changed to *Godzilla vs. the Thing,* with ads showing Godzilla in mortal combat with an enormous question mark. For the most part, *Godzilla vs. the Thing* was Americanized with care. The dubbing is among the best in the series. The only major discrepancy between the Japanese and United States editions involves a sequence in which the U.S. navy attacks Godzilla with "Frontier Missiles," specifically commissioned by AIP to add stateside appeal. Sekizawa wrote the scene and Tsuburaya filmed it during production of the film, yet the sequence appears only in the American release. In other words, this was an occasion in which the Americanized version included actual special effects material featuring Godzilla filmed by Toho but available only to American viewers (and has to date not been included on any Japanese video release of the film).[8]

In promoting the U.S. release, AIP encouraged theater owners to "spot all places where buildings have been wrecked or razed ... or where pre-construction digging is going on and post signs on surrounding fences reading: 'Godzilla fought the Thing here.'" Lest one find this advertising campaign insensitive, consider that in 1961 Columbia Pictures asked exhibitors showing *Mothra* to display radioactive materials in the theater lobbies.[9]

Although not as big a hit as *King Kong vs. Godzilla,* *Mothra vs. Godzilla* earned enough both in Japan and abroad to ensure that Godzilla would return yet again. In the immediate sequel, Sekizawa and Honda would revisit the "brotherhood of man" theme in a twisted and bizarre way. Mothra's generosity in fighting Godzilla would be remembered; the next time Japan faced an unstoppable monster, they knew who to call.

# Chapter 12

# Ghidrah, The Three-Headed Monster

## San Daikaiju Chikyu Saidai no Kessen
## (Greatest Giant Monster Battle on Earth)

*Attention all citizens. The space monster discovered in Kurobe Gorge last night has been identified. It is Ghidorah. All proper measures are being taken to render him harmless. However, in the interest of public safety the city must be evacuated at once.*

— police warning

Japanese version: 92 minutes, Released December 20, 1964 (Champion Festival Release: *Gojira, Mosura, Kingu Ghidorah: Chikyu Saidai No Kessen* [Godzilla, Mothra, King Ghidorah: Greatest Battle on Earth], 73 minutes)

U.S. version (Continental Distributing/Walter Reade-Sterling): 81 minutes, Released September 13, 1965, double-billed with *Harum Scarum*, Original U.S. release title: *Ghidrah, The Three-Headed Monster*

Color, Widescreen

Produced by Tomoyuki Tanaka; U.S. version produced by Walter Reade-Sterling; directed by Ishiro Honda; U.S. version dubbing directed by Joseph Belluci; screenplay by Shinichi Sekizawa; music by Akira Ifukube; Song "Call Happiness" composed by Hiroshi Miyagawa with words by Tokiko Iwantani; cinematography by Hajime Koizumi; art direction by Takeo Kita; edited by Ryohei Fujii; special effects by Eiji Tsuburaya; special effects assistant director Teruyoshi Nakano; special effects cinematography by Sadamasa Arikawa and Motoyoshi Tomioka; special effects art direction by Akira Watanabe; optical effects by Hiroshi Mukoyama, Yokio Manoda, and Taka Yuki

Starring Yosuke Natsuki (Shindo), Yuriko Hoshi (Naoko Shindo), Hiroshi Koizumi (Professor Murai), Takashi Shimura (Dr. Tsukamoto), Emi and Yumi Ito (The Shobijin), Akiko Wakabayashi (Princess Salno), Hisaya Itoh (Malness), Akihiko Hirata (Detective Okita), Kenji Sahara (Editor), Ikio Sawamura (Fisherman), Eiji Okada (Geologist), Yoshifumi Tajima (Ship Captain), Eisei Amamoto (Princess' Aide), Kazuo Suzuki, Susumu Kurobe, Toru Ibuki (Henchmen), Kozo Nomora, Yoshio Kosugi, Minoru Takada, Yuriko Hanabusa, Haruya Kato, Nakatiro Tomita, Shigeki Ishida, Shin Otomo,

Yukaka Nakayama, Senkichi Omura, Somamasa Matsumoto, Senya Aozora, Ichiya Aozora, Henry Okawa, Junichiro Mukai, Yoshiniko Furuta, Shoji Ikeoa, Hideo Shibuya, Kenchiro Katsumoto, Koji Uno, Daisuke Inoue, Ooshio Miura, Tamami Urayama, Takuzo Kumagaya, Mitzuo Tsuda, Yoshio Hattori, Kenji Tsubono, Kazoo Imai, Suburo Kadowaki, Kenzo Echigo, Toku Ihara, Bin Furuya, Jun Kuroki, Yutaka Oka, Koji Urugi, Haruya Sakamoto

GODZILLA portrayed by Haruo Nakajima; MOTHRA portrayed by Katsumi Tezuka; RADON portrayed by Masashi Shinohara; KING GHIDORAH portrayed by Shoichi Hirose

*Worried that Princess Salno will be assassinated on her journey to Tokyo, allowing her imperial homeland to become a communist state, Japanese Intelligence assigns Detective Shindo to protect her highness from the assassins. However, en route to Japan, Princess Salno has vanished.*

*Shindo's sister Naoko, a reporter for the TV show Mysteries in the 20th Century, interviews a mysterious prophetess claiming to be from Mars, only to realize it is Princess Salno, clad in a man's fishing clothes. She foresees the imminent arrival of Godzilla and Rodan — and worse, the arrival of an even more powerful creature from space she calls Ghidorah.*

*Indeed, Godzilla and Rodan come ashore, fighting as always, and a meteor shower in Kurobe Gorge has brought an enormous three-headed dragon. With assassins still pursuing the princess, whoever she thinks she is, and giant monsters tearing Japan to shreds, Professor Murai has a bright idea: "As you know, Godzilla and Mothra once had a fight. And as all of you know, Godzilla lost that fight. I think Mothra might help us in this fight with Ghidorah."*

*Mothra is no match for the space monster. But what if she can persuade Godzilla and Rodan to cooperate?*

*Ghidrah, The Three-Headed Monster* was rushed through production under a grueling schedule, and arrived in theaters a scant nine months after *Mothra vs. Godzilla.* To call it a rush job, though, misses the point.

From 1961 to 1964, Toho turned out eight lavish science fiction spectacles: *Mothra, Gorath, King Kong vs. Godzilla, Atragon, Matango, Mothra vs. Godzilla, Dogora the Space Monster,* and *Ghidrah, The Three-Headed Monster*—of which the last three appeared in 1964 alone. As the decade progressed, the pace of production only increased.

Every one of those eight big pictures during those four years was produced by Tomoyuki Tanaka and directed by Ishiro Honda, with effects by Eiji Tsuburaya. Akira Ifukube scored seven of the eight, and Shinichi Sekizawa wrote the screenplays for six. In fact, the production team is exactly the same for all of the ones made in 1964: the same writer, director, producer, special effects crew, soundtrack composer, cinematographer, art director, and editor. In the casts of those three films, there are eight actors who appeared in at least two. Toho was a factory in the 1960s, and the fact that some of the films are true classics of the genre is an astounding testament to the folks behind them, given the pressures under which they worked.

*Mothra vs. Godzilla* premiered on April 29, 1964. *Dogora the Space Monster* followed on August 11, 1964, not quite four months later. *Ghidrah* came along on December 20, 1964, four months after that. The distance between these premieres is insufficient to actually complete the work within; a movie of this scale could not be made in four months. Inevitably these projects overlapped. They were produced in tandem but finished in serial. Thus, of their common elements, there must have been cross-pollination behind the scenes.

One obvious feature shared by both *Dogora* and *Ghidrah* is that each features a space monster. There are only so many times a nuclear bomb test could revive a prehistoric beast, and Sekizawa had already tried giant animals worshipped as gods on a remote island ... so where else could a giant monster come from? How's about outer space?

Dogora was a sort of space amoeba mutated by exposure to nuclear satellites. It looked like a cross between a jellyfish and an octopus, for no evident reason, and it eats diamonds, for even less reason. To complete the hat trick of irrationality it is defeated by bee venom. Boiled down to its essence like that, it may sound like Sekizawa was off his meds, but the film is actually even stranger than that, because all the monster stuff is shoved off into the background while the center stage is occupied by a cops vs. gangsters plot inspired by the popularity of yakuza action thrillers.

Like *Dogora,* *Ghidrah* mixes traditional monster vs. monster action with a different thriller genre—in this case 007-inflected spy stories. *Ghidrah* has it all: assassins, revolutionary conspiracies, secret agents, hidden identities, shootouts and narrow escapes, all against a backdrop of giant monsters battling for the planet.

*Ghidrah* and *Dogora* share five cast members, as well as several physical structures: Both movies make use of the same police station set, for example. One of the shared actors is Hiroshi Koizumi, who had the distinction of playing essentially the same scientist character in all three of Toho's effects films of 1964. Toho had groomed him as a star for years, through a program called New Faces. Something vaguely like *American Idol,* the New Faces program was a system by which one of Japan's biggest and most prolific movie studios sought out undiscovered talent. Ordinary members of the public, untrained amateurs, would enroll in this competition, and the studio picked out those they thought had star potential. The winners would then receive acting training while being put before the public in various films, starting with small roles, to see who "clicked." Koizumi had been working as a TV announcer when the New Faces program catapulted him into starring roles in teen-oriented pictures in the 1950s. He made his Godzilla debut as Tsukioka, the courage-challenged cannery pilot of *Godzilla Raids Again,* and made his biggest mark on the franchise as gentle anthropologist Chujo in *Mothra.* Koizumi would be typecast as the nerd hero forevermore.[1]

For all intents and purposes, Koizumi plays the same role in *Ghidrah* that he had in *Mothra vs. Godzilla*—that of Professor Murai. His name is spelled slightly differently, but no other attribute of his character has changed. Curiously, in both *Dogora* and *Ghidrah*, Koizumi's role is one of the axes of a defanged romantic triangle. In both films, there is a heroine, linked between the Koizumi's scientist character and a policeman character played by Yosuke Natsuki. One is her boyfriend, one is her brother. The only thing that changes between the two films is which one is the brother, Koizumi or Natsuki, and the actress playing the girl.

For this film, that actress is Yuriko Hoshi, revisiting the reporter heroine role she handled in *Mothra vs. Godzilla*. If Koizumi has been cast in a repeat performance, though, Ms. Hoshi has been given a substantial upgrade — as will be discussed shortly.

Yosuke Natsuki stars as Detective Shindo, the nominal hero. Primarily a journeyman actor, Natsuki did appear in two of Toho's science fiction flicks, both in 1964. He didn't return to the genre until 1984 for *The Return of Godzilla*, released in the United States as *Godzilla 1985*. Interestingly, he did so in a role originally written for Akihiko Hirata, who in *Ghidrah* appears briefly as Natsuki's superior officer. After work began on *The Return of Godzilla*, Hirata was felled by cancer and his old friend Yosuke Natsuki stepped in to take over his role.[2]

Originally, the brilliant and criminally underrated character actor Yoshio Tsuchiya was supposed to appear as Malness, the assassin sent to kill Princess Salno. Tsuchiya was one of Ishiro Honda's most favored performers. Akira Kurosawa also admired Tsuchiya, and that sometimes created scheduling conflicts. Tsuchiya was already committed to Kurosawa for *Red Beard* (1965) and ultimately had to drop out of *Ghidrah*. Hisaya Ito took over the part of Malness.[3]

Another of the actors who straddled between Kurosawa's arthouse classics and Honda's monster pictures was the distinguished Takashi Shimura, who had already brought his gravitas to the original *Godzilla*. For that, critics could forgive him, but his continued gyrating between the two worlds discomfited American critics for whom a clear distinction, however arbitrary and artificial, was believed to exist between serious cinema and slummy exploitation fare. Shimura worked for Kurosawa on the likes of *Seven Samurai* and for Honda on *Ghidrah* and *Frankenstein Conquers the World*. Like Yoshio Tsuchiya, Shimura was part of the *Red Beard* cast, but managed to take a day off to shoot his one scene for this picture.

The 007 vibe is carried in no small part by the strikingly beautiful actress Akiko Wakabayashi, one of several actors pulling double duty with *Dogora*. In that other film, she played a hard-bitten femme fatale, while in *Ghidrah* she plays the enigmatic Princess Salno. Not long afterwards, she graduated to full-fledged 007 antics as a Bond girl in 1967's *You Only Live Twice*, partly filmed in Japan at Toho's studio with a few familiar Toho faces alongside Sean Connery. *You Only Live Twice* features a memorable line ("In Japan, men always come first, women come second") moments before James Bond gets a full body massage from Akiko Wakabayashi.

But that's a Western movie, with a Westerner's fetish of what Japanese women are like. Wakabayashi sashays her killer body through both *Dogora* and *Ghidrah*, stealing diamonds, grubby clothes, and scenes as she does—and would never be caught dead surrendering so submissively to a man.

Japan is a much more patriarchal nation than the United States, but the depiction of women in movies sometimes displayed more progressive thinking than actual day-to-day life. Since the original *Godzilla*, much had changed for female characters in the series. Emiko in the 1954 film had little more to do than worry about loving one man when she was betrothed to another. Her character was defined in terms of her relationships to the males: daughter of Yamane, betrothed to Serizawa, lover of Ogata. In the sequel, Hidemi at least had a job, but she too was defined by her relationships to her father and her beloved. Sitting at her radio mike, she never participates directly in any of the proceedings. Fumiko in *King Kong vs. Godzilla*, little more than sister and beloved to the more prominent male leads, only participated in the action in so much as she was menaced by the monsters and needed to be rescued by the men.

As Sekizawa's influence grew, things changed. He took the monsters—once so noble, fearsome, and imposing—and turned them into slapstick comedians. And then, he took the women characters—victims and bumblers—and gave them pride of place. Take for example Yuriko Hoshi as the girl reporter Naoko. In *Mothra vs. Godzilla*, Hoshi was a supporting player cast as the incompetent photographer Junko. She was a Japanese Lucille Ball, too dim-witted even to remember to remove her lens cap. But in *Ghidrah*, Hoshi is a full-fledged reporter, a central heroine in a woman-positive story.

She is good at her job; when a choice assignment like covering the Martian prophetess comes along, her editor unhesitatingly gives it to her. (In the original Japanese version, she is a print reporter rather than a television producer, and she proves her skills by beating her male colleagues to the scoop.) She may be Shindo's sister, but she is in no way defined by that relationship; she defines herself. Her brother and mother chide her for what they take to be her romantic interest in Professor Murai, but in fact she is only following a lead. She actively participates in the story, even managing to take charge of Princess Salno while her brother bumbles around.

Princess Salno is an interesting heroine herself. She throws away her royal heritage, arguably a symbol of a patriarchy. She asserts her uniqueness to the world while wearing men's clothes, and spends much of her screen time dressed as a man. Once Naoko gets her back in womanly attire, Salno reverts to a retiring and meek figure carted around by the male characters, as if the clothes made the woman.

While emboldening all of the female roles, Sekizawa also uses the women characters as narrative devices to explain the monster action. Princess Salno gives Ghidrah its name and explains its origins. The Shobijin translate Mothra's call for Rodan and Godzilla to join the fight. Naoko, most importantly, gives voice to these other, somewhat supernatural women, whose warnings are not being heeded by the men.

In both of their previous appearances, Mothra's fairies were abused, mistreated, and victimized—forced against their will to perform on stage. Here, they are introduced in the story once again on stage but *this* time they are voluntarily appearing before an appreciative audience. People genuinely want to hear what they have to say. Their introductory scene is nothing less than a parody of the two previous Mothra films, even though this parody was written by the same author as the originals. The tiny girls develop an action plan and take charge of the situation: rescuing others, fighting bad guys, and ultimately proposing and enacting the very plan that will save the world. No victims they.

For their reappearance in *Ghidrah*, a new song was written for the Peanuts, "Cry for Happiness" by Hiroshi Miyagawa, the composer who had worked with the twins on their earlier film *Young Comrades*. (In the American version, dubbing supervisor Joseph Bellucci hired Annie Sukiyaki to read, along with the song, a vague English translation.)

This scene also features a pair of Japanese comedians named Senya Aozora and Ichiya Aozora—and unlike the Peanuts, these two are not actually related. They were a comedy team, and these were stage names. Their word-play and back-and-forth verbal patter has been compared to vaudeville and Abbott and Costello; it was not unique to the Aozoras, but was a comedy tradition called manzai. Yoshihito Sakai, the real name of the one billed as Senya Aozora, was a coal miner who left home for the big city with the classic dream of making it big in show business. He paired up with Ichiya to form the Aozora team, and they won a manzai competition in 1960. They appeared on television throughout the 1960s and released some albums, but never developed a meaningful film career. In terms of charting the presence of comedy in Godzilla, the arrival of a pair of known comedians basically replicating their stage act is notable.[4]

When *Ghidrah* was distributed in the United

States in 1965, it was primarily on a double bill with Elvis Presley's musical comedy *Harum Scarum*. The advertising screamed, "The Beat and the Beast make a holiday feast!" Even back home, *Ghidrah* had already been paired with a comedy. It was released in Japan on a double bill with *Samurai Joker*, directed by Kajiro Yamamoto, the venerable director who taught Honda and Akira Kurosawa the craft of filmmaking. *Samurai Joker* was part of a franchise called the Crazy Cats. While not well known to Western viewers, such comedies were a much bigger part of Toho's output than the sci-fi thrillers. There was a lot of overlap in cast between Ishiro Honda's monster flicks and the Crazy Cats comedies, and after a while the Crazy Cats comedies even started to take advantage of Eiji Tsuburya's special effects expertise. [5]

Straining under the demands of producing effects-laded spectacles at a steadily increasing pace, Tsuburaya's skills faced new challenges. It is often said that the decision to relocate much of Godzilla's monster-on-monster bouts in the countryside was a cost-conscious choice intended to reduce the demand for detailed city miniatures. In order to put some numbers to this claim, consider the climactic battle between the monsters in *Ghidrah*. The set for the base of Mt. Fuji took 12 thousand man hours to build — that's 500 man days or nearly 1½ man years, and it's just *one* of the miniature sets seen in the film. This was a raised set, so that the cameras could be positioned low compared to the monster actors, to help give the scene a proper sense of size. It was built in 1/25th scale, with actual bonsai trees and small plants mixed in with fake ones to create the foliage. The miniature buildings had actual working sliding doors and working lights — but were built backless, to be seen from one direction. The ones that were intended to be crushed by the monsters were pre-cut and stressed to break in specific, predictable ways. Buildings that were not supposed to break could be reused, repositioned in later setups on other sets.[6] In all, the enormous effort involved in the Mt. Fuji set belies the notion that countrysides were chosen simply to save costs. More likely, as Sekizawa re-tooled the franchise to be funnier and more appealing to youngsters, moving the battles away from population centers reduced the need for the films to deal with casualties and deaths.

The legendary "Big Pool" was constructed on Toho's lot in 1959 under Tsuburaya's direction. Approximately 43,000 square feet in size, 262 feet wide at its widest, 210 feet deep at its deepest, the massive thing has a 46-foot high concrete wall serving as the sky, which could be painted as needed. Electric motors generated artificial waves. Since water cannot be miniaturized, to help disguise the scale of the water Tsuburaya would work in the largest scale miniatures he could manage, and film at fast frame rates so the action would be slowed down, lending a sense of gravity and size. Unfortunately for the crew, fish lived in the tank, despite all attempts to remove them. Between the fish and the real bugs that were attracted to the water, nature had a way of intruding and ruining many an expensive shot. During one of Godzilla's tussles with Rodan, the edge of the tank was revealed by accident in one shot. Tsuburaya tried to conceal the tank by superimposing some trees over it.[7]

While the Godzilla suit had been recreated for each of the monster's previous film appearances, that process typically took as much as three months. Given how quickly *Ghidrah* went before cameras following production on *Mothra vs. Godzilla*, not enough time existed for a full-scale redo of the Godzilla suit. During filming on *Mothra vs. Godzilla*, Nakajima slipped and crashed into one of the model buildings, dislodging the foam cheeks inside the suit's head. For the suit's second outing later that year, Toshimitsu's suit-building team decided to renovate the damaged head. They added radio-controlled eyeballs where the head previously held glassy-looking painted wooden eyes. The mechanics, and the process of installing them, flattened out the head a bit. Although the suit had been used in the water tank, it had not suffered unduly, and managed to survive in storage better than some of its cousins. This is partly because rather than being left to rot, it was used in various public appearances and publicity outings; it was the first Godzilla costume ever exhibited to the public in this way. In later years, the special effects unit would manufacture cheaper, cruder suits expressly for public appearances rather than use one of the actual filming suits.

The Mothra larvae costume used in *Ghidrah* is one of the two props left over from the previous film. Amazingly, there was a performer inside the thing: the experienced monster actor Katsumi Tezuka. However, it was no longer possible to use the 1956 Rodan costume, which had rotted and been discarded long ago. Even if the old Rodan suit had been available, it would not have been right to use it. Compared to the prehistoric elegance of the original, the suit used here looks goofy—comparisons to Don Knotts and Stan Laurel are not inappropriate. But that is actually the point. The 1956 Rodan was a tragic creature, a monster modeled after King Kong as a noble savage out of place in the modern world. The 1964 Rodan is a slapstick character, and should look the part.

The star of the show, however, and the monster whose name graces the title, is Ghidorah — or Ghidrah, depending on how you choose to transliterate the Japanese characters into English sounds. Written Japanese uses characters that represent vowels or consonant-vowel pairs, but there are no stand-alone consonant characters. Which means that in written Japanese, it is not possible to write a word that ends in a consonant or abuts two consonants against one another. This however applies to *written* Japanese, not necessarily the spoken form of the language, which is spoken very quickly. Interstitial vowels are often aspirated or swallowed, so the word written as Ghi-do-rah could easily be said as Ghi-d'rah. Indeed, the name was written as "Ghidrah" in the original English-language release and that spelling persisted for many years before Toho started stipulating "Ghidorah" as the preferred rendering. The "rah" sound at the end is the Japanese character ラ, the very same character used for so many monster names: Mothra, Ebirah, Hedorah, Gaborah, Gamera — not to mention Godzilla himself (or Gojira, if we're being precise). The had by now come to serve the same function in Japanese that its English variant "zilla" did

for Americans: an all-purpose suffix connoting enormous size.

Shinichi Sekizawa coined the name, and in the screenplay described the monster: "It has three heads, two tails, and a metallic roar like a bell." From this legendary description onwards, Sekizawa exerted an unprecedented level of involvement in the creation of what was to become Toho's second most popular monster. He advocated to Tsuburaya the use of lighter-weight silicon-based materials in the manufacture of the suit so that the actor inside could move more easily, facilitating more energetic fight sequences. This level of collusion was unusual, and it grew out of Sekizawa's genuine enthusiasm for his job. He loved doing these movies and wanted them to be the best they could be, and so disregarded the conventional boundaries of a writer's role.[8]

Ghidorah's golden scales were originally only expected to coat the body, while the wings were planned to have a rainbow hue. Based on imagery of Japanese mythological dragons, Ghidorah was largely designed by Akira Watanabe. The artist had created a relatively similar beast in 1959 for *The Three Treasures*, a historical fantasy chronicling the myth of Japan's creation. That film featured an eight-headed dragon called Orochi. With fewer heads but more menace, Ghidorah is an even more striking design. The immensely popular monster would rival Godzilla in its enduring popularity.[9]

Inside the suit was stunt actor Shoichi Hirose, AKA Solomon Hirose. He was a burly man's man who'd started his suitmation career in 1962 playing King Kong opposite Nakajima as Godzilla. Like Nakajima, he was versed in both judo and karate, and like Nakajima his ability to use those techniques on screen was limited by the extraordinary circumstance of having 180 pounds of rubber caked around his body. As Ghidorah, he was even more compromised. Inside the body of the suit, he was hunched over, grasping a bar for balance. The various wings and heads were all operated like marionettes by a team of puppeteers. If he moved too quickly or in the wrong direction, the wires would get tangled up with each other. Even if he moved with precision, sometimes the wires got caught in the scales of Ghidorah's golden skin. The whole endeavor was so complicated, it took much longer to film Hirose's scenes for Ghidorah than it had for Kong even though he had much less screen time.[10]

Ultimately, Hirose had overall less screen time in Toho's special effects extravaganzas than he might have wished, because he angered Tsuburaya. Nakajima was a loyal company man, committed to giving more than was asked, ever obedient to Tsuburaya. Hollywood had made overtures to Nakajima about work in America, but before accepting such a tempting offer, he asked Tsuburaya's opinion. The Old Man made it plain that without Nakajima, the whole *kaiju eiga* enterprise was doomed — and in deference to his colleagues, Nakajima turned Hollywood down. However, Hirose did not demonstrate the same feelings of obligation, and he accepted an offer for work on another Japanese studio's movie. For this act of selfish betrayal he was essentially blacklisted. Tsuburaya never hired Hirose again, replacing him in future movies with Hiroshi Sekida.[11]

*Ghidrah* would be among the last Godzilla films to be radically altered for stateside distribution. Not until New World got its hands on *Godzilla 1985* would anything this extensive be done to alter a Godzilla picture for American audiences. That said, the dubbing job is uniformly excellent: The light touch of Sekizawa's character-based comedy and his more slapsticky moments both are expressed best to non–Japanese speaking audiences through the American voice talents. Part of the reason for this success was that it was more than just a straight dub job: The film was reedited, as well.

The cuts fall into two categories. The first category relates purely to the dubbing process. One of the reasons that the studio dub jobs commissioned by American distributors sound so much better and more convincing than the cheaper ones offered by Toho itself in the decade to come was that the studios would often cut the picture to match the new voices — a few frames here, a few seconds there, move a reaction shot from one place to another to cover up a line of English dialogue that could not be made to fit the lip movements. These changes never altered the basic stuff of the movie, but helped greatly to smooth out the new English language soundtracks in relation to the onscreen performances.

The second category of edits was more intrusive. Many of the changes made to the U.S. version have to do with advancing Ghidorah's arrival in the story, and generally tightening everything up. For example, during the opening sequence at the space observatory, a shot of Ghidorah's fireball crashing in the mountains was moved from later in the film to coincide with the meteor shower, to more explicitly connect Ghidorah's arrival with the meteor storm and to bring ominous excitement to the very opening of the picture.

The American cut also drops a pair of scenes involving the press. The original cut introduces Detective Shindo in a scene between him and a reporter, before Akihiko Hirata's character shows up to assign Shindo to the princess. The Continental version drops this, and skips a later scene with Naoko's pressroom discussing how to handle the prophetess story. Such moments were not essential to advance the plot.

Both versions muddle the chronology regarding when Professor Murai is on the mountaintop investigating Ghidorah's meteorite and when he's back in town hanging out with Naoko, and how he gets back and forth. The American cut resequences some scenes so he only appears to leave the site *once* and then return, rather than leave it twice.

One purpose of the American cuts had to do with the personalities of Godzilla and Rodan. Toho in general and Sekizawa in particular were changing the characters of these once dreaded forces of mindless destruction into more or less heroic figures, defenders of Earth, the good guys. This movie stands as a crucial transition point; with few exceptions, Godzilla would be from now on the hero of his movies. The American cut helps that process along, by not having the audience feel too uncharitably towards the monsters in the first half of the film, before Mothra recruits them into a band of brothers. In the Japanese original, Godzilla tramps ashore and for no apparent reason engages in willful property damage — his modus operandi from previous films. He spies Rodan in the air and decides to spend most of the rest of the film fighting him. The U.S. cut yanks a clip of Rodan back to when Godzilla first rears his head out of the water, to motivate his rampage right from the beginning as a rivalry with Rodan. It softens his character slightly for his violence to at least be motivated rather than random.

The most significant alterations wrought on the U.S. version reorganized the sequence of events in the thrilling midsection of the film. In the original Japanese theatrical release, Ghidorah does not emerge from the fireball until after Princess Salno has prophesized it, whereas the American cut brings that moment forward to occur at the halfway point, right after Godzilla and Rodan begin to engage. One can see the logic behind the change: Get the titular menace into the movie as soon as possible. Critics of the Americanized version often point to the fact that the change weakens Salno's standing as a prophet, and rightly ask just what it is Ghidorah spends his time with after breaking free of the meteorite before he gets around to attacking Matsumoto City. The original cut goes directly from Ghidorah's birth to his rampage.

However, in defense of the Americanized edition, it is worth noting the following: Godzilla fights Rodan at night. Salno makes her prophecy in broad daylight, and Ghidorah attacks Matsumoto City in broad daylight. Yet Ghidorah's birth on the mountaintop is staged at nighttime. This appears to have been a continuity error, something that Honda tried to cover up by having Ghidorah's birth from the fireball fade out, so the abrupt switch in lighting between juxtaposed scenes was less obvious. By changing the order of scenes around, the U.S. cut has Godzilla and Rodan fighting at night, Ghidorah emerges later that night, and the following morning all hell breaks loose. The continuity problem is solved, Ghidorah enters the film at the earliest possible point, and the only cost is a minor tweaking of Salno's psychic gifts. Ghidorah's emergence from the fireball is a signature moment not just for the film but the series as a whole, and would then be recycled as stock footage every time Ghidorah reappeared in future movies.

Some of the American changes were later retroactively reintroduced to the film for a Japanese reissue. As mentioned earlier, Toho re-released a package of classic Godzilla films to the Champion Festival in digest versions cut down by Honda himself. In the case of *Ghidrah*, Honda's recut faithfully duplicated many of the cuts made by the American version, emphasizing Ghidorah as the primary threat, and showing Godzilla and Rodan's battle more as pointless roughhousing between giant monster toddlers than as a serious menace to the planet.

Whereas most of the American cuts make sense, there is one major change that defies excuse. Akira Ifukube's thrilling score was virtually jettisoned in favor of stock library cues. His artistry had done much to support Tsuburaya's effects sequences with epic grandeur, yet more often than not American distributors felt his work was dispensable. Given the crushing workload of scoring two hundred films over the span of sixty years, it was all but inevitable that Ifukube would occasionally recycle themes. In fact, the signature theme for Ghidorah in this film was originally scored in 1958 for *Varan*.

In the briefing at the Diet Building, Murai brings the Shobijin to discuss Mothra's possible cooperation. During the debate, Salno's prophecy is mentioned. An army general rolls his eyes and says something condescending about the so-called "Martian." This scene highlights a central incongruity of the Godzilla series. The characters accept the existence of monsters as a given; even the arrival of a space monster is greeted with anxiety but not disbelief. However, the idea that Salno is a Martian tests their credulity. Monsters and miniature people, sure, but a Martian? *That*, they say, is preposterous. Even a steady stream of evidence supporting Salno's claim makes little impact. She repeatedly accurately predicts the future, she identifies Ghidorah, and she shows no sign of recognition or fear of the treacherous communists who killed her father. Only reluctantly, after prolonged psychological testing, do they concede she may have a point.

She explains that a handful of Martians fled

to Earth before Ghidorah's attack, and the Martian strain gradually dissolved into the human population, leaving a residual trace of prophesy in Martian descendants. This idea has much in common with Nigel Kneale's *Quatermass and the Pit* (1958), a BBC television serial that was made into a feature by Hammer Films in 1968. Professor Quatermass discovers a relic of a Martian spacecraft in a geologic strata dating back five million years. He gradually deduces that the Martians, recognizing the coming death of their world, tried to emigrate to Earth. Unable to survive in Earth's atmosphere, they interfered with the evolution of the apemen to introduce their genes into humankind. Some modern humans, then, retained such Martian traits as telekinesis. The possibility that Sekizawa was directly influenced by Nigel Kneale is intriguing.[12]

Some reviewers have criticized *Ghidrah* for inadequately weaving the human and monster plots together. This criticism rests on an expectation derived from the previous films. In the other series installments, the monsters' actions provide the context for the humans'. The love triangle of *Godzilla* and the inner turmoil of Dr. Serizawa take their epic dimensions from the fact that Godzilla threatens to destroy their world. The battle between Godzilla and Anguirus shows the tragic consequences of warlike conflict on innocent parties. King Kong, Godzilla, and Mothra provide metaphors for the destructive impact of unrestrained greed. Seen in this light, the human plot of *Ghidrah* has little to do with the monster battle. However, the relationship exists, it has merely been switched: the human plot gives the context for the monster plot, not the other way around.

The real story of *Ghidrah* involves the decision on the part of Godzilla and Rodan to join Mothra in combating the space monster. Sekizawa's development of his female characters pales in comparison to the unprecedented humanization he here applies to the monsters. The "brotherhood of man" theme from *Mothra vs. Godzilla* has now become the brotherhood of monsters. Mothra's argument to Godzilla and Rodan mirrors what Sakai said to Mothra's people before.

The very idea that Mothra could reason with Rodan and Godzilla would have been laughably out of place in any previous film. To understand the innovations Sekizawa made to the monster movie genre, consider the history of monsters in American pictures. In the classic American monster movies of the 1930s, monsters were representations of the monstrous dark natures lurking inside outwardly civilized human beings. To quote horror film historian Frank Dello Stritto:

> One of the most common elements of the early horror films is superhuman, inhuman sexual repression and denial. All of these films fall into two basic plots. In the first, into a staid, sterile setting comes a protagonist — a monster — who ignores the social constraints and sates his lusts. In the second, the protagonist suffers incredible repression and finally breaks free in horrifying vengeance. All the monsters, whether "highbrows" (the noblemen, the doctors) or "lowbrows" (the monsters, Moreau's animal men, Browning's freaks) have appetites and desires which can no longer be satisfied.[13]

The American monsters of the 1930s had personalities, and could even arouse audience identification and sympathy. However, by the 1950s, monsters were no longer human in form but usually giant animals. American giant monsters now came to represent our collective fears and guilts: namely, the fear that we would destroy the world, and our guilt for being so stupid as to do just that. Monsters in this new tradition, then, sprang forth not from human sexual repression, but instead were loosed upon the world by scientific hubris. As such, distinct anthropomorphic personalities were no longer appropriate. Giant monsters were evil demons to be destroyed. Depicting them as human, or human-like, would contravene their narrative and thematic function.

Japanese filmmakers, in an almost perverse contrast, anthropomorphosed giant monsters in ways American filmmakers never would have. While American monsters, big and small, stood as representations of something else, Japanese monsters were characters in and of themselves. This approach reaches its peak in the infamous "monstertalk" scene. Mothra weaves a silky web around Rodan and Godzilla to get their attention — and then, Mothra starts talking.

> NAOKO: It looks like they're having a conversation. Oh, Shindo, what do you think they're saying to one another?
> SHINDO: Huh? How would I know? Do you expect me to understand monstertalk?
> MURAI: Hey, the fairies do. What's he saying?
> SHOBIJIN: He's trying to persuade them, but he's having trouble. They won't agree. He's saying all three of us should fight together against this new monster to save the Earth.
> NAOKO: And what's Rodan saying now?
> SHOBIJIN: He's saying it's none of their business if the Earth perishes. And Godzilla agrees with him. Now Rodan says he'll just fly away. And Godzilla says they have no reason to try and save mankind. They've always had trouble with men and men hate them. And Rodan says yes, he's right. But Mothra's still trying. Oh, it looks like it's no use. Godzilla and Rodan want to fight each other. They're both so bull-headed. But Mothra is still trying.
> SHINDO: Ah, these monsters are as stupid as human beings.

Although silly in the extreme, the monsters have to be able to talk in order to become full-fledged movie heroes. Although off-putting to many American viewers, it is this essential difference in approach that defines and distinguishes the Godzilla series. This happens to be a defining theme for Ishiro Honda's movies. Time and again, regardless whether Sekizawa or Kimura penned them, Honda returns to the notion that in the face of some common enemy, we will need to reach out to former rivals in the name of humanity. Of course here it's monsters, but the sentiment is the same.

Nineteen sixty-four was the year that Japan threw open its borders to the world for the Tokyo Olympics. It was the year that Japanese engineers launched the bullet train. It was also the year that their neighbor China tested their first nuclear weapon. In summary, 1964 was a year that the once famously cloistered and hermetic nation reached out tentatively into a brave new world, full of promise and danger. In the guise of a monster movie, chock-a-block with silliness, the filmmakers react to this zeitgeist with a bold statement of mutuality.

And it was heard. The July-August 2000 edition of the *Bulletin of Atomic Scientists*, a journal for national security policymakers, featured an article by Janne Nolan entitled "When Three Heads Are Better Than ... Three Heads" analyzing *Ghidrah, The Three-Headed Monster* as a useful parable for understanding serious issues facing real-world nuclear powers. "[Mutant strategic culture], according to this logic, is too primitive for conflict prevention or resolution, and mutants lack the skills for even rudimentary tension reduction, such as confidence-building measures or Track II diplomacy. In *Ghidrah*, the introduction of a new mutant into the trilateral rivalry [between Mothra, Rodan, and Godzilla] changes these dynamics significantly," Nolan writes, only partially tongue-in-cheek. "They engage in a joint operation using overwhelming and decisive force and drive Ghidorah shrieking into space in a humiliating retreat. *Ghidrah* is a clear demonstration that even mutants, despite tiny brains and a Darwinian environment, can understand the imperatives of cooperative security when survival is at stake. Maybe policy-makers will be next."[14]

Godzilla's transformation into a heroic defender of the Earth was more than just the softening of a once terrifying movie monster into a fun family-friendly icon. The change represented something about Japan as a nation. Like Japan, Godzilla was sometimes right, sometimes wrong, but always acting on the same underlying principle: the defense of its territory. Depending on against what that territory is being defended at times put Japan on the wrong side of various global conflicts. In 1964, it was still a pressing and current issue of how to reconcile patriotism, nationalism, and self-pride in Japan with being honest about how wrong and destructive Japanese military aggression had been in the war. Perhaps, in some way, the fictional construct of Godzilla helped provide a metaphor for that process, to show that great forces can have both good and bad effects in the world, without being all of one or the other.

## Chapter 13

# Invasion of Astro-Monster*
### KAIJU DAISENSO (GREAT MONSTER WAR)

*We need an exterminator.*

— Controller of Planet X

Japanese version: 96 minutes, Released December 19, 1965 (Champion Festival Release: *Kingu Ghidora tai Gojira*, 73 minutes)

U.S. version (UPA): 92 minutes, Released July 29, 1970, MPAA rating: G, double-billed with *War of the Gargantuas*, original U.S. release title: *Monster Zero*

Color, Widescreen

Produced by Tomoyuki Tanaka; U.S. version produced by Henry G. Saperstein and Reuben Bercovitch; directed by Ishiro Honda; assistant director Koji Kajita; screenplay by Shinichi Sekizawa; music by Akira Ifukube; cinematography by Hajime Koizumi; art direction by Takeo Kita; edited by Ryohei Fujii; special effects by Eiji Tsuburaya; special effects assistant director Teruyoshi Nakano; special effects cinematography by Sadamasa Arikawa and Motoyoshi Tomioka; special effects art direction by Akira Watanabe; optical effects by Yukio Manoda and Sadeo Izuka

Starring Akira Takarada (Fuji), Nick Adams (Glenn), Kumi Mizuno (Namikawa), Jun Tazaki (Dr. Sakurai), Akira Kubo (Tetsuo), Keiko Sawai (Haruno Fuji), Yoshio Tsuchiya (Controller of Planet X), Yoshifumi Tajima (General), Goro Naya, Takamaru Sasaki, Noriko Sengoku, Toru Ibuki, Kazuo Suzuki, Yasuhida Tsutsumi, Masaaki Taghibana, Kamayuki Tsubono, Somamasa Matsumoto, Takuzo Kumagaya, Yoshizo Tatake, Gen Shimizu, Mitzuo Tsuda, Hirgo Kirino, Hideki Furukawa, Rioji Shimizu, Toki Shiozawa, Yutaka Oka, Minoru Ito, Rinsako Ogata, Fuyuki Murakami, Koji Uno, Tadashi Okabe

GODZILLA portrayed by Haruo Nakajima; RODAN portrayed by Masashi Shinohara; GHIDORAH portrayed by Shoichi Hirose

*When a mysterious planet is discovered beyond Jupiter, Earth launches an exploratory spaceship. That ship, the P-1, carries the intrepid astronauts Glenn and Fuji towards Planet X, a seemingly uninhabitable wasteland under relentless attack by Ghidorah. The Xians want to borrow Godzilla and Rodan to drive Ghidorah away from Planet X, and offer a miracle drug that can cure all disease in return for the right to subcontract Earth's mightiest monsters.*

*Once Godzilla and Rodan have vanquished the space monster, the people of Earth realize that instead of a recipe for eternal health, the Xians only give up a dire ultimatum: "Earth will continue to exist only as a colony of Planet X." Unless the peoples of Earth surrender in 24 hours, the Xians will unleash the full fury of Godzilla, Rodan, and Ghidorah—all now under Xian control. Glenn is outraged: "In defense of Earth we're gonna fight to the last man, baby!"*

*But that will mean finding a way to get Godzilla and Rodan back on the home team...*

From the perspective of Japanese audiences, one of the most important, influential, and enduringly popular science fiction films ever to come from Toho Studios was not a Godzilla picture, was not even a monster movie at all, and predated the arrival of Shinichi Sekizawa. In 1957, *Chikyu Boeigun* ("Earth Self-Defense Force"), known here as *The Mysterians*, heralded Ishiro Honda's and Eiji Tsuburaya's first foray into full-color, widescreen spectacle. It

---

*Toho has stipulated that the film previously known in the U.S. as Monster Zero and Godzilla vs. Monster Zero is now to be called by its official English title, Invasion of Astro-Monster. The Japanese language does not use articles or plurals, and such linguistic distinctions are conveyed through context. In all likelihood, this English title was meant to be The Invasion of the Astro-Monsters, which is indeed the title the British distributors used, amending the name Toho supplied with the missing English modifiers. Despite the fact that, in English, Invasion of Astro-Monster is virtually nonsensical, this is the title now officially used in nearly all situations, including the DVD, and so I reluctantly use it here without the modifiers.*

tells the story of how the scientists and armies of the Earth unite to repel an invasion by aliens determined to mate with human women. *The Mysterians* spawned a cycle of space-oriented films that included *Battle in Outer Space* and *Gorath*, and introduced the "maser" cannon that would become as much an icon of Toho's sci-fi universe as any of its monster characters. *The Mysterians* even employed a giant robot mole called MOGERA, which would return to the Godzilla series many years later.

Honda saw in *The Mysterians* an opportunity to express plainly his optimistic philosophy that through science, mankind could come together across cultural and political barriers to join in common causes. It should not escape our note, however, that the vehicle Honda used to convey this sunny faith can also be read more cynically: Beware those who proclaim brotherhood and peace, because they may be enemies in disguise.

In most space alien invasion movies, especially those made in Hollywood, the threats come out swinging. Martians in tripods decimating cities, extra-terrestrial ships that blast the White House to smithereens—their hostile intentions are never in doubt, and the need for the heroes to rally a defense is also unquestioned. From *The Mysterians* onward, Toho's filmmakers explored trickier territory, in which otherworldly visitors with superior firepower and advanced technology initially spout pretty words about mutual cooperation, all while maneuvering to conquer. The inescapable moral: The best thing to do in one's defense is to be ever vigilant and distrusting of outsiders.

The political crisis that exploded in Japan not long after the release of *The Mysterians* put these ideas into stark relief. In 1951, as part of the postwar reconstruction of Japan, the United States had signed a mutual security pact with its former enemy, each side promising to maintain its military capabilities in order to work together, should the need arise, in common defense. Since Japan was constitutionally forbidden to send forces abroad, regardless of the reason, this treaty presupposed that the threat in question would be attacking the Japan islands directly. As the decade drew to a close, and negotiations began for a renewal of the treaty, a powerful minority started to make its displeasure known, objecting very publicly to this abrogation of Japan's sovereignty. The Japanese people had decided that America's appearance as an ally was not to be taken at face value, and commitments binding the nation to that alliance were dangerous acts of naïveté. The treaty was eventually renewed against a backdrop of such intense public hostility that President Dwight Eisenhower canceled plans to visit Japan.[1]

The films *Mothra vs. Godzilla* and *Ghidrah, The Three-Headed Monster* exhibit Honda's more hopeful attitudes—first a brotherhood of man, then a brotherhood of monsters—while *Invasion of Astro-Monster* injects a note of caution. As in the previous film, the space monster Ghidorah will threaten the world, and mankind will warily turn to its homegrown monsters for help. But this time that monster war will be fought inside the context of an alien race that makes happy noises about the brotherhood of "intergalactic humanity" and promises a cure-all for all disease, none of it sincere.

It is easy, and tempting, to read into this an allegory of Japanese American relations, but it must be pointed out that the dual U.S.–Japanese flags planted by the American and Japanese astronauts on Planet X visually highlight the international co-production that led to *Invasion of Astro-Monster*. Unlike *Godzilla, King of the Monsters* and *Gigantis the Fire Monster*, which were remade by U.S. producers for their American release, *Invasion of Astro-Monster* saw the input of American producer Henry G. Saperstein from the start. Consequently, the Japanese and American versions are virtually identical.[2]

United Productions of America (UPA) was a cartoon studio founded in 1941 by a group of disgruntled ex–Disney animators who set up their own shop, to produce daringly inventive and highly influential cartoon shorts distributed by Columbia. The Red Scare of the 1950s took a sad toll on the once proud studio, when much of its staff fell afoul of blacklists and Congressional investigations into Communists working in Hollywood. By the early 1960s, the company was seemingly on its last legs, when former television producer Saperstein bought its assets and retooled it for a new life. Saperstein sold off the cartoon library and focused his attention on mimicking the successful AIP model of exploiting teenage audiences with genre films. He started forging a business relationship with Toho to acquire their splashy science fiction films for American distribution.[3]

Saperstein befriended Toho's filmmakers and took a personal role in the production process. He was as much a smitten fanboy admirer of Tsuburaya's as anyone. But what Saperstein had in enthusiasm for Toho's products, he lacked in a strong business model of what to do with them once he had them.

His first acquisition was *Mothra vs. Godzilla*, though he was unable to distribute it on his own and merely sold it on to AIP. Undaunted, Saperstein took a direct role in shaping *Frankenstein Conquers the World*, which co-starred American actor Nick Adams with the Japanese cast and set the stage for a continued co-production arrangement with Toho. Along with *Frankenstein Conquers the World* and *Invasion of Astro-Monster*, Saperstein co-produced *War of the Gargantuas*, *All Monsters Attack*, and *Terror of Mechagodzilla*, and helped negotiate the deal with TriStar for the 1998 American *Godzilla*.[4]

UPA was not a distribution company, however, and relied on relationships with other firms to get their movies into theaters. Saperstein's relationship with AIP was commercially productive to both outfits but personally strained, and by 1965, Saperstein had broken off ties with AIP's Samuel Z. Arkoff. This meant that *Invasion of Astro-Monster* and *War of the Gargantuas*, produced back to back, were left without American distribution while Saperstein went looking for a new partner. That took him nearly five years; the double bill of the two pictures did not make it to American screens until 1970.[5]

When they did arrive, American audiences finally had a chance to see a more American approach to storytelling integrated into the original construction of Toho's genre films. Saperstein felt Sekizawa's scripts had become formulaic. "Most of the pictures ... opened up with a press conference or a government conference of scientists and officials," Saperstein explained in an interview. "The exposition always went on forever from there, telling the viewer all about what the story was and what was about to happen.... We convinced them that we needed to get into the picture a lot quicker. The conference could take place later on. [*Invasion of Astro-Monster*] jumps right in. Otherwise we might lose the attention of the American TV audience, which doesn't want to wait for all that."[6] The injection of American storytelling techniques rejuvenated what had developed into an almost ritualistic collection of plot ideas and characters.

Star Akira Kubo plays inventor Tetsuo with a nerdy goofiness, in a role clearly patterned after Kenji Sahara's Fujita from *King Kong vs. Godzilla*. Both were boyfriends of the hero's sister, both faced some degree of coldness from that hero-brother, and both invented something that would be used to defeat the monsters. Tetsuo is an awkward character without the confidence American heroes usually display in abundance. Ironically, astronaut Fuji does not want his sister to marry Tetsuo because he doubts the geeky inventor can make any money off his creation. Tetsuo does not make any money; in fact, he saves the world.

Kubo began his long and successful acting career at the age of eleven. Although he never received formal, professional acting training, he was a popular child star, and went on to become one of Akira Kurosawa's players. After he appeared with Toshiro Mifune in Kurosawa's *Throne of Blood* (1957) and *Sanjuro* (1962), Toho passed him to Ishiro Honda.[7] His celebrity status having been earned with such teen dramas as *The Sound of Waves* (1954), he surprisingly began taking small supporting roles in science fiction films like *Gorath* (1962), *Matango* (1963), and *Invasion of Astro-Monster*. Soon, he joined stars like Akira Takarada and Kenji Sahara as the leading man in Toho's fantasy films. He would later play the lead in *Son of Godzilla*, *Destroy All Monsters*, and *Space Amoeba*, gradually evolving into a suave, dashing hero.[8]

One of Saperstein's most significant suggestions was the inclusion of an American star to help market the film in the States. Japanese films had occasionally included some characters played by Westerners living in Japan, but in those cases the performers were chosen for their ethnicity and not their acting ability. American stars had been inserted after the fact into *Godzilla*, *Half Human*, and *Varan the Unbelievable*. Saperstein recommended Toho cast a professional American star to appear with the Japanese cast in the original version. Through a long, odd, and ultimately tragic path, that role came to be filled by Nick Adams.

Adams was a second-string American actor, confined to supporting roles in films as varied as *Rebel Without a Cause* (1955), *Pillow Talk* (1959), and *The Interns* (1962). He had also appeared in two unremarkable television series, *The Rebel* and *Saints and Sinners*. By 1963, Adams was desperate for higher billing, and he lobbied feverishly for an Oscar nomination for his performance in *Twilight of Honor*.

He explained publicly, "A nomination for me means that *Twilight of Honor* will bring in another million dollars and supply more funds for Hollywood pictures. Next, it means that I, as a Hollywood star, can make more films in Hollywood and stop this runaway production which is killing Hollywood. I will never make a picture abroad."[9] When Melvyn Douglas won the Best Supporting Actor for his role in *Hud*, Adams promptly left Hollywood to make pictures abroad.

After appearing with Boris Karloff in the British production *Die, Monster, Die!* (1965), he moved to Japan to appear in *Frankenstein Conquers the World*, Saperstein's first involvement with Toho. In both *Frankenstein* and *Astro-Monster*, Adams costars with Kumi Mizuno. Honda had a special liking for Mizuno, and said that unlike most of her peers in the Japanese film world, she had the right stuff to play a Westernized heroine, more sexual and aggressive than the typical Japanese woman of the time.[10] Playing lovers onscreen, Adams and Mizuno allegedly began an offscreen affair as well. In February 1965, Adams appeared on TV's *The Les Crane Show* where he announced

he was divorcing his wife Carol. She, however, had heard nothing of this decision prior to the broadcast. For the next two years, they battled out their private lives very publicly. In order to stay close to Mizuno, Adams began living in Japan.[11]

After multiple divorces and remarriages with Carol, Nick eventually returned to Hollywood in 1966. He committed suicide on February 6, 1968, only 37 years old. Some have speculated the impetus for his suicide was Mizuno's rejection of continuing their affair.[12] Some believe his drug overdose was an accident and not a suicide at all, and cite the lack of any suicide note as supporting evidence of this claim.[13]

Of Adams, Saperstein has nothing but praise, "Nick Adams was terrific, a real professional. Very cooperative, always on time, ready with his lines, available, totally cooperative. He loved being there."[14]

August Ragone and Guy Tucker, writing for the fan journal *Markalite*, recounted:

> Yoshio Tsuchiya [who played the Controller of Planet X], an inveterate practical joker ... started Adams' Japanese lessons by teaching him to say, "I'm starving!" for "Good morning," and later "How's it hanging?" for "Pleased to meet you"—this latter incident reportedly caused a group of wealthy ladies to shrink from him in horror. Adams quickly learned to dish it back, learning the real Japanese for "You're overacting!" during Tsuchiya's scenes as Controller of Planet X. Adams very much admired Tsuchiya, partly due to his work with Kurosawa, and asked if he could arrange for Toshiro Mifune to dub Adams' voice for the Japanese version. The reply: "Sure, can you get Henry Ford to do mine?"[15]

As the Controller, the famously eccentric Yoshio Tsuchiya punctuated his dialogue with strange hand gestures that underscore his alienness. Tsuchiya also invented some dialogue for himself in "Xian."[16]

Keiko Sawai plays the now *de rigueur* role of the sister, a comedown from the improved gender roles of *Ghidrah* and a return to the helpless-female days of *Godzilla Raids Again* and *King Kong vs. Godzilla*.

The best female role went to Nick Adams' costar and real-life love interest Mizuno. As an

Xian agent, she imprisons Tetsuo and helps betray Earth. However, her decidedly un–Xian emotions for the astronaut Glenn lead her to betray her people and save the Earth. Although the film reveals that all the Xian women look alike (but not the men), it ironically turns out to be one of the cloned women who proves to be the only true Xian individual. Other writers would borrow elements of her character for future films; Takeshi Kimura created an army of emotionless space women to invade Earth in *Destroy All Monsters*, and *Terror of Mechagodzilla*'s screenwriter Yukiko Takayama devised an emotionless cyborg who turns out to have the capacity to love after all. However, Miss Namikawa, played with style and grace by the great Kumi Mizuno, was both first and best.

One strikingly foreign aspect of *Invasion of Astro-Monster* is the mention of people who are willing to surrender to the Xians to avoid war. Glenn's brash "We're gonna fight to the last man, baby!" is the typically American response. It is hard to imagine an American film that would feature any contemplation of surrendering to the invaders without a fight. Not only does the screenplay mention such people, but suggests their numbers are large enough to cause significant controversy in the world's reaction to the ultimatum.

As with *King Kong vs. Godzilla*, *Mothra vs. Godzilla*, and *Ghidrah*, the Japanese government refuses to allow the use of nuclear weapons against the monsters. In past films, nuclear weapons were forgone in favor of some kind of electric fence. Although the electric fence never worked, at least it was not a nuclear device. For American viewers, whose real-life society constantly threatened the deployment of nuclear weapons in its defense, this strenuous avoidance of such a defense in the Godzilla films seems bizarre. Americans never faced first-hand the consequences of nuclear war, and could rationalize the proposed use of their super-weapons as a necessary evil. The Japanese had no such luxury.

A more successful alternative to the electric fence was the pitting of monsters against one another. The monsters thus became symbols of super-weapons. More terrible and more destructive than nuclear weapons, monsters were also less predictable. The Xians claimed to control Ghidorah at all times, yet the three-headed monster destroyed their water plant, much to the Controller's dismay.

By this point in the series, the human heroes had learned the best way to fight a monster was to get an even bigger monster, for example asking Mothra for help against Godzilla and later against Ghidorah. Godzilla has now assumed the heroic role Mothra formerly held, and indeed no mention is made of Mothra's role in previously defeating Ghidorah. The Xians' request to "borrow" Godzilla and Rodan puts an interesting twist on the scenario developed in past films. The Japanese, used to asking Mothra's people for help, find the shoe on the other foot. The distrust they feel towards the Xians shows the Japanese heroes what Mothra's people must have felt towards them.

Elements in *Ghidrah, The Three-Headed Monster* suggested a conscious alien force behind the threat, and some dialogue in *Invasion of Astro-Monster* directly connects the two films. The magnetic waves emanating from Planet X could have been the cause of the unseasonal heat wave in *Ghidrah*, for example. Furthermore, the Xians know a great deal about Godzilla's last encounter with Ghidorah, implying the events in the previous film may have been part of the Xians' invasion plan. The Xians run the World Education Corporation as a front for their Earth-based operations, only a minor variation on the vilification of corporations in *King Kong vs. Godzilla* and *Mothra vs. Godzilla*. The alien-invasion theme would become the formula for Godzilla films in the '70s, and Sekizawa would reuse the notion of invading aliens running a corporation in *Godzilla vs. Gigan*.

The special effects measure up to Tsuburaya's standards and improve on the average American fantasy film of the period. The look of the picture, unrestrained by Western concerns with realism, perfectly captures the mid–1960s idea of the space age. In many ways, this is one of the more representative science fiction fantasies of the sixties. Akira Watanabe's lovely set designs for Planet X echo Chesley Bonestell's famous astronomical paintings.

Realism was clearly not the driving motivation for the special effects staff when Haruo Nakajima as Godzilla was allowed to dance a victory jig on Planet X after pummeling Ghidorah into submission. The controversial scene, resisted by much of the film's crew, pays homage to the Japanese comic "Ahso Matsu-kun," which Tsuburaya is said to have liked.[17] This admittedly ridiculous moment, however, met with stern disapproval with Honda, who objected to such comic portrayals of the monsters. "It's a disgrace," he declared.[18]

With the all-time attendance record set in 1963, the Godzilla series continued with dwindling ticket sales. Concordantly, costs were cut. The greatest expense, of course, came as a result of Tsuburaya's effects work, but as they were also the key to the series' appeal, they could not be cut altogether. This tension between cost-cutting and the natural expense of special effects would continue throughout the first series. *Invasion of Astro-Monster* recycles shots from *Rodan*, which never look like the new footage. *Rodan* was shot in the Academy aspect ratio, while *Invasion of Astro-Monster* is a widescreen film, necessitating footage from *Rodan* being photographically enlarged and cropped, resulting in a marked increase in the film's grain. Astute viewers can also spot changes in Rodan's appearance (especially coloration) between old and new scenes. The reuse of existing special effects footage would increase steadily over the coming years, especially in films like *All Monsters Attack* and *Godzilla vs. Gigan.*

With Honda's confident direction and another superb score by Akira Ifukube, *Invasion of Astro-Monster* would be the last Godzilla film made by the Tanaka-Honda-Tsuburaya-Sekizawa-Ifukube team. The series would continue, but gradually a new team would take over.

## Chapter 14

# Monsters Inc.

*I'll repeat the news bulletin that has triggered this alert: Gargantua came ashore thirty minutes ago at the mouth of the Sakai River. Land, sea, and air units of the nation's defense force have gone into action in an effort to prevent the huge green monster from retreating back into the ocean. And, of course, to destroy him.*

— newscaster, *War of the Gargantuas*

It is only with hindsight that we can look back on a coherent Godzilla franchise. When *King Kong vs. Godzilla* was made, there was no reason to suspect that the Godzilla character would appear in more films—and indeed the king of the monsters had been dormant for seven years. Looking at the first decade of Toho's *tokusatsu* output (that is, "special effects" films in general), it was simply a question of Toho's executives discovering that their people were quite gifted at making a peculiar kind of movie that happened to sell well at home and abroad. But within those parameters it was not yet the case that anyone had decided to prioritize Godzilla features over other special effects showcases—which included space epics, alien invasion films, gloomy sci-fi head-scratchers, action thrillers, and various other giant monsters.

Then, in 1962, the team of Tanaka, Honda, Tsuburaya, Sekizawa, and Ifukube lent their considerable talents to a movie that broke all box office records and remains to this day the most commercially successful in the franchise; forty years afterwards, it would continue to serve as the benchmark by which all subsequent films in the genre would be judged. Yet whereas the preceding *tokusatsu* efforts had been fairly uniformly serious in tone, *King Kong vs. Godzilla* revels in its silliness and makes no excuses about being a comedy. The experiment succeeded; *King Kong vs. Godzilla* thrilled 12.6 million Japanese viewers.[1] Before 1962, Godzilla was a sporadic enterprise with an uncertain future, and after 1962 was a veritable pop cultural juggernaut.

*King Kong vs. Godzilla* so far outstripped the other productions in terms of popularity, it forced the studio to streamline and retool the formula: Drop the dour, brooding stuff that tended not to make as much money and instead focus on big all-star monster smash-ups.

Tsuburaya responded to the increasingly comic screenplays by allowing greater amounts of comedy into the effects sequences. But his principal understudy, Teruyoshi Nakano, also resisted the change of tone. Stuart Galbraith interviewed Nakano, who said, "The first Godzilla had such a social impact, because Godzilla was the aftermath of the bomb. I wasn't sure if it could be turned into something that was entertaining and comical. But commercially it was very successful, and after that the Godzilla series became one monster-vs.-monster movie after another. But it was totally opposite to what the first film was about. It was a little confusing to me. It had been hard, but after that Godzilla movies became soft."[2]

Sekizawa's self-imposed mission to fill Godzilla movies with jokes met with resistance from Honda, who was not as keen on allowing the monsters to be humanized. Honda said, "I don't think a monster should ever be a comical character."[3] Had he been working in Hollywood, Honda, one of the most commercially successful Japanese filmmakers of all time, would have had the clout to prevent changes with which he did not agree. In the top-down movie factories of Japan, Honda was denied any such say in his fate.[4]

That audience figures for the successive sequels fell steadily, and that the budgets for Toho's *kaiju eiga* also dropped are facts that, if taken out of context, can be quite misleading. Three years after *King Kong vs. Godzilla* beat out *101 Dalmatians* and *El Cid* to place as the fourth highest grossing film in Japan, *Invasion of Astro-Monster* finished as the ninth top-grossing Japanese-made film in Japan for 1965 (with Akira Kurosawa's *Red Beard* taking the top slot). Heavy competition from American imports meant that the top-earning films increasingly were Hollywood ones.[5]

It is often said by commentators of the genre that dwindling audiences forced the studio to slash its budgets, which in turn compromised the quality of the product, which in turn cost the films more viewers, in a self-feeding cycle of decline. This book's narrow focus on Godzilla movies in and of themselves risks contributing to this misperception. Only by stepping back to take in a wider context is it possible to see that there is an additional layer of detail missed by that analysis.

*Mothra* and *King Kong vs. Godzilla* were more than just unique twists on the genre; they were unique films in the marketplace, unchallenged by anything else at the time. *Mothra* was the only science fiction film released by Toho in all of 1961; the only thing remotely similar to it on Toho's roster that year was *The Last War*, a speculative drama about a nuclear war which featured Tsuburaya's effects but no real science fiction or fantasy component. *King Kong vs. Godzilla* was one of just two science fiction films from Toho the following year, competing only against *Gorath*, a space epic about a runaway star on a collision course with Earth.

The box office records set by these two films established a sort of baseline of the total audience available for a *kaiju eiga*. We can think of that audience as a pie. *King Kong vs. Godzilla* had that pie all to itself, and gorged on nearly 13 million viewers. It would be hard to top that achievement. By comparison, in 1966, Toho released two major monster movies: *Godzilla vs. the Sea Monster* and *War of the Gargantuas*. These had to share the nation's screens with *Gamera, Gamera vs. Barugon, Daimajin, Wrath*

*of Daimajin, Return of Daimajin, Yokai Monsters: Along with Ghosts, Yokai Monsters: 100 Monsters, The Magic Serpent,* and *Terror Beneath the Sea*—all the while, Ultraman battled giant monsters on weekly television. Add to that the eight major Japanese giant monster films theatrically released by various studios in the four years between 1962 and 1966. This level of aggressive competition only increased. The pie was now being split among many hungry rivals.

Even discounting the competition from enemy studios, Toho's own staff had good reason to compete against themselves. Investing all of their efforts in a single lavish production, *a la King Kong vs. Godzilla*, not only meant that the film stood to reap all of the potential rewards of success, but also risked catastrophic losses if something went wrong. Distributing the risk across a number of smaller monster movies meant that no single film was likely to be a huge blockbuster, but at the same time there was a better chance that some of them would be modest successes. *King Kong vs. Godzilla* had been a one-of-a-kind moment, a lavish production celebrating the studio's thirtieth anniversary; it had little competition and some unique marketing advantages. Its successors would be instead an array of diversified product lines of reduced expectations but greater volume. Monsters had become big business.

Tomoyuki Tanaka spent the 1960s making as many science fiction films as humanly possible, with an eye towards economy and efficiency, in the hopes of finding something else that "clicked."

The case of *Matango* was especially instructive. Released in the summer of 1963 (and distributed in the United States under the title *Attack of the Mushroom People*), this grim fable is frequently cited by Japan's top film critics as one of the best Japanese films of all time.[6] Written by Takeshi Kimura and directed by Ishiro Honda, *Matango* tells the tale of a ragtag bunch of shipwreck survivors—a neat cross-section of contemporary Japanese society—stranded on an uncharted island with no hope of rescue. There is no food on the desolate rock, save for a nasty fungus that, while technically edible, has serious psychotropic effects. Eating the mushrooms not only induces delirium, it gradually corrodes the soul until the person literally becomes a mindless fungus—you are what you eat. In other words, you can only survive by voluntarily surrendering your humanity.

It was a deeply personal film for both Honda and Kimura. Honda used what leverage he had earned as the master of Godzilla to earn the right to indulge himself. Despite *Matango*'s profitability (it earned double its cost), Toho's decision makers prohibited further indulgences of its kind. As a thinly veiled parable about selling out, the fate of *Matango*'s creators was doubly ironic: Honda and Kimura would now be forced to abandon such personal projects in favor of assembly-line monster pictures. Kimura made his unhappiness known, and refused to sign his name to any of his future screenplays. After *Matango*, he insisted on using the pseudonym Kaoro Mabuchi, to signal that he did not consider the work "his" any more.[7]

By 1965, Tanaka had learned to focus all of his team's attention on giant monsters, all the time. Godzilla was now the established brand name for the monster movie product line, and viable monster stars had been cultivated in Rodan, Mothra, and Ghidorah. If new hit monsters were to be added to that line-up, then the chances were best if the hit-makers were assigned to that task; the Godzilla films could afford to coast for a while, and might even benefit from a fresh influx of new talent. Rather than put the company's flagship product entirely in the hands of newcomers, Shinichi Sekizawa was left on the Godzilla team as the experienced old hand. Joining Sekizawa would be director Jun Fukuda (whose action film *Young Guy in Hawaii* was considered by Toho to be the real reason why its co-feature *Matango* did as well as it did), and Fukuda's regular staff including director of photography Kazuo Yamada and composer Masaru Sato. Meanwhile, Honda took his DP Hajime Koizumi and composer Akira Ifukube with him to join Takeshi Kimura on a parallel set of monster flicks.

Since the Honda-Sekizawa team had mined so much treasure already out of the gold mine that was *King Kong vs. Godzilla*, the Honda-Kimura team returned to that source to see what else had been left unexploited. The story outline that Willis O'Brien had originally generated for that film had called for King Kong to battle a suitably oversized Frankenstein Monster. Meanwhile, American distributor Brenco had been so happy with their purchase of Honda's 1960 insubstantial man picture *The Human Vapor* that they had requested a sequel. Tanaka initially asked Kimura to work up a scenario for *Frankenstein vs. the Human Vapor*. This evolved into *Frankenstein vs. Godzilla*, and then, with the decision to segregate the Godzilla unit, into *Frankenstein vs. Baragon*.[8]

Henry G. Saperstein arranged a full-fledged co-production deal with Toho for the film, the first of its kind (and prior to *Invasion of Astro-Monster*). Nick Adams flew to Japan for the first of his Toho collaborations, proudly trumpeted in Japanese ads as "Hollywood star Nick Adams."[9] The film was released almost to the day on the twentieth anniversary of the bombing of Hiroshima; Kimura's screenplay emphasizes the connection.

In a wonderfully cinematic and nearly wordless opening sequence, Nazi soldiers in World War II commandeer the still-beating heart of Frankenstein's Monster from a reluctant scientist in Frankfurt, crate the thing up, and ship it to Japan. The Japanese doctors, aspiring to use the heart as a sort of 1940s stem cell research into new therapies for human injury and disease, take it to, of all places, Hiroshima on August 6, 1945.

The atomic blast destroys the lab but leaves the still-living heart. A feral boy, orphaned by the bomb and desperate for food, later finds and eats it. Fifteen years later, a guilt-ridden American doctor (Adams) sets up shop in Hiroshima to treat the victims of radiation poisoning and cancer caused by his government's actions, only to find a teenage boy rapidly going through the worst parody of puberty imaginable, mutating into a giant freak whose body regenerates after any injury.

That the film also features a radioactive dinosaur with the ability to shoot blasts of energy from his horn and a cross-racial love affair between Adams and the luscious Kumi Mizuno is just icing on the cake. Saperstein thought that Toho's original ending, in which Frankenstein and Baragon are sucked into a volcano, lacked punch, and asked Tsuburaya to shoot an alternate ending in which Frankenstein also takes on a giant octopus. Saperstein found few interested takers for his *Frankenstein vs. the Giant Devilfish*, eventually selling the picture to AIP who proceeded to remove Saperstein's ending, restore the original Japanese conclusion, and retitle it *Frankenstein Conquers the World*. Toho happily kept Saperstein's devilfish finale for their release, however.[10]

Following their collaboration on *Invasion of Astro-Monster*, the Saperstein-Honda-Kimura team returned to their Frankenstein creation with an eye to a sequel. What started as *The Frankenstein Brothers* turned into *Battle of the Frankensteins* and then into *Duel of the Frankensteins*, before going before cameras as *Frankenstein's Monsters: Sanda vs. Gaira*—and is known today as *War of the Gargantuas*. Again, the film revolves around a hero scientist trying to rehabilitate the reputation of "his" monster, falsely accused of crimes and mayhem actually caused by a different creature. The good and bad monsters meet, and special effects ensue.

As a sequel, *War of the Gargantuas* is an odd beast. Kumi Mizuno returns in basically the same role, but her character has been unaccountably renamed. Kenji Sahara has taken over the role previously played by Tadao Takashima (and received a name change of his own in the process). The American hero doctor is no longer kindly Nick Adams, but grumpy Russ Tamblyn. On paper, one can see why Saperstein might have felt Tamblyn a better choice: Where Adams was something of a punchline to American audiences with a decidedly B-list stature at best, Tamblyn was and remains today a busy actor with a strong résumé of major roles in highly respected productions. Tamblyn was a better marquee name—but that is as far as that goes. Say what you will about Adams as an actor, he was a sincere, possibly even naïve, young man whose enthusiasm cloaked his faults—like Michael Scott of *The Office*. He studied the Japanese language and Japanese business etiquette, befriended his costars (and even at times acted like a starstruck fan), and invested his entire being in his work for Toho. He may have been a troubled man whose private life was crumbling, but he took his work for Ishiro Honda very seriously indeed.[11] Tamblyn took the easier route, and clearly saw his assignment to *War of the Gargantuas* as a comedown unworthy of too much effort.

The screenplay (the English language version of which was written by co-producer Reuben Bercovitch) gave the character of Dr. Paul Stewart dialogue rich in sarcasm and factitiousness. Tamblyn says those lines flatly, with a hint of contempt, which turns potentially casual-sounding lines into unduly harsh words. Adams developed genuine chemistry with his Japanese co-stars; Tamblyn might as well check his watch on screen, so eager is he to leave the proceedings.

In addition to cast changes, *War of the Gargantuas* fiddles with the monster characters as well. The Japanese dialogue alternates between calling them "gargantuas" and "Frankensteins," but neither monster looks much like the Frankenstein seen in the previous film. The script posits that skin tissue from a Frankenstein can regenerate into a new creature. This process is how the evil Green Gargantua came into being, a sort of clone of his brother with brown fur. Whether the Brown Garagantua is meant to be a similarly regenerated product derived from the carcass of the previous Frankenstein, or that same monster in a new costume, is neither clear nor especially important. Toho's fantasy filmmakers had spent over a decade playing fast and loose with logic and continuity, and felt no compulsion about imposing any new restrictions on themselves now that they had hit their stride.

Saperstein felt otherwise, and was troubled by the pointed lack of continuity connecting the ostensible sequel to its predecessor. *Frankenstein Conquers the World* had not enjoyed the kind of success that would have somehow earned it a monopoly on the name

Frankenstein; if anything, Western audiences would connect the name Frankenstein to Peter Cushing long before images of Haruo Nakajima in fur underwear. Realizing that there was nothing to gain in playing up the film's status as a sequel, he had references to the previous film omitted from the English dubbing and retitled it.

On a double bill with *Invasion of Astro-Monster*, *War of the Gargantuas* terrified American audiences and thrilled a generation of youngsters. This was Toho fantasy filmmaking at its finest, with every department firing on all cylinders. Akira Ifukube's ominous and syrupy soundtrack perfectly underscores Eiji Tsuburaya's wall-to-wall effects sequences (which were later recycled into other films more than any other Toho production). The two Gargantuas are fast-moving, intelligent brutes, unlike the reptilian monsters typically populating such films. The Green Gargantua even has the disquieting habit of eating people—and spitting out their clothing! In one unforgettable scene, a hapless pop singer at a rooftop nightclub belts out "The Words Get Stuck in My Throat," possibly the most annoying song ever written, unaware that an enormous green whatsit is coming into view behind her, with every intention of getting *her* stuck in its throat.

In the raucous finale, the two Gargantuas sink into a volcano—an ambiguous ending not dissimilar to the one that capped *Frankenstein Conquers the World*. The stage was set for yet another sequel ... but the Gargantuas have remained dormant ever since.

In Germany, *Frankenstein: Der Schrecken mit dem Affengesicht* (the German title for *Frankenstein Conquers the World*, which translates as "Frankenstein: The Freak with the Face of an Ape") had been a huge hit. Constantin Films was only too happy to play up the link, and released the sequel as *Frankenstein: Zweikampf der Giganten* (with a little poetic license, it means "Frankenstein: War of the Gargantuas") in March of 1968. However, in the process, it was as if the logic centers of their brains were severed and henceforth Japanese imports would all find some bizarre connection to Frankenstein! Having crossed that Rubicon, there was no turning back.

*King Kong Escapes* became *King Kong: Frankensteins Sohn* (King Kong: Frankenstein's Son), *Godzilla vs. the Sea Monster* became *Frankenstein und die Ungeuheur aus dem Meer* (Frankenstein and the Monster from the Sea), *Son of Godzilla* became *Frankensteins Monster Jagen Godzillas Sohn* (Frankenstein's Monster Hunts Godzilla's Son), *Destroy All Monsters* became *Frankenstein und die Monster aus dem All* (Frankenstein and the Monster from Space), *Godzilla vs. Hedorah* became *Frankenstein Kampf Gegen Teufelsmonster* (Frankenstein vs. the Devil's Monster), and *Godzilla vs. Gigan* became *Frankensteins Höllenbrut* (Frankenstein's Hellish Children). Somehow the name Frankenstein had morphed into an all-purpose moniker for giant monsters.

What of the name Godzilla, then? To German distributors, it seemed to be a general reference to some kind of giant reptile. Thus: *Gamera vs. Barugon* became *Godzilla, der Drache aus dem Dschungel* (Godzilla, the Dragon from the Jungle), *Gamera vs. Gyaos* became *Frankensteins Kampf der Ungeheuer* (Frankenstein's War of the Monsters), *Gamera vs. Jiger* became *Frankensteins Dämonen bedroht die Welt* (Frankenstein's Demons Threaten the World), *Gappa* became *Frankensteins Fliegende Monster* (Frankenstein's Flying Monster), and the Korean Godzilla knock-off *Yongary* became *Godzillas Todespranke* (Godzilla's Hand of Death).

Constantin's titling staff noticed that in *Godzilla vs. Mechagodzilla*, Godzilla battled a robot duplicate of himself—an idea similar to the one used in *King Kong Escapes*, which they had sold as *King Kong: Frankensteins Sohn*. On the logic that "King Kong" then must refer to a giant robot, Godzilla's first encounter with Mechagodzilla became *King Kong Gegen Godzilla* (King Kong vs. Godzilla), and *Godzilla vs. Megalon* turned into *King Kong: Dämonen aus dem Weltall* (King Kong: Demon of the Universe).

It was not until the 1990s that German distributors started using reasonably translated German titles for Japanese monster imports.

Monster names, so freighted with cultural meaning, had markedly different connotations for different audiences. In the United States, the name King Kong still stood for the Eighth Wonder of the World, and America's most acclaimed homegrown monster hero. Kong was conspicuous as the one facet of *King Kong vs. Godzilla* not yet exploited for reuse by Toho—but their hands were tied, so long as the rights to the ever-popular monster were not their own.

Those rights belonged to RKO, and in 1966 RKO licensed the character to cartoon producers Arthur Rankin Jr. and Jules Bass for a Saturday morning television series. *The King Kong Show* has the curious distinction of being the first American cartoon series animated in Japan. Rankin/Bass subcontracted the animating to Toei Studios for the cycle of 26 episodes, which aired between September 1966 and August 1969. Japanese kids got in on the fun, too, as Toei aired the show on Japanese TV from 1966 to 1967.

As written by Lew Lewis, Bernard Cowan, and Ron Levy, *The King Kong Show* depicted the adventures of explorers Professor Bond, his daughter Susan, and son Bobby on a tropical island home to a giant ape. Their lives are imperiled by various threats, from dinosaurs to the villainous Dr. Who (clearly modeled after James Bond's Dr. No)—but always rescued by their friend King Kong. The premise of a group of scientists befriended by a giant monster would resurface in the following decade in Hanna-Barbera's cartoon *Godzilla*.

Rankin/Bass' license included the option to make a theatrical feature adapted from the TV cartoon, and for that the company approached Toho. Delighted to have a second crack at a King Kong movie, Tomoyuki Tanaka asked Shinichi Sekizawa to develop a scenario. Sekizawa returned with *King Kong vs. Ebirah: Operation Robinson Crusoe*. Sushi aficionados will surely recognize the word ebi as Japanese for shrimp, and as discussed the "rah" character ラ is equivalent to the "zilla" suffix, so "Ebirah" is basically "Shrimpzilla." Arthur Rankin Jr. did not think Sekizawa's idea captured the essence of his show, and rejected it. Never one to let anything go to waste, the economical Tanaka had Sekizawa cross out the name "King Kong" on the script, change it to "Godzilla," and hand it over to director Jun Fukuda more or less as is.

Takeshi Kimura took over the King Kong gig and hewed closer to the American original. His script borrowed heavily from the existing cartoon scripts, even down to Dr. Who's giant robot duplicate of Kong, Mechani-Kong—an idea that would later become a staple of the Japanese monster genre, but born in the minds of American cartoon producers.[12]

*King Kong Escapes* (1967) was six ways from crazy, and probably the most childish of all the *kaiju eiga* up to that point. American critics gasped in horror (and willfully ignored the fact that this supposed Japanese abomination was really nothing more than an American abomination that had been outsourced).

As the decade grew closer to its end, Toho had valiantly tried to duplicate the magic of Godzilla, but without lasting success. No other monster caught on as tenaciously with audiences, no other franchise got started. There was something special about Godzilla, regardless of who was at the helm.

# Chapter 15

# Godzilla vs. the Sea Monster

## GOJIRA, EBIRAH, MOSURA: NANKAI NO DAI KETTO
## (GODZILLA, EBIRAH, MOTHRA: BIG DUEL IN
## THE SOUTH SEA)

*Be quiet! Get back to work and stop praying!*

— Red Bamboo captain

Japanese version: 87 minutes, Released December 17, 1966 (Champion Festival Release: 74 minutes)

U.S. version: 82 minutes, U.S. Television release by AIP, 1968, limited theatrical release as *Ebirah, Horror of the Deep*

Color, Widescreen

Produced by Tomoyuki Tanaka; directed by Jun Fukuda; screenplay by Shinichi Sekizawa; music by Masaru Sato; cinematography by Kazuo Yamada; art direction by Takeo Kita; edited by Ryohei Fujii; special effects by Sadamasa Arikawa; special effects supervised by Eiji Tsuburaya; special effects assistant director Teruyoshi Nakano; special effects art direction by Akira Watanabe; optical effects by Hiroshi Mukoyama, Yukio Manoda, and Sadao Iizuda

Starring Akira Takarada (Yashi), Toru Watanabe (Ruta), Hideo Sunazuka (Mita), Kumi Mizuno (Daiyo), Jun Tazaki (Commander), Akihiko Hirata (Captain), Toru Ibuki (Yata), Chotaro Togano (Ichiro), Eisei Amamoto (Red Bamboo Officer), Pair Bambi (Shobijin), Ikio Sawamura (Slave)

GODZILLA portrayed by Haruo Nakajima; EBIRAH portrayed by Hiroshi Sekida

*Anxiously seeking his brother, presumed dead at sea, teenager Ruta tries to enter a dance marathon in hopes of winning a seaboat. He falls in with a crowd of unlucky dance contestants who wander the marina late at night. On a lark, they board a yacht, unaware that it is a stolen ship hiding fugitive bank robber Yashi. Convinced the circumstances are divine providence, the reckless Ruta steals the boat himself, setting his motley group of acquaintances to sea in search of his missing brother.*

*Shipwrecked on a remote island, they discover several surprising things. First is the secret hideout of the Red Bamboo terrorist organization, using slave labor to manufacture a strange yellow juice. Second is the purpose of the juice: to pacify and control the giant monster Ebirah, who patrols the island destroying any ships that approach. Third is the presence of Mothra's people among the slaves. And fourth, the hibernating body of Godzilla concealed in a cave. With the right pluck and moxie, these ragtag survivors can set the monsters against one another to free the slaves and defeat the Red Bamboo. When their sabotage efforts accidentally trigger a countdown to a nuclear holocaust, the situation takes on a new urgency...*

Jun Fukuda was one of the young guys behind *Young Guy*, a venerable franchise of teen-friendly films starring musician Yuzo Kayama. Eleven years younger than Ishiro Honda, Fukuda was a filmmaker with a flair for action and light comedy, and whose *Young Guy* efforts had in recent years brought in fat profits for Toho. He had served as Honda's assistant on *Rodan*, and had taken over *The Secret of the Telegian* from Honda a few years later. Honda was a director of deeply held convictions who found ways to express himself through the genre and exploitation films he tackled; Fukuda was destined to be a more superficial stylist. Honda's personal indulgence, *Matango*, survived at the box office largely thanks to its co-featured partner, *Young Guy in Hawaii* by Fukuda. But Fukuda's contribution to the insubstantial man cycle, *The Secret of the Telegian*, was the most expensive and least popular of the lot and ended the series. As a replacement for Honda, Fukuda was at once a natural choice and a mixed bag.[1]

Nineteen sixty-five, the year that Honda first began exploring the world of giant Frankensteins, found Fukuda directing one of his best films, *100 Shot, 100 Killed*. A wildly entertaining spoof of James Bond movies, it stars Akira Takarada as a jet-setting and madly charming yet slapstick-prone secret agent, facing down a villainous cabal led by Akihiko Hirata and a femme fatale played by Mie Hama. Full of spectacular action, explosions, chases, shoot-outs, daring escapes, sexy bikini-clad assassins, gadgets, secret lairs, and broad comedy, all set to a jaunty jazz-fueled score by Masaru Sato, it was a stand-out film for the era. When Rankin/Bass rejected Shinichi Sekizawa's proposed *King Kong vs. Ebirah*, Tanaka had him retool it as a Godzilla vehicle and handed the project over to Fukuda. In turn, Fukuda reunited nearly all of his *100 Shot, 100 Killed* team for a "new generation" Godzilla picture that would be ostentatious in its novelty. Fukuda described the difference in approach, saying, "I generally think of my movies as action dramas."[2]

Fukuda brought in composer Masaru Sato to take over from Akira Ifukube. Sato had scored *Godzilla Raids Again*, but his name is venerated among soundtrack aficionados as the musical voice of Akira Kurosawa's greatest works. Sato was an eclecticist who freely mixed instrumentation and musical styles in a freestyle, irreverent way. He and Fukuda had been longtime friends and collaborators, and Sato recycled a handful of cues from his work on *100 Shot, 100 Killed* for the *Sea Monster* soundtrack.

In this action-packed spectacle, the heroes go from one lucky escape to another with scarcely a breath in-between. In a refreshing break with the traditions established in the past, the film omits the usual roster of reporters, police detectives, or government scientists. Pulled into the action as much by coincidence as by anything else, the heroes of *The Sea Monster* are a young man who steals a boat, two refugees from a dance marathon, a plucky escaped slave, and a bank robber. This unlikely group of characters shows a resourcefulness and bravado in the face of danger that sets them apart both from the confident authority figures of films like *Ghidrah* and the anxious, timid protagonists in *Godzilla Raids Again*.

Sekizawa's script is obviously influenced by the James Bond movies, a genre Fukuda had been riffing on for some time. The Bond series found popularity not only in the West, but in Japan as well. In 1967, Toho Studios provided facilities and personnel to the producers of the 007 adventure *You Only Live Twice*, which featured Akiko Wakabayashi (Princess Salno from *Ghidrah*) and Mie Hama (from *King Kong vs. Godzilla* and *King Kong Escapes*) along with star Sean Connery.[3] The 007 influence on *Godzilla vs. the Sea Monster* surfaces in one especially Bond-like sequence as Akira Takarada's character desperately tries to deactivate the nuclear self-destruct system. As he struggles to extend his arm towards the big red button, it slowly drops ever farther out of reach.

Takarada obviously relishes his chance to play against type. It is his most Cary Grant–like of performances. Yashi the bank robber comes off as more interesting, complex, and believable than the clean-cut heroes Takarada played in previous installments (or his slapsticky action hero role in *100 Shot, 100 Killed*). Toho's fantasy films often included cops-and-robbers, most prominently in non–Godzilla entries like *The H-Man* and *The Human Vapor*, but also in *All Monsters Attack* and *Ghidrah* as well. Unlike Toho's usual robber villains, Yashi is a sympathetic hero who never gets his comeuppance; the qualities that make him a successful bank robber are the very qualities that serve him well in fighting the Red Bamboo.

Also defying typecasting, Akihiko Hirata plays the captain of the mysterious Red Bamboo faction, again donning an eyepatch like the one he wore as Dr. Serizawa, but with less hammy exuberance than he showed as the villain of *100 Shot, 100 Killed*. Whether the Red Bamboo represent fascists or communists is never clear, but also irrelevant. Shinichi Sekizawa has little interest in the reasons behind the events, and the fun of the movie comes from watching the action unfold for its own sake.

Kumi Mizuno returns, again playing a strong female. Unlike her role as Miss Namikawa in

*Invasion of Astro-Monster*, though, her character is a real human being, and her strengths are
not associated with villainy. Daiyo is afraid of
no man; afraid of Godzilla, sure, but no mere
man. Her bravery stands out particularly in
comparison to the cowardly Mita, played by
Hideo Sunazaka.

As the naïve yet courageous young man who
brings the others into the action, Toru Watanabe gets a meatier role than his walk-on part in
*100 Shot, 100 Killed*, and provides a refreshing
new face in a cast increasingly comprised of a
Godzilla stock company.

Godzilla's "entrance" scene is one of the most
memorable in the cycle, and the most unusual.
Godzilla does not rise up out of the ice/water/
land roaring and bruising for a fight. Instead,
the heroes come to the realization that Godzilla
lies asleep practically under their feet. This introduction occurs long before the monster even
stirs. The tension derives from the unspoken
realization of what could happen if Godzilla
awakes, a tension that gives the scene a powerful emotional punch.

The late switch from King Kong to Godzilla
left Godzilla's characterization very close to
Toho's version of Kong. Notably, Godzilla is revived by electricity, which in *King Kong vs.
Godzilla* was shown to be a source of energy for
the great ape. By contrast, *King Kong vs. Godzilla*
and *Mothra vs. Godzilla* depict Godzilla as somewhat vulnerable to electricity. Another nod to
Kong-like behavior occurs when Godzilla traps
Daiyo on a mountainside.

There is superb tension as Daiyo freezes in
place while Godzilla meditates. Godzilla, a
creature that can crush an entire building with
a single step and incinerate a foe with his
breath, seems more terrifying and powerful
when compared to a defenseless, tiny person, all
alone. The scene does, though, beg the question, why does Godzilla *meditate?*

In the post–*Ghidorah* films, Haruo Nakajima
played Godzilla with a charming mix of brash-
ness and moxie, more anthropomorphic than
monstrous. Although at times hammy, this performance gives a personality to the suitmation
creature and lets Godzilla be a full movie character along with his human co-stars, who can

sometimes seem lifeless and uninteresting in
the comparison. In his second bout with Ebirah, Godzilla rips the sea monster's claws off. As
Ebirah retreats back into the sea, Godzilla claps
the severed claw at him in a cruel taunt. This
gesture, at once triumphant and threatening,
perfectly suits Nakajima's Godzilla persona.

Mothra, absent in the last film, returns in a
significantly reduced role. Although still intelligent, courageous and generous, she no longer
takes center stage or top billing, as she had in
1964. Godzilla has now taken over as the unquestioned monster star, and also assumes
much of Mothra's heroic qualities as well. Not
yet a full-fledged hero, as he would become in
1969, Godzilla has already come a long way
from the menacing terror of his 1954 debut.
Mothra's somewhat diminished role in the film
has more than a little to do with the new ac-
tresses playing her fairy priestesses. The
Peanuts did not return for this film; the Shobijin roles were handed to another set of twins
named Pair Bambi. It would be the last appearance of Mothra's fairies until 1992.

Eiji Tsuburaya received a mostly honorary
credit as supervisor for the effects, which were
in fact handled by Sadamasa Arikawa, who
took the opportunity to experiment and innovate a variety of new techniques. With most of
Toho's attention and budget going to *War of
the Gargantuas*, Arikawa was forced to economize. There is little monster action, and what
there is takes place largely in the Big Pool, with
little property destruction. One novel sequence
found suitmation actors Haruo Nakajima and
Hiroshi Sekida battling entirely underwater,
with offscreen aqualungs allowing the actors to
snatch a breath between takes.[4]

While the series got a new look, Godzilla
himself did not. The *Astro-Monster* suit reappears here, tattered and flabby, and the Mothra
marionette was one of the five puppets made
for use in *Mothra vs. Godzilla*.[5] The Ebirah costume, however, is well-designed and colorful,
and far more lifelike than the appalling giant
crab monster Toho created for 1970s *Space
Amoeba*.

Sekizawa griped that he was being made to
turn out monster scripts at too grueling a pace,

and that between Toho gigs and writing for *Ultraman* he had long ago run out of original concepts. His attempts to encourage Toho to hire another writer fell on deaf ears at a studio looking to cut costs.[6] Inevitably, Sekizawa returned to some familiar ideas in his screenplay for *The Sea Monster*, including a new version of his magical liquid. Again he presents the monsters as super-weapons and as gods, with a super-weapon Godzilla and monster-god Mothra.

Of course, of all the Polynesian peoples they could have enslaved, why did the Red Bamboo select the one society with an authentic giant monster as a god? Not to mention, this god has a well-documented track record of saving her people from this kind of injustice. If they had not all been eaten alive by their monster protector, the Red Bamboo's top brass would certainly have fired whoever made that moronic decision.

*Godzilla vs. the Sea Monster* never received any wide-scale American theatrical distribution. Continental Pictures released it in a few theaters as *Ebirah, Horror of the Deep*, but the only major release stateside came from AIP's television release in 1968.[7]

The American version does not differ greatly from the Japanese edition. Just as cost-cutting measures prompted Toho to scale back the productions of Godzilla's movies, the same economic motivations encouraged American distributors to tamper as little as possible with the films. Excessive recutting and reworking of the films cost money, without necessarily improving revenues. Beginning with the UPA co-production of *Invasion of Astro-Monster*, the Godzilla movies began appearing in the United States with only minor alterations.

One ill-conceived edit in *Ebirah, Horror of the Deep* sticks out: While the original begins slowly with a gentle introduction to the small fishing community and a mother's worried search for a missing son, the American version starts with a dramatic bang. The footage intended to represent the fate of Yata's boat was taken from Ebirah's subsequent attack on the stolen yacht *Yahlen*. Consequently, the boat in the beginning sports the name *Yahlen* very clearly inscribed on its hull.[8]

In the mid–1960s, Toho started creating English dubbed versions of their fantasy films using a Hong Kong–based dubbing firm. These editions were termed "international versions," because they were of especial use in making European sales. Distributors in France, Germany, Spain, and Italy were accustomed to dubbing English-language imports from Hollywood into their local tongues, but translating Japanese required specialized talents and knowledge that were not always readily at hand. European distributors were happier working from an English-language print, and so in making such things available, Toho was increasing their ability to make international sales. The English dubbing done in the United States by companies like AIP and UPA was far superior, but the existence of an already dubbed version did make it possible for English-language distributors to skip that step: While Henry Saperstein struggled for five years to work out distribution for his version of *Monster Zero*, the international cut *Invasion of Astro-Monster* was shown in the U.K. The American-produced dub of *Ebirah, Horror of the Deep* improved greatly on the international version *Godzilla vs. the Sea Monster*, but changed the continuity of the picture. In recent years, the original cut has been restored, which has necessitated the abandonment of the American dubbing in favor of the complete, but more poorly voiced, international cut of *Godzilla vs. the Sea Monster*.

Fukuda complained that he had to drastically cut sequences to fit them into the proscribed running time, likening the process to "pouring two cups of water into one." Dissatisfied with the result, he disowned it and quickly returned to work on his television pilot. He was asked to return to direct *Son of Godzilla*, and took over the series in the seventies, but Fukuda never enjoyed the task. Feeling no sequels should have been made to the original *Godzilla*, and bristling at the half-size budgets Toho gave him, Jun Fukuda later told an interviewer that he liked none of his Godzilla films. Preferring to direct comedies in the *Young Guy* mold, Fukuda would nevertheless remain attached to Tomoyuki Tanaka's popular series until 1974.

# Chapter 16

# Son of Godzilla

## Kaiju Shima no Kessen: Gojira no Musuku
## (Monster Island's Decisive Battle: Son of Godzilla)

*Godzilla and its youngster and the Gimantises and now a Spiega — it's an island of monsters!*
— Goro

Japanese version: 86 minutes, Released December 16, 1967, (Champion Festival Release: 66 minutes)

No U.S. theatrical release; U.S. television version (AIP): 84 minutes, 1969

Color, Widescreen

Produced by Tomoyuki Tanaka; U.S. version produced by James H. Nicholson and Samuel Z. Arkoff; directed by Jun Fukuda; screenplay by Shinichi Sekizawa and Kazue Shiba; music by Masaru Sato; cinematography by Kazuo Yamada; art direction by Takeo Kita; edited by Ryohei Fujii; special effects by Sadamasa Arikawa; special effects supervised by Eiji Tsuburaya; special effects assistant director Teruyoshi Nakano; special effects cinematography by Motoyoshi Tomioka; special effects art direction by Akira Watanabe; optical effects by Yukio Manoda and Sadao Iizuda

Starring Tadeo Takashima (Dr. Kusumi), Akira Kubo (Goro Masaki), Beverly Maeda (Riko), Akihiko Hirata (Fujisaki), Yoshio Tsuchiya (Furukawa), Kenji Sahara (Morio), Kenichiro Maruyama (Ozawa), Seishiro Kuno (Tashiro), Yasuhiko Saijo (Suzuki), Susumu Kurobe (Aircraft Captain), Kazuo Suzuki (Pilot), Wataru Ohmae (Radioman), Chotaro Togane (Surveyor)

GODZILLA portrayed by Haruo Nakajima and Kiyoji Onaka; MINILLA portrayed by Little Man Machan

*At a research station on Solgell Island in the South Pacific, a United Nations research team headed by the stubborn Dr. Kusumi is testing a method for controlling the weather. Three months on duty in this steamy jungle has left the crew irritable and nervy. At last, the preparations begin on the test, which, if successful, will freeze the island. Just as the end is in sight, some of the men begin to crack.*

*Into this volatile situation parachutes Goro Masaki, an intrepid reporter who claims the island is not as uninhabited as they think: He insists he saw a native girl swimming nearby. The others dismiss Goro's claim, certain the only other animal life on Solgell are its monsters, notably a group of giant preying mantises (Kamacuras, in the Japanese version).*

*Mysterious radio interference affects the test, causing a radioactive storm which drastically raises the temperature, wrecks much of the equipment, and mutates the Kamacuri to humongous size. They unearth a giant egg, which hatches to reveal a baby Godzilla (Minilla, in the original). It was the source of the interference, sending out an emergency radio call to the full-size Godzilla.*

*Goro finds the native girl, Riko Matsumiya, who befriends the baby Godzilla and helps the increasingly anxious scientists hide from yet another monster — Spiega, a giant spider (Kumonga, in Japanese).*

*Hunted by Spiega, sickened by radiation, and trapped underneath a raging battle between the Godzillas and the mutant mantises, all hope seems lost for the humans. Dr. Kusumi seizes their only hope: try the test again and hope to freeze the island and the monsters with it...*

We should not be too surprised that science fiction movies display rampant scientific ignorance. The people who make motion pictures—screenwriters, directors, studio executives—are trained in the arts and humanities, or business school. It is very rare that someone with a degree in a scientific field decides to go to work in show business. Science fiction movies are sculpted to be dramatic, and the science is shoehorned in as an afterthought, as doublespeak and jargon to sound impressive and provide the justification for the fantastic events depicted, misrepresented with confidence that the scientifically illiterate audience won't notice the difference.

Even on *Star Trek*, which has inspired numerous viewers to become real engineers and physicists, the situation is the same. The screenwriters pen the tales with the emotional conflicts and drama, and where a scientific explanation is needed, the writers leave a blank. Later, someone charged with maintaining consistent usage of the show's trademark terminology inserts the proper jargon. So, the things that happen in their stories are driven first and foremost by dramatic purpose and the "science" is made to conform as needed.[1]

Scientist characters rarely surface in American movies except in science fiction. Mainstream dramas and comedies think nothing of showing the lives of architects, photojournalists, real estate agents, teachers, race-car drivers, or chefs. But a scientist cannot appear in a movie without the film suddenly taking a position on the relative merits and dangers of scientific research.

Scientist characters in American sci-fi movies generally fall into one of two categories. The first is the scientist advisor. This is a secondary role, brought in to help the heroes identify their problem and devise a solution. The real heroes are cops, military types, or reporters—average Joes. To emphasize the gulf between the heroes and the smart guy, the scientist advisor speaks in ten-dollar words, laced with smug superiority that the people he advises don't know what he's saying. Such movies assume scientists and average folks do not even share a common language.

Indeed often they do not: The advisor role is often a foreigner. The accent may be nothing more exotic than British, but the point is made that the scientist is not a normal American.

To further separate the scientist from the hero, he is usually an old professor type (substitute the absent-minded professor cliché for some comic relief if needed). In addition to being old and foreign and possessed of uncommon intelligence, the advisor is cold and detached. We will not see any real emotional outburst from him when innocent people are killed, nor see him in love or anything so common. The only emotional display may be a gush of excitement over the discovery of an alien invader, mutant creature, or whatever—just what he needs to get the fame and reputation that moviemakers assume all scientists crave.

The second primary scientist character type is the mad scientist, the only leading man scientist character—so we may see more in the way of action, dashing good looks, love affairs, and the like. But he is not a hero. He may be a *protagonist*, but he is the villain or the anti-hero of the story, too—the root cause of the evil, creator of monsters.

The mad scientist shows more emotion, but it is uncontrolled and wild. He is narrowminded in his pursuit of his goal, and willfully ignorant of the possible unpleasant consequences. He works alone in a basement lab, having been kicked out of the academy for some egregious transgression that has left him with a lingering bitterness. "I'll show those fools who laugh at me!"

The most important identifying feature of the mad scientist is the fact that his research is pushing the boundaries of knowledge into some dangerous new terrain. Watch enough mad scientist movies in a row and over and over again you will hear some variation of the words, "He tampered in God's domain, asking questions man was not meant to know."

The message hammered home by these character types is that scientists are a dangerous bunch of egotistical, amoral, emotionless know-it-alls quite unlike regular people. What sets them apart is their fanatical devotion to the pursuit of knowledge, without any regard for decency or tradition.

The clue to the source of this cultural attitude lies in the wording of the ubiquitous phrase "Things man was not meant to know." More than just the age-old conflict between science and religion, this is the essence of Original Sin. Adam and Eve were tempted by the Tree of Knowledge—knowledge God had placed off limits from mankind. By caving in to curiosity, they were cast out of Paradise, and all of us must face the horror of death as a consequence.

Looked at purely as a narrative, stripped free of religious significance, the story of Adam and Eve is a derivation of the earlier myth of Prometheus, a Greek god who defied Zeus' will and gave mankind the knowledge of fire — the very beginnings of science and technology.

Mary Shelley subtitled her novel *Frankenstein* "A Modern Prometheus," and so all of the mad scientists fashioned in Frankenstein's image carry with them the ancient heritage of these myths. Scientists are dangerous because they dare to intrude into the realms God has declared off limits.

Logically, then, the way to defeat monsters is to demonstrate to God that we have learned our lesson, to show some humility. In most monster flicks, the demons loosed by unrestrained science are ultimately contained by looking backwards to simpler things—fire, the common cold, salt water. These are the tools by which we keep monsters at bay. This is how we show God that we understand not to push our limits.

Notably, most of the classic monster movies were made during the height of the Cold War's obsessive investment in military research and development. Instead of exploiting science fiction movies as propaganda platforms offering cinematic justification for all the billions spent in the military industrial complex, however, these movies are resolute Luddites, arguing that we have everything we need already.

Ironically, what counts as the status quo changes as we move forward in time. Electricity created monsters in the 1930s, but by the 1960s electricity is used to stop monsters created by newer technologies. There were a number of early German horror movies based on the story of Alraune, in which a mad scientist experiments with "artificial insemination" and thereby creates a soulless killer. These movies seem ludicrously quaint by modern standards, with people in the audience conceived by artificial insemination who would attest from personal experience that it does not create monsters at all.

If our culture's distrust of science is a by-product of Christian theology, though, we should expect to see different attitudes expressed in Eastern cultures. Godzilla movies do display such a difference. Godzilla movies are blessedly free of Original Sin anti-science, and we can finally see scientists save the day with *new* research and technology.

Part of this, to be sure, is the result of Ishiro Honda's personal biases. He believed that scientists were best equipped to overcome the petty nationalistic thinking that keeps nation poised against nation. He wanted his movies to depict a utopian ideal, where in the face of adversity scientists could unite divided people to defend their world. It's a wonderful vision, but a distinctly personal one. Compare it to *Independence Day*, in which in the face of adversity it is the American military that unites the world.

Honda's first foray into monster movies was, of course, *Godzilla*. At first glance, *Godzilla* seems to fall into the well-worn tradition of mad scientist tales. Dr. Serizawa even looks like an archetypal mad scientist — his eyepatch marks him physically as different from normal people, and he is so engrossed in his work that he has no time for anything as lowly as human romance, losing his betrothed Emiko to the suave young hero Ogata as a result. Ogata is a seaman, not some aloof nerd. And Serizawa toils away in his basement lab on secret research that he refuses to tell anyone about.

In true mad scientist fashion, Serizawa has discovered something really dangerous. Just as research into subatomic particles led to the development of nuclear weapons, his experiments with what will later be called micro-oxygen have yielded a practical application as a weapon — a weapon of such awesome destructive power that it surpasses A-bombs and H-bombs.

If Godzilla is a monstrous omen from the gods punishing mankind for tampering with the atom, then the American sci-fi model would require that mankind be chastised, and demonstrate newfound humility by turning backwards to simpler tools. But as it happens, Dr. Serizawa's Oxygen Destroyer is what *stops* Godzilla. Given the "mad scientist" characterization of Serizawa, American viewers would normally be conditioned to think his Oxygen Destroyer is a bad thing, not the salvation of the world.

*Godzilla* is a real cinematic work of art, and its densely allegorical story is cluttered with Honda's idealism, the historical parallels to the

A- and H-bombs, and the holdovers from American sci-fi caused by copying such films as *King Kong* and *The Beast from 20,000 Fathoms.* We should not draw any final conclusions from analyzing just this one movie, since there is too much background noise. But *Son of Godzilla* is a quickie exploitation programmer made to cash in on the Godzilla franchise. It is the seventh sequel, so all pretenses to originality and art have long since fallen away. That is not to say *Son* is a bad film, just that it is a simple-minded one.

*Son of Godzilla* also has the distinction of being made by Jun Fukuda, who had little interest in making Godzilla movies, so the end result is very much a by-the-numbers, manufactured product. In this way, we can see underlying cultural attitudes more clearly, since there are no strident artistic visionaries dominating the film.

The story concerns scientists on Solgell Island, working to develop technology that will control the weather. This has to be one of the most extreme encroachments into God's domain imaginable; most early religions developed as a way of explaining the weather. The Greek gods wielded tools of weather like lightning as their mystical powers. The weather is the most tangible evidence of Nature's power in our lives.

If this were an American sci-fi flick, this audacious act of human arrogance would not go unpunished. Sure enough, the first time the Solgell team fire up their machinery, it goes disastrously wrong and starts a radioactive storm, leaving the island overrun by giant monsters. And if the insects or the various Godzillas don't trample the humans underfoot, they'll kill each other off since months of being copped up in this steamy South Pacific hellhole has driven them to their wits' end. Lesson learned?

No, because the only way they are going to save themselves is by uniting, overcoming their differences, and perfecting the weather control device. They run the experiment again, and this time it works: It freezes the island and subdues the monsters. So, attempting to control the weather unleashes monsters but successfully controlling the weather puts the monsters back again. That has nothing at all to do with Original Sin. Far from cautioning us to be satisfied with the status quo, *Son of Godzilla* advocates continued research. We can expect some hiccups along the way, a few monsters here or there, but stay the course because only through progress can we secure the future.

Real life demands difficult choices, and scientists like all normal people face those responsibilities with conscience. Unfortunately, mainstream American science fiction has been reluctant to depict this.

Jun Fukuda never went on record the way Honda did regarding his feelings about science or scientists. He may not have had much of an opinion on the matter. However, examining another of his films may illuminate some of the workings of Fukuda's mind. *The Secret of the Telegian* was Fukuda's first science fiction effort, and arguably his best. In *Telegian*, the mad scientist role is split into two characters. One is Dr. Nikki, who invented a matter teleporter. Despite having been betrayed, blown up, left to die, and forced to live in exile, Nikki bears no grudges and seems content with his lot. Nikki may be responsible for creating a dangerous new technology, but he is not misusing it in the way a typical mad scientist would. Instead, his assistant, Lance Corporal Suto (not a scientist at all) has the mad desire for revenge. Suto teleports himself around town on a vengeful killing spree, but he did not invent the teleporter.

Lest we tarnish Nikki with this association, the film also presents a benign Professor Miura (who is also a reporter — always a Japanese SF fave) who used to be a scientist and now covers the science beat for the newspaper. In the end, Suto meets his end, but not as a result of his abuse of this menacing new technological marvel, but a volcanic eruption. Just one of those things that happen in a land beset by natural disasters.

Fukuda had barely let the developing chemicals dry on the prints of *Godzilla vs. the Sea Monster* before he was heard moaning that "all of the variations of monster movies had been used up." Tomoyuki Tanaka approached Shinichi Sekizawa with an idea: "'How about writing a movie about the son of Godzilla for the New Year, Mr. Sekizawa?' So I went off and wrote one," Sekizawa recalled.[2]

Similar in many ways to *Godzilla vs. the Sea Monster*, this attempt at a "new direction" was also set on a tropical island, dispensing with expensive miniature metropoli. There is a native girl, some strife between the male heroes, a secret research station, an island full of unexpected monster life, a colored liquid with mysterious powers, and a sentimental ending as the escaping heroes look back at Godzilla left behind. Still playing with the balance between human plots and monster action, and between comedy and horror, Sekizawa this time plays the human story completely straight and reserves all his slapstick for the monsters.

Again as in *Sea Monster*, the humans have unwittingly involved themselves in monster affairs. The U.N. installed all that expensive equipment on what turns out to be Godzilla's home island. The scientists insist they checked the island thoroughly, but somehow none of them noticed the giant spider Kumonga, Kamacuras, Minilla's egg, Godzilla, or the refuge Riko. When the survivors reach civilization, somebody is going to lose his job.

Riko is an odd character. No reason is ever given for her to have hidden from her countrymen. Once found, she quickly joins them as a colleague. She also has a way of providing useful information just a little late. Fever runs rampant before she announces that the island's pools of red water are a cure, and she lets Spiega's siege thoroughly depress everyone before revealing a secret exit to the cave. Even after the secret exit is discovered, no one uses it to escape the monsters. They all just sit around, waiting for the roof to cave in.

There are several fine scenes, though. Godzilla's arrival, the tense atmosphere as the cave begins to collapse, and the gradual disintegration of morale are all very effectively handled. The effects work is outstanding. As before, Tsuburaya received nominal credit as "supervisor," but the actual work was overseen by Sadamasa Arikawa, who indulged in techniques both new and old for a film full of ambition. Compared to *Sea Monster*, *Son of Godzilla* was an indulgent undertaking with a healthy budget and wall-to-wall monster action.

The giant mantises and Kumonga were elaborate marionettes, and according to Tsuburaya's protégé and successor Teruyoshi Nakano, extraordinarily difficult to operate.[3] The effort pays off, as they are authentic in appearance and behavior. In one memorable moment, Goro and one of the other men flee the site of Godzilla's bout with the mantises as the severed limb of one of the insects is hurled ahead of them, aflame from Godzilla's atomic ray.

Unfortunately, the high quality of the giant insect effects only serves to highlight the low quality of the Godzilla effects. Godzilla's scenes are the most embarrassing ever filmed. Part of the blame must go to the eponymous creation, the Son of Godzilla himself. Minilla (Minizilla?) is atrocious.

As soon as the egg cracks open, Goro instantly recognizes the thing inside as a baby Godzilla. Later, he even mistakes it for the real Godzilla. Poor Goro must need glasses. Some effort was evidently put into making Minilla appear to develop over the course of the film, as he is seen in at least three distinct stages. He hatches, still fairly embryonic. As the film proceeds, his features become more distinct. In the end, he looks like a ratty teddy bear. Critic Don Glut said he looked like "something out of a medical book of human freaks."[4] At no point, though, does he look like anything other than rubber.

Initially, a rubber puppet Minilla hatches from the egg, an effect along the same lines as the Gimantises, only much less effective. Later, a suitmation Minilla appears courtesy of midget actor Little Man Machan.[5] Machan may have been the right size for the role, but he does not behave like an animal, or like a monster, for that matter. Godzilla fares scarcely better. The costume has been redesigned with bulbous eyes spaced close together atop his squashed-in face, looking like some kind of giant frog.[6]

Ishiro Honda, commenting on his absence from these two films, said he would have a hard time humanizing Godzilla in the way Toho wanted.[7] When Honda returned to his creation, it would be for a return to first principles, and an all-out celebration of the monster world he and his collaborators had spent fifteen years building.

## Chapter 17

# Destroy All Monsters

## KAIJU SOSHINGEKI (MARCH OF THE MONSTERS)

*On land, all of the Earth's monsters have been collected and are living together in a place called Monsterland.*

— narrator

Japanese version: 89 minutes, Released August 1, 1968, double-billed with a reissue of *Atragon* (Champion Festival Release: *Gojira Dengeki Taisakusen* [Godzilla Electric Battle Masterpiece]), 74 minutes

U.S. version (AIP): 86 minutes, Released May 23, 1969, MPAA rating: G

Color, Widescreen

Produced by Tomoyuki Tanaka; U.S. version produced by James H. Nicholson and Samuel Z. Arkoff; directed by Ishiro Honda; assistant director Seiji Tani; U.S. version dubbing directed by Salvatore Billiteri; screenplay by Takeshi Kimura and Ishiro Honda; music by Akira Ifukube; cinematography by Sadamasa Arikawa; art direction by Takeo Kita; edited by Ryohei Fujii; special effects by Sadamasa Arikawa; special effects supervised by Eiji Tsuburaya; special effects art direction by Akira Watanabe; optical effects by Yukio Manoda and Sadao Iizuda

Starring Akira Kubo (SY-3 Captain Katsuo Yamabe), Jun Tazaki (Dr. Yoshido), Yoshio Tsuchiya (Dr. Otani), Kyoko Ai (Kilaak Queen), Kenji Sahara (Nishikawa), Yukiko Kobayashi (Kyoto), Andrew Hughes (Dr. Stevenson), Chotaro Togane (Okada), Yoshifumi Tajima (General Sugiyama), Hisaya Ito (Tada), Yoshio Katsude (Young Scientist), Henry Ohkawa, Kenichiro Maruyama (Engineers), Ikio Sawamura (Farmer), Yutaka Sada (Policeman), Hiroshi Okada (Doctor at Hospital), Hideo Shibuya, Yutaka Oka (Reporters), Ken Echigo, Yasuhiko Saijo, Seishiro Hisano, Wataru Ohmae (SY-3 Engineers), Hiroo Kirino, Kamayuki Tsubono, Naoya Kusagawa (Detectives), Rinsaku Ogata, Haruya Sakamoto (Officers), Susumu Kurobe, Kazuo Suzuki, Minoru Ito, Toru Ibuki (Control Room Staff), Yukihiko Gondo (Soldier), Michiko Ishii (Kilaak), Keiko Miyauchi, Atsuko Takahashi, Ari Sagawa, Yoshio Miyata, Kyoko Mori, Midori Uchiyama, Wakako Tanabe, Nadao Kirino, Kazuo Suzuki

GODZILLA portrayed by Haruo Nakajima; MINILLA portrayed by Little Man Machan; GHIDORAH portrayed by Susumu Utsumi; RODAN portrayed by Teruo Nigaki; ANGUIRUS portrayed by Hiroshi Sekida

*By the year 1999, all ten of the world's monsters have been collected on Ogasawara Island in a compound known as Monsterland. For the monsters there is no escape, but researchers ensure the monsters are satisfied in their artificial environment.*

*The United Nations Scientific Committee operates a moonbase, with regular flights from Earth. Katsuo, captain of the SY-3 moon shuttle, calls his girlfriend Kyoto from the moon. She has just joined the staff of Monsterland to conduct a thorough study of the giant creatures. Katsuo remarks to his sweetheart that he has found evidence of possible monstrous life on the moon, but before he can elaborate, there is a grave malfunction at Monsterland.*

*Once the U.N. reestablishes communications with Monsterland, they find the island now a deserted wasteland, conquered by aliens from the planet Kilaak. The queen of the Kilaaks intends to build a new technologically advanced civilization on the rubble of human society. The Kilaaks have turned the Monsterland scientists into brainwashed zombies and now control the monsters as well. She sends her monster drones out to destroy the world's capitals, while Katsuo leads the SY-3 back to the moon in hopes of bringing the fight to the invaders.*

*If they can free Godzilla and the other monsters from the Kilaaks' mind control, perhaps then they will have a defense against the Kilaaks' ultimate weapon: King Ghidorah.*

In the sixties, two essential conflicts shaped the Godzilla series. The first was the tension between Shinichi Sekizawa's increasingly absurd scripts and Ishiro Honda's desire to keep the dignified seriousness of the early *kaiju eiga*. The second conflict was the dilemma of reducing the expenses involved in the special effects without lessening the appeal of the movies. In the decade to come, these tensions would be summarily resolved, and the careful balancing act that produced classics like *Mothra vs. Godzilla* and *Ghidrah, The Three-Headed Monster* would end, leaving an imbalance that would produce such turkeys as *Godzilla vs. Megalon*. *Godzilla vs. the Sea Monster* and *Son of Godzilla* pointed the way the franchise would go in the seventies, with decreased budgets and increased silliness, but *Destroy All Monsters* returned, briefly, to the style and tone of the early sixties, with a lavish buffet of special effects.

It was the first Godzilla film since *Godzilla Raids Again* not written by Shinichi Sekizawa. The script by Takeshi Kimura and Ishiro Honda is essentially a retread of Sekizawa's *Invasion of Astro-Monster*. An alien menace takes control of Earth's monsters to spearhead their invasion. When blackmail fails and the monsters are freed from alien mind control, they must unite to battle Ghidorah. The Achilles heel of the invaders is discovered and the Earth is saved. What sets *Destroy All Monsters* apart, aside from its lack of deliberate humor, is the concept of Monsterland (called Monster Island in future films).

Films like *Rodan* and *Mothra* had been produced with no prior intent to tie in with the Godzilla universe. By pairing these monsters in films like *Mothra vs. Godzilla* and *Ghidrah*, Toho tied those worlds together after the fact. Thus, by 1967, the fictional Japan of the movies was a land beset by the likes of Godzilla, Rodan, Mothra, Kumonga and the Kamacuri, Ebirah, King Kong, Anguirus, and occasionally the unwelcome extraterrestrial visitor King Ghidorah. Honda and Kimura looked at this fictional world and came up with a solution that was inspired. The most rational solution to this major public safety problem would be to intern the lot of them on some faraway island where they can be kept nicely pacified. Dr. Yamane of *Godzilla* would be pleased to note that Monsterland staff members are finally getting to study these monsters.

Monster Island became as memorable an icon as Godzilla himself, and would feature in most of the subsequent films. Not all of the monsters are here; there is no sign of Ebirah or King Kong, for example. However, as a compensation for this oversight, several monsters are interred on Monster Island that were not previously part of the Godzilla universe. Manda (from 1963's *Atragon*), Baragon (last spotted wrestling with the Frankenstein monster in 1965) and Varan were originally created by Eiji Tsuburaya and Ishiro Honda for existence in their own self-contained fictional worlds.

Of course, both Baragon and Varan appear so fleetingly that only the most attentive observer will catch them. The costumes deteriorated so badly that they could not stand up to extended use. While money existed to update the Manda and Anguirus suits, Toho had to draw the line somewhere. The Baragon suit underwent several alterations for use on Tsuburaya's *Ultraman* television series and was not in good enough condition for more than a fleeting cameo appearance, although the script called for the creature to attack France. Gorosaurus (from 1966's *King Kong Escapes*) filled in for Baragon's scenes, but the dialogue in the script was never changed. In both the English and Japanese language editions, the newscaster incorrectly identifies the monster attacking Paris as Baragon.[1]

Tsuburaya was by now too ill to participate. The Old Man had finally earned his nickname, and so Sadamasa Arikawa led the team in staging an array of effects simply astonishing in their sheer number and creative design. This is the ultimate *kaiju eiga* spectacle, with no fewer than eleven rampaging monsters. Numerous low-angle shots make the monsters seem truly gigantic, and overhead tracking shots are also used in abundance. Godzilla's attack on the SY-3 crew as they search Mount Fuji on foot is a masterpiece of miniature set design and optical compositing. The re-use of Ghidorah's fiery "birth" scene is the only recycled footage in the film. (Chunks of *Destroy All Monsters* would be reused in the seventies films.[2])

The Kilaaks appear to be an all-female race, and their queen is the second female villain for the series. Unlike *Astro-Monster*'s Miss

Namikawa, the Kilaak queen never changes from her ultimatum-spewing, gloating persona. She does seem to lose her self-confidence slightly when she hears Godzilla tearing his way into her base, but then, who *wouldn't*? Interestingly, some of the strongest women characters in the first series are emotionless space aliens: Princess Salno, Miss Namikawa, and the Kilaak queen. Evidently the filmmakers find something about self-confidence, courage, and intelligence incompatible with being a real human female. Fortunately there are characters like Naoko in *Ghidrah* and Daiyo in *Sea Monster* to prove that real human females can be resourceful, brave, and active.

The only human woman in *Destroy All Monsters* is the hero's girlfriend, and once she is freed from alien mind control she simply sits around politely and keeps her mouth shut. She is only released from Kilaak dominance when Katsuo physically rips the control spheres from Kyoto's bleeding ears. Through violence, the man regains control of the woman, silencing her and removing her individuality. Katsuo realizes that only under the influence of *the other* does Kyoto exhibit such assertiveness, and it is his duty to free her from that alien influence so that she can return to her "natural" role as a submissive female.

The Americanized edition stays very close to the Japanese original. AIP released it in the United States shortly after the Japanese release, the first new Godzilla film in American theaters since 1965's *Ghidorah*. (*Invasion of Astro-Monster* having been delayed until 1970, and both subsequent films were dumped unceremoniously directly to TV.[3]) AIP recommended that exhibitors display wrecked cars outside theaters with signs declaring, "A Victim of *Destroy All Monsters.*" AIP also encouraged exterminators to participate in cooperative advertising with the slogan, "We destroy all monsters, too—but not the variety seen in *Destroy All Monsters.*" Additionally, AIP proposed placing ads in the classified sections of newspapers saying, "Wanted—Men, women or young adults to help *Destroy All Monsters!*"[4]

Some have called *Destroy All Monsters* the "last hurrah" of Toho's classic *kaiju eiga*, others called it the "last gasp," the difference mainly lying in whether the reviewer in question liked the film or not. Either way, the consensus was that *Destroy All Monsters* represents the last of the line. An attempt by Toho to win back the adult audience that had gradually deserted the series over the course of the decade, *Destroy All Monsters* nevertheless continued the declining ticket sales of the series. *Invasion of Astro-Monster* brought in 3.8 million Japanese viewers, *Sea Monster* 3.4 million, *Son of Godzilla* 2.5 million, and *Destroy All Monsters* only 2.6 million.[5] Tomoyuki Tanaka fully expected to call it a day and let Godzilla end on this last, glorious outing.[6]

And so it would have ended, if Gamera had not pointed to a new path.

# Chapter 18

# *All Monsters Attack*

## ORU KAIJU DAISHINGEKI* (ALL MONSTERS ON PARADE)

*How d'ya like that, weirdo?*

— Minilla

Japanese version: 70 minutes, Released December 20, 1969, double-billed with *Kuso Tengoku* (Fancy Paradise)

U.S. version (UPA): 69 minutes, 1971, double-billed with *Island of the Burning Damned*

Color, Widescreen

Produced by Tomoyuki Tanaka; U.S. version produced by Henry G. Saperstein; directed by Ishiro Honda; assistant director Masaki Hisumatsu; screenplay by Shinichi Sekizawa; music by Kunio Miyauchi; cinematography by Motoyoshi Tomioka; art direction by Takeo Kita; edited by Masahima Miyauchi; special effects by Eiji Tsuburaya (actually Ishiro Honda); special effects assistant director Teruyoshi Nakano; special effects cinematography by Sadamasa Arikawa and Motoyoshi Tomioka; special effects art direction by Akira Watanabe; optical effects by Yukio Manoda and Sadao Iizuda

Starring Tomonori Yazaki (Ichiro), Eisei Amamoto (Toy Consultant Inami), Kenji Sahara (Ichiro's Father), Yoshifumi Tajima (Detective), Sachio Sakai and Kazuo Suzuki (Bank Robbers), Machiko Naka (Ichiro's Mother), Chotaro Togin (Assistant Detective), Ikio Sawamura (Bartender), Shigeki Ishida (Landlord), Yutaka Sada (Train Engineer), Yutaka Nakayama (Painter)

GODZILLA portrayed by Haruo Nakajima; MINILLA portrayed by Little Man Machan; GABBARA portrayed by Hiroshi Sekida

*Ichiro, a latchkey child of working class parents, lives in an industrial apartment complex. Tormented by bullies led by the mean Gabbara, Ichiro retreats into daydreams about his favorite movie monsters. While his parents are away at work, their neighbor, an inventor named Inami, looks after Ichiro. Inami shows his young friend a new toy, a "computer" that Ichiro uses to launch an extended fantasy voyage to Monster Island. In his happy dream, Ichiro meets Minilla and watches as Godzilla battles the evil mon-sters of Monster Island. However, Minya is tormented by a bully, too, a giant goblin not coincidentally also named Gabbara.*

*Meanwhile, two bank robbers hole up in an abandoned factory near Ichiro's apartment complex. Ichiro wanders into the factory, looking for broken bits of vacuum tubes to play with. Seeing him as a potential threat, the robbers kidnap Ichiro during the night.*

*In his fantasy world on Monster Island, Ichiro sees Godzilla teach Minilla how to fight his own battles. Inspired by Minilla, Ichiro decides to take on the robbers — and his own bully Gabbara — himself.*

The economics of Godzilla (Godzilla-nomics?) no longer made sense. What had begun as a tight-knit team of gifted artists and major movie stars working with fat budgets to create fantastic spectacles for mass audiences had seen its market all but vanish.

Tsuburaya was on his deathbed, receiving honorary credits on films he never touched. Cinematographer Hajime Koizumi and assistant director Koji Kajita, both important collaborators of Ishiro Honda's, had been fired. Shinichi Sekizawa openly complained he had run out of ideas. Honda had lost interest as the films had become increasingly ridiculous. Without the prestige value that Godzilla films once commanded, access to A-list movie stars had dried up. Competition from TV and other studios had splintered the monster movie audience. Partnerships with major American media companies like Columbia and AIP ended, shutting off a critical source of capital.

In short, the potential revenues that could be reasonably anticipated from the release of a

---

*There is no Japanese word "Oru"; rather, this is an attempt to represent in Japanese characters the English word "All."

new Godzilla movie were now too small to justify the expense of making any more.

Or, so it appeared. Over at Daiei Studios, producer Hidemasa Nagata, screenwriter Nisan Takahashi, and director Noriaki Yuasa had boldly forged a completely different business model. It began in 1965 with *Gamera*, a self-conscious rip-off of *Godzilla*. There is that familiar rah symbol ラ again, making this a "turtle-zilla." Gamera is a giant irradiated reptile, mutated by exposure to nuclear bombs, who breathes fire and tramples Japanese cities; *Gamera* is a brooding black and white horror film that was imported to the United States in a heavily Americanized version featuring newly added footage of an American actor shoved into the Japanese plot. Having established their challenger *kaiju*, Daiei set to cycling through Godzilla's back catalog in their own sped-up, hyperactive way. The Gamera films quickly became brightly colored action films about a superhero monster identified as "a friend of all children," and with his own catchy theme song. Logic played no role in the proceedings; Takahashi's writing makes even the craziest Sekizawa script seem sober by comparison. Working with an effects budget that may have been single-digit, the Gamera team abandoned worries about realism and just had fun.

By the fourth Gamera film (in just three years!), the already impoverished budgets had been slashed further. Yuasa was obliged to assemble significant sections of *Gamera vs. Viras* out of scraps of footage culled from previous films—including the original, which was in black and white. The monochrome shots are just dropped into *Viras* anyway. The whole thing is told from the point of view of two children, and feels like it was written by kids, too.

Tomoyuki Tanaka eyed *Gamera vs. Viras* with great interest. While it may have been true that the economics of Godzilla, as it was practiced in the 1960s, had collapsed, the Gamera films abandoned the expensive, prestigious, artistic aspects altogether and just made monster action for its most dedicated audience. Godzilla could survive, too—if it followed suit.

"Tanaka asked me, 'Well, Mr. Sekizawa, can you write up a script based on bits and pieces of other films?'" Sekizawa remembers, "And I replied, 'Of course, Mr. Tanaka, that's what I do best—I *am* a good editor!'"[1]

*All Monsters Attack* (released theatrically in the United States by UPA as *Godzilla's Revenge*) adapted the *Gamera vs. Viras* solution to the world of Godzilla. It is the story of a child, facing problems familiar to his contemporaries in the audience, who fantasizes about Monster Island. Most of those fantasies are compiled from excerpts of previous films. Eiji Tsuburaya's health was now perilous, and he would pass away a month after the release of the film. Tsuburaya's name appears in the credits out of respect, as Ishiro Honda directed the few new monster scenes himself.[2]

Although the appeal of the Godzilla movies lies in the monster scenes, *All Monsters Attack* delivers very little in this regard. Ichiro, a fine representative of the Godzilla fans in the audience, certainly would not like this movie. Compared to the dramatic effects of the previous year's *Destroy All Monsters*, the reruns of scenes from *Sea Monster* and *Son of Godzilla* are a steep comedown. Since the audience knows from the outset that the film is cleaving to that hoary movie cliché that it was only a dream, the Monster Island scenes lack tension.

The monster fights cheat in more ways than one, since so little of the effects footage is new. The few new scenes are done well enough but are not very interesting. The intense reliance on recycled footage causes problems of its own, since Godzilla changes in appearance noticeably from battle to battle. The Godzilla suit underwent such a severe redesigning for *Son of Godzilla* that any cross-cutting between shots from that film and any other footage, new or old, calls attention to itself. In one sequence, Ichiro and Minilla watch Godzilla lumber across Monster Island from a bout with Ebirah to a match with the giant mantises, and the king of the monsters appears to mutate before their very eyes.

As a sharp contrast to the previous year's *Destroy All Monsters*, which featured all of Toho's monsters existing in the same world, in *All Monsters Attack* the existence of monsters is ambiguous. Shinichi Sekizawa's screenplay remains circumspect as to whether monsters exist in Ichiro's world or are fictional movie characters as in the real world. In so doing, *All Monsters Attack* breaks the loose continuity that held the first seven films together, and allowed the series to diverge in new directions in the ensuing decade.

Ichiro's dubbed voice in the UPA version *Godzilla's Revenge* comes from what is obviously an adult forcing an awkward whine, quite unlike any human child. The limited number of voice performers used in the American dubbing prevents adequate differentiation between the characters. The performer voicing Minilla's annoying drawl also voices one of the bank robbers, allowing a bizarre and certainly unintended interpretation: Since the monster Gabbara is a fantasy version of the human bully Gabbara, is the monster Minilla then just Ichiro's fantasy version of the bank robber?

Godzilla historians Stuart Galbraith and Greg Shoemaker faulted Shinichi Sekizawa's screenplay for its apparent message, namely that Ichiro ultimately fends off his bullies only by becoming "an even bigger bully."[3] By the end of the film, Ichiro has become quite a little monster himself, terrorizing an innocent painter solely to win the approval of a gang of street kids.

On the other hand, more than a few critics staunchly defend *All Monsters Attack*. Jeff Rovin calls it his favorite of the sequels, "a modern morality tale [starring] a lovable little kid. *Godzilla's Revenge* is better, by far, than most of the Saturday-morning TV cartoon tripe."[4]

*All Monsters Attack* is purely a children's film and needs to evaluated by a different set of criteria than the more inclusive all-ages films that preceded it. Sekizawa and Honda have done an admirable job depicting in Ichiro precisely the kind of obsession felt by Godzilla's young fans. As Ichiro's inventor friend Inami says, "This child is inspired by the monster," which pretty well sums up the worldview of many in the audience. When Ichiro recommends that Inami include recordings of the various monster roars in his children's "computer," it's a good marketing move; Godzilla fans the world over would certainly buy one. Additionally, the ambiguity regarding the existence of monsters enhances the connection between Ichiro and the real-life Ichiros in the audience, as both can find Godzilla only in the world of fantasy, not the real world.

As for the moral of the story, that the best defense is a good offense, the film cannot simply be evaluated on a plot level alone. How Honda and Sekizawa tell that rather brutal life lesson makes a significant difference. Sure, *All Monsters Attack* posits a world where viewing monster movies encourages antisocial behavior, but it does so within a historical context that deserves mention.

Whether Ichiro's world contains a Monster Island may be up for debate, but one thing is certain about his environment; it is *profoundly depressing*. Honda packs the film with shots of industrial pollution and decay. Little Ichiro lives in a dingy semi-industrial area, with thick black smog and burned-out factories. His apartment building has dirty walls and metal doors. His toys are vacuum tubes he finds along the dusty road he walks to school. This is an industrial wasteland, a man-made environment designed for machines and not human habitation. The desolation of Ichiro's home contrasts vividly with the lush jungle paradise of Monster Island.

Ichiro is a prototypical *kagikko*, what we in English would call a latchkey kid. His parents work around the clock, leaving him home alone for days on end. In his otherwise favorable review, critic Rovin misses an important point, faulting the parents for not being "concerned enough to sacrifice a few hours at the factory to be home with their son."[5] Ichiro's folks simply have no choice in the matter. Sacrificing a few hours is clearly out of the question, since the family appears to be on the verge of poverty already. The fault lies not with the parents, but with the entire social situation.

In an interesting parallel, Godzilla leaves Minilla alone and unattended as much as Ichiro's folks leave Ichiro. Godzilla, too busy with his profession of combating his fellow Monster Island detainees, scarcely has the time to teach Minilla how to breathe radioactive fire. Ichiro's father, played by Kenji Sahara, has nothing quite so useful to teach his son, but no more time in which to teach it. Both children must take the responsibility of raising themselves.

The first large housing developments of the kind depicted in *All Monsters Attack* began construction in 1964, a period of increasing urban density and crowding. Rising real estate prices pushed housing projects farther out into the suburbs, which in turn inflated the numbers of workers obliged to commute long distances to their jobs. More and more adults found themselves sitting in traffic jams, on crowded buses and trains, while the children were left to fend for themselves far away. By 1966, fully half of the Japanese public expressed dissatisfaction with their housing conditions, saying that it was inadequate for child rearing. These issues were pressing political concerns in the mid- to late 1960s, and it was to audiences obsessed with these problems that *All Monsters Attack* appeared in 1969.[6]

In the 1980s, Toho released several of Godzilla's adventures in severely condensed formats as a twelve-volume videocassette set, *Toho SPFX.* Honda edited the Godzilla films down to ten-minute digests, and in the case of *All Monsters Attack* made a significant and telling cut. The full-length version of the film concludes with Ichiro reassuring his mother that he is happy now. Although she weeps in shame for having to leave him alone, he hurries out to play with his friends. In the truncated version, Honda ends the film with the mother crying, not a happy ending at all.[7] The essential problem has not been resolved, and cannot be. Ichiro's happiness is a form of self-delusion. He does not recognize the bleakness of his existence because he can escape to his fantasy world of Monster Island. In this way, *All Monsters Attack* resembles Terry Gilliam's dark satire *Brazil* (1986), which also concludes with the hero in a happy delusion, unable to change the cruelty and harshness of his real world.

Toho historian Guy Tucker wrote, "Some movies are so psychologically perfect that one doubts their creators ever knew how deep they were going. *All Monsters Attack* is one."[8] Robert Biondi and John Rocco Roberto, writing for the

Godzilla magazine *G-Fan*, claimed that *All Monsters Attack* dealt with "what Honda viewed as the most important subject: the nature of the relationship between father and son." Biondi and Roberto note how Honda filmed Ichiro and his father such that they almost never appeared in the same shot together, and always had a significant physical distance between them. They also note that Honda reshot the infamous scene in which Godzilla teaches Minilla how to breathe radioactive energy rather than reuse Tsuburaya's existing footage of the same scene from *Son of Godzilla* because Honda wanted to alter the relationship between Godzilla and Minya, making them less warm and close.[9]

The villains of the piece, the two bank robbers on the lam, combine the genres of the Godzilla series with another popular Japanese genre, the gangster (or *yakuza*) film. Many of Toho's other, non–Godzilla, science fiction releases included yakuzas or similar criminal types: *The Invisible Avenger* (1954), *The H-Man* (1958), *The Human Vapor* (1960), *The Secret of the Telegian* (1960), *Atragon* (1963), and *Dagora, the Space Monster* (1964). Yakuza-like elements also appear in *Ghidrah* and *Godzilla vs. the Sea Monster*, and would surface in such future installments as *Godzilla vs. Megalon* and *Godzilla vs. Mechagodzilla*. In *Godzilla Raids Again*, a handful of convicts escape in a stolen truck and accidentally crash into an oil refinery, causing a massive explosion. The light from the blast attracts Godzilla to Osaka, ruining the until-then successful efforts of the authorities to lure him out to sea. This sequence highlights the essential villainy of the criminal character in Japanese films: They act in selfish ways that defeat the common good. By trying to elevate their own personal gain over that of the whole, the convicts in *Godzilla Raids Again* make the situation worse for everyone. Countering these individualistic villains, then, are teams of law enforcement officials working cooperatively, unlike the loner heroes usually seen in American crime dramas. The yakuza genre in Japan usually reinforced communitarian social norms, by depicting the triumph of teamwork over individualism.

In *All Monsters Attack*, however, Sekizawa and Honda reevaluate that social norm. The gangsters target a young child, who is alone and helpless. Ichiro has no team to back him up, no larger social network to rely on. In the end, Ichiro has to act as a selfish individual to protect himself, and in so doing undercuts the usual message of the genre. His bullying actions at the conclusion of the film show the deleterious consequences of such selfish thinking. Ichiro's transformation into a bully comes about not simply as the result of his fantasies about Godzilla, but as a direct result of a society that has left him parentless and alone in an environment of very real danger. Society has failed Ichiro, and he learns to rely on no one but himself.

*All Monsters Attack* was released directly to the Champion Festival in December 1969, an acknowledgment that this was the way of the future.[10] In the 1960s it had been typical for Godzilla films to be paired in Japan on double bills with teen-oriented action films. In the coming decade, Godzilla would be doubled up with cartoons.[11]

Long-time fans of Godzilla have faced the ridicule heaped upon their hero from all sides. Fans try to explain their obsession and justify their fandom to those who do not understand, but the appeal runs very deep to an innocence of childhood that some individuals never lost. Mike Bogue, writing for the magazine *Wonder*, called it the "inner ten-year-old."[12] Perhaps what makes *All Monsters Attack* such a polarizing experience is that it is so obviously aimed at such a young audience that it makes adults uncomfortable. Watching other Godzilla films allows adult fans to sate the desires of that inner ten-year-old without breaking the veneer of the mature adult. *All Monsters Attack* asks the viewer to regress too far, to an inner six-year-old maybe, and so fans protest.

For those who give in to its entreaties, though, an unsettling subtext awaits. In the final installment of the sixties, Sekizawa and Honda crafted a subtle and provocative critique of Japanese industrial society and an accurate look at the psychology of the series' fans, woven into an escapist film for children. Honda left the series until 1975's *Terror of Mechagodzilla*, and Tsuburaya died in 1970. The original team of Tanaka, Honda, Tsuburaya, and Sekizawa had completed their final collaboration. For better or worse, the Godzilla series had taken a new course, and the ensuing decade would see even greater changes wrought.

# Part Three

# Something Funny's Going On
# (1970–1975)

Fans and film critics generally regard the 1970s as a period of decline for the Godzilla series. With a new team in place and a desire to break new ground, the five Godzilla movies made between 1971 and 1975 experiment with new approaches to the character and the theme, ultimately finding popular success only by returning to the formula established in the 1960s. With Japanese audiences down to a fraction of what they were in the beginnings of the kaiju eiga cycle back in the 1950s, Toho threw in the towel and the first Godzilla series came to an end.

# Chapter 19

# Survival of the Silliest

*I don't think any sequels to the first Godzilla movie should have been made.*

— Jun Fukuda[1]

To say that Godzilla movies went into decline in the 1970s is true, but painfully narrow in focus. It is a bit like saying that in late 2005, New Orleans tourism dropped. In order not to miss the forest for the trees, it is important to realize that in the 1970s, the *entire* Japanese film industry collapsed, and never really recovered. The drop in quality on movies about giant rubber-suited monsters was but one, small symptom of a much larger phenomenon.

The economic miracle of the 1960s did wonders for much of Japanese culture, but the film industry did not share in the bounty. The film business actually hit its financial peak in 1960, when six major movie studios sent out 537 domestic productions to some 900 Japanese theaters.[2] By 1964, the rug had been yanked out.

That was the year of the Tokyo Olympics, and in happy celebration nearly every Japanese household got a television set with which to become part of the experience. The sudden proliferation of TVs provided a new wrinkle of competition to Japanese cinema, already struggling against Hollywood imports.

Between 1960 and 1970, 75 percent of the theater-going audience disappeared.[3] The mass audience was gone forever. Half of the studios in Japan went out of business altogether; those that remained were deracinated ruins all but obliged to abandon the movie business. Companies like Toho still made films, but only as one facet of a diversified business that drew most of its income from real estate, railroads, baseball, grocery stores, etc. The only movie company that still found the film business to be a functioning business was Nikkatsu, which had switched over exclusively to making pornography.[4]

To the extent that movies were still made and shown in Japan, they had to become leaner, more ruthlessly commercial, more narrowly targeted. Films aimed at mass audiences were aimed at a target that no longer existed, so genre films dominated, made to stifling genre templates carefully honed to appeal to the most die-hard true believers. Many genres died off; yakuza films and the so-called "youth pictures" were the first to go.[5] Many long-running franchises crashed onto the rocky shores of 1970: The Crazy Cats, Young Guy, Station Front, and the Boss series all ended by 1971.[6]

Somehow, despite this, Godzilla movies continued — the only long-running cycle to survive from the 1960s into the 1970s. This it did in part because the underlying formula was so profoundly popular. Godzilla proved himself the heartiest weed in the garden, but survival was not easy.

The Godzilla movies of the seventies drew Japanese audiences of between 900,000 and 1.8 million ticket buyers, compared to 3.5 to 4.3 million ticket buyers in the mid-sixties.[7]

Indeed, the vast majority of fantasy or horror genre productions that had thrived in the 1960s had all run aground in the mid- to late 1970s. It wasn't just Japanese monsters closing up shop, but Hammer horrors, Roger Corman's Edgar Allan Poe cycle, spaghetti westerns, blaxploitation films, kung fu chop-sockys, etc. The exhibition venues that once hosted these genres in America were primarily drive-ins and specialized hardtop cinemas. The distribution chains that fed them had started off as larger, more reputable companies, too. As the decade wore on, most of those exhibition venues started to close, and the distribution companies became increasingly unreliable.

Where Toho had once been doing business with companies like Columbia, AIP, or UPA, they now found themselves forced into arrangements with fly-by-night companies who were, for their part, struggling to make bookings at fewer and less reliable outlets.

The major Hollywood studios like Warners and Columbia could no longer participate in the 1970s because they were undergoing wrenching institutional transformations and had ceded the field to independents like Brenco and Cinema Shares. By mid-decade, Hollywood's studio system was overtaken and overrun with a new generation of filmmakers with an entirely different attitude about pulp movies. For years, genre filmmaking had been primarily something done by indies and B-movie makers, outsiders. Then, suddenly, in the mid- to late 1970s, Hollywood started making genre films, and making them very well. A new age of blockbusters was ushered in, with *Jaws*, *Star Wars*, *Superman*, and *Alien* leading the way.[8]

In their heyday in the 1960s, Toho's science fiction spectacles had been extremely competitive, with higher production values and greater entertainment than the low-budget American dreck in the same category. But even the finest example, say *Mothra vs. Godzilla*, would have had little chance against the likes of *Star Wars* or *Jaws*.

To put it simply: It almost doesn't matter what kind of Godzilla movie Toho was making in 1975. The channels of distribution and exhibition that had been critical to the American success of the cycle was drying up, and facing grueling competition from big-budget, heavily hyped fare targeting the same kind of audience. In Japan, the entire movie industry across the board had crumbled, studios were going bankrupt, and directors slept on friends' sofas, unable to make a living making movies. The odds of a film franchise specifically predicated on expensive and specialized special effects work holding its own in that environment was slim to none.

In 1970, Tomoyuki Tanaka oversaw the last non–Godzilla monster movie Toho would make for almost a generation. *Space Amoeba*

(originally released in the U.S. as *Yog, Monster from Space*) is as nutty as they come. Director Ishiro Honda and composer Akira Ifukube tried valiantly to bring a sense of gravitas to the outing, but their sincerity was undermined by a crazy script and Gamera-level special effects. Eiji Tsuburaya had passed away just after the release of *All Monsters Attack*, and *Space Amoeba* would mark the first time Sadamasa Arikawa took sole credit for his work. It was also, as it happened, the last. Arikawa's request to append a credit to the film in honor of the late Tsuburaya was rejected by the studio, and in bitter protest Arikawa quit. Honda retired, or something awfully close to that. Suitmation actor Haruo Nakajima put everyone on notice that he had no intention of continuing long without Tsuburaya.[9]

Other behind-the-scenes personnel departed in the seventies as well. Art directors Takeo Kita and Akira Watanabe left to pursue careers as special effects directors for other studios. Cinematographers Motoyoshi Tomioka and Hajime Koizumi and editor Ryohei Fujii departed the series, and composer Akira Ifukube would not write an original Godzilla score again for many years. Partway through the seventies era, even Godzilla himself (Haruo Nakajima) retired.

Toho had previously operated as a classically oriented movie studio, with a company of actors on contract, obliged to take whatever assignments their producers handed out. That contract system ended in 1970, and Toho was now obliged to hire actors on a per-movie basis. The familiar players who had populated the Godzilla films of the sixties—Akihiko Hirata, Kenji Sahara, Akira Takarada, Jun Tazaki, Yoshio Tsuchiya, Akira Kubo, Hiroshi Koizumi, Takashi Shimura, Akiko Wakabayashi, Kumi Mizuno, and Yuriko Hoshi—were replaced by new, much cheaper actors, who arguably lacked the same screen charisma.

Jun Fukuda had been groomed as Honda's likely replacement. Fukuda placed a greater emphasis on action, but generally disliked his assignment, preferring instead to direct crime-dramas and comedies.[10] Tsuburaya's long-time assistant Teruyoshi Nakano took over the special effects department after Arikawa's departure, but never exhibited the perfectionism or drive of his mentor.[11] By the 1970s, the creative forces behind the "Golden Age" of the Godzilla series had been replaced by a B-team of lesser talents.

Fans and critics sometimes blame the decline of the Godzilla series on Fukuda and Nakano, working with half-size budgets, lacking the talent, skill, and motivation of their predecessors. Certainly, creative individuals doing what they love with ample funding are capable of greater achievements than people whose limited ambitions are further limited by lack of resources. However, this line of argument is unfairly harsh on Fukuda and Nakano, and overlooks the bright spots that do exist in the seventies era movies.

Fukuda strongly desired to find a new approach for the Godzilla movies, to break new ground.[12] Much of the bad reputation of the seventies era Godzilla movies comes from the fact that Toho continued to experiment, and viewers differ on the effectiveness of these experiments.

A shift in the depiction of Godzilla and his monster opponents occurred in the seventies films. Beginning with 1964's *Ghidrah*, the filmmakers began to rehabilitate Godzilla from a demonic destroyer to a heroic figure. In the seventies, Godzilla became an outright superhero, exhibiting a level of intelligence far beyond that previously ascribed to him.

In the sixties films written by Shinichi Sekizawa, monsters were frequently depicted as super-weapons that were deployed in order to resolve disputes between human or humanoid opponents. When threatened by a monster, Japan (or the world) enlisted a monster of their own (Mothra or Godzilla) to combat it on their behalf. Godzilla's battles with King Kong, Mothra, Ghidorah, and Ebirah were arranged by human forces. In the seventies, Godzilla acts as a free agent who battles monster foes for his own reasons. Godzilla's opponents in the seventies still appear to be super-weapons, whose attacks on Earth have been commissioned by invading space aliens, but Godzilla fights on his own.

In the sixties, Godzilla's opponents were either mutated dinosaurs (Anguirus, Rodan) or enormous animals (Mothra, Ebirah, Spiega, King Kong). The space monsters of the seventies (Hedorah, Gigan, Mechagodzilla) sport weird, abstract appearances that did not follow the design logic of natural animals. Consequently, Teruyoshi Nakano's special effects department could create opponents for Godzilla that did not need the kind of detailing required to make, say, a giant shrimp look convincing. The bizarre creations of the seventies were an attempt to work around the limitations of the smaller special effects budgets. Furthermore, the popularity of television programs such as Tsuburaya Productions' *Ultraman*, which pitted a superhero against space monsters, demonstrated the commercial appeal of more inventive monster designs .

Another advantage of using space monsters, aside from the reduced cost of abstract costume designs, involved international politics. The late sixties and early seventies saw the height of the Cold War's influence on popular culture. In the West, fictional heroes like James Bond played out the international tensions less as a Cold War than as a Hot War. Conflicts were resolved not with diplomacy or compromise but with guns, explosions and stunts. A tense and anxious public vicariously acted out the battle between good and evil and saw the unqualified triumph of good. James Bond, however, was a peculiarly Western pop hero.

In Japan, the same tensions existed but the culture could not create a hero quite like Bond. World War II still loomed too large in recent memory for the Japanese to feel comfortable idolizing aggressively militaristic characters. Geographically and culturally Eastern but economically and politically allied with the West, Japan straddled between the two poles of the Cold War. Japanese viewers desired the kind of catharsis that fictionalized combat, such as that of James Bond, could bring. TV shows like *Ultraman* and movies like the Godzilla series provided that pop cultural catharsis. With the enemy identified as invading space aliens, the battle between good and evil was effectively depoliticized. Neither the Americans nor the Russians, nor any others, would see themselves symbolized in the giant cockroaches of *Godzilla vs. Gigan* or the ape-men of *Godzilla vs. Mechagodzilla.* Any idolizing, then, of the Japanese Defense Forces or their monster-god protector Godzilla was safe and politically neutral.

The last five first-series Godzilla films are a mixed bag: at times pathetically derivative, at other times startlingly different. Anchoring the seventies at both ends are films that attempt to hark back to the original *Godzilla. Terror of Mechagodzilla* (1975) consciously attempted to recreate the original's mood and theme, with Honda returning from semi-retirement to direct. Although *Terror of Mechagodzilla* displays a refreshingly different visual style than its immediate predecessors, it is one of the most formulaic and predictable of the entire series, making for a somewhat disappointing conclusion to a decade that began with *Godzilla vs. Hedorah*, a bold rewrite of the Godzilla myth for a new age, recreating the themes the 1954 original in the form of the sequel least like any of the others.

# Chapter 20

# Godzilla vs. Hedorah

## Gojira Tai Hedorah (Godzilla Against Hedorah)

*Atomic bombs, Hydrogen bombs and radioactive fallout falls into the sea, / Poison gas, man's garbage, everything into the sea, / Thrown by you and me, / Godzilla would rage if he could see, / He'd turn the page and clean it for you and me.*

— Ken's poem for school

Japanese version: 85 minutes, Released July 24, 1971

U.S. version (AIP): 85 minutes, Released July 1972, MPAA rating: G, double-billed with *Frogs*, original U.S. release title: *Godzilla vs. the Smog Monster*

Color, Widescreen

Produced by Tomoyuki Tanaka; U.S. version produced by Samuel Z. Arkoff; directed by Yoshimitsu Banno; U.S. version dubbing directed by Salvatore Billiteri; screenplay by Takeshi Kimura (a.k.a. Kaoru Mabuchi) and Yoshimitsu Banno; music by Riichiro Manabe; U.S. version's English lyrics for the song "Save the Earth" by Adryan Russ; cinematography by Yoichi Manoda; art direction by Yasuyuki Inoue; edited by Yoshitami Kuroiwa; special effects by Teruyoshi Nakano; special effects assistant director Koichi Kawakita; optical effects by Yukio Manoda

Starring Akira Yamauchi (Dr. Yano), Hiroyuki Kawase (Ken), Toshie Kimura (Mrs. Yano), Toshio Shibaki (Yukio Keuchi), Keiko Mari (Miki Fujiyama)

GODZILLA portrayed by Haruo Nakajima; HEDORAH portrayed by Kenpachiro Satsuma

*Marine biologist Dr. Yanno and his young son Ken discover a strange new species of creature, a mutant sea animal that thrives on garbage and pollution. No sooner has Ken named the thing Hedorah than it has grown to enormous size, capsizing ships, killing fish and people alike, and filling the air with toxic fumes. Each piece of the monster has a life of its own, and the tiny parts can fuse together into a larger beast. There is no limit to its potential size, and plenty of pollution from which to grow.*

*Godzilla confronts the Smog Monster, but their first battle ends in a draw. Hedorah mutates into a stingray-like thing that flies around emitting poisonous sulfuric acid that rusts buildings and corrodes hu-*

*mans into skeletons. As the bodies pile up, Hedorah takes to swallowing cars.*

*The army launches an attack on the premise that pure oxygen will prove to be lethal to a creature that consumes poisoned air. The oxygen bombs fail, and Hedorah destroys the army helicopters. Dr. Yanno jerry-rigs a machine designed to dehydrate Hedorah, but when Godzilla and Hedorah tumble down the mountainside in battle, they knock out the power plant. The Smog Monster walks into the trap, which now cannot be turned on. Their last chance has come and gone.*

*Godzilla fires his atomic ray to power the electrodes. When at last the monster has been destroyed, torn to bits, and burned to dust, Godzilla turns malevolently to the humans, as if warning, "Don't make me come after you next." Then he returns to Monster Island through enough sludge and waste to make many more Smog Monsters.*

Words cannot do justice to the experience of watching *Godzilla vs. Hedorah*, a delirious 85 minutes of dream sequences, musical numbers, animated cartoons, drug-induced hallucinations, abstract symbolic imagery, a black and white sequence, dancing skeletons, distorted "monster-eye" viewpoints, and a series of television-like images of people whose voices rise into a cacophony as their faces transform into flashing lights. This is a movie in which *Godzilla flies*.

The advance trailers promoting the film proudly declared that filmmaker Yoshimitsu Banno was the man who would reinvent Godzilla for a new generation.[1] He was a young stage actor who had made the transition behind the camera to serve as Akira Kurosawa's assistant director on *Throne of Blood, The Bad Sleep*

*Well, The Hidden Fortress*, and *Lower Depths*. As if this was not substantive enough of a résumé, Banno won a special place in Tomoyuki Tanaka's heart when he helped stage an important publicity event at the Mitsubishi Pavillion for the 1970 Osaka Expo. Tanaka was so impressed with the wildly creative and energetic Banno, he asked him to take on the next Godzilla picture.[2]

It would be a rough go. Banno had a tiny budget and an untested special effects team. To simplify matters and economize, Banno took the unprecedented step of collapsing the drama and effects units into a single team with a single director of photography. In all, he employed less than half the usual number of staffers, and oversaw the entire project himself, over a crushing 35-day production schedule.[3]

Banno was frustrated that Takeshi Kimura (still refusing to use his real name on his work) had slapped together a less than inspiring screenplay. "You're not really getting sincere about this," Banno berated Kimura. "You're not working hard to make this thing work." So Banno rewrote the script himself.[4]

The ecological premise tapped into very current fears rippling through Japan at the time. "Pollution is a different kind of murder," explained special effects director Teruyoshi Nakano. "If we do nothing about it, the human race may be destroyed. So I figured, if we were making a statement about pollution in the movie, bold expression would be necessary. Mr. Banno and I were still young back then, so we just went all-out."[5]

The soundtrack by Riichiro Manabe, a student of Akira Ifukube's,[6] suits this "anything goes" visual approach. Instead of Ifukube's grand marches or Sato's lyrical melodies, Manabe's irritating score leaps about between wildly different tempos, featuring a horn fanfare, a patriotic march, and a twangy mouth harp.

Although *Godzilla vs. Hedorah* looks and sounds like no other Godzilla film (or any other monster movie for that matter), in many ways it is truer in spirit to the original *Godzilla* than any of the sequels. For *Godzilla Raids Again*, director Motoyoshi Oda had copied some of the more obvious surface elements of the orig-

inal film, but approached the story from a very different perspective. *Godzilla vs. Hedorah* has surface parallels to *Godzilla* as well, but is the only first series sequel to also duplicate the underlying theme.

As with *Godzilla*, the monster's presence is first felt by fishermen. There is no love triangle, but there are two young lovers, one of whom is killed in the climax. Dr. Yanno is a scientist-hero like Dr. Serizawa. With half of his face bandaged as a result of acid burns caused by the Smog Monster, Dr. Yanno even looks like the one-eyed Dr. Serizawa. In fact, one scene forms a visual rhyme with a memorable sequence from *Godzilla*. Yanno has a tank of prized tropical fish in his lab. Hedorah's sulfuric acid mist affects the tank, darkening the water as the fish die. Yanno's wife recoils in horror at the sight of the dying fish. The staging strongly resembles Dr. Serizawa's test of the Oxygen Destroyer in a fish tank.

*Godzilla vs. Hedorah* is also the only film other than the original to depict the deaths of innocent people onscreen. The other sequels sanitized the effects of monster attacks. Certainly there were people inside each stomped tank, each jet grabbed out of the sky, each building incinerated by an atomic ray, but those deaths were only implied. The audience never saw the mourning friends and families of those slain in the monster's path. In a clear break with tradition, *Hedorah* highlights bloodshed. From the mah jongg players killed in a warehouse to an infant sinking into sludge, the deaths are numerous and unpleasant. Hedorah even attacks a cat. Ken, evidently somewhere around nine years old, races home alone and defenseless as his city is destroyed around him. He comes upon the slimy bones of the recent dead, corroded by acid. Screaming, he covers his eyes. This is not pretty.

*Godzilla* took the idea that humanity threatened to poison the world (via nuclear technology) and embodied that threat in the symbolic form of a monster (Godzilla) who could mete out a form of poetic justice by directing that threat in an exaggerated way back onto modern society. The monster Godzilla never differentiated between innocent or guilty in his attacks just as the movie *Godzilla* never placed the blame for the monster's existence on any specific person or group. Everyone shared responsibility for creating such a monster, and so everyone shared in its destructive wrath. When the monster was ultimately defeated, Dr. Yamane warned that unless we all mend our collective ways there will be more such monsters. Hedorah embodies and symbolizes humanity's poison (industrial pollution). The name, hedoro + rah, means "sludge-zilla." This symbol never pins responsibility on any one person or group. With the defeat of the monster comes the acknowledgment that we must somehow see to it that we do not create another smog monster. As with *Godzilla*, there is no reason to believe we will mend our ways.

By returning to the series' roots, Banno and co-author Takeshi Kimura undid much of the influence Shinichi Sekizawa had developed through the last decade. By writing most of the sixties-era scripts, Sekizawa rewrote the Godzilla myth in his own terms. He was the first writer to conceive of the monsters as characters in their own right, but he used those monster characters within a fairly rigid context, as super-weapons or protector-gods (or both). The battles between Godzilla and other monsters grew out of human conflicts, with monsters recruited by human interest groups to fight on their behalf. Interest groups could be individuals seeking to right a moral wrong (*Mothra vs. Godzilla*, *Godzilla vs. the Sea Monster*) or nations united against a common outside foe (*Ghidorah*, *Invasion of Astro-Monster*). Even the Takeshi Kimura–authored *Destroy All Monsters* kept this approach, so great was Sekizawa's influence.

In *Godzilla vs. Hedorah*, Godzilla is not recruited by any human interest group. In fact, Godzilla saves the human race only as a side effect of battling Hedorah, which Godzilla does for his own reasons. Hedorah threatens his world, so Godzilla acts to save it.

Godzilla has a narrative link to Ken, who seems to understand Godzilla's motivations. Ken also accurately predicts Godzilla's behavior, as if he has some kind of psychic bond with the monster. He does idolize Godzilla in much

the same way as Ichiro from *All Monsters Attack*. Ken, being higher up the social ladder than the working class Ichiro, has the money to collect Godzilla toys. He sports a vast collection of figures, mostly Godzillas, with at least one King Ghidorah thrown in for good measure. His ability to predict when Godzilla will appear recalls the prophecy of Princess Salno from *Ghidorah*, and his understanding of Godzilla's thought processes recalls the Shobojin from the same film.

Ken also is very close to his father, Dr. Yanno. The two can communicate better with one another than with any other character. While the other adults laugh at Ken's ideas, Dr. Yanno accepts them immediately. They are the only people to suffer injuries from Hedorah yet survive. Among the first to encounter the monster, they quickly identify it, conceive of a defense, and implement it. Their single-minded heroic defense of Earth against the Smog Monster stands as a stark contrast to the other human characters, whom the film ridicules and derides throughout.

Authority figures especially do not come off well. The police initially ignore reports that Hedorah has come ashore, arguing Hedorah is a "water monster." Later, they issue a public statement that Hedorah will only attack at night, which also turns out to be false. The proposal that Hedorah be choked with pure oxygen fails. Everything anyone in authority says turns out to be lethally wrong.

The Self-Defense Forces fail miserably, too. Of course, in all of these films, the Self-Defense Forces are powerless against the monsters; that is simply part of the formula. However, the *way* in which the Self-Defense Forces fail here is important. This is not a question of tanks firing useless cannons at a monster's impregnable skin, nor is it a question of jets being grabbed out of the air by a monster's claws. The soldiers have a routine task to do: hook up Dr. Yanno's giant electrodes before Hedorah walks into the trap. Godzilla and Hedorah have knocked out the main power supply, and a truck on its way to tap the power from elsewhere has been crushed underfoot by the Smog Monster. Plan A and Plan B have failed, which means the soldiers have to repair the damage from the only available electrical towers, and they have only a few short minutes. It seems a hopeless task. However, this is the sort of challenge that, in movies, heroes always accomplish. A race against time is a personal challenge, and if the individuals in question are efficient, they will succeed. Here, they do not. In fact, they finish their repairs ludicrously late, only to have the generator promptly shut down as soon as they switch it on. Godzilla reacts to this display of profound incompetence by ruefully shaking his head.

Dr. Yanno's wife never seems to fully understand the significance of events. She only seems capable of understanding them within the context of how they relate to her personally. When the TV reporters come to interview Yanno about Hedorah, she is ashamed that the world will see his scars. Later, as the scientist struggles to comprehend this new menace, she tells him to get some rest. He tries to explain that the future of all life on Earth depends on his research, but she simply does not get it. When Hedorah gasses Fuji, leaving the bones of thousands of dead piled up in the streets, killing their fish, and almost blowing Ken to little bits, her only reaction is concern that her gymnastics class had a hard time breathing.

The most surprising ridicule, however, is directed against the teenagers in the film. Miki, in body paint and a skintight suit, simply looks absurd. Her boyfriend Yukio, though, is something else altogether. Drunk and apparently on acid, he hallucinates that his friends have fishes for heads. Later, Yukio reacts to the apocalyptic mood by proposing a music festival on Mount Fuji with "all the hip kids" to protest pollution. How this protest party is meant to help matters is unclear. When he and the others arrive at Mount Fuji, they discover the media did not show up to cover the event. Yukio does not seem concerned, although the only *possible* benefits this protest party could have had depend on influencing public opinion. Absent media coverage, their party is politically useless. When Yukio first proposes it, he says they should hurry before Hedorah conquers the world, implying that he does not re-

ally expect to change the course of events at all, merely to have fun before the end of the world.

As it happens, the party is even counterproductive, since in order to get there, the "hip kids" must drive in cars, which have been banned by the government in a desperate bid to reduce pollution. After polluting their way up Mount Fuji, Yukio and the others set a bonfire, which cannot be of much benefit to the environment, either. Director Banno suddenly cuts to a shot of a group of ghostly unidentified figures watching the teenagers frolic around their bonfire. These old men (rural villagers? spirits of the dead?) watch the proceedings without emotion, making the teenagers' behavior seem even more alien and irrational.

Possibly attracted to the pollution, Hedorah arrives at Mount Fuji, which stops the party cold. Ken had repeatedly predicted that Hedorah would climb Mount Fuji and that Godzilla is on his way, but no one bothered to listen. In the ensuing panic, Yukio announces, utterly without justification, that Hedorah is afraid of fire. He leads a group in hurling torches at the Smog Monster. The torches are absurdly small compared to the giant creature, which shows no sign of fear. Instead, Hedorah turns and swiftly kills Yukio and many others. Yukio's death does not come off as tragic. If anything, it almost feels as if he got what he deserved.

The teenage characters are depicted as stupid, self-absorbed, and self-destructive. Their response to the problem is laughably inappropriate and ineffective. They make no impact on public opinion, they make no headway towards reducing pollution, and they do not assist in any way towards defeating the monster. Their only tangible impact on events is to marginally *increase* pollution, and to get themselves killed.

By presenting the protest party on Mount Fuji as absurd and self-defeating, *Godzilla vs. Hedorah* bites the hand that feeds it. Environmentally aware teenagers are among those most likely to go see an environmentally oriented Godzilla movie. During the late sixties and early seventies, the age of the hippies and Woodstock, staging a music festival to protest pollution is exactly the kind of response such a group would have had. The teenage philosophy of that era *sincerely* believed in the power of music and good feelings to effect social change. Events like Woodstock were premised on the philosophy that, through their music, youth culture could change the world for the better. *Hedorah* spits in their faces, both literally and figuratively.

Yoshimitsu Banno's film is a cynical and depressing, with no real hope for the future. The authorities are as stupid and incompetent as the countercultural youth movement. Industry, which caused the problem in the first place, makes no effort to redress their wrongs. Absent a government decree, they are apparently unwilling to sacrifice a penny of profits even if it means the certain death of all life on Earth. Once the national crisis is over, there is no reason to suspect they will pollute any less. Science, as embodied in Dr. Yanno, is at best a faint ray of hope. However, another scientist interviewed on TV has disastrously incorrect theories of his own, which result in the deaths of two helicopter crews. There is no theme of scientists banding together for the common good, as in earlier films. Dr. Yanno is a maverick who must argue with his wife to even have the opportunity to save the Earth.

In the end, Dr. Yanno's invention does not even work as advertised. Only in conjunction with Godzilla's atomic ray does it have any effect on Hedorah. In other words, Hedorah, a symbol of all that is wrong with modern society, is defeated only by Godzilla, who is also a symbol of all that is wrong with modern society, who uses human technology, which is presumably also something wrong with modern society. If the concentrated-oxygen bombs had killed Hedorah, there would have been a neat Nature vs. Technology dichotomy, and also a clear value judgment between them. As it stands, in this battle between technology's monstrous waste products, victory of one waste product over another brings with it no clear value judgments, leaving the issues unresolved and ambiguous.

The movie is full of symbolism, some of it obvious, some of it oblique. Banno places particularly heavy emphasis on fish imagery. The opening montage, repeated at the end, shows an oil slick packed with the silvery bodies of dead fish. Later, a concerned fisherman presents the Hedorah tadpole to Yanno, and then looks around Yanno's lab at the bottles full of mutated fish. The fisherman remarks, "Fishing in the bay is dumb now. All we bring up are monsters." Yanno's lab also sports a tropical fish tank which gets considerable screen time. Miki hallucinates humanoid fishes dancing around him at the club. Banno also revels in eye imagery, or rather injured-eye imagery. Yanno loses an eye to Hedorah, then later grinds up the tadpole's eyeball for microscopic examination. Hedorah injures one of Godzilla's eyes with a smoking gooey spitball. In response, Godzilla puts his fist through one of Hedorah's eyes.

The battle between Godzilla and Hedorah brought together, for the first time, two of the actors most associated with Godzilla: Haruo Nakajima and Kenpachiro Satsuma. Then known as Kengo Nakayama, Satsuma began his acting career as a contracted player with Mifune Productions. Because of his Kyushu accent, casting directors never hired him for speaking roles, and he became increasingly frustrated with playing non-speaking bit parts. In 1971, Satsuma got his big break, although he did not recognize it at the time. Teruysoshi Nakano had heard of Satsuma's strength and good physical condition, and called him for an interview at Toho Studios. Satsuma recalled the interview:

> So, Mr. Nakano told me his story and I started to ask him some questions. "So, what type of role should I take in this film, sir?" Mr. Nakano replied, "Oh yes, it's a very powerful role, Mr. Nakayama. There's a meteorite which falls into Tagonoura Bay in Shizuoka Prefecture and it grows into a huge 50-meter monster named Hedorah. OK? And I want you to do the monster, Hedorah." [*Long silence and dumbfounded look*] Well, I was extremely disappointed, to say the least.[7]

Although wearing the 330-pound rubber Hedorah suit was a difficult and unpleasant experience, Satsuma became friends with Nakano and worked for him again on the next two Godzilla films.

Yoshimitsu Banno planned a sequel, in which Godzilla was to face Hedorah again in

Africa; this would have been a rare example of a Godzilla film set outside Japan. The original Japanese version, in anticipation of this planned sequel, concludes with a title card that reads, "Will there be another?" AIP removed that title card from the otherwise faithful Americanized release, which would be the final Godzilla film distributed by AIP.[8]

The rematch never happened. Banno had made his film, perhaps the most personal work of art ever to carry the name of Godzilla, without any supervision from Tomoyuki Tanaka, who was hospitalized with an illness. When Tanaka was discharged from the hospital and finally saw the result of the trust he placed in the young auteur, his jaw hit the floor. Teruyoshi Nakano recalls Tanaka's reaction: "He told Mr. Banno, 'You ruined the Godzilla series!'"[9] Banno was banned.

Approximately 1.7 million Japanese viewers attended *Godzilla vs. Hedorah*; while this was only a fraction of the attendance records set in the early sixties, it was one of the better turnouts for the seventies.[10] The film's reputation has suffered, largely because it differs from the established format and formula so greatly that it defeats just about any possible viewer expectation. As a one-of-a-kind experiment, *Godzilla vs. Hedorah* was reasonably commercially successful, but nothing in the first series ever tried to emulate its heavy-handed symbolism, ambiguous approach to its material or disorienting avant-garde style.

## Chapter 21

# Godzilla vs. Gigan

## CHIKYU KOGEKI MEIREI: GOJIRA TAI GAIGAN
## (EARTH DESTRUCTION DIRECTIVE:
## GODZILLA AGAINST GIGAN)

*In the tower, we're building a museum. It will be the first one ever of its type. It'll be devoted solely to the monsters — Western and Oriental. All sorts of monsters — ancient and new.*

— Kubota

Japanese version: 89 minutes, Released March 12, 1972

U.S. theatrical version (Cinema Shares): 89 minutes, Released August 1977, MPAA rating: G, original theatrical release title: *Godzilla on Monster Island*

Color, Widescreen

Produced by Tomoyuki Tanaka; directed by Jun Fukuda; assistant director Fumikatsu Okada; screenplay by Shinichi Sekizawa; music by Akira Ifukube (prerecorded, not an original score); Song "Godzilla's March": music by Danro Miyaguchi, lyrics by Shinichi Sekizawa and Jun Fukuda; cinematography by Kiyoshi Hasegawa; art direction by Yoshifumi Honda; edited by Yoshio Manoda; special effects by Teruyoshi Nakano; special effects art direction by Yasuyuki Inoue; special effects cinematography by Motoyoshi Tomioka; optical effects by Toshiyuki Tokumasa and Saburo Doi

Starring Hiroshi Ishikawa (Gengo Kotaka), Yuriko Hishimi (Tomoko Tomoe), Tomoko Umeda (Machiko Shima), Minoru Takashima (Shosaku Takasugi), Kunio Murai (Takashi Shima), Susumu Fujita (Fumio, World Children's Land Chairman), Toshiaki Nishizawa (Secretary Kubota), Wataru Ohmae (Employee), Kuniko Ashiwara (Woman), Kureyoshi Nakamura (Priest), Akiyo Muto (Comic Book Editor), Gen Shimizu (Defense Forces Commander)

GODZILLA portrayed by Haruo Nakajima; ANGUIRUS portrayed by Yukietsu Omiya; KING GHIDORAH portrayed by Kanta Ina; GIGAN portrayed by Kenpachiro Satsuma

*Aspiring comic book artist Gengo presents his latest creations to the World Children's Land, a non-profit amusement park-cum-museum devoted to monsters. The company is located inside the Godzilla Tower, a building constructed to look like the famous monster. World Children's Land plans to destroy the monsters on Monster Island after creating duplicates of them for display in the museum.*

*Suspicious of his employers' talk of "perfect peace," Gengo joins up with young Machiko and her hippy friend Shosaku to search for Machiko's brother, a computer scientist who disappeared after expressing his fears that the company was engaged in something nefarious. Machiko plays a stolen audiotape they think holds the secret to the mystery, but the garbled electronic noise is unintelligible.*

*Unintelligible, that is, except to the monsters on Monster Island. Godzilla speaks his mind: "Hey, Anguirus! Something funny's going on. You better check!" Godzilla and Anguirus break out of Monster Island and head for the mainland. The broadcast reaches into deep space where it activates King Ghidorah and Gigan. As the monsters converge on World Children's Land, Gengo and his friends head there, too, determined to stop the chairman, whoever he really is.*

*In reality, Kubota and the chairman are extraterrestrial cockroaches whose home planet was so polluted by the dominant humanoid species that it became uninhabitable. Expecting the human race to pollute itself into self-destruction soon, the cockroaches from Nebula M Spacehunter have come to claim the Earth as their own. Only Godzilla stands in their way, and so they have enlisted the space monsters to do away with him. But better monsters have tried this tactic before, and failed.*

When Gengo breaks into the Godzilla Tower looking for Machiko's brother, he bluffs his way out of an awkward encounter with Kubota, playing the fool. After he leaves, the chairman sizes Gengo up: "He's stupid but at the same time cunning." The assessment could just as easily apply to *Godzilla vs. Gigan*, a severely flawed movie with an incongruously intelligent streak.

After Tomoyuki Tanaka saw the indescribably bizarre *Godzilla vs. Hedorah*, he quickly brought back Jun Fukuda with the specific mission to return the series to "normalcy." Two story ideas were developed, both reviving the immensely popular King Ghidorah. *Kingu Ghidorah no Gyakushu* ("King Ghidorah's Counterattack") was to feature a battle between Godzilla, Rodan and Varan against Ghidorah, Gigan, and a monster called Mog. This idea was rejected in favor of *Gojira tai Uchu Kaiju: Chikyu Boei Meirei* ("Godzilla vs. the Space Monsters: Earth Defense Directive"), which pitted Godzilla, Anguirus, and a monster called Majin Tsuru against Ghidorah, Gigan, and Megalon.[1]

Screenwriter Shinichi Sekizawa was also brought back, and he dropped two of the monsters. Megalon would be put off until the next film, and the Majin Tsuru (based on the Daiei company's Giant Majin series) was abandoned altogether. The screenplay, now called *Chikyu Kogeki Meirei: Gojira tai Gaigan* ("Earth Destruction Directive: Godzilla vs. Gigan"[2]), reworked Sekizawa's *Invasion of Astro-Monster* script in many ways: an alien race chooses to colonize the Earth once their home world becomes environmentally damaged. Using mind control techniques, they enslave the space monster Ghidorah in their quest to kill Godzilla, the one monster that could spoil their invasion plans. Eventually, the alien's control is broken and Godzilla defeats the now independent space monster(s).

In addition to recycling an old story, *Godzilla vs. Gigan* also raids the history of Godzilla for its presentation. Tanaka decided to keep production costs on the film exceptionally low, which turned out to be a wise approach. *Godzilla vs. Gigan* earned almost as much in ticket sales as *Godzilla vs. Hedorah*, but cost much less, thereby netting higher profits. In order to keep expenses down, Tanaka asked Fukuda not to commission an original score, but to rely instead on existing recordings of Ifukube's music.[3] Some of the musical cues, including the opening title theme, were borrowed from Ifukube's score for *The Birth of the Japan Islands* (directed by Yoshimitsu Banno, no less).[4] The more familiar Godzilla and Ghidorah themes came from previous Godzilla entries.

Along with the recycled music, Teruyoshi Nakano relied heavily on existing footage for the effects scenes. Footage from *Ghidorah, Invasion of Astro-Monster, Son of Godzilla, War of the Gargantuas, Destroy All Monsters*, and *Godzilla vs. Hedorah* reappears here. Unlike the use of recycled footage in *All Monsters Attack*, where old scenes would be played pretty much in their entirety, the stock footage in *Gigan* has been carefully edited with new footage to create new scenes.

When the alien's "tape of peace" is broadcast into space, it activates Ghidorah and Gigan. Fukuda and Nakano very successfully build up the suspense for the space monsters' appearance. At this point, though, King Ghidorah appears as a completely immobile model. Without flapping its wings or shifting any of its three heads, Ghidorah flies to Earth, where it and Gigan circle the Godzilla Tower. When they begin their attack on Tokyo, both monsters suddenly and inexplicably increase in scale. When their battle with Godzilla and Anguirus returns them to the Tower, they are now as big as the building that previously dwarfed them.

Another inconsistency arises in edits between new footage of the almost catatonic Ghidorah and stock footage (from *Ghidorah* and *Destroy All Monsters*) of a violent, hyperactive dragon. Casual viewers would be forgiven for concluding that there were two Ghidorahs, one in combat and the other standing by the sidelines, doing nothing but watching. That these errors most severely mar what should be the dramatic centerpiece of the film (the arrival of the space monsters) is a sign of the fatigue underlying this blatantly commercial effort.

Godzilla appears in the same costume used since 1968, now looking quite tattered.[5] This was Haruo Nakajima's final performance in the series. Kenpachiro Satsuma, who would inherit Nakajima's role many years later, plays the cyborg Gigan, a monster with the bizarre attribute of a circular saw in its abdomen.

While the innovations of *Godzilla vs. Hedorah* are debatable, at least Banno's film shows a sincere creative effort. By contrast, *Godzilla vs. Gigan* is a pastiche of fragmentary bits appropriated from other works. However, lurking beneath the surface of this Godzilla collage lies a self-referential, post-modern theme which almost saves the movie. Sekizawa's "stupid but cunning" screenplay is about the role of monsters in society, monsters as legendary icons and marketing tools. Or as the alien Kubota puts it, "all sorts of monsters—ancient and new."

Perhaps no writer was in a better position to address this theme. Sekizawa in the sixties had singlehandedly reinvented the role of monsters in giant monster movies. The series' earliest writers, Shigeru Kayama and Takeo Murata, presented monsters in the American mold, nothing more or less than mindless, destructive juggernauts. Sekizawa permitted Toho's monsters to develop individual personalities, moral faculties, and the ability to communicate and reason.

Much of the appeal of the Godzilla series rested on the ability of its pantheon of famous monsters to be interpreted in various ways. Viewers with a penchant for symbolism could read Godzilla as a statement on Hiroshima, others could find references to the Lucky Dragon accident, and the very intrepid could find even more obscure significance. However, viewers with no such inclination could enjoy the films on the surface level, as exciting science fiction action movies.

By the early seventies, a new role for monsters had developed, outside the narratives of the films themselves. This new role was as marketing tools. Although attendance for the Godzilla films dropped in the seventies, the franchise proved financially worthwhile because it kept Godzilla alive as a cultural icon who could be exploited for profit in comic books, soundtrack albums, toys, and so on. Godzilla was especially popular among children, a fact Sekizawa had recognized very early. In 1962's *King Kong vs. Godzilla*, Sekizawa included a brief scene where a small boy enthusiastically asks his terrified mother if they can

go see Godzilla. Well aware that it would mean certain death, she anxiously declines.

By 1969, references to Godzilla's popularity among children no longer suggested a morbid death wish, and *All Monsters Attack* starred a child who idolized Godzilla and who owned a Godzilla toy. In 1971, *Godzilla vs. Hedorah* featured many shots of the child hero's extensive Godzilla toy collection. The evil marauder of *King Kong vs. Godzilla* had been rehabilitated into a hero that children could safely admire, and wish to take home as a playmate.

*Godzilla vs. Gigan* is a product of that marketing strategy. With budgets slashed so harshly that quality work was virtually impossible, *Gigan* was an obvious attempt to keep Godzilla alive in the public imagination so that more toys could be sold. Bringing back popular co-stars such as Anguirus and Ghidorah not only helped bring viewers into the theater, but helped keep those monster designs current (*Hedorah*'s Ken owned at least one Ghidorah doll). The introduction of the new monster Gigan, too, reflected both the desire to give audiences something new to watch as well as to provide a new character for merchandising. This approach succeeded, and Gigan became one of Godzilla's more popular opponents, immortalized in numerous Gigan toys.

Sekizawa, who had so memorably pilloried these kind of crassly commercial attitudes in *King Kong vs. Godzilla* and *Mothra vs. Godzilla*, managed to encode a critique of the commercial motives behind *Gigan* within the movie *Gigan* itself. This post-modern self-referential argument was accomplished through the fact that *Gigan* introduces *three* new monsters, not one: In addition to the titular monster, there are Shukra and Mamagon, created by cartoonist Gengo. Of course, Shukra and Mamagon do not deserve to share the stage with Godzilla, Anguirus, Ghidorah and Gigan. Nevertheless, they remain highly visible throughout the film, both as the prominently displayed layout sketches in Gengo's apartment and as plot devices. Whenever Gengo is caught snooping around World Children's Land, he makes up some excuse related to his monster designs.

To understand why Shukra and Mamagon

are unsuccessful monster designs is to address the issue of marketing.

The movie opens with Gengo presenting an unfinished comic book layout to a potential editor, who rejects it. The editor is at first upset that the monster Shukra is invisible. In fact, Gengo simply has not finished drawing yet. During the early sixties, Toho produced a cycle of movies about invisible monsters. Although the insubstantial man movies succeeded in frightening audiences, Toho abandoned them altogether. Invisible monsters are very hard to market, since every kid in Japan can claim to already own a Transparent Man figure.

As Gengo explains to the editor what Shukra will look like, he recounts some advice the editor apparently gave him earlier: "You said, 'Find out what the kids hate most and visualize whatever it is as a monster.'" Consequently, Gengo created Shukra as "the homework monster." The editor scoffs, "It's far too simple! Kids are much too sophisticated for that now!" To some extent, the editor has identified the problem with Shukra. Unlike Godzilla, Shukra lacks the ability to be interpreted by different viewers in different ways. As Honda intended, viewers around the world over forty years have found multiple levels of enjoyment in Godzilla, a character that can adapt to the changing fears and desires of its international audience. A homework monster is altogether too superficial in conception.

Gengo's other creation, Mamagon, the monster of "too-strict mothers," is also superficial in concept. However, Gengo has added an additional layer to Mamagon in that he has designed it to resemble his girlfriend Tomoko. Tomoko refers to herself as "the boss," a far more flattering nickname than the crude obscenity Gengo calls her. A black belt in karate, aggressive, she is the only one of the human heroes with a shred of common sense.

Women's roles in the Godzilla series being frequently limited to superfluous girlfriends and sisters or villainous space dominatrixes, a strong human heroine like Tomoko stands out as an exception to the rule. The fact that portrayals of strong women were either suppressed or attached to negative images of evil space women reflects a deeper ambivalence about gender roles in Japan. This discomfort with women who do not stay in their proscribed places manifests itself through Gengo's hostile epithet and satirical drawing of her. Although Mamagon, like Shukra, never gets off the page, her presence in the story invokes more issues than Shukra and demonstrates the value of having more than one interpretation.

While the comic book publishers have no use for Shukra or Mamagon, the invading aliens from Nebula M Spacehunter apparently do. In the name of "perfect peace," the World Children's Land plans to replace all the real monsters of the world with model duplicates for display in their monster museum. On a strictly narrative level, this plan is necessary to get Godzilla and other potential opposition out of the way before their invasion. On a thematic level, though, the plan addresses the marketing of monsters.

In the world outside the narrative, monsters can represent important issues (Cold War nuclear policy, capitalism, communism, environmentalism), which can pose a threat to authority figures who may wish such issues not be discussed. By replacing monsters with models, the cockroaches can limit their expressive power. When the cockroaches talk of "perfect peace," they mean it. The messy internecine squabbles that keep the Earth a place of violence and war arise from differences of opinion between groups who have the ability to employ weapons (literal or monstrous) to settle the argument rather than debate civilly. If Godzilla were replaced with a mere model, in the world within the story humanity would be effectively "disarmed," while in the world outside the story moviemakers would be "silenced." A totalitarian state enforces peace by suppressing differences of opinion and stifling debate on controversial issues.

Visitors to the monster museum will learn what World Children's Land chooses to teach. When the cockroaches announce that Shukra and Mamagon are excellent ideas, and plan to include them among the Monster Island detainees in the museum, they reveal their preference for monsters with easy-to-package, superficial relevance. Lacking ambiguity, Shukra and Mamagon are less politically threatening that something like Godzilla. Toho makes money off selling the likeness of a character whose popularity was established in movies that often criticized the profit motive. Godzilla's expressive power as a symbolic figure is at odds with his value as a commercial icon. Reduced to a mere commodity, Godzilla no longer raises uncomfortable questions.

The monster museum proposes to reduce all monsters to mere commodities: lifeless objects whose images can sell things. The aliens have their base inside a building designed to look like Godzilla, a design choice selected precisely for its ability to appeal to consumers.

When Godzilla encounters the Godzilla Tower, he is momentarily fooled. His confusion is endemic: Throughout *Gigan*, characters routinely mistake things for other, often significantly dissimilar things. Cockroaches from space are mistaken for human beings, and their plan for invasion is mistaken for a plan for world peace. Gengo mistakes a corncob for a gun. The aliens mistake an empty car for the heroes' getaway car. In one especially telling moment, the aliens mistake a black and white cartoon for the heroes.

This last confusion seems absurd and implausible (although we have no reason to suspect cockroaches from outer space perceive color or depth the same way we do) but is consistent with the recurring theme of comic books. If a drawing of people can be mistaken for real people, than drawings of Shukra and Mamagon are perhaps not so far away after all from being as "real" as Gigan and Ghidorah. In fact, the Japanese version accomplished the infamous scene in which Godzilla speaks by showing cartoon-style word balloons above his and Anguirus' heads. In the American version, however, the monsters actually speak English, although so heavily distorted by synthesizer noise that some viewers might not even notice.

A newly formed company called Cinema Shares bought the rights to distribute *Godzilla vs. Gigan*, as well as *Godzilla vs. Megalon* and *Godzilla vs. Mechagodzilla*. They opted not to replace the flat, monotonous Hong Kong dubbing commissioned by Toho for its international edition; Cinema Shares instead spent their effort in removing the bloodletting and profanity that had now become standard in the Godzilla films. Excising Gengo's "hard bitch" line and the shots of Gigan's buzzsaw slicing bloody wounds into Godzilla and Anguirus, apparently on the theory that American children need more protection from such stuff than their Japanese counterparts, Cinema Shares released the film theatrically as *Godzilla on Monster Island*. In 1988, New World Video restored the film to its uncut state as *Godzilla vs. Gigan* for home video release.[6]

The 1.8 million Japanese ticket buyers who attended *Godzilla vs. Gigan* earned it a higher profit than the comparatively more expensive *Godzilla vs. Hedorah* had earned with only 1.7 million viewers.[7] Tanaka succeeded, and the Godzilla series had thrown off the arthouse trappings of its last installment. Buried within a recycled plot made from recycled footage and music, Shinichi Sekizawa had planted some seeds of a post-modern, ironic acknowledgment of the market forces that were now controlling the series' destiny, but his ideas do little more than lend the movie a strange, quirky attitude. The glory days of the early sixties seemed a long way behind, and things were to get much worse before they got better.

# Chapter 22

# *Godzilla vs. Ultraman*

*The first generation of kids to watch* Ultraman *has grown up and now has kids of its own. So* Ultraman *gives families a basis for communication. Parents can talk to their children about the monsters because they saw the same monsters 20 years ago.*

— Noburu Tsuburaya[1]

Eiji Tsuburaya's son Noburu was employed at Fuji Television in the summer of 1962 when he started hearing rumors that the company was looking to make a special effects–driven TV program. Seizing the opportunity, Noburu got all the right people in the room together to hammer out a deal between Fuji and his father's company Tsuburaya Enterprises to make a weekly series highlighting the kinds of things people associated with the name Tsuburaya.

Gradually, that show began to take form as *Woo*, about a friendly space alien. Meanwhile, in 1964, Tsuburaya made a bold purchase of an Oxberry 1200 optical printer — the most advanced of its kind in the world. It was essential equipment for his team and would prove invaluable on assignments both for Toho's *tokusatsu* spectaculars and his budding television work, but it was also staggeringly expensive. The only way to justify the cost was to make it part of the budget for the nascent series— and Fuji refused to pay their portion of a bill they had not intended to incur. With one purchase, Tsuburaya had killed his TV show.

Over at TBS, Fuji's biggest competitor, more forward-thinking minds ruled. The TBS bosses were quite content to foot the bill for the printer if it meant they could have Tsuburaya working for them; the only thing they were not so keen on was the silly idea for *Woo*. Writer Tetsuo Kinjo, a friend of Shinichi Sekizawa's, wrote a new scenario for *Unbalance*, a sort of *Twilight Zone*–styled anthology series. As *Unbalance* developed, it was gradually retooled to emphasize a recurring cast of characters and more special effects. By the time it went before

cameras in September of 1964, it had been christened *Ultra Q* (the Q stands for "Question").[2]

*Ultra Q* concerned the exploits of a group of elite scientific researchers investigating weird happenings (read: monsters) in Japan. Tsuburaya produced the series, with the day-to-day effects work handled by Sadamasa Arikawa and photographed by Hajime Koizumi. Toho Studios was part of the board of Tsuburaya Enterprises, and *Ultra Q* was packed with Toho staffers both on and off screen.[3]

Tsuburaya was now handling effects for three major Toho features and *Ultra Q*. The pressure of cranking out a weekly program on a TV budget taught his staff crucial lessons in economy. New ideas were pioneered, practiced, refined, and perfected — and then ported over to the more demanding world of features.

*Ultra Q* ran from January to July of 1966. During the course of its broadcast, its makers could not help but notice the spike in ratings every time the program featured giant monsters. Quick to respond, Tsuburaya Productions adapted the often grim black and white *Ultra Q* into the colorful eye-candy of *Ultraman*, which took *Ultra Q*'s timeslot just weeks after the original series retired. Where *Ultra Q* relied on clever writing, *Ultraman* focused on action. Over the course of its year-long run, *Ultraman* told the story of a space-policeman from Nebula M-78 who fuses with a human named Hayata to help protect the Earth from space monsters. When Hayata, a member of the Science Patrol, uses the Beta Capsule, he transforms into Ultraman, a powerful superhero. *Ultra-*

128

*man* became a phenomenal hit with ratings higher than the less sensationalistic *Ultra Q.* Thus was Tsuburaya a major creative force behind the development of two of Japan's most prominent pop cultural icons, Godzilla and Ultraman.[4]

Since his first appearance on April 9, 1967, Ultraman has starred in numerous television series and feature films. *Ultra Q, Ultraman, Ultra 7, Return of Ultraman, Ultraman Ace, Ultraman Taro, Ultraman Leo, Ultraman 80, Ultraman Great, Ultraman Powered, Ultra 7-2-1,* and so on have so far covered hundreds upon hundreds of individual episodes.[5] Ultraman merchandise grew into a multimillion dollar industry. Noboru Tsuburaya, who took over *Ultraman* after his father's passing, proudly asserts, "Ultraman has had a tremendous social impact in Japan."[6]

Reporting on Ultraman's continued impact on Japanese popular culture, Michael Ross noted *Ultraman*'s

> function as [a vehicle] for the communication of cultural values and mores. For one thing, unlike their American counterparts, Japanese supermen are not individuals, lone crusaders for truth, justice, and the Japanese way. Ultraman ... and other Japanese superheroes work in teams, as members of family groups, teaching youngsters early lessons about the importance of cooperation and conformity in an intensely group-oriented society. The individual is the monster — he who opposes the interests of the group and tries to destroy the social order.[7]

To keep up with the demands of supplying new and exciting monsters for Ultraman to battle each week, Tsuburaya frequently adapted existing Toho monster suits to create new creatures, although for copyright reasons Toho monsters could not appear as "themselves" in a Tsuburaya Production. This process resulted in the Baragon suit from 1965's *Frankenstein Conquers the World* being so altered for use in *Ultraman* that his scheduled appearance in *Destroy All Monsters* had to be curtailed.[8] Among the costumes Tsuburaya adapted for his television show was, naturally, Godzilla.

Godzilla's first small screen appearance came in the very first episode of 1966's *Ultra Q,* "Defeat Gomess." For Gomess, Tsuburaya redressed the 1964 Godzilla suit with armor plates, hair and horns. The tenth *Ultraman* episode (also 1966) featured that Godzilla suit again, now repainted blue and yellow with a frilly fin around the neck as the monster Kira.[9]

The connection between Ultraman and Godzilla also ran the other way. Whereas the Godzilla series had once been the trendsetter for the monster genre, the seventies era Godzilla borrows extensively from the competition. In an effort to mimic Daiei's successful Gamera series, Godzilla had become proactively friendly to children. In response to *Ultraman* and other such TV shows, Godzilla came to be a superhero, no longer brought into battle by human agents or by the silver tongue of Mothra. Also, Godzilla now fought evil space monsters, often controlled by alien invaders. Godzilla's ally in *Godzilla vs. Megalon,* Jet Jaguar, was about as close as Toho could come to putting Ultraman on the screen alongside their superstar.

In another nod to the popularity of small screen superheroes, the seventies era Godzilla films featured "theme songs" (*Godzilla vs. Hedorah*'s "Save the Earth," "Godzilla's March" from *Godzilla vs. Gigan,* Jet Jaguar's theme song, and the King Seesar theme song sung by the Azumi prophetess in *Godzilla vs. Mechagodzilla*).

Many American fans enjoy watching these television shows, yet few of the programs have ever been officially released in North America. As it happens, most fans can enjoy such programs as *Kamen Rider,* most of the *Ultraman* series, *Kikaider,* and others only on Japanese imports, lacking English dubbing or subtitles. This language barrier presents little problem because the storylines are so simplistic and formulaic that non–Japanese speakers miss little. Unfortunately, this simplistic plotting began to appear in Godzilla as well, and the seventies era films in particular display a Mad Libs–style approach to screenwriting (fill in the blanks with name of reporter, name of monster crawling out of mountain, name of invading alien's home planet, etc.). This dumbing-down of an already simplistic, formula-driven series only served to cheapen it.

*Ultraman*'s success in his various TV incarnations was such that other producers quickly rushed to fill Japanese television with more superhero shows. *Johnny Sokko, Space Giants, Kikaider 01, Star Wolf, Mighty Jack, Kamen Rider* and *Zone Fighter* competed with *Ultraman* for the attention of Japanese youngsters, and the more successful ones reached American children, too.

Some of these *Ultraman* rip-offs would find international success. Perhaps the most famous of these appeared in 1967. Toei's *Giant Robot*, which ran from October 11, 1967, through April 1, 1968, aired in the U.S. almost simultaneously under the title *Johnny Sokko and His Flying Robot*.[10] Like most Japanese superhero shows, its premise concerned a power-mad alien dictator using an army of monsters to invade the Earth, and the efforts of an elite group of technologically empowered superheroes to stop him. The dictator in this case was Emperor Guillotine, whose Gargoyle Gang has enlisted human turncoats in their efforts to conquer the world. Unicorn, a super-secret organization, is investigating the Gargoyle Gang's sea monster when a little boy named Johnny Sokko gets caught up in the action by accident. Johnny Sokko and Unicorn Agent U3 are captured by the Gargoyle Gang and taken to an underwater lair where a human scientist is being forced to construct a giant robot. The scientist has designed the robot to obey only the orders of the first voice it hears, and little Johnny precociously takes the control unit and shouts, "Hey, robot!" into it. A television legend was born.

The trend continued into the 1980s with such offerings as *Dimensional Warrior Spilvan* and *Super Machine Metalder*. The 1990s saw *Blue Swat, Fiveman, Birdman Jetman, Gridman,* and the continued variations of Toei Studios' *Rangers*.[11]

In 1975, Toei premiered the first incarnation of the *Rangers*, called simply *Five Rangers*, to cash in on the *Ultraman* craze. Noting the growing number of color televisions in Japan, Toei Studios dressed each of their five superheroes in a different color uniform and then sent them into battle against the alien dictators and monsters required by the genre. Every year,

Toei revamped the show, changing it into such versions as *Turbo Rangers, Goggle Five Rangers,* and *King Rangers*. The program soon rivaled *Ultraman* for the hearts of Japanese children, and went on to become a favorite for more than twenty-five years. In the 1990s, the American production company Saban bought reruns from Toei. Instead of dubbing the programs as had been done in the past to *Ultraman* and its clones, Saban shot new footage with American actors and used only the special effects scenes from the Japanese original. In this way, Saban managed to convince American children and critics that *The Mighty Morphin Power Rangers* was a recent American creation.[12]

The phenomenal stateside success of *Mighty Morphin Power Rangers* was attributed as much to its Americanization as to its Japanese effects footage, creating a trend. Footage from *Gridman* became *Superhuman Samurai Syber-Squad*. Saban compiled the Toei shows *Dimensional Warrior Spilvan, Super Machine Metalder,* and *Space Sheriff Shaider* into *VR Troopers*, and turned *Kamen Rider* into *Masked Rider*.[13] In none of these "American" series is a Japanese face to be seen.

By the seventies, Toho had become Japan's leading producer of television programming, and the boom in superhero programs was tempting. Superhero shows appealed to the same audience they were courting with monster movies, but TV tolerated cheaper production values than the big screen would allow. On April 2, 1973, Toho's *Zone Fighter (Ryusei Ningen Zone,* which translates as "Human Meteor Zone" and is also known as *Meteor Man)* broadcast its first episode.[14]

While copyright issues kept the real Godzilla from starring with Ultraman, Godzilla and his enemies could appear in Toho's own superhero vehicle, produced by Tomoyuki Tanaka and directed by Ishiro Honda and Jun Fukuda.

Over the 26 episodes of *Zone Fighter*, the villainous Baron Garoga attempts to conquer the universe using an army of space monsters. Baron Garoga destroys the planet Peaceland, leaving only the members of the Sakimori family as survivors. The Sakimoris, able to transform into the Zone Angel, Zone Jr. and Zone

Fighter, arrive on Earth and defend it from Garoga's monster army.[15]

Production on the series took place in 1973, immediately following *Godzilla vs. Megalon.* Teruyoshi Nakano and Koichi Kawakita directed the special effects.[16] Godzilla appeared in episodes 4, 11, 15, 21, and 25, played by suitmation actor Teru Kawai wearing the mid–70s puppydog-like costume. King Ghidorah stars solo in episodes 5 and 6, while Gigan fights Godzilla in episode 11.[17]

Years later, an interviewer asked Fukuda for his memories of working on *Zone Fighter.* Fukuda responded, "You don't have to mention that show!"[18]

Although the juvenile series is little more than a footnote in Godzilla's career, it is noteworthy for its illustration of how far Godzilla had fallen. The series that had spawned *Ultraman* was now imitating *Ultraman.* Godzilla's days as a pacesetter were over.

# Chapter 23

# Godzilla vs. Megalon

## GOJIRA VS. MEGARO (GODZILLA AGAINST MEGARO)

*I guess he realized he had to hold the monster somehow. So he just programmed himself in some way to increase his own size.*

— Goro

Japanese version: 83 minutes, Released March 17, 1973
U.S. theatrical version (Cinema Shares): 81 minutes, Released April 1976, MPAA rating: G; Public domain video version: 79 minutes
Color, Widescreen
Produced by Tomoyuki Tanaka; directed by Jun Fukuda; screenplay by Shinichi Sekizawa and Jun Fukuda; music by Riichiro Manabe; cinematography by Yuzuru Aizawa; special effects by Teruyoshi Nakano; special effects art direction by Yasuyuki Inoue; optical effects by Yukio Manoda
Starring Katsuhiko Sasaki (Goro), Hiroyuki Kawase (Rokkuchan), Yutaka Hayashi (Jakavin), Robert Dunham (Seatopian Leader), Kotaro Tomita and Wolf Otsuki (Seatopian Agents), Mori Mikita (Truck Driver)
GODZILLA portrayed by Shinji Takagi; GIGAN portrayed by Kenpachiro Satsuma; JET JAGUAR portrayed by Tsugitoshi Komada; MEGALON portrayed by Hideto Odachi

*An underground nuclear test triggers worldwide geological instability, unsettles the detainees on Monster Island, and causes untold damage to a peaceful civilization no human even knew existed. Inventor Goro, his kid brother Rokkuchan, and his friend Jakavin encounter agents determined to steal Goro's robot, Jet Jaguar.*

*Deep under the surface of the Earth lies the civilization of Seatopia, an Atlantis-like undersea world. Peaceful for three million years, the Seatopians are now reeling from nuclear tests which obliterated a third of their nation. In retaliation, they reluctantly declare war on the surface world. The Seatopian leader prays to their god Megalon to awake and avenge them. Using Jet Jaguar to guide Megalon, the Seatopians send the monster to destroy Tokyo.*

*Rokkuchan despairs, "It's a pity we can't send Jet Jaguar to go and get Godzilla." Goro thinks this is a capital idea, and just happens to have designed a back-*

*up remote control unit in case the main computer ever malfunctioned. Goro regains control of Jet Jaguar and commands it, "Get Godzilla! You'll find him on Monster Island."*

*Reacting to this change in fortune, the Seatopians contact the cockroaches of Nebula M Spacehunter and request Gigan. The cockroaches agree to loan their space monster to the Seatopians' cause. As the various monsters, mutants, and cyborgs converge to battle, the fate of two civilizations hangs in the balance.*

The Japanese film industry was in dire straits. Toho's flagship franchise — the only one to survive into the seventies at all — was in freefall; the number of available theaters had been decimated and those that remained preferred Hollywood imports. Television had co-opted the monster genre and stolen its audience; the only people who still reliably attended movies in theaters were kids. For many adults, movie tickets had become an extravagant expense they could forgo, but they were not about to deny their children anything.[1] The once proud industry of Japanese monsters had all but gone bust. In just a few years, what had been a free-for-all melee of Toho, Toei, Daiei, Shochiku, and Nikkatsu scrambling to fill theaters with the latest exploits of every imaginable mutated monstrosity had dwindled to the point that when *Godzilla vs. Megalon* was sent out, it was the lone representative for its genre for that entire year.

The logic seemed obvious at the time: If the audience wanted television superheroes, then the next Godzilla movie would be a theatrical version of a television superhero show. Aimed squarely at kids, reviving the popular Gigan alongside a new and equally lunatic monster (with Godzilla as Earth's Defender, teamed with an Ultraman-clone called Jet Jaguar), the whole thing was lashed together for about as much money as a comparable outing on TV. The bets were hedged all around.

In hindsight, it's easy to spot the failures. Toho's Godzilla movies had once been the gold standard of the genre, the prestigious vehicle all other comers hoped to emulate. By compromising quality for economy and copying its own copycats, *Godzilla vs. Megalon* degraded itself. Why would audiences pay to see what they could see on TV for free? Godzilla movies needed to do more than their TV competitors, to offer a kind of entertainment otherwise unique. But desperate times call for desperate measures, and *Godzilla vs. Megalon* is a work of desperation.

Shinichi Sekizawa had by now been hung with his own rope. In his heyday, the man wrote crackling satires that appealed to all ages and wrapped serious ideas around absurd visions full of spectacle. Writing *Godzilla vs. Megalon* with director Jun Fukuda, those ideas now appear as clichés, hollow routines trodded through by rote. The dramatic opening scene provides an excuse for the heroes to decry nuclear testing ("What the hell are they trying to do? Wipe us all out or something?"), but never connects to the rest of the film. In fact, nothing at all ever seems to connect. Nuclear tests get the story going and provide a quick explanation for why Godzilla has to fight Megalon. The *raison d'etre* of the film is Godzilla's fight with Megalon — a plot description masquerading as a title. The fight's foregone conclusion carries no emotional or political significance whatsoever.

As a peaceful civilization wronged by nuclear testing and forced to call their monster-god to defend them, the Seatopians mirror the similar plight of Mothra's people. Sekizawa had shown an aptitude for developing this kind of complex conflict, with no easy answers. Unfortunately, Sekizawa and Fukuda make no effort at all to depict the conflict between Godzilla and Megalon, or by extension the conflict between human civilization and Seatopia, as an am-biguous battle in which either side's victory would necessarily be bittersweet. Instead, the Seatopians are evil and so is their monster, plain and simple. Jakavin's naive suggestion at the end that they could "warn the scientists to be more careful" cannot be taken seriously.

The Seatopians, we are told, fell into the sea three million years ago. The Seatopian agent explains, "They managed to create their own oxygen supply and later were able to construct their own sun." One supposes that they created their own oxygen supply, then, during the three or four minutes of human lung capacity they had before they all drowned.

In fact, the Seatopian agent tells Jakavin (Yu-taka Hayashi) this miraculous tale without even the remotest motivation to do so. Jakavin escapes shortly afterwards, leading the agent to call his superiors and warn, "He's aware of the whole story of our mission here!" Well, whose fault is that? Of course, in formulaic movies like this one, bad guys always tell their prisoners exactly what their evil plots are, because it's a lazy way to convey that information to the viewer.

The laziest piece of scripting, and one of the most blissfully logic-impaired moments in the entire storied franchise, occurs when Goro's heroic robot Jet Jaguar suddenly becomes as gigantic as the monsters. This he does because that's what Ultraman does, and it's what the audience expects. The only shred of explanation offered, however, is that he must have "programmed himself somehow to increase his own size." While that absurd plot development suddenly renders the human characters irrelevant to the story, it is questionable what they were contributing to the proceedings before this point. The only relevant answer to that question: They provide story padding.

An example: Jakavin and the little boy Rokkuchan want to stop the Seatopian agent who has taken control of Goro's lab. This they accomplish by running off to a local hobby shop, stealing a model airplane, assembling it, returning to the lab, throwing the plane at the bad guy's head and knocking him out. They then *leave the lab with the agent still there*! Since the agent has no power over any of the monsters, knocking him out achieves nothing, and leaving him achieves less than nothing — not to mention that they could have saved time by knocking him out with a rock or something that had been nearby at the time. When they later return to the lab, for no reason other than to say some dialogue somewhere other than the hillside, the agent is gone. Perhaps he went to a drugstore to buy some aspirin.

Fukuda brings no more professionalism or attention to detail to his end of the endeavor. One notorious scene finds the actors standing motionless until Fukuda calls for "Action!" This kind of appalling mistake could be easily edited out, but evidently no one bothered. Not until a late 1990s reissue was this obvious error finally corrected.[2]

There are two chase scenes, both packed with stunts, yet neither chase ever amounts to anything dramatic. Exploding cars, flipped motorcycles, and cars driving perilously down a flight of stairs should be interesting, but without characterization or logical motivation, these exploits lack emotional power and leave the viewer cold. Much of the film takes place supposedly at night, achieved through underexposure and blue filters in the day-for-night technique. Unfortunately, the scenes are still obviously shot during the day, ruining the effect, while the dark blue coloring obscures the actors' faces.

Teruyoshi Nakano simply did not have the money to even try to pull off a quality result. Despite such reduced circumstances, however, he does manage a few nice scenes. The opening sequence with Rokkuchan nearly sucked into a whirlpool is especially creepy, and sets a standard the rest of the film cannot meet. Megalon's attack on the dam also shows some modicum of effort, but quickly turns sour as Megalon fights a stock footage army.

Not only that, but the stock footage army has been cobbled together from a sequence yanked out of War of the Gargantuas that had been used in exactly the same way just the previous year in Godzilla vs. Gigan. Gigan itself was plundered for clips, along with Ghidorah, Destroy All Monsters, Godzilla vs. the Sea Monster, and Godzilla vs. Hedorah.

What new footage Nakano has crafted takes place on a barren landscape devoid of detail, with the monsters wrestling as anthropomorphically as they ever would. The new Godzilla suit, which would be used for the rest of the decade with only slight modifications, simplified Godzilla's look and made him downright cute. With big, Muppet-like eyes and puffy cheeks, Godzilla resembled a puppy. Briefly replacing the now-retired Haruo Nakajima inside the suit, stuntman Shinji Takagi even acts like a rowdy house pet.

Godzilla's co-stars were likewise made as unthreatening as possible. Jet Jaguar was an obvious Ultraman lookalike, and Gigan's behavior has been tamed for younger viewers. Megalon, a roach-like insect with power-drill arms, a lightning rod on his forehead, and the ability to spit explosive spitballs, was too bizarre a monster to be very scary. The climactic confrontation between the four monsters is played strictly for laughs.

A children's film, Godzilla vs. Megalon needs to be evaluated on different terms than the more adult-oriented pictures of the sixties. However, Megalon displays such a shocking lack of care that it appears to be a cynical attempt to excuse shoddy work as being good enough for undemanding children. Sekizawa's improbable and unmotivated story, Nakano's reuse of existing and well-worn effects footage, and Fukuda's lackluster direction get no help from Riichiro Manabe's obnoxious score, which revives some of the less successful themes from his Hedorah soundtrack. In every respect, this film represents the creative failure of its production team.

When Cinema Shares distributed Godzilla vs. Megalon theatrically in 1976, their promotional poster showed Godzilla and Megalon astride the twin towers of the World Trade Center, an image that deliberately mimicked the advertising campaign for Dino De Laurentiis's concurrent remake of King Kong but bore no relationship to anything in the movie itself. Cinema Shares promoted Godzilla vs. Megalon as "All New! Never Before Seen!" and claimed that it was Godzilla's first color-and-widescreen film. Only viewers who were unaware of any of the other sequels could be fooled by any of those claims.[3]

Weirdly, some American critics, including Vincent Canby of *The New York Times*, praised the ridiculous result. *Variety* wrote that "the miniature and technical effects are superb, reflecting a creative understanding of the camera." Phil Hardy wrote, "[T]he effects are expertly done, and it looked as if the series was beginning to revive." That these same critics disliked the special effects in the original films from which *Megalon* borrowed its footage is puzzling, and suggests that some critics do not bother to watch the movies they review.[4]

Cinema Shares' lack of concern for consistency or authenticity continued with their other major piece of promotion: a slim comic book issued to some theaters in which Gigan was called "Borodan" and Jet Jaguar referred to as "Robotman."

Because Japanese kids' films were freer with violence, bad language, and fleeting sexuality than would ever have been acceptable in the United States, even something like *Godzilla vs. Megalon* needed some censorial trims to be made usable in the drive-in circuit. The American release keeps the crude "international" dub track but deletes shots of extreme violence, as well as some shots of nude pinups in the cab of a truck. This sanitized 82-minute American version underwent more editing for American television. The storyline was such that large sections of the film could be deleted without upsetting the overall plot. For example, the opening sequence in which Goro, Rokkuchan, and Jakavin experience an earthquake while having a picnic, one of the few effective and dramatic sequences in the entire movie, bears no relationship to any of the events that follow. This scene is often cut, and the plot never suffers for the loss. In fact, *all* of the scenes could be removed with no loss of entertainment value.

In 1977, NBC broadcast *Godzilla vs. Megalon*, hosted by *Saturday Night Live* star John Belushi wearing a Godzilla costume designed by Robert Short for use in the film *Hollywood Boulevard* (1976). This high-profile prime time national television premiere brought Godzilla an unprecedented American audience. The one-hour time slot required the film to be almost cut in half in order to fit. Presented by a comedian with a smugly superior attitude and deliberately campy approach, almost any Godzilla film would have come off poorly, but as the series' nadir, *Godzilla vs. Megalon* never had a chance.[5]

Eventually, one edited print, cut down to 79 minutes, fell into the public domain, having been published without copyright protection. Any company could sell videos of this version without paying royalties. Consequently, many companies began to market low-cost, low-quality dubs of this drastically edited *Godzilla vs. Megalon* across North America. By 1994, Video Treasures reported that *Godzilla vs. Megalon* was one of their best-selling public domain titles. The public domain videos became so prevalent that although a higher quality, unedited, copyrighted print has long been available, none of Toho's various American video licensors have ever attempted to market it here.[6]

When Goro regains control of Jet Jaguar, Megalon becomes briefly confused and starts leaping around in an emotional fit. His random jumping provides a neat visual metaphor for the movie that bears his name. *Godzilla vs. Megalon* was the series' least financially successful effort to that point, and widely regarded to be its creative worst as well.[7] That it is probably the most accessible and best-known Godzilla film among Americans is truly a shame.

Chapter 24

# Godzilla vs. Mechagodzilla
## GOJIRA TAI MEKAGOJIRA
## (GODZILLA AGAINST MECHAGODZILLA)

*Two Godzillas? What does it mean?*

— Prof. Wagura

Japanese version: 84 minutes, Released March 21, 1974

U.S. theatrical version (Cinema Shares): 80 minutes, Released March 1977, MPAA rating: G; original theatrical titles: *Godzilla vs. the Bionic Monster*; *Godzilla vs. the Cosmic Monster*: 84 minutes

Color, Widescreen

Produced by Tomoyuki Tanaka; directed by Jun Fukuda; assistant director Jozaburo Nishikawa; screenplay by Hiroyasu Yamamura and Jun Fukuda; story by Shinichi Sekizawa and Masami Fukushima; music by Masaru Sato; cinematography by Yuzuru Aizawa; art direction by Kazuo Satsuya; special effects by Teruyoshi Nakano; special effects art direction by Yasuyuki Inoue; special effects cinematography by Motoyoshi Tomioka and Takeshi Yamamoto; optical effects by Yukio Manoda

Starring Masaaki Daimon (Keisuke Shimizu), Kazuya Aoyama (Masahiko Shimizu), Hirosihi Koizumi (Prof. Wagura), Akihiko Hirata (Prof. Miyajima), Reiko Tajima (Saeko Kaneshiro), Mori Kishida (Interpol Agent Namura), Goro Mutsu (Commander for Conquest of the Earth), Hiromi Matsushita (Iko Miyajima), Masao Imafuku (Azumi Priest), Barbara Lin (Azumi Prophetess), Takayasu Torii (Interpol Agent), Daigo Kusano (Kawa Yanagi), Kenji Sahara (Ship Captain), Yasuzo Ogawa (Construction Workshop Supervisor)

GODZILLA portrayed by Isao Zushi; MECHAGODZILLA portrayed by Kazunari Mori; ANGILAS and KING SEESAR portrayed by Momoru Kusumi

*Ominous portents of imminent doom accumulate: The discovery of a hitherto unknown metal coincides with a prophecy that foretells the apocalypse — making specific predictions that, one by one, come true. As scientists confirm the metal is of extraterrestrial origin, an earthquake hits, a regular phenomenon of late.*

*Some people attribute them to a monster moving underground.*

*The underground monster emerges: Godzilla, seemingly intent on destruction. An Azumi priest in Okinawa remarks that the only thing that could stop Godzilla is Okinawa's ancient monster god King Seesar, but he cannot be revived easily.*

*Godzilla attacks an oil refinery but encounters another Godzilla — the real one. The impostor sheds his fake skin to reveal his space-titanium armor. Godzilla and Mechagodzilla prove to be a match for each other, and soon both are down for the count. Bleeding profusely, Godzilla falls into the sea, and Mechagodzilla returns to his underground cave for repairs.*

*Mechagodzilla is the creation of an invading force of space aliens from the third planet inside the Black Hole. In order to get it operational quickly, the space aliens need the help of the Nobel Prize–winning scientist Prof. Miyajima. Using his daughter as leverage, they blackmail him into repairing the cyborg.*

*As a freakish red moon appears on the horizon, it seems the doomsday prophecy is coming true. Since Godzilla cannot defeat Mechagodzilla alone, the only hope for humanity's survival is if King Seesar can be revived from his ancient slumber.*

*Godzilla vs. Megalon* had been a disaster. Cutting the budget to the bone, dropping the standards of quality to the floor, and unabashedly chasing the youngest and least discriminating of viewers—these were crass moves that then did not even pay off. *Megalon* brought the worst box office return for the series up to that point. A course correction was needed.

Toho was desperate to mint new monster stars, to keep fueling the most profitable aspect of the enterprise—the merchandising. Gigan was kept alive as a TV villain on *Zone Fighter*, but none of the other monsters created in the 1970s had connected in any meaningful way with audiences. When asked to pen a twentieth anniversary outing for Godzilla, Shinichi Sekizawa shrugged in despair, "There aren't any monsters *left*." Teruyoshi Nakano suggested, in the spirit of helpfulness, that a mechanical monster would be easier (and cheaper) for the special effects staff than mutated animals were. With that nudge, Sekizawa realized he still had a monster or two left in him after all.[1]

The shooting script was credited to Jun Fukuda and Hiroyasu Yamamura, from Sekizawa's story outline. Sekizawa called it quits after that scenario, and would not write another screenplay ever again. The resulting script, however, bears more than a passing resemblance to the TV series *Johnny Sokko and His Flying Robot*. In *Johnny Sokko*, and most Japanese superhero TV shows for that matter, the hijinks involve an evil alien dictator attempting to conquer the world through a monster. *Johnny Sokko*'s Baron Garoga enslaved a human scientist to build a giant robot; the commander of the apes from the Black Hole enslaves a human scientist to repair Mechagodzilla. Baron Garoga kidnapped biologist Dr. Dorian's granddaughter to blackmail him into helping the aliens' evil schemes; *Mechagodzilla*'s commander kidnaps Prof. Miyajima's daughter as hostage to ensure the scientist's compliance. *Johnny Sokko* features the super-secret security force Unicorn; *Mechagodzilla* has Interpol.

Mechagodzilla even looks a lot like Johnny Sokko's Giant Robot. Both shoot laser beams from their eyes and missiles from their fingers. Both fly, despite their singularly un-aerodynamic design. When the apes launch Mechagodzilla from their underground cave, his take-off looks exactly like the oft-repeated special effects sequence from *Johnny Sokko* showing the Giant Robot's liftoff from Unicorn HQ.

Equally derivative is the idea that the alien invaders are ape men disguised as humans. *Planet of the Apes* (1968) had already spawned four theatrical sequels in the United States, all of them hits in Japan, the last of which was released in the same year as *Mechagodzilla*. Tsub-

uraya Productions would take a stab at adapting the popular notion for Japanese audiences as *Ape Corps* (1975), a television miniseries that was later edited into a feature-length movie called *Time of the Apes* (1987).[2]

Befitting the formulaic nature of this screenplay, the heroes fit neatly into the now-standard stereotypes: the scientist, the reporter, the sister/daughter/girlfriend, the swashbuckling police agent (here, an Interpol agent). As stereotyped hero-figures, they lack the emotional dimension of well-developed characters, coming across merely as shallow narrative devices. Akihiko Hirata's Prof. Miyajima is the only character to experience any complex emotions during the film, and his feelings of guilt at having assisted the aliens, even under the duress of blackmail, provides the only meaningful character development.

In his heyday, Sekizawa could fill a script with quirky character details, witty dialogue, and interconnected dramatic conflicts. Add to that the fact that Toho's contract roster in the 1960s was full of charismatic movie stars, most of whom could bring charm even to an underwritten role. By now, the creative exhaustion is all too evident: *Godzilla vs. Mechagodzilla* is packed with characters who fail to connect with the audience meaningfully. The action never lets up, but it is empty spectacle.

While the previous seventies era films starred a new cast of performers that did not include the familiar players who had formed something of an informal Godzilla repertory company in the sixties, *Mechagodzilla* sees the welcome return of Hirata and Hiroshi Koizumi, playing their familiar roles as kindly scientists. Also returning, albeit in a very brief cameo, is Kenji Sahara, as a ship captain. The starring roles, however, go to players who came up through the ranks of the very superhero shows that inspired the script. Masaaki Daimon, previously the star of various crime thrillers, plays Keisuke; he went on to roles in *Zone Fighter* and *Ultraman*. Mori Kishida, as the Interpol agent Namura, was an ex–*Ultraman* star who had made his name as Toho's Dracula in a cycle of 1970s horror films. Goro Mutsu, here as the alien commander, previously appeared in Tsuburaya Productions' *Mighty Jack* and *Fireman* series. Kazuya Aoyama plays Masahiko, having previously been the fabled "Young Guy" himself, but his more relevant credit here may be his tenure as Zone Fighter himself in Toho's own Ultraman-clone.[3]

The few original elements in *Mechagodzilla* screenplay, stemming from the Azumi prophecy, do not bear close scrutiny. The prophecy makes specific predictions about freak atmospheric conditions (a black mountain above the clouds, a red moon, a western sun) that do occur, but without any explanation. None of these occurrences seem to be connected with the alien invasion; however the prophecy's doomsday monster is clearly Mechagodzilla, so the viewer is left to wonder whether the aliens simply waited until they saw these weather patterns to go ahead with their invasion.

The aliens are keen to get hold of the statue of King Seesar. At some point during all the commotion of the plot, hero Keisuke miraculously finds the time to have an exact duplicate of the statue made, and substitute it without ever letting his companion Saeko know. He could have spared himself the bother if he had noticed that the prophecy is also very clear that the doomsday monster will in fact be defeated by two other monsters.

As with *Godzilla vs. Gigan*, the script ruminates on mistaken identity. Keisuke's fake statue is mistaken for the real one. Godzilla is mistaken for the doomsday monster. Apes from the Black Hole are mistaken for humans. An Interpol agent is mistaken for a villain. Most importantly, Mechagodzilla is mistaken for the real Godzilla. As for why the aliens bothered to disguise Mechagodzilla as Godzilla, the Godzilla fanzine *G-Fan* editors J.D. Lees suggests, "[P]erhaps ... because it was a cool thing to do. Can't aliens have a sense of humor?"[4]

Despite the flimsy story, Jun Fukuda manages several masterful set pieces that highlight his skill as a director. This would be Fukuda's final involvement with Godzilla, and he sends himself off with a bang. There are several standout action sequences, including a hand-held chase scene on a steamship and two fist-fights. A strong sense of menace ripples through the film, with a growing sense of urgency as the elements of the prophecy come true.

One particularly effective sequence occurs as the Interpol agent rescues Miyajima and the others from the alien base, and they climb into a car to make their escape. As the key is turned in the ignition, the car is engulfed in flames. Suddenly we see that the heroes are not in the car at all, but have turned the key by wire while standing safely far away. The editing of the scene achieves maximum impact while conveying with economy the idea that they have recognized the booby-trap. This is a truly cinematic scene, and stands in marked contrast to the blandly literal-minded treatment of a parallel moment in *Gigan* when the aliens destroy an empty getaway car believing it to be occupied by the human heroes.

Teruyoshi Nakano also shows off his talents in several scenes, and clearly has a higher budget with which to work. For the first time in years, the effects sequences are all-original footage. Godzilla's revival by a lightning storm is a powerfully visual moment that takes full advantage of Nakano's skill with pyrotechnics, also highlighted in Godzilla's first encounter with his cyborg double at the oil refinery. Despite similarities in design to *Johnny Sokko*'s Giant Robot and similarities in concept to *King Kong Escapes*' Mechanikong, Mechagodzilla became one of Godzilla's most popular opponents and one of Toho's enduring monster icons.

King Seesar fares less well. The leonine monster, a demonic god from authentic mythology, has a ragged look. Because the actor inside the suit performs so energetically, dashing around like a boxer, the hairy costume shimmies and shakes in a most unnatural fashion. Unlike the angular and powerful Mechagodzilla, King Seesar did not win many fans.

Sporting one of the best original soundtracks of the seventies era films, *Mechagodzilla* saw the return of Masaru Sato as composer. His jazzy, upbeat score also contains a level of menace and doom missing from his scores for *Sea Monster* and *Son of Godzilla*. Just as this was the last Godzilla film for Fukuda and Sekizawa, this would be the last time Sato scored for the series.

*Gojira tai Mechagojira* first appeared in the United States courtesy of Cinema Shares as *Godzilla vs. the Bionic Monster*. Universal Pictures threatened to sue, claiming the title infringed on their copyright of *The Six Million Dollar Man* and *The Bionic Woman*. Cinema Shares dutifully changed the title to *Godzilla vs. the Cosmic Monster*,* but not before milking the publicity for all its worth.[5]

The Cinema Shares theatrical version deleted four minutes' worth of credits, profanity, and blood-letting, but did so without trying to smooth over the edits. The jarringly cut-up end product did little to persuade critics that the film deserved to be taken seriously. In 1988, New World Video restored the film on video, issuing a complete and unedited international print.[6]

Moderately successful both in the United States and Japan, *Godzilla vs. Mechagodzilla* vindicated Nakano, and gave both Fukuda and Sekizawa a face-saving departure from the series. Significantly, this renewal involved improved production values, but a less ambitious script than usual for the seventies, an era of experimentation for the Godzilla series. *Smog Monster* experimented the most, both in content and style. *Gigan* saw an effort to return to the complex subtexts that had given Sekizawa's sixties scripts such depth, but now in a self-referential context. *Megalon*, for all its flaws, actively courted a different, younger audience. *Mechagodzilla* returns to the safe formula hammered out over the years, but without the nuances and subtexts that had breathed life into that formula, making *Mechagodzilla* one of the most shallow of the series' adult-oriented entries.

*There is some controversy about whether the movie was ever actually shown under the name* Godzilla vs. the Bionic Monster, *or if it was merely advertised that way. I saw the film in 1976, at a drive-in theater in Raleigh, North Carolina, double-billed with* Godzilla vs. Megalon. *I distinctly remember that it was advertised as* Godzilla vs. the Bionic Monster, *even as late as 1976. I have acquired a copy of the trailer using the* Bionic Monster *title, and it matches my memories. However, I was not attentive to whether the film bore the same onscreen title when I saw it, or if in fact I saw it as* Cosmic Monster. *I have acquired a copy of the film with* Cosmic Monster *titles, but have not yet found one with* Bionic Monster *titles, and so cannot resolve this dispute myself.*

## Chapter 25

# Terror of Mechagodzilla

## MECHAGOJIRA NO GYAKUSHU
### (MECHAGODZILLA'S COUNTERATTACK)

*Your heart is frozen and dry. Who'd love a cyborg? A person who is not a person. So remember, forget about Earthlings. They're no concern of yours.*

— Alien captain

Japanese version: 83 minutes, Released March 15, 1975

U.S. theatrical version (Bob Conn Enterprises): 79 minutes, Released in 1978, MPAA rating: G, original theatrical title: *Terror of Godzilla*; U.S. television version (UPA): 89 minutes, Released March 1977

Color, Widescreen

Produced by Tomoyuki Tanaka; U.S. version produced by Henry G. Saperstein; directed by Ishiro Honda; assistant director Kenshou Yamashita; screenplay by Yukiko Takayama; music by Akira Ifukube; cinematography by Motoyoshi Tomioka; art direction by Yoshibumi Honda; edited by Yoshitami Kuroiwa; UPA's "History of Godzilla" prologue edited by Richard Bansbach and Michael McCann; special effects by Teruyoshi Nakano; special effects art direction by Yasuyuki Inoue; optical effects by Yukio Manoda and Kazunobu Mikame

Starring Katsuhiko Sasaki (Akira Ichinose), Tomoko Ai (Katsura Mafune), Akihiko Hirata (Dr. Shinji Mafune), Katsumasa Uchida (Murakoshi), Goro Mutsu (Commander Mugan), Kenji Sahara (Army Commander), Tomoe Mari (Yuri Yamamoto), Shin Roppongi (Wakayama), Tadao Nakamaru (Tagawa), Kotaru Tomita (Tada), Masaaki Daimon (Captain), Ikio Sawamura (Mafune's Butler), Kazuo Suzuki and Yoshio Kirishima (Aliens), Toru Ibuki, Yasuzo Ogawa, Hiraya Kamita, Taro Yamada, Masaichi H., Haruo Suzuki, Saburo Kadowagi, Shigeo Kato, Kazuo Imagi, Kiyoshi Yoshida, Toshio Hosoi, Masayoshi Kikuchi, H. Ishiya, Shizuko Higashi

GODZILLA portrayed by Teru Kawai; MECHAGODZILLA portrayed by Kazunari Mori; TITANOSAURUS portrayed by Tatsumi Fuyamoto

A submarine, unsuccessfully searching for the wreckage of Mechagodzilla, is attacked and destroyed by what the black box recording calls "a giant di-nosaur." Interpol agent Murakoshi and his friend, marine biologist Ichinose, think the dinosaur that destroyed the sub might be the same one Dr. Shinji Mafune claimed to have found fifteen years earlier.

Years earlier, Dr. Mafune was a well-respected marine biologist, but was then rejected by his peers for his unorthodox claims that he had not only discovered a living dinosaur but was able to control it. Mafune lost his research position and became isolated from the rest of the world. Mafune persisted in his work, now funded by the alien invasion force. In an experiment testing his ability to control his dinosaur, Titanosaurus, his daughter Katsura was electrocuted. She was resurrected by aliens from the Black Hole, as a cyborg.

The aliens reveal their true identity to Dr. Mafune, hoping that he will feel indebted to them for saving his daughter's life. He agrees to work with them on the reconstruction of Mechagodzilla, since his fifteen years of isolation have cultivated a strong sense of resentment and hatred towards the human race. His Titanosaurus project and their Mechagodzilla project are similar in concept, and the aliens welcome Dr. Mafune aboard as a collaborator.

Ichinose and Katsura fall in love, which is especially problematic, since she is a humanoid robot programmed to hate all humans, and her mechanical brain controls Titanosaurus on its rampage of destruction. She is torn between conflicting loyalties and unfamiliar emotions.

Godzilla comes after Titanosaurus, while the aliens keep Mechagodzilla in reserve. They hope that Godzilla will be so weakened by his bout with the dinosaur that he will be an even easier foe for Mechagodzilla. That is, as long as Katsura plays along.

The most important genre film made in Japan in the 1970s did not feature Godzilla, nor any other giant monster for that matter. In fact, *The Submersion of Japan* (1974) was in effect a monster movie without monsters—a special effects–driven epic that allowed Teruyoshi Nakano to do what he did best (explosions, miniatures, miniature explosions) without those things that vexed him most (guys in rubber monster suits beating on each other). Produced by Tomoyuki Tanaka, it was the *Gojira* of its day. In the guise of a somber horror movie, it tackled real issues of national identity and international politics. For the first time in years, if not decades, a Toho special effects movie acknowledged that the destruction of a city was a catastrophe with terrible human costs— that the bloodless evacuations of Tokyo in so many Godzilla flicks had been a glib fantasy. Relentlessly grim, overwhelming in scope, humorless and self-important, *The Submersion of Japan* was the biggest Japanese blockbuster of all time.

The word "blockbuster" hardly does it justice, since its box office performance outdid things like *King Kong vs. Godzilla*, a product of happier times when there were many more theaters and many more theater-goers. To actually hit it so big during such a sallow era was nothing short of astonishing.

Like *Gojira* before it, it made its way to American screens in an altered form. New World hacked away a full hours' worth of character development and narrative detail to leave just the effects and melodrama, linked by some new footage of Lorne Greene as an American diplomat. Titled *Tidal Wave*, this recut version did respectable but unremarkable business on the drive-in circuit.

Back in Japan, though, the aftershocks of *Submersion*'s success continued. Toho had found a winning formula that emphasized impersonal spectacle over characterization, and Tanaka sought to replicate the formula.

Toshio Masuda's *The Prophecies of Nostradamus* (released in the U.S. as *The Last Days of Planet Earth*) and Jun Fukuda's *ESPY* followed quickly later the same year, continuing the serious trend signaled by *Submersion of Japan*. As Guy Mariner Tucker notes, much of Toho's genre output for the next twenty years would be informed by the ponderous *Submersion of Japan*. Already, *Godzilla vs. Mechagodzilla* had taken baby steps towards a more adult tone; now Tanaka wondered what it

would take to go all the way back to the apocalyptic atmosphere of the 1954 original.[1]

And who better to helm such a return than ... Yoshimitsu Banno?

In the years that followed his angry complaint "You ruined Godzilla!" Tanaka had come to reflect differently on Banno's contributions. In hindsight, *Godzilla vs. Hedorah* now stood as one of the most popular and profitable Godzilla movies of the decade, and its bizarre style was at least a coherent artistic vision by a singular creator expressing deeply held convictions. More to the point, Banno had worked as assistant director on *Last Days of Planet Earth* and had demonstrated his understanding of the new genre direction.

Banno figured this would at last be a chance to make good on the sequel promised by *Hedorah*'s closing titles, and to pit Godzilla against the Smog Monster once again, this time in the deserts of Africa.[2]

Such plans had no future. Toho was already on the fence about whether to continue Godzilla movies at all. It no longer made sense to make monster features. Toei had killed off almost all competition with its ruthlessly cheap special effects TV shows. As fecund as weeds, Toei drowned out all others by sheer volume. At the theaters, Hollywood imports bested Japanese films so consistently that the only truly popular and profitable genre left for Japan to pursue was anime, a field skyrocketing to international success with such artists as Hayo Miyazaki. Old-timey man-in-a-suit monster films no longer had a place on Japanese movie screens. With fewer and fewer films being made, why squander scarce resources on anything but the most profitable?

To give the next Godzilla feature a greater chance at standing out in the marketplace, Toho decreed that it was time to bring back Ishiro Honda, and to blend the old guard with the new. Although Honda had worked with Godzilla fairly recently, on TV's *Zone Fighter*, this would mark his first theatrical assignment in five years.

"It was a whim of the executives that I got to do it at all," Honda recalled, "I found the story getting away from me."[3]

That story may never have been much in his hands to start with. With Sekizawa gone, the studio announced a company-wide contest to develop a script for the new Godzilla picture. Novice writer Yukiko Takayama, the series' first woman screenwriter, won the competition. A recent graduate of an independent screenwriting academy, Takayama was hired to develop the outline into a screenplay.[4] Honda found her work intriguing, but sloppy: "Her story was psychological—you could even call it poetic—but not terribly cinematic."[5] He was obliged to rewrite it extensively. The result was yet another "superhero" Godzilla squaring off against a space monster controlled by alien invaders, not much of a return to first principles.

This injection of new blood may have done little to lift the series out of its storytelling rut, but still provided something new: a female perspective. For the first time (and of this writing, the only time), one of the primary creative forces behind the scenes was a woman. Notably, her screenplay focuses on a female character. Katsura, the cyborg, paradoxically fills both heroic and villainous narrative roles, and as such stands as one of the most complex female characters in the series.

In many ways, Katsura resembles Miss Namikawa from *Invasion of Astro-Monster*. Both are alien robots whose loyalty is ultimately split by an unexpected love for a human man. The relationship between Katsura and Ichinose is a classic "star-crossed lovers" setup. Both Ichinose and Katsura endure constant interference from their immediate peers encouraging each to give up on the other. Murokoshi tells Ichinose to forget about Katsura, who in turn must listen to the alien's speech urging her to feel nothing but hatred towards humans. Ichinose is so blinded by love that he overlooks the inconvenient facts that Katsura has openly lied to him, is the most likely suspect for the sabotage of Interpol's only weapon against Titanosaurus, and has been seen consorting with the spacemen near their mountain base. In turn, Katsura maintains tender feelings towards Ichinose despite the intense pressure around her.

Like the warring Capulet and Montague families pitted in eternal rivalry, the humans and the aliens are locked in battle for control of the Earth. Ichinose is a true-blooded human. However, as a cyborg constructed from alien technology in the image of a once-human girl, Katsura lies somewhere between the two worlds of the humans and the aliens. The aliens provoke Katsura in her vengefulness by asserting that no human could ever love such a creature as her. When Ichinose cradles her in his arms and says gently, "Even if you're a cyborg, Katsura, I still love you," he proves otherwise. He does so not as a representative of humanity, since all other human characters considered her an enemy. Instead, Ichinose acts as an individual whose power of love transcends the obvious barriers of nationalism. He should hate her as a traitor, yet he forgives her for any complicity she had with the aliens' plans. This scene, then, shows the *male* character as overlooking national allegiances in favor of love, and thus turns the sexist *Astro-Monster* paradigm on its head.

Takayama said that the most important aspect of the script to her lay in the central theme of a cyborg that retained human emotions.[6] Takayama's Katsura combines elements of Miss Namikawa and the queen of the Kilaaks. Like Namikawa, Katsura has a redeemable, human soul. Yet, like the Kilaak queen, she never has to renounce her position. She is depicted throughout as uncomfortable with the aliens' exploitation of her "gentle dinosaur," but even when faced with having to kill Ichinose to protect her father's dreams, she does not falter. Ichinose forgives her without her ever having apologized.

When Toho began a new series of Godzilla movies in the 1980s, the audience included larger numbers of women than had been the case for the original series. To keep those women viewers, the new series would enhance the on-screen roles for its female characters, giving human heroines the strong characteristics previously reserved for space women villains. Additionally, many of the films featured women controlling the monsters, an idea borrowed from Katsura's control of both Titanosaurus and Mechagodzilla.

Given how much of the screenplay was actually written by Honda, it is hard to say for certain who was responsible, but the opening sequence of *Terror of Mechagodzilla* seems to make explicit reference to *The Submersion of Japan*. Both pictures begin with a submarine searching for something at the bottom of the sea, making unexpected discoveries that portend disaster ahead. In the case of *Terror of Mechagodzilla*, the sub is on the hunt for the wreckage of the cyborg that Godzilla dropped into the ocean off Okinawa Island at the end of the previous film. However, Interpol's crew is looking off the coast of Manazuru Island. Little surprise, then, that they cannot locate the monster.

Toho's monster pictures were never strong on continuity, and while *Terror of Mechagodzilla* supposedly takes place on the heels of the events shown in *Godzilla vs. Mechagodzilla*, there is no more connection between this film and the last than there was between *War of the Gargantuas* and *Frankenstein Conquers the World*. Certain events in *Terror of Mechagodzilla* make little or no sense when seen as extensions of the story told in the previous film. In *Mechagodzilla*, Commander Mugan went to great lengths to blackmail Professor Miyajima into assisting with the Mechagodzilla project. Yet in *Terror of Mechagodzilla*, the aliens apparently have been associated with Dr. Mafune for a good portion of the last fifteen years. So at the time Prof. Miyajima was brought in, Dr. Mafune was hard at work nearby. Why would the aliens bother with Miyajima when a willing ally was already close at hand?

Furthermore, during the years of association between the aliens and Dr. Mafune, they never revealed their true identities. Mafune expresses surprise to learn who they really are. However, Mafune has harbored a fifteen-year-long hostility towards the human race, because of their rejection of his dinosaur theories. For many years, though, the aliens have supported his dinosaur research. Unless Mafune knew his financiers were not human, why would he not have let their obvious belief in him assuage his feelings of anger? In any case, why was he not the least bit suspicious when they revived his daughter after a fatal electrical shock?

The filmmakers evidently did not care much about logical consistency. The audience was expected merely to be swept along. Consequently,

the movie essentially remakes the previous film: Mugan manipulates a scientist's daughter to ensure his cooperation because that is what happened last time.

There is also the curious presentation of Mafune's controversial dinosaur theories. No date is given onscreen, but the clothing styles and cars depicted suggest that *Terror of Mechagodzilla* occurs in the mid-seventies, concurrent with its production. Fifteen years previous would be around 1960—by which point in our fictional universe, Japan had already experienced two Godzillas, Anguirus, and two Rodans. The revelation that yet another living dinosaur had been discovered may well have been greeted with some skepticism, but in what way could it have been so controversial as to have justified firing Mafune from his research institute? Even if his theories were before their time, surely in the intervening years as Mothra, King Kong, Manda, Baragon, Ebirah, Minilla, Kumonga, some giant mantises, and Gorosaurus were discovered, someone should have given the poor doctor an apology. Even his theories regarding monster control eventually ended up a part of Japanese public policy, as the way to keep the monsters on Monster Island. Not only does the fact that the scientific community rejected Mafune despite the known existence of other living dinosaurs seem implausible, but the flashback shows Mafune's peers *physically assaulting* him. What did the man say that was so objectionable?

Instead of trying to concoct a strong story with plausible character motivations, the priority obviously lay in improving on-screen production values. The much vaunted return of Honda (along with his former director of photography, Motoyoshi Tomioka) highlighted this attitude. Aside from the opportunity to herald the return of the prodigal director in advertisements, though, Honda's presence adds little new to the mix. In fact, he seems to be trying to channel the spirit of Jun Fukuda—fast cutting, zooms, handheld shots, moving cameras, and a level of energy more in keeping with Fukuda's breathless style than Honda's more stately approach.

Emboldened by his stunning work on *Sub-*

*mersion of Japan*, Teruyoshi Nakano is in top form. The new monster Titanosaurus is a beautiful, colorful, highly detailed creation that harks back to the giant animal designs of the sixties, rather than the bizarre monster designs of the seventies. Even in conception, as a gentle beast forced against its will to commit evil acts of violence, Titanosaurus displayed a depth of character more reminiscent of the monsters of the sixties than the one-dimensional evil space monsters of the seventies.

Nakano photographs his monsters several times from a low angle, against a real sky. Such shots succeed in creating a believable illusion of monumental monsters wreaking havoc in a real world. Other scenes show thoughtful design, too. When Godzilla first appears, he is silhouetted by an explosion in a dark cityscape in one of the more effective first-appearance scenes in the series. During the climactic final assault on Tokyo, Mechagodzilla fires missiles from his fingers towards the camera. They erupt in the street, sending buildings and cars flying towards the viewer. Although the miniatures lack convincing detail, the sheer violence of the well-staged sequence more than compensates.

Also returning to the series after a long absence, Akira Ifukube composed his first original Godzilla score since *Destroy All Monsters* in 1968. It is a sweeping work full of sad themes and grandeur. Far from relying on his immense back catalogue of existing compositions, Ifukube wrote a new march for Mechagodzilla, emphasizing the power of the giant robot. His elegant theme for Titanosaurus musically conveyed the monster's tragic role as an unwilling destroyer.

The cast overlaps with the previous film, with the same actors brought back to play new roles. Akihiko Hirata returns as the mad scientist, for his last appearance in the series. His role as Dr. Mafune serves a similar narrative role as his role as Professor Miyajima a year earlier, but he plays the two characters very differently. As Mafune, Hirata overacts tremendously. His hammy performance undercuts the production team's attempts to return to the somber atmosphere of the early films, and makes for a sad swan song for this very capable actor. Worse, the Americanized version adds a sinister and stereotypical laugh to the character not present in any other version.[7]

Kenji Sahara makes a brief return appearance as a general, continuing to put notches in his belt as Toho's most-seen actor in Godzilladom. Also back is Masaaki Daimon, star of *Godzilla vs. Mechagodzilla*, in what amounts to a cameo appearance as a man whose larynx was cut by the aliens. Goro Mutsumi, who dubbed Russ Tamblyn's voice in the Japanese version of *War of the Gargantuas*, reprises his role as the alien commander.

Taking the lead role is Katsuhiko Sasaki, *Godzilla vs. Megalon*'s hero inventor. Sasaki also starred in one of Toho's attempts to encroach on Hammer Horror territory, *Evil of Dracula*, as well as *The Last Days of Planet Earth*. Of all of Toho's new generation of stars, he had the easiest charm and marquee looks. Sasaki would return to the Godzilla series in the next cycle of films, in the late 1980s and early 1990s.

In 1978, Henry Saperstein released *Terror of Mechagodzilla* to television in an 89-minute version that added a six-minute prologue created from clips of previous UPA-owned Godzilla films. This "History of Godzilla" sequence purported to tell how Godzilla came into being, and why the one-time villain of the early films was now depicted as a superhero. This led into the opening credits and a virtually complete version of the film. UPA left Toho's "international" dubbing intact, with the exception of transferring some of Mugan's sinister laughter to a shot of Dr. Mafune. Otherwise, the only change UPA made to the film occurred in the scene where the aliens implant the Mechagodzilla controls in Katsura's chest. Although not a true nude scene for actress Tomoko Ai, the scene did depict what were supposed to be her naked breasts (although the breasts looked somewhat fake and rubbery). Saperstein deleted two such pseudo-nude shots, and released its version to television.

At about the same time, Bob Conn Enterprises handled a theatrical release, although on a very limited basis. Bob Conn's version sported the title *Terror of Godzilla* and lacked UPA's prologue. However, even without glimpses of Katsura's naked chest, UPA's version contained extensive profanity and considerable violence, which would have garnered a PG rating from the MPAA. Realizing that Godzilla's audience in the West consisted largely of children, Bob Conn drastically edited *Terror of Godzilla* for a G rating, cutting it down to just under 79 minutes.[8] This theatrical version lacked all gunplay, which unfortunately left the action-packed movie rather confusing. The edits were made crudely, leaving jumps in the music track and changing the meaning of the movie. Shots of violence and death were unceremoniously dropped, which was quite destructive to a movie that was otherwise supposed to be full of death and violence. At one point, Mafune thanks Mugan for saving his daughter's life. Since the scenes of her being shot and her subsequent operation have been cut, Mafune's comment makes no sense.

Worst of all, in the climactic final battle, Mafune and Katsura die, but in the 79-minute version, *who* shot them is unclear. Katsura's tragic suicide at the end, to save the world from the evil she controls, makes for a nice bookend to the series; Ishiro Honda, directing both the first and last of the original series, mirrors the suicide of Dr. Serizawa with Katsura's selfless act. However, this moment, despite its emotional and historical significance, does not appear in the edited American version. Instead, the impression is that Murakoshi killed Katsura. Bob Conn clearly only wanted to delete images of graphic violence, but as a result leaves the viewer thinking that Murakoshi killed his best friend's true love, a disturbing implication for what was supposed to be a children's movie.

For several years, the more complete UPA version remained the version shown on television, but by 1984, the shorter theatrical version had somehow replaced it. In the process, the difference between the two titles *Terror of Godzilla* and *Terror of Mechagodzilla* became academic, as the 79-minute version lost its on-screen title altogether. The complete (and extended length) UPA version of *Terror of Mechagodzilla* did not resurface in America until 2006.

This film was to be Honda's final monster movie. Although his science fiction films had garnered greater international attention than his other, dramatic works, Honda never expressed anything but pride in his achievements:

> A lot of things can be expressed by literature or painting, but cinema has a particular advantage in its visual aspect. I try to express in films things that other arts could not approach ... Monster films permit me to use all these elements at the same time. They are also the most visual of any kind of film.[9]

Despite the professionalism and artistry of Honda, the production team behind the Godzilla series had dropped their standards throughout the seventies. In the final shot of *Terror of Mechagodzilla*, Godzilla wades into the ocean, his face twisted into a grotesque toothy smile. This nightmarish grinning Godzilla shows actor Teru Kawai wearing an exhibition costume never intended for use on screen.[10] Poorly designed and startlingly unlike the Godzilla costume used in the rest of the film, its use in this final shot of the final film of the first series highlights the carelessness that had come to the surface during the seventies.

Such sloppiness took its toll. In its Japanese release, *Terror of Mechagodzilla* drew a paltry 980,000 ticket buyers, a mere tenth of the audience for the original *Godzilla*.[11] Instead, the Japanese box office success for 1975 was the American import *The Towering Inferno*. That year marked an ominous historic moment: For the first time, foreign films out-earned domestic features at the Japanese box office.[12]

"We tried to make Godzilla fearsome," recalled Teruyoshi Nakano, "but he wasn't so scary in the end. We all kept thinking about the children too much, we couldn't get away from that."[13]

Honda retired to a small house in the suburbs, next to a golf course. As if to bookend his career, his new neighbor was none other than Akira Kurosawa. By day, the two old men played golf, hung out with Yoshio Tsuchiya, and plotted a return to the movies. *Kagemusha the Shadow Warrior* (1985) gradually took shape on the links. An era had ended, but another was waiting in the wings.[14]

Godzilla returned to Monster Island, and the series came to its end.

# Chapter 26

# The Crook, the Geek,
# the Reporter, and His Lover

*As long as the arrogance of human beings exists, Godzilla will survive.*
— producer Tomoyuki Tanaka[1]

From the gritty black and white realism of *Godzilla* to the colorful fantasy of *Terror of Mechagodzilla*, Toho's trademark film series had come a long way over the course of 21 years.

The seminal early films, somber in tone and aimed at a mature audience, used monsters as narrative devices to discuss controversial issues in an allegorical fashion. With Shinichi Sekizawa's *Mothra*, however, a new approach began to develop. For the first time, a giant movie monster displayed intelligence, moral faculties, and compassion. For the first time, despite the destructive power of the monster in question, mankind was not compelled to destroy the monster, but rather reasoned with it and learned to co-exist. Toho's monster movies, in a move that separated them from all other contemporaries, created monsters with distinctive personalities.

This not only separated Toho's work from the competition, but forced writers to adapt their stories. Giant monsters whose charisma formed part of the movie's appeal were naturally more likely to engender audience sympathy, and as such came to be recast as heroes, not as evil destroyers. A growing focus on "good" monsters pitted against "bad" encouraged a move away from allegorical storylines to more superficial action-adventures.

As Godzilla and Rodan were revamped into Mothra-style heroes, their monster opponents changed from Earth-based dinosaur-like monsters into space monsters and cyborgs. This move freed Toho's designers to create monsters with more powerful weaponry and more out-landish appearances. The Darwinistic struggle of mutant dinosaurs, each fighting the other out of natural aggression, gave way to a monstrous reenactment of nationalistic conflicts, where the two sides fight one another over the control of land.

Villainy, then, came to be represented in human, or humanoid, form. The early human villains were greedy, ruthless businessmen, communist insurgents, paramilitary terrorists, or bullies. This evil, whether embodied by a respected entrepreneur or a member of the criminal underground, grew out of selfishness and individualism. Villains were those who prized their own needs and desires above the common good, and would steal trucks, kidnap people, and threaten children if it served their interests. Gradually, human evil gave way to humanoid evil, as invading space alien dictators took over as the main villains. These oppressors carried with them no direct connotations to any particular human group. They could represent Americans or Soviets, capitalists or communists, fascism or militarism of any kind, any political or national interest group — idealized manifestations of oppression, dissociated from any specific example.

Human heroes tended to fall into a handful of professions: reporter, scientist, or police agent. In the opening sequence of his aborted *Agon: The Atomic Dragon* show, Shinichi Sekizawa gathered his anxious heroes at a beach, waiting with bated breath as the giant monster lumbered out of the sea: a reporter, a scientist, and a policeman. He followed the template ever after, and bequeathed it to his heirs.

Reporters and scientists, as seekers of objective truth, exemplified the positive aspects of modern civilization. Mankind's technological progress might, at times, contribute to the creation of terrible monsters, but in the end the films upheld the fundamental values of continued progress. Police agents received slightly harsher treatment, often seeming like bumbling fools. Nevertheless, their good-intentioned defense of Japanese land and culture against all manners of human and monstrous threats could succeed when they collaborated with the scientists and reporters.

The scripts often limited female roles to sisters and love interests. Active female heroes appeared in the early sixties, but by the seventies, the Godzilla films had become a very male-dominated enterprise. (*Godzilla vs. Megalon* featured no women at all.) On occasion, though, the series created memorable women characters, yet these roles were usually villainous space women who would betray their own cause and commit suicide in order for the male hero to win.

As the series evolved, it also devolved. The high-water mark in terms of both commercial success and creative accomplishment occurred in the early 1960s. As audiences shrunk, revenues shrunk with them, which forced budget cuts that hit special effects hardest. Behind the scenes, the creative team endured significant shake-ups. Individuals with limited enthusiasm and little desire to innovate assumed the primary creative responsibilities.

Godzilla also faced increasing competition from other sources. Television heroes like Ultraman and rival movie monsters like Gamera cut into Godzilla's audience, while Americans increasingly saw the series as Grade-Z bad movies aimed at children, unfit to be taken seriously.

In the wake of major Hollywood genre blockbusters like *Star Wars*, the bar for fantasy and special effects–driven entertainment was raised higher than the increasingly impoverished Japanese film industry could manage. In the 1950s and '60s, Eiji Tsuburaya and his peers were trendsetters for the world, but their techniques looked anachronistic and embarrassing when compared against the work of Industrial Light and Magic. In 1977, Toho put out *War in Space*, a bald-faced *Star Wars* knock-off directed by Jun Fukuda with effects by Teruyoshi Nakano. It was cobbled together from ideas cribbed from previous, better Toho spectacles but bringing nothing new of value. The decrepit state of the Japanese film industry by that point meant its measly box office performance of a million tickets sold actually looked pretty good, and the endeavor was deemed a success—commercially, if not creatively.

There was no incentive to do any better. Japanese filmmakers found they could make money by making inexpensive films of low ambition. The better the industry got at this, the harder it would be to try to appeal to a broader, international audience. The world of Japanese genre film would remain insular and isolated for years to come.

*Part Four*

# The Return of Godzilla
# (1977–1995)

Ten years after Godzilla last waded into the sea, a second series began, with a new creative team. Although their efforts found commercial success in Japan, they would remain inaccessible in the United States until nearly the end of the century. Instead, the relationship between this Japanese popular cultural icon and audiences in North America would grow more complex, as American producers attempted to develop a new American Godzilla specifically for American consumption. This Hollywood project would influence Toho in many ways, and would ultimately lead to the death of Godzilla (but not necessarily the death of his series).

## Chapter 27

# Waiting for Godzilla

## (Godzilla in America, Part Two)

*Godzilla in Japanese means half gorilla and half something else. What I felt was that in order to do Godzilla right, it had to be a dinosaur.*

— Steve Miner, director[1]

*One point that should be made clear, King Kong is a real animal, whereas Godzilla is a monster born from radiation.*

—from the Japanese version of *King Kong vs. Godzilla*

Godzilla's absence from the silver screen did not preclude his continued prominence in other media. Toho, in fact, found considerable profits in licensing their monster icon to various companies for all manner of spin-offs and merchandising. Some of these spin-offs were produced by American companies for American fans.

From 1977 to 1979, Marvel Comics published a Godzilla comic book. Since Marvel's license agreement related only to the character of Godzilla himself, his comic book foes came from the imaginations of Marvel artists rather than Toho's established monster roster. Over the course of twenty-four issues, Godzilla battled Yetrigar, Batragon, Ghilaron, Lepirax, Centripor, and the Mega-Monsters. In the Marvel comic, Dr. Yuriko Takiguchi, a survivor of Godzilla's 1954 attack on Tokyo, joins the American security force SHIELD in order to prepare a defense against the giant mutated dinosaur. SHIELD's cigar-smoking agent Dum-Dum Dugan became a continuing human hero in the protracted battle against Godzilla. Although Marvel Comics attempted to create a marauding, evil Godzilla, on several occasions he was depicted as a sympathetic, anthropomorphic character similar to Toho's 1970s version.

As drawn by Herb Trimpe, Marvel's Godzilla was a giant green dinosaur with back plates extending all the way up his head. He more closely resembled a Tyrannosaurus Rex than any of the screen incarnations. At one point, Dum-Dum calls the monster a "blasted overgrown salamander," a not-inaccurate description.[2]

The comic ended after two years of middling sales. It had occasionally highlighted existing Marvel superheroes like Spider-Man and the Fantastic Four in the stories; longtime Toho fans had grown weary of their hero being misused. Fans of Marvel's familiar characters, too, found the confrontations between their human-sized heroes and an opponent larger than a building to be unsatisfying.[3] Marvel Comics editor Stan Lee considered his original creations to be superior to this character licensed from a foreign movie company, and that attitude influenced the development of the Godzilla comic.[4] In responses to fans' letters, Lee described the *Godzilla* comics line as "lighter, more 'fun,'" compared to "'serious' books like *Masters of Kung Fu*."[5] Toho became frustrated with Marvel's treatment of their icon, and did not renew Marvel's license agreement.[6]

In 1978, Hanna-Barbera developed a Saturday morning animated television series for NBC. This short-lived program of 26 half-hour episodes initially aired under the title *The Godzilla Power Hour*, and later as *Godzilla and the Super 90*. It subsequently reran as *The Godzilla Show*, *The Godzilla-Globetrotters Ad-*

151

*venture Hour*, *The Godzilla–Dynomutt Hour with Funky Phantom*, and finally *The Godzilla–Hong Kong Phooey Hour* before leaving the air in May 1981.

The producer of Hanna-Barbera's *Godzilla*, Doug Wildey, had made a name for himself in the world of American animation as the creator of the popular prime-time series *Jonny Quest*. *Quest* followed in the footsteps of Hanna-Barbera's previous prime-time programs (*The Flintstones*, *The Jetsons*, and *Top Cat*) but with one noteworthy innovation: Wildey's animation team drew the weekly adventures of *Jonny Quest* in a realistic style. Although *Jonny Quest* only ran its 26 original episodes from late 1964 through 1965, it drew a loyal following and stayed in reruns through 1978, by which time it had become part of *Godzilla Super 90*.

*Jonny Quest* followed the globe-traveling adventures of 11-year-old Jonny Quest, his scientist father Dr. Benton Quest, Jonny's tutor "Race" Bannon, Jonny's adopted East Indian brother Hadji, and their pet bulldog Bandit. Race's gal pal Jezebel Jade, a shadowy character with suspicious alliances, joined the team on occasion. When Wildey began work on *Godzilla* over a decade later, he borrowed the same format. *Godzilla* depicted the exploits of the crew of the *Calico*, a research vessel equipped with a hovercraft, a bathysphere, and other hi-tech equipment recalling the similar obsession with gadgets that characterized *Jonny Quest*. Captain Majors served as the skipper of the *Calico*, and Dr. Quinn Darian supervised most of the scientific research. Rounding out the *Calico* team were Brock and the youthful Pete, whose presence helped achieve the same racial, gender, and age representation of *Jonny Quest*'s cast. Instead of a pet dog, the *Calico* had Godzilla's son Godzooky, and in times of trouble they could count on the King of Monsters himself to come to their rescue. Among the *Calico*'s useful gadgets was a signal box that called Godzilla from his resting place deep in the ocean.*

Wildey depicted his Godzilla as a superhero,

much like Toho had during the seventies, but contrasting with the somewhat menacing monster of Marvel's comic series. The human crew of the *Calico* relied on Godzilla as a trusted ally, and the giant monster seemed willing to obey their instructions. Wildey and co-designer George Wheeler drew Godzilla with simplified back plates, green skin instead of Toho's charcoal-gray, and a dog-like face with pronounced nostrils. Godzilla roared with a leonine growl supplied by Ted Cassidy (who also played Lurch on the *Addams Family* television series), a sound effect that owed nothing to the familiar screech originally created by Akira Ifukube.

Ensuring Godzilla's obedience, the *Calico* crew kept Godzooky as a sort of pet. Like Bandit before him, Godzooky provided comic relief and frequently blundered into peril, requiring the human characters to rescue him. Godzooky had the ability to fly, quite unlike Minilla, and even unlike Hanna-Barbera's own Godzilla. Godzooky's Scooby-Doo–like voice came from voice artist Don Messick.[7]

Both Marvel's and Hanna-Barbera's versions glossed over the central issue of Godzilla's nuclear heritage. In the original 1954 *Godzilla*, Dr. Yamane clearly stated that Godzilla is a "child of the H-Bomb." Twenty-five years later, this issue had been all but forgotten. As Toho's creative team felt that nuclear radiation no longer held the same place in the public imagination as it had in the mid-fifties, they let the movie series expand to address other issues instead. However, to the extent that radiation did still play a part in the continuing mythology of Godzilla, American middle-men obscured it from the view of American audiences.

While Tomoyuki Tanaka continued to search for the right project to bring his monster star back to the screen, an American filmmaker decided to develop an American feature film version of Godzilla. In 1983, director Steve Miner (director of *Friday the 13th Part 3D*) hired screenwriter Fred Dekker (writer and director of *Night of the Creeps*, *Monster Squad* and *RoboCop 3*) to write *Godzilla, King of the Mon-*

*There are certainly similarities to the Rankin/Bass* King Kong *cartoon here as well, but the linkage to* Jonny Quest *is the more overt.*

*sters in 3D*. The screenplay invites comparisons to *Gorgo* and the never-made *The Volcano Monsters*. Surprisingly little influence came from the various extant Godzilla movies by Toho.[8]

In Dekker's script, a nuclear accident involving an orbital missile platform uncovers an enormous, dead creature. The animal is a "proto-saur," a nuclear-powered ancestor of dinosaurs. Named Godzilla after a Japanese legend of a fire-breathing dragon, the creature turns out to be only a baby. A fully grown adult Godzilla destroys much of San Francisco searching for the baby, only to become further enraged upon discovering it to be dead. Experimental "Dragon" missiles, designed for use against nuclear weapons, are used against Godzilla. As a nuclear-powered "proto-saur," Godzilla strongly resembles a living nuclear bomb. A Dragon missile fired down his throat appears to kill him.[9]

Miner brought on artist William Stout to draw production art to help visualize the project. From Stout's illustrations, cartoonist Dave Stevens began work on the storyboards. Miner quickly found the support of the American special effects community. A special screening of the original Japanese *Gojira*, subtitled in English, was arranged in Century City. Jim Danforth brought top stop-motion animation specialists to the screening, an event which caused excitement and enthusiasm among the special effects artists. Rick Baker looked forward to developing a cable-controlled head while David Allen agreed to head the stop-motion animation team. Steve Cherkis built a three-foot stop-motion model of Godzilla, based on Stout's new Godzilla design, which more closely resembled a dinosaur than Toho's version but kept the trademark dorsal plates.[10]

With approval from Toho and Saperstein, Miner began pursuing financing from Hollywood. Although producers like Jon Peters and Keith Barish showed interest, the project never came to fruition. Hollywood believed Godzilla appealed only to children, and resisted spending $25 to 30 million on what would have been, in their opinion, a children's movie.[11]

Miner's proposed *Godzilla, King of the Monsters in 3D*, although unmade, offers considerable insight into American attitudes towards Godzilla. Dekker's script keeps the nuclear issue, but weakens it. The nuclear explosion that revives Godzilla is an accident, unlike the deliberate test explosion that awakened the 1954 Godzilla. Furthermore, as a "proto-saur," Godzilla is not a mutation caused by mankind's splitting of the atom; he was Godzilla already, tens of millions of years ago. Even the legend that gives him his name refers to a fire-breathing dragon.

The next proposed American Godzilla film would go even farther in changing the mythology. Early in the 1990s, TriStar Pictures, a division of Columbia Pictures, announced plans to develop a big-budget American version of Godzilla. Under a deal brokered by Henry G. Saperstein, TriStar optioned the rights to create an entirely new Godzilla series, divorced from its Japanese origins. The first draft screenplay by Ted Elliott and Terry Rossio (who together wrote Disney's *Aladdin*) presents Godzilla as a genetically engineered creature created by space aliens and placed in hibernation on Earth as a defense against the "doomsday beast," another alien monster capable of cobbling together genetic material from its victims into a super-monster called the Gryphon. In elements recalling Dekker's earlier script, Godzilla is revived by a nuclear accident and proceeds to attack San Francisco. In other similarities to Dekker's version, Elliott and Rossio depict a Godzilla whose powers existed independent of the nuclear accident which awoke him. In another striking similarity, an author writing a book called *The Waking Dragon*, a study of the world's many myths of fire-breathing dragons, names the creature Godzilla after a Japanese legend. The author joins the anti–Godzilla St. George Project, named for the legendary slayer of dragons.

The multiple dragon references in both scripts is no accident. As with Marvel and Hanna-Barbera's versions, American producers recreated Godzilla as a fire-breathing dragon. In the Marvel comic and in the Hanna-Barbera cartoon, Godzilla breathes flames, not an atomic ray.

An American Godzilla toy sold at the same

time, the Shogun Warrior Godzilla, was an 18-inch-tall plastic figure with a spring-loaded fist that could be launched by a push-button in the elbow, and a lever at the back of the head that emitted a plastic flame "tongue" from Godzilla's mouth.

This trend extended back as far as 1956, when Warner Brothers' release of *Gigantis the Fire Monster* referred to Godzilla's ray as "fiery breath." In the book *Legendary Horror Films*, Peter Guttmacher describes Godzilla's "searing radioactive breath," but merely writes that Gigantis "breathes fire."[12]

Critics Tom Shales and Rick Kogan number among the many who have inaccurately called the monster a fire-breather in their reviews.[13] Henry G. Saperstein licensed a Godzilla cigarette lighter in 1986; "It's great," Saperstein proudly announced. "You press the tail fins and the flame comes out of Godzilla's mouth."[14] In 1995, a springtime run of Godzilla movies on Ted Turner's TNT Network was advertised with a montage of scenes, concluding with a shot from *Terror of Mechagodzilla* in which billowing flames had been carefully superimposed in place of Godzilla's glowing blue ray.

Whenever possible, American companies had substituted fire for the atomic ray or obscured the nature of the ray. In his American incarnations, Godzilla had become a fire-breathing dragon instead of a symbol of the horror of nuclear war. Certainly the legend of a fire-breathing dragon carries rich connotations, with a mythological heritage much older than the Cold War. Nevertheless, Godzilla's role as a symbol of the nuclear age is central to the series, making Godzilla distinctive. Altering that aspect of Godzilla's character does violence to Toho's creation.

Cultural differences between Japan and America underlie this American transformation of Godzilla into a fire-breathing dragon. American monster movies in the 1950s and 1960s so overused the gimmick of radioactive mutation that it lost its expressive power and became a cliché. The makers of American monster movies, from upscale entries such as *Them!* and *The Beast from 20,000 Fathoms* to cheap quickies like *Attack of the Crab Monsters*, never used their films as platforms for discussions about nuclear policy. The moral dimensions of their films simply cautioned against scientific hubris of any variety. Radioactive-monster movies were largely indistinguishable from movies that used electricity, glandular transplants, or genetic experimentation as narrative gimmicks.

By contrast, the Japanese makers of *Godzilla* deliberately used their film to address Japanese fears and memories of nuclear war. As the only country in history to have experienced nuclear war firsthand, Japan's perspective on such issues naturally differed from the United States'. Japan's filmmakers worked in a country that did not manufacture, purchase, or test nuclear weapons. They made films for audiences living in a country whose military existed for the *sole* purpose of defending Japan from hostile outside forces. American filmmakers and American moviegoers, though, lived in a society that did manufacture, stockpile, and test nuclear weapons as a *proactive* defense against foreign enemies. The American culture that believed in a moral imperative to actively defend its national interests with nuclear weapons was fundamentally at odds with the very attitudes Ishiro Honda wanted Godzilla to symbolize.

American distributors and licensees did not actively censor Godzilla. There was no formal body reviewing Godzilla's subversive subtexts and declaring them anti–American. Instead, those individuals and companies who brought Godzilla to American theaters, television screens, and comic book shelves failed to recognize the subtext because of their cultural conditioning. Not seeing any particular value in Godzilla's back fins lighting up, a distributor might conclude that such an image detracted from the iconic familiarity of a fire-breathing dragon. Why use a glowing blue ray when American audiences would better respond to fiery breath?

Another aspect of this transformation of Godzilla into a dragon involved the shifting of responsibility away from human beings. The Japanese series clearly indicted human society as the creators of this terrible monster. Both the Dekker and the Elliott-Rossio screenplays posit a Godzilla independent of humanity. Dekker's version is a "proto-saur," whose nuclear characteristics are natural for his species. The TriStar Godzilla is the product of alien bioengineering, created especially to protect the Earth. Consequently, neither American Godzilla carries the allegorical weight of Toho's monster.

Even the design of the American Godzillas differed from Toho's icon. Iwao Mori and Ryosaku Takayama based the original Toho Godzilla on the then-common image of dinosaurs as upright beasts whose tails dragged on the ground. Over time, paleontologists revised this image, such that the modern depiction of dinosaurs like the Tyrannosaurus Rex shows a creature leaning forward with a stiff tail aimed backwards as counterbalancing support. Both American Godzilla designs adapted Godzilla to conform to this more-accurate dinosaur posture, abandoning the character's familiar silhouette.

Discussing *Godzilla, King of the Monsters in 3D*, director Miner said,

> Our goal was, instead of remaking a classic and automatically pissing off the people who loved the original, to take a good idea that we felt had not been executed very well and to do the film state of the art, Spielberg-style, using stop-motion animation and puppetry.[15]

Although Miner did not want to remake the original, he did say specifically that he wanted to provide Hollywood production values to "a good idea." Since Dekker's script contains none of the narrative or thematic ideas present in the Japanese Godzilla series, one can only conclude that the "good idea" Miner refers to is simply the idea of a giant monster attacking a metropolis. Of course, there have been many well-done American-made movies about giant monsters attacking cities. Calling another entry in that generic tradition "Godzilla," without utilizing the concepts that distinguished Godzilla from that tradition, is cynical.

The Hollywood attitude in 1983 saw Godzilla as an icon that only appealed to children. Most Americans know Godzilla more for *Godzilla vs. Megalon* than the more sober, sophisticated films of the early '60s. With this campy image of Godzilla as the standard public expectation, TriStar obviously needed to distinguish their version as being a serious, adult-oriented movie.

Ironically, this return had already occurred in Japan. *The Return of Godzilla* started a second cycle of films that ignored all of the original sequels, creating instead a new history for their monsters. The new films sported higher budgets, high-quality special effects, and Western-style realism.

While American producers attempted to recreate Godzilla in a form they hoped would appeal to adult Americans, little attention was paid to the fact that on the other side of the world, Godzilla had already come of age.

# Chapter 28

# The Return of Godzilla
## GOJIRA (GODZILLA)

*It's not every day monsters appear.*

— Prof. Hayashida

Japanese version: 103 minutes, Released December 15, 1984

Color, Widescreen

Produced by Tomoyuki Tanaka; associate producer Fumio Tanaka; directed by Koji Hashimoto; assistant director Takao Okawara; screenplay by Shuichi Nagahara; story by Tomoyuki Tanaka; music by Reijiro Koruko; Tokyo Symphony Orchestra conducted by Katsuaki Nakaya; songs: "Goodbye My Love" music by Takashi Miki and lyrics by Toyohisa Araki, sung by Yasuko Sawaguchi, "Godzilla" music by Reijiro Koroku and lyrics by Linda Henrick, sung by the Star Sisters; cinematography by Kazutami Hara; art direction by Akira Sakuragi; edited by Yoshitami Kuroiwa; special effects by Teruyoshi Nakano; special effects cinematography by Takeshi Yamamoto and Toshimitsu Oneda; special effects art director Yasuyuki Inoue; optical effects by Takeaki Tsukuda, Yoshio Ishii, Takeshi Miyanishi, and Yukio Manoda

Consultants to the production: Hitoshi Takeuchi (Professor Emeritus, Tokyo University), Hideo Aoki (military consultant), Yorihiko Ohsaki (Doctor of Engineering), Klein Uberstein (science fiction author), Sohichiro Tahara (journalist)

Starring Keiju Kobayashi (Prime Minister), Ken Tanaka (Goro Maki), Yasuko Sawaguchi (Naoko Okumura), Shin Takuma (Ken Okumura), Yosuke Natsuki (Professor Hayashida), Taketoshi Naito (Chief Cabinet Secretary Takegami), Tetsuya Takeda (Bum), Eitaro Ozawa (Finance Minister Kanzaki), Mizuho Suzuki (Foreign Minister Emori), Junkichi Orimoto (Defense Secretary Mori), Shinsuke Mikimoto (Chief of Staff Kakurai), Mikita Mori (Internal Affairs Secretary Okouchi), Nobuo Kaneko (Home Affairs Minister Isomura), Kiyoshi Yamamoto (Science and Technology Agency Director Kajita), Takeshi Kato (Internal Trade and Industry Minister Kasaoka), Yoshifumi Tajima (Environmental Director General Hidaka), Yasuhiko Kono (Maritime Forces Chief of Staff Imafuji), Isao Hirano (Air Force Chief of Staff Kiyohara), Kunio Murai (Secretary Henmi), Kenichi Urata (Secretary Ishimaru), Hiroshi Koizumi (Geologist Minami), Kei Sato (Chief Editor Godo), Takenori Emoto (Desk Editor Kitagawa), Takero Morimoto (Newscaster), Takashi Ebata (Yahata Maru Captain), Shigeo Kato and Sennosuke Tahara (Yahata Maru Crew), Shinpei Hayashiya (Cameraman Kamijo), Sho Hashimoto (Super X Commander Hagiyama), Kenji Fukuda (Super X Lieutenant), Yumiko Tanaka (Akemi), Tetsuya Ushio and Kensui Watanabe (Operators), Walter Nichols (Ambassador Chevsky), Luke Johnston (Captain Kathren), Dennis Falt (Soviet Submarine Captain), Nigel Reed (Soviet Sub Lieutenant), Terry Sonberg (Parasebo Crew Member), Koji Ishizaka (Nuclear Power Plant Technician), Hiroshi Kamayatsu (Shinkansen Passenger)

GODZILLA portrayed by Kenpachiro Satsuma

*An accident involving a Japanese fishing vessel reveals that the monster Godzilla, which attacked Tokyo 30 years ago, is still alive. Reporter Goro Maki finds that his story about Godzilla has been quashed by the government, afraid of starting a panic. When Godzilla destroys a Russian nuclear sub and nearly starts World War III in the process, the prime minister has no choice but to reveal the terrifying truth.*

*The Russian and American ambassadors lobby for the right to drop nuclear bombs on Godzilla, which Japan fervently resists: "We will not make, possess, or allow nuclear weapons. We cannot make an exception." Realizing that Godzilla feeds off radiation, the Self-Defense Force proposes sending in the Super X, an experimental flying tank, to shoot cadmium missiles down the creature's throat to poison his nuclear metabolism. As a backup plan, Professor Hayashida thinks he can trick Godzilla's natural homing instincts and lure the monster into a volcano.*

*When a Russian nuclear strike is accidentally triggered, despite the prime minister's firm objections, the situation becomes even more dire.*

Godzilla's long absence from the screen was not the result of any formal cancellation of the series. At no point did Toho's decision-makers sit down, review the declining box office performance of monster movies over the past decade, and say, "Okay, we're done with that." In fact, in the years between *Terror of Mechagodzilla* and *The Return of Godzilla*, several Godzilla projects were mooted, at various levels of seriousness. It is a long-standing practice for exploitation filmmakers to announce a title, maybe even publish an ad or two on the trade press, and then see what kind of interest gets stirred up. If enough potential buyers come forward to make the idea profitable even before the film has been made, then the exhibition commitments would be used as collateral to raise the funds to actually go and make the "pre-sold" film.

This strategy was tried on various occasions both by Toho itself and by American licensing partner Henry Saperstein. Toho put out feelers on behalf of *Space Godzilla*, *Minilla's Revenge*, and (in a nod to *The Exorcist*) *Godzilla vs. the Devil*.[1] UPA tried to drum up support for *Godzilla vs. Gargantua*, *The Resurrection of Godzilla*, and a feature version of Hanna-Barbera's cartoon series.[2]

The failure of the late-seventies films was a stumbling block that needed to be overcome. The licensing of the monster's image for merchandising had turned into a $33 million-a-year industry.[3] T-shirts, comic books, record albums, beach sandals, and dolls bearing the likeness of Japan's most internationally recognizable pop cultural icon brought Toho substantial profits.[4]

An estimated 65 million people had seen Godzilla's movies, and some 200,000 of them belonged to Godzilla fan clubs (there were several hundred). Of these, 10,000 formed a coalition called the Godzilla Resurrection Company which gathered over 40,000 signatures on a petition demanding a new Godzilla movie.[5] What turned the tide, strangely enough, was Disney.

In 1980, Toho Studios signed a deal with Disney to be the Japanese licensor of all Disney films, from its back catalogue of animated classics to its continuing output of live-action fam-

ily films. Distributing Disney films turned into one of the studio's most reliable sources of income.[6] At the same time, Toho took to reissuing some of its own past classics, like *Mothra vs. Godzilla* and *Invasion of Astro-Monster*. These drew surprisingly large crowds.[7] For Toho's 50th anniversary in 1982, they celebrated with a film festival, in which Godzilla movies drew larger crowds than other films like Akira Kurosawa's *The Seven Samurai*.[8] Most significantly, they held their own against the reissues of *Bambi* and *Pinocchio*.[9]

On December 26, 1983, Toho officially announced Godzilla's return.[10]

Tomoyuki Tanaka realized that there was money to made and artistic rewards to be reaped by resurrecting the monsters of the past in serious horror movies aimed at paranoid adults. The evidence was all around him: Filmmakers were constantly digging up the SF tropes of the mid-century and giving them a darker edge for a new era. *King Kong* had been revived for a 1976 remake with a grimmer tone, 1958's *It! The Terror from Beyond Space* was redressed as *Alien* (1979), Philip Kaufman put a nihilistic spin on his 1978 *Invasion of the Body Snatchers*, and John Carpenter's 1982 *The Thing* was so much more nightmarish than its 1951 source that it scarcely bears comparison. The future of Godzilla depended on returning to the darker style of the early, allegorical *Gojira*. Certainly *King Kong vs. Godzilla* held the record for audience size, but *Gojira* had a more attractive audience demographic composition. In order to win back the adult viewers who had defected during the seventies, Tanaka decided to abandon the fantastical approach. In fact, the new series of Godzilla movies would pick up where *Gojira* ended, thereby pretending that the preceding sequels never happened.

"This character change was responsible for his decline," Tanaka would admit later. "It was a mistake."[11] "The fans did not like Godzilla when he was good," agreed Toho spokesperson Masaru Yabe.[12]

Tanaka drafted a story outline with writer Akira Murao, *The Return of Godzilla*, introducing the idea that Godzilla needs to eat nuclear material and featuring a sequence in which he attacks a nuclear power plant. It was an idea that first surfaced in the Gamera films of the 1960s and Shochiku's *Guilala: The X from Outer Space*, but was so brilliant, so obvious, it was a wonder it had not been part of the Godzilla formula all along.

From this outline, Shuichi Nagahara wrote the screenplay. Nagahara also borrowed elements from Fred Dekker's unproduced *Godzilla, King of the Monsters in 3D*, namely the orbital missile platform, the Cold War tensions between the Soviets and the Americans, and the anti-nuclear missiles fired down Godzilla's throat. Familiar ideas from the past also returned, including an opening sequence on a fishing boat that could have been taken straight from *War of the Gargantuas*, and a familiar collection of reporters, scientists, and government officials. In structure and tone, the script owed much to *The Submersion of Japan*—a disaster movie framework that explores international politics with great earnestness. Like *Submersion of Japan*, *The Return of Godzilla* jumps around between special effects footage of a catastrophe, the ineffectual institutional response, the diplomatic relations with the rest of the world, and young lovers caught up in the chaos.

Ishiro Honda turned down Tanaka's request to direct the new *Gojira*. Honda felt very strongly that the series should have ended with the passing of his creator, saying, "Godzilla died when Eiji Tsuburaya died."[13] Honda also still smarted from the difficulties he faced during *Terror of Mechagodzilla*, when Tanaka often overruled his ideas and the script underwent numerous revisions while he was shooting.[14] Also at this time, Honda was involved in renewing the career of his longtime friend Akira Kurosawa, serving as assistant director on Kurosawa's 1980 comeback film *Kagemusha* and the 1985 Academy Award–winning *Ran*.

Akira Ifukube also declined to participate. Perhaps also unhappy about the creative decline of the series since his original involvement, Ifukube remained skeptical of the whole affair. Once informed of Godzilla's new height, 30 meters taller than his original 50-meter size, Ifukube replied, "I do not write music for 80-meter monsters."[15]

Ultimately, Tanaka hired Kohji Hashimoto to direct the new picture. His only other science fiction experience was 1983's *Sayonara Jupiter*, adapted from a novel by *Submersion of Japan* author Sakyo Komatsu. Although *Sayonara Jupiter* was an embarrassing commercial flop, it showed Hashimoto had the ability to supervise a special effects–driven production in the ponderous style that was now the rage. That Hashimoto had been on the crew of *The Submersion of Japan* was an important résumé item as well.

Certainly Hashimoto approached his task seriously. "In the first Godzilla movie in 1954 ... the message was against nuclear testing. This time the theme is broader — the risk of nuclear energy in all its forms. This is the message I want to spread to the world through this film."[16]

Indeed, *The Return of Godzilla* shoves the nuclear issue aggressively to the front of its stage, perhaps more forcefully than any other Godzilla movie. "Godzilla is the son of the atomic bomb. He is a nightmare created out of the darkness of the human soul. He is the sacred beast of the apocalypse," Tanaka said.[17]

The original *Gojira* allowed Japanese filmmakers to discuss Hiroshima, Nagasaki, and the Bikini Island tests in a sort of code, using Godzilla as a symbol for ideas that were too painful to address directly. The 1984 *Gojira* offered a similar opportunity. "We wanted to show how easily a [nuclear] incident could occur today, but vivid images of nuclear war are taboo," explained Tanaka. "Godzilla, on the other hand, can bring the message to light and still be entertaining."[18]

In addition to illuminating Cold War nuclear fears, *The Return of Godzilla* allowed Toho's creative team to comment on Japan's economic prosperity. After the traumatic devastations of the 1923 earthquake, the firebombings of Tokyo, and the atomic bombings of Hiroshima and Nagasaki, the Japanese people came to view their society's prosperity as fragile. Godzilla's attack on the modern, Western-style skyscrapers of Tokyo's Shinjuku section, what Tanaka called "the vain symbols of these abundant days," pointedly demonstrated how easy it could be to undo that prosperity.[19] In one scene, the finance minister frets aloud to the prime minister that if Godzilla attacks Tokyo, it would mean the end of Japan's economy. Tanaka hoped to make the Japanese audiences experience that crisis vicariously: "Japan is rich and people can buy whatever they want. But what is behind that wealth? Nothing very spiritual. Everyone's so concerned with the material, and then Godzilla rips it all apart. I suspect that is good for us to see."[20]

One striking and memorable sequence involves the prime minister's decision to forbid the use of nuclear weapons against Godzilla. In the original series sequels, a spokesperson for the government usually announced that no nuclear weapons would be used against the monster, but such scenes were usually dismissed without any elaboration. *The Return of Godzilla* shows the audience for the first time the difficult debate behind this announcement.

First, the Soviet and American ambassadors make their case to the prime minister (Keiju Kobayashi). Kohji Hashimoto stages this scene with powerful visual compositions, as the prime minister is seen in profile as the ambassadors rant at him from the far left and far right of the screen. We cannot see the prime minister's face, but we feel the pressure he faces. The only thing the Americans and the Soviets have agreed on in decades of Cold War is that nuclear missiles should be dropped on Japan.

The scene cuts to a private meeting as the prime minister asks his cabinet ministers for their advice. They estimate the total damage caused by a nuclear attack would probably be less than that caused by Godzilla. On the other hand, they cannot accurately predict the long-term damage caused by fallout. Further complicating the matter, Godzilla's attacks could ruin Japan economically. They cannot be certain that nuclear bombs would kill Godzilla, yet refusing the Americans and the Soviets would isolate Japan diplomatically. There is no obvious answer, only grave doubts and fears.

The prime minister returns to the diplomats and restates Japan's famed "three principles": non-production, non-possession, and non-introduction of nuclear weapons into Japan. "We cannot make an exception," he intones. The American ambassador is enraged: "This is no time to be discussing principles!" The prime minister replies, "No, it is the right time when principles are at stake."

Neither ambassador accepts the answer, leaving the prime minister to negotiate with the Soviet and American leaders directly. As he later describes it to an aide, "I said that if Godzilla appeared in your countries, decided to attack your cities, would you have the courage to use nuclear weapons knowing that many of your people would be killed?"

Keiju Kobayashi was the star of *The Submersion of Japan*, and he brings the same gravitas to this role. He plays the prime minister with restraint and dignity. With little dialogue, he expresses the awesome responsibility this man faces as he tries to save his country from an almost supernatural foe. Joining Kobayashi on the cast are several familiar faces from the original series. Yosuke Natsuki, best known as Detective Shindo from *Ghidrah, The Three-Headed Monster*, portrays Professor Hayashida, a man who lost his family to Godzilla in 1954 and has been studying the creature ever since. (It is tempting to see him as having been based on Dr. Takiguchi from the Marvel Comics series.)

Yoshifumi Tajima and Kunio Murai play government ministers, and Hiroshi Koizumi makes a brief appearance as geologist Minami. One almost imagines that Koizumi should have earned an honorary degree in geology from some Japanese university, given how often he played one on screen.

Unfortunately, Kobayashi's understated performance stands out from the lifeless characterization of the young heroes Goro and Naoko, played by Ken Tanaka and Yasuko Sawaguchi. The cast take their parts seriously and with sincerity, but never achieve much emotional depth.

Instead, the strength of the film lies in its thoughtful script and effective visuals. "We spared no expense in creating a Godzilla for the '80s," Tanaka boasted.[21] Much of the film's record-setting $6 million budget was spent on Teruyoshi Nakano's special effects. Nakano himself considered the film his favorite of the

Godzilla films and the best example of his work in the genre.[22]

Noboyuki Yasamaru, the veteran suit-maker whose monster creations included Gorosaurus, Hedorah, and Gigan, designed the new Godzilla costume. He brought back design features not seen since the 1950s: ears, four toes per foot, staggered rows of dorsal plates, and fangs. His Godzilla sported a long tail with a rough underside, red-brown eyes, and no musculature around the shoulders. Yasamaru included a system of pneumatic tubes inside the costume so that the operator could manipulate the eyes and jaw, as well as snarling the upper lip. For the first time, Godzilla could show facial expression on screen.[23]

The completed rubber suit weighed 240 pounds. Kenpachiro Satsuma, who played Hedorah and Gigan in the seventies, took over the role of Godzilla. In fact, Satsuma had not been the first choice to assume the role, and Yasamaru had designed the costume for actor Hiroshi Yamawaki, a larger man than Satsuma. When Yamawaki backed out at the last minute, Nakano turned to Satsuma. This meant that the actor had to perform inside a costume that was too large for him. "It was hell to act in it," Satsuma remembers.

Satsuma requested that tiny holes be drilled in the fingers so that his sweat could drip out of the costume. A man in phenomenal physical condition, proficient at karate, judo, and horseback riding, Satsuma could withstand only ten minutes inside the suit at a time. Toho's special effects staff estimated that a normal person would faint after two minutes.[24] Performing the role of Godzilla was so physically taxing, Satsuma lost twelve pounds during filming.[25]

In addition to the traditional suitmation techniques, Teruyoshi Nakano also built a mechanical robot for use in some scenes. The 18-foot fully articulated robot, called a "cybot" in Toho's press releases, could display a sophisticated degree of motion and facial expression. Toho proudly boasted that the hydraulically operated, computer-controlled cybot would appear in 70 percent of the special effects scenes. In fact, the cybot served largely as a marketing ploy, receiving significant press exposure. The cybot went on a promotional tour to advertise the movie, but appeared on screen only for close-ups of Godzilla's face.[26]

In the thirty years since Godzilla was first designed, Tokyo's architecture had grown. In order to better match the taller skyscrapers of downtown Tokyo, Nakano increased Godzilla's height from 50 to 80 meters (260 feet). This forced Nakano to decrease the scale of the miniatures from $\frac{1}{25}$ down to $\frac{1}{40}$, with a corresponding decrease in detailing. Nakano tried to disguise the less realistic miniatures with clever staging and careful compositions.[27]

The return to high-speed photography, abandoned in the seventies for cost reasons, helped greatly to restore a sense of scale. Borrowing from his innovations in *Terror of Mechagodzilla*, Nakano shoots Godzilla consistently from a very low angle, often back lit. The monster scenes are also staged at night, a throwback to the original *Gojira*, helping to both build the mood and hide flaws in the miniatures. Sound effects, too, helped make the visuals convincing. In a return to the 1950s production values, Godzilla's footsteps now echoed with a forceful boom.

Complementing the visuals, Reijiro Koruko provided the score. After Ifukube's refusal, Tanaka's decision to hire Koruko surprised many. Like director Hashimoto, Koruko lacked experience in the genre. In a sharp contrast to the small orchestras used by Ifukube and Sato, Koruko scored his music for the Tokyo Symphony Orchestra. The full, lush sound filled out the stereophonic soundtrack admirably; it is arguably the best non–Ifukube score in the series. Koruko composed a lyrical, elegiac piece for the end of the film, and the mournful music, combined with images of Godzilla trapped in lava, mirrored the ending of *Rodan* in some respects.

On top of the $6 million spent in production, Toho also poured in $1.7 million in promotion. Taking a cue from the Americans' method of promoting movies through merchandising, Toho licensed a wide array of products from chewing gum to T-shirts. A special telephone number was set up for fans to call and hear Godzilla's trademark roar.[28]

As Godzilla's thirtieth anniversary film, and the first in nine years, the new *The Return of Godzilla* earned considerable international publicity. For the week of its December 15 opening, *The Return of Godzilla* drew 800,000 viewers across 234 theaters.[29] Competing with *Ghostbusters* and *Gremlins* for its audience in the highly competitive Christmas holiday season, *The Return of Godzilla*'s eight-week run ultimately brought in 1.7 billion yen ($6.2 million), making it the second highest grossing Japanese-produced feature of the year.[30]

With some bold decisions and savvy strategies, Tomoyuki Tanaka and his team had successfully reinvented Godzilla, and put the problems of the past behind them. The problems of the future, though, would be a different story.

## Chapter 29

# *Godzilla 1985*
## GOJIRA (GODZILLA)

*He's the product of civilization. Men are the only real monsters. Godzilla is more like a nuclear weapon.... A living nuclear weapon, destined to walk the Earth forever. Indestructible. A victim of the modern age.*

— Prof. Hayashida

U.S. version (New World Pictures): 91 minutes, Released August 23, 1985, MPAA rating: PG
Color, Widescreen
U.S. version produced by Anthony Randel; directed by R.J. Kizer; screenplay by Lisa Tomei; additional music for U.S. version by Chris Young; additional U.S. cinematography by Steve Dubin; edited by Michael Spence
U.S. version also stars: Raymond Burr (Steve Martin), Warren Kemmerling (General Goodhue), James Hess (Colonel Rascher), Travis Swords (Major McDonough), Crawford Binion (Lieutenant), Justin Gocke (Kyle), Bobby Brown, Patrick Feren, Mark Simon, Shepard Stern, Alan D. Waserman

*A Russian nuclear submarine is destroyed, inflaming international tensions. As the Cold Warriors step up their angry rhetoric, the Japanese government reveals that Godzilla, thought dead for thirty years, has returned. The Pentagon seeks out retired reporter Steve Martin, a firsthand witness to Godzilla's original attack. His advice: there's nothing you can do.*

*The Japanese military unveils an experimental flying fortress called the Super X, which engages Godzilla in battle in downtown Tokyo and seemingly subdues him. The situation changes when a Russian nuclear missile is launched from space at Godzilla, threatening all of Japan. The Americans succeed in exploding the bomb in the stratosphere, but the resulting electromagnetic pulse revives Godzilla.*

*The last hope for mankind is Professor Hayashida's device to lure Godzilla into the volcano at Mt. Mihara...*

The dubbed international version of *The Return of Godzilla* played in the United Kingdom soon after the Japanese premiere. However, the film did not arrive in the United States until a year later. At first, Toho approached Hollywood with an asking price of $5 million. After meetings with Paramount and Universal, Toho spokesperson Kei Nakagawa announced that Hollywood's best offer was a mere $2 million. For months, the impasse blocked any agreement.[1]

A variety of important factors influenced these negotiations. From Toho's standpoint, *Gojira*'s remarkable commercial success in Japan proved the film's worth. Toho felt the $5 million price for foreign distribution rights was perfectly reasonable for such a demonstrably popular movie.

The Japanese film industry never faced the kind of antitrust legislation that had forced American movie studios to sell their theaters. In the United States, movie studios acted only as producers and distributors, while independent third parties owned the theaters. In Japan, the film companies were vertically integrated. Toho Studios was and is Japan's most powerful studio, owning 25 percent of all Japanese theaters, 36 of which stand on prime real estate in Tokyo, Osaka and Nagoya. Toho's real estate holdings, in fact, are estimated to be worth 510 billion yen. Toho's powerful grip on theaters is so vast that Toho makes 64 percent of their total revenues from motion pictures, while competitive studios like Nikkatsu and Toei earn less than 25 percent of their total profits from movies, and Shochiku relies on movies for less than half of their income. This vertical integration means that most of *Return of Godzilla*'s 1.7 billion yen earnings in box office receipts went directly to Toho.[2]

By contrast, the United States has frowned on such monopolies. Independent theater companies therefore keep a large percentage of the box office gross before it passes on to the distributor and producer. From Toho's standpoint, the commercial success of Godzilla movies in the United States put money in the pockets of Americans far more than it returned profits to the Japanese producers. Toho's insistence on a high price for the distribution rights to *Gojira* reflected their intent not to be cheated.

Across the ocean, Hollywood companies approached the negotiations from a very different standpoint. Only two years earlier, Steve Miner had approached the same studios with the proposal for *Godzilla, King of the Monsters in 3D*. That film and *The Return of Godzilla* targeted the same audience. Hollywood had rejected Miner on the grounds that his projected $25 million budget was too high for the kind of business they expected to get from children and the exploitation-movie audience to which Godzilla traditionally appeals. Were a major studio to have picked up *Gojira* at the $5 million price tag, they would then have had to pay for distribution expenses, such as prints and advertising. Hollywood studios generally spent around $10 million on those expenses at that time, which would have brought the total bill up to $15 million, not much less than the amount they already decreed too high for an American-made Godzilla movie.

Toho was not likely to find a sympathetic ear at the major Hollywood studios. Instead, their best chance lay with a smaller, independent distributor. Smaller distribution companies have the ability to market movies to specialized audiences with inexpensive promotional techniques that the major studios, burdened with high overhead costs, rarely employ. Godzilla's past efforts had been distributed in North America by smaller indie companies like Embassy Pictures, AIP, and UPA. By the mid-eighties, none of these were options.

Meanwhile, an upstart distributor called New World struggled to establish itself. Roger Corman had started New World Pictures in the 1970s, and under his guidance the company had turned Toho's *Submersion of Japan* into *Tidal Wave*, and perfected the art of acquiring foreign-made genre pictures on the cheap and turning them into profitable exploitation fare, often with heavy editing and substantial alterations.

Corman sold the firm in 1983 to a pair of entertainment lawyers, Lawrence Kuppin and Harry Evans Sloan.[3] When Kuppin and Sloan bought New World for $12 million, they reasoned that the market was ripe for a new exploitation film distributor to take up the slack left by the passing of AIP and Embassy. Under Corman, New World earned annual profits between three and four million dollars. Under Kuppin and Sloan, however, the company lost $4.8 million in 1983 and barely broke even in 1984.

Hoping to turn their fortune around, Kuppin and Sloan brought in longtime film industry veteran Robert Rehme as CEO. Under Rehme, New World bid for Toho's *Return of Godzilla*. Unaccustomed to spending even as much as $1 million for the rights to the movies they distribute, they balked at Toho's asking price. In the end, New World purchased the North American distribution rights for only $500,000, far less than Toho had wanted, and only a quarter of what big Hollywood had offered.[4]

New World got a bargain. The film, retitled *Godzilla 1985* for its American release, turned out to have many inexpensive routes for marketing. One route was the thirtieth anniversary, which somehow managed to last three years. The true anniversary occurred in 1984, thirty years after the Japanese release of *Gojira*. Even though the American press had given considerable coverage to the Japanese anniversary the previous year, *Godzilla 1985* rode a wave of publicity for the anniversary as well. The publicity continued into 1986, the thirtieth anniversary of the American release of *Godzilla, King of the Monsters*.

Some of the marketing overlapped Toho's efforts in Japan, including the promotional tour by the cybot Godzilla. In a significant windfall for New World, Dr Pepper had *already* signed an agreement with Toho and Henry Saperstein to use Godzilla in a television commercial campaign. The $10 million campaign had in fact already been negotiated before New World bought *Godzilla 1985*.

When New World's senior vice-president of publicity and promotion, Rusty Citron, heard about the Dr Pepper deal, he flew to Dallas to meet with Dr Pepper's executives. After a three-hour meeting, Dr Pepper agreed to combine their advertising campaign with New World's marketing.[5] Dr Pepper financed New World's extensive reworking of the film, and in return New World prominently featured Dr Pepper in the new, American-shot sequences.[6] The Godzilla–Dr Pepper television and radio commercials, with the catch-phrase "Out of the Ordinary," also promoted the movie.[7] Additional tie-ins were arranged with Konica Film, Hallmark Cards, and Scope mouthwash(!).[8]

Citron took pride in finding a "singular and cost-efficient approach" to marketing each of New World's releases. "We are rediscovering the lost art of publicity," he declared. With publicity budgets 40 percent lower than other distributors, New World relied on Citron's eight-person staff to devise the kind of inexpensive publicity-grabbing stunts that characterized the exploitation film distributors of the 1950s and 1960s.[9]

To this end, Citron found what was to be perhaps his second most fortuitous piece of free publicity, after the Dr Pepper tie-in. Just as Joseph Levine shot new scenes with Raymond Burr as reporter Steve Martin to Americanize *Gojira*, Citron brought Burr back to reprise his role 30 years later. New World producer Anthony Randel hired screenwriter Lisa Tomei to rework the Japanese version and include new scenes with Burr and Dr Pepper. Randel recognized the promotional value of Burr reprising his role: "It's a revitalization of '50s nostalgia, that sort of Saturday matinee fun type of picture." Randel found Burr eager to participate: "He liked it, thought it had philosophical merit and decided to take the part."[10]

Burr recalled:

> They called me on the phone, said, "We have another picture, we're going to cut it the same way we did the first one...." For the first one I

got paid a great deal of money for one day's work. The second one was also shot in one day, and I also got a great deal of money for that. But when they asked me to do it the second time, I said, "Certainly," and everybody thought I was out of my mind. But it wasn't the large sum of money. It was the fact that first of all, I kind of liked *Godzilla*, and where do you get the opportunity to play yourself 30 years later? ... I wasn't bad in the second *Godzilla*. I wasn't good. I was just nothing in it. We didn't call him Steve Martin any more; we called him Mr. Martin in the second picture because Steve Martin the comedian came up in between times.[11]

Burr's return provided a useful hook for the American press, and newspaper coverage for *Godzilla 1985* included detailed descriptions of the connections between the new film and the original. At the same time, NBC asked Burr to return to his role as Perry Mason for a made-for-TV movie. Press coverage for *Perry Mason Returns* also reported Burr's concurrent role in *Godzilla 1985*, thus providing New World with even more free publicity.[12]

As critic Tom Shales noted, Burr appeared in the original *Godzilla* "as [a] reporter ... who always seemed to be occupying a window with the best possible vantage point on the carnage, yet never met any of the other lead characters." For *Godzilla 1985*, screenwriter Tomei kept Mr. Martin even farther away from the action, as he spends the movie watching the events unfold on a giant TV screen in the Pentagon. This meant the Japanese footage did not have to be re-edited around a character who could not be seen in the same shot as the other actors, and provided an excuse for reporter Martin not to interact with the Japanese cast. Although Burr played the role with the same graveness and sincerity as Keiju Kobayashi, the rest of the new American footage injected a note of self-conscious humor ill-suited to the deadpan Japanese footage.

Producer Randel and editor Michael Spence began by recutting the Japanese footage to suit New World's needs. According to R.J. Kizer, the director they hired to shoot their new material, "[T]he editorial decisions fell under four categories: (1) have Godzilla appear earlier in the story; (2) slant the story to a pro–American, anti–Russian attitude (the management of New World was cozying up to Reagan and his "evil empire" outlook); (3) eliminate any miniature effects that looked hokey; and (4) tighten up running time."[13]

Spence disputes Kizer's claim that any political slanting was imposed by New World's management, but agreed that the changes they made shifted the film's tone. "I think it was felt at New World that the picture was too concerned with the anti-nuclear issues and too 'talky.' Our instructions were to make it play like a [genre] picture. Emphasize the action, etc."[14]

The Americanized *Godzilla 1985* changed the original in many significant respects. Bob Briggert, supervising sound editor, recut the soundtrack, moving Koruko's music around and adding new music by Chris Young. Some of Nakano's best effects shots (including a beautiful shot of Godzilla reflected in the glass windows of a skyscraper) were deleted, and the rest were re-edited. In the original, a crowd of rubberneckers gather at Godzilla's feet after his apparent death from the Super X cadmium missile assault. Revived by the nuclear pulse, he rises up and casts an ominous shadow across the crowd as they flee in panic. In the American version, the shot of Godzilla's shadow falling on the panicking crowd is inserted into Godzilla's arrival in Tokyo, although in all of the wide shots of that sequence it is clear that there is no crowd on which the shadow could fall. In their reediting, New World damaged the continuity, logic, and believability of the original version.

In the original, a giant sea louse attacks Goro aboard the shipwreck, and it later turns out to be a once-normal creature that lived parasitically off Godzilla. After consuming enough of Godzilla's irradiated blood, the bug mutated to monstrous dimensions. In *Godzilla 1985*, no explanation is ever given for the giant louse, leaving the opening sequence a baffling anomaly.

Even fundamentally important elements of the plot, logical and well-developed in the original, became silly in the American version. In the Japanese cut, Professor Hayashida theorizes that Godzilla possesses a homing instinct similar to that of birds, and his sudden departure from the power plant was a natural instinctive reaction he and the nearby migrating bird flock experienced simultaneously. In the U.S. edition, Hayashida announces Godzilla is attracted by bird calls, a theory that seems much less plausible, and less consistent with what audiences expect from such a gargantuan god-like creature.

Whereas some of these changes created continuity errors where there were none, left plot elements unexplained, and reduced the logic of the story, some changes were dictated by the political climate. Many critics recognized the strong political statements inherent in the original. Reviewing the Japanese edition of *Gojira*, Don Richie told the Reuters Press Service, "Poor little Japan is shown in the middle. The United States is on one side, the Soviet Union on the other, and both want to use Japan as a nuclear testing ground. It's all political status quo, a fable of Japan's present predicament."[15]

Tanaka believed the political allegory to be at the core of the film: "The main difficulty is the control of nuclear weapons because man made them and controls them and man can't be trusted."[16]

In developing this theme, the original version makes clear that no one side has either the moral authority to use such weapons, or even the full control over the arsenal they have. Both the Soviets and the Americans seem trigger-happy in their desperate demands to bomb Godzilla, and their extreme reluctance to yield to Japan's prime minister. In the end, the Soviets launch a missile by accident, and although the Americans manage to stop it from hitting Tokyo, the after-effects revive Godzilla and destroy Japan's only successful military defense, the Super X.

By depicting the Americans and the Soviets as moral equals, and the Japanese as principled victims caught in the crossfire, Toho's version was unlikely to find a sympathetic audience in Reagan's America. In order not to offend American patriotic sensibilities, New World altered the relative roles of the two Cold War superpowers. Godzilla's attack on the Russian submarine was shortened and the Russian dialogue subtitled differently so that the Soviets now fired on their attacker with little provocation. The scene in which the American ambassador points to the Soviet ambassador and shouts, "He's right!" ended up on the cutting room floor, as did his line, "This is no time to be discussing principles!" (although reviewers ended up quoting the line in the American press anyway). Gone, too, was the dramatic and thoughtful sequence showing the prime minister's behind-the-scenes debate considering whether or not to allow a nuclear strike.

In the American version, when the prime minister refuses to permit the use of nuclear weapons against Godzilla, the American ambassador agrees without reluctance and the prime minister never has to argue directly with the U.S. president. By contrast, the Russians double-cross the Japanese, agreeing to the prime minister but then preparing a missile for launch anyway. The sequence on the Soviet ship in Tokyo Bay keeps the Russian language dialogue from the Japanese version, but with new subtitles. Whereas the original shows a Russian soldier heroically sacrificing his life in an attempt to prevent the missile launch, *Godzilla 1985* depicts a callous, duplicitous soldier boasting, "I'm the only one who can do it. I've got to launch that missile."

Cultural critic Anthony Enns notes that *Godzilla 1985* creates "a fantasy that rationalizes the need not only for nuclear weapons, but also for America's role as the defender of the free world.... At the same time the viewer witnesses the horror of using such weapons, they are simultaneously encouraged to believe that these weapons are necessary."[17]

Although this alteration better conformed to Rambo-era American attitudes, New World's newly shot sequences undermined even that. The Pentagon officials appear stupid and insensitive, buffoons compared to the Soviet foes. Worst of the lot, Travis Swords' Major McDonough responds to footage of Godzilla's rampage with such remarks as, "That's quite an urban renewal program they've got going over there." Such facetious retorts were the stuff of John Belushi's *Godzilla vs. Megalon* on NBC or Comedy Central's *Mystery Science Theater*

*3000*; to incorporate them directly into the film itself subverted the drama.

According to director Kizer:

> My understanding of the original incarnation of New World's *Godzilla 1985* was to have it played as tongue-in-cheek. Not so much with the Japanese footage, but most definitely with the new American footage. The first American script I read was filled with *Dr. Strangelove*–like dialogue. When I was first asked to come on to the project, the actor they were considering to star was Leslie Nielsen. This was mainly because they thought Raymond Burr would either be uninterested or too expensive. By the time I was hired, Mr. Burr did agree to star in the film, and suddenly the whole tone of the enterprise shifted.
>
> In fact, when I first met Mr. Burr at the Mondrian Hotel the evening before the shoot, he answered the door with words to the effect of, "Godzilla is a symbol of the nuclear menace threatening mankind." His tone and manner clearly told me that he took the allegorical aspects of Godzilla quite seriously indeed. Prior to this meeting, weeks had been spent watering down the "humor." What I found interesting was that Tony Randel's interpretation had shifted. Before, he was gung-ho for the *Dr. Strangelove* approach, but after Mr. Burr was hired he started back-pedaling away. It was decided to let the major be the comic foil, while all the others characters would be played straight. All this led to the alienation of the writer.[18]

Nevertheless, the American edition has its strengths. The dramatic opening title sequence by Ernest D. Farino, Jr., rates as the best in the series, and far more imaginative than the Japanese version. New World emphasized Godzilla's indestructibility, making him more powerful and awesome than in Toho's film. On a related note, the *Rodan*-inspired ending seems awkward in the Japanese cut — with Keiju Kobayashi almost in tears over the defeat of a terror that laid his nation to waste. The American version provides a better lead-up to this ending, with Godzilla clearly depicted as both a sympathetic character and a deadly menace. Burr provides a elegy for the beast as its screeches a painful cry from the volcano (a speech which, by the way, Burr wrote himself):

> Nature has a way sometimes of reminding Man of just how small he is. She occasionally

throws up the terrible offsprings of our pride and carelessness to remind us of how puny we really are in the face of a tornado, an earthquake, or a Godzilla. The reckless ambitions of Man are often dwarfed by their dangerous consequences. For now, Godzilla, that strangely innocent and tragic monster, has gone to earth. Whether he returns or not or is never again seen by human eyes, the things he has taught us remain.

Another American improvement relates to the revisionist history of the new series. Toho hoped to jump back to the original *Godzilla* and pick up without any acknowledgment of the previous sequels. However, *Godzilla* ended with the affirmative death of Godzilla at the hands of Dr. Serizawa, with its sequels following the exploits of a second Godzilla, introduced in 1955. *The Return of Godzilla* made claim to being the continued adventures of the same creature seen thirty years earlier, with no explanation given for its remarkable resurrection. *Godzilla 1985* provides a scene with Mr. Martin cautioning his Pentagon colleagues, "Just for the record, 30 years ago, they never found any corpse." Far from a satisfying answer (did the dying Dr. Serizawa hallucinate that skeleton?), it is at least an answer.

The whipsaw turns between contradictory tones left *Godzilla 1985* a confused mess. The seriousness of the Japanese version remains, for the most part, alongside self-consciously campy scenes with joking Pentagon officials slurping Dr Pepper. Spence put together a terrific trailer, playing up the camp aspects with a dry wit that earned the ad an Honorable Mention at the 1985 Key Art Awards[19]:

*(In white letters printed on a black screen, accompanied by the deep voice of a narrator:)*

In 1956 ... he first appeared on motion picture screens across the country.

His impact on audiences was instantaneous and unprecedented.

His acting technique was revolutionary. His presence ... overwhelming.

He possessed more raw talent than any performer of his generation.

He soon became an international legend, a giant who took the world by storm.

Then, suddenly, at the height of his fame, he retired from motion pictures.

*Now he is back.*

And he's more magnificent, more glamorous, more devastating than ever.

Prepare yourself.

The greatest star of all has returned.

*Godzilla 1985!*

In theaters and on videotape, New World preceded the film with Marv Newland's extremely brief animated short *Bambi Meets Godzilla*, a black and white cartoon from 1969 showing Godzilla stomping on Bambi.[20]

In its North American theatrical run, *Godzilla 1985* barely broke even. New World spent a total of $3 million on the rights, new footage, and advertising.[21] With all of the serendipitous promotion from the thirtieth anniversary, the Dr Pepper campaign, and NBC's *Perry Mason Returns*, New World managed to get more publicity than they paid for. When New World released *Godzilla 1985* on home video in 1986, they again benefited from free publicity.

In 1986, ongoing Perry Mason movies on NBC kept *Godzilla 1985* in the papers via interviews with Raymond Burr.[22] Even more helpful was the true American anniversary of Godzilla, thirty years after Joseph Levine's release. Henry Saperstein, president of UPA, celebrated the event with Godzilla-themed retrospective film festivals at the New York Museum of Art, Washington's Kennedy Arts Center, Boston's Emerson College, Philadelphia's Theater of Living Arts, Chicago's Facets Multimedia, and several major universities. Dr Pepper continued its Godzilla-based "Out of the Ordinary" campaign, introducing "Newzilla," a love interest for the giant monster. New World's video release of *Godzilla 1985* coincided with video releases of *Godzilla, King of the Monsters, Mothra vs. Godzilla, Godzilla vs. Monster Zero* (a.k.a. *Invasion of Astro-Monster*), and *Terror of Mechagodzilla*.[23] In this climate of strong interest in Godzilla, the video version of *Godzilla 1985* brought $2 million in profits back to New World, a third of the company's profits for the entire year.[24]

*Godzilla 1985* turned New World around, bringing the struggling company back to financial security. After the film's success on home video, New World's stock doubled in value.[25]

However, with all of the free publicity, New World only realized meaningful profits on the video release. Without the benefit of so much related promotion, future Godzilla movies would not likely be so successful.

For the long run, several bad precedents had been set. The clumsy Americanization of *Godzilla 1985* invited a severe thrashing from movie critics. Tom Shales felt "the comic trailer was more entertaining than the picture," and complained, "[O]ne can laugh at the bad dubbing of Japanese actors ... for just so long before the jokiness pales."[26] Also writing for the *Washington Post*, Michael Hill called it "the long-unawaited sequel."[27] Rick Kogan, film critic for the *Chicago Tribune*, decreed it "a thundering dud," and concluded, "[H]eavily laden with antinuclear messages, bad dubbing and worse dialogue, *Godzilla 1985* is a pale imitation of the original film."[28] *Playboy*'s Bruce Williamson wrote of "the god-awful *Godzilla 1985*," "[T]he Japanese-to-English dubbing is so out of sync and ludicrous that I half expected an end credit giving a nod of acknowledgment to Woody Allen."[29] An uncredited syndicated reviewer summed up the feelings of most critics: "[T]his updated ... production seems too colorful and slick to maintain the campy effect that marked the black and white versions."[30]

In the minds of most American reviewers and moviegoers, Godzilla's appeal lay in campy, "So-Bad-They're-Good" B-movies.[31] Whatever seriousness of purpose or creative effort the Japanese filmmakers put into their work went by American viewers without notice. Although *The Return of Godzilla* eschewed the silliness of past entries, *Godzilla 1985* counteracted it with a promotional campaign highlighting the campy aspects, of which there were few. New World set up unattainable audience expectations.*

Many of the criticisms leveled at the picture actually apply only to New World's Americanization. This distinction, however, was too subtle for most reviewers to make. Many sources claimed New World had actually produced *Godzilla 1985* themselves[32]; others believed that Toho had shot the scenes with Raymond Burr out of a fear that Americans could not relate to an all–Japanese cast.[33] *The Detroit News'* Peter Ross even asserted that the dubbing was intentionally bad.[34]

For the United States, Godzilla had been firmly entrenched as a campy star of low-grade movies aimed at an exploitation audience. Ironically, Toho meanwhile aggressively revamped the series into a mature, highly political one aimed at adults. The two markets had started to diverge and, with the next film, would split apart completely. The second Godzilla series would continue, but without an American audience.

---

*In an interesting coincidence, as part of Toho's 50th anniversary celebrations in 1982, a subtitled, unedited print of the original* Gojira, *sans Raymond Burr, played at the Joseph Papp Public Theater in Manhattan and the Hirshhorn Museum in Washington, D.C., along with several classics by Akira Kurosawa. In a subtitled form, this oft-ridiculed monster movie received the same treatment as an art movie.*

# Chapter 30

# Godzilla vs. Biollante

## GOJIRA VS. BEORANTE*
## (GODZILLA AGAINST BIOLLANTE)

*Godzilla and Biollante aren't monsters. It's the unscrupulous scientists who create them who are monsters.*

— Dr. Shiragami

Japanese version: 104 minutes, December 16, 1989
Color, Widescreen
Produced by Tomoyuki Tanaka; associate producer Shogo Tomiyama; directed by and screenplay by Kazuki Omori; assistant director Hideyuki Inoue; story by Shinichiro Kobayashi; music by Koichi Sugiyama, arranged and conducted by David Howell; Godzilla themes by Akira Ifukube; cinematography by Yudai Kato; art direction by Shigekazu Ikuno; edited by Michiko Ikeda; special effects by Koichi Kawakita; special effects assistant director Kyotaka Matsumoto; special effects art direction by Tetsuzo Osawa; special effects cinematography by Kenichi Eguchi; optical effects by Yoshiyuki Kishimoto and Horiaki Hojo; computer graphics by Tetsuo Obi, Hisashi Kameya, and Satoshi Mizuhata; animation by Michiaki Hashimoto
Starring Kuniko Mitamura (Kazuhito Kirishima), Yoshiko Tanaka (Asuka Okouchi), Masanobu Takashima (Major Kuroki), Megumi Odaka (Miki Saegusa), Tohru Minegishi (Lt. Goro Gondo), Ryunosuke Kaneda (Seido Okouchi), Koji Takahashi (Dr. Shirigami), Yasuko Sawaguchi (Erika Shirigami), Toshiyuki Nagashima (Technical Division Director Seiichi Yamamoto), Yoshiko Kuga (Chief Cabinet Secretary Keiko Owada), Manjhat Beti (SSS9), Koichi Ueda (Self Defense Agency Chairman Yamaji), Isaho Toyohara and Kyoka Suzuki (Super X2 Operators), Kenji Hunt (John Lee), Derrick Holmes (Michael Low), Hirohisa Nakata (Director General of the Defense Agency), Katsuhiko Sasaki (Director of Science Technology Takeda), Kenzo Hagiwara (Ground Forces Staff Officer), Kazuyuki Senba (Maritime Staff Officer), Koji Yamanaka (Air Force Staff Officer), Iden Yamanruhl (Abdul Saulman), Hiroshi Inoue, Kazuma Matsubara, Ryota Yoshimitsu, Tetsu Kawai, Yasunori Yumiya (JSDF Officials), Shin Tatsuma (Director of Giant Plant Observation Akiyama), Abdula Herahl (Researcher), Curtis Kramer, Brian Wool, Robert Conner (American Commandos), Beth Blatt (CNN Newscaster Susan Horn), Makiyo Kuroiwa (Nurse), Haruko Sagara (TVC-TV Reporter), Hiromi Matsukawa (Newscaster), Demon Korgure (Himself), Isao Takeno (Chief of Super X2 Repair Crew)
GODZILLA portrayed by Kenpachiro Satsuma, Shigeru Shibazaki and Yoshitaka Kimura; BIOLLANTE portrayed by Masao Takegami

*Godzilla's raid on Tokyo has left untold devastation but one curious benefit: a shred of Godzilla's skin, found in the rubble, offers genetic researchers access to the monster's unique biology. It is now possible to synthesize some of Godzilla's traits — such as the ability to consume radioactivity, or to regenerate after injury — into other organisms. Dr. Shiragami works to develop a plant capable of enduring even the harshest climate, while Dr. Kirishima engineers a bacterium that eats nuclear fallout. Either discovery could save mankind — and radically tip the balance of power. After suffering so long as victims of Godzilla, is there not some poetic justice in Japan finally getting something positive from their monster?*

*There are powerful vested interests keen to suppress or steal these discoveries. They will stop at nothing to end Shiragami's and Kirishima's research — whether that means theft, sabotage, murder, or even loosing Godzilla from his volcanic prison on Mt. Mihara.*

*The Japanese Self-Defense Force have spun off a*

---

*Beginning with this film, the original Japanese versions began using the English abbreviation "vs." in the titles in place of the Japanese word "tai" (which means "against"). The title would still be spoken aloud as "Gojira tai Beorante," but the "vs." familiar from the Americanized films had now been accepted by the Japanese as their own.

*Godzilla Countermeasures Unit specifically to handle the monster's return. Their remit will be sorely taxed by the additional arrival of Biollante, a monstrous creation resulting from the splicing of Godzilla's genetic information into an ordinary garden rose.*

*As the two great beasts prepare to face down, Shiragami muses, "I think now I may have made a mistake."*

It is a conversational convenience often used in the West to divide up recent history into decades. Speak about "the sixties," or "the eighties," and instantly a set of commonly understood assumptions spring to mind. Exactly what ideas are connoted by any given decade may vary from culture to culture; what Britons think of "the forties" is certainly going to differ from what the French associate with the same period. But the habit of dividing up time by units of ten remains constant. In the course of discussing the storied history of Japanese film icon Godzilla, this author has adhered to this culturally informed predilection: The 1950s was driven by the reissue success of *King Kong* and a host of imitators, of which Japanese films were but one facet. The 1960s saw the development of Japanese monster films in a unique direction (led in large measure by screenwriter Shinichi Sekizawa) that codified the *kaiju eiga* as a discrete form. The decline of the Japanese film industry in the 1970s forced the series to survive only as a shell of its former self...

It must be noted that with thousands of years of unbroken history behind them, the Japanese are more accustomed to thinking in broader terms. Rather than reflexively carve up their experiences into decades, Japan tends to use imperial epochs instead. The Showa Period covers the reign of Emperor Hirohito, from 1926 to 1989. The ascendancy of Emperor Akihito in 1989 inaugurated a new epoch, the Heisei Era.

Thus, when we speak of the "original" or "first" Godzilla series, running from 1954 to 1975, we are talking about the Showa series of Godzilla films. Similarly, Godzilla fans and cultural critics alike also refer to a Heisei Series of Godzilla films. Technically, this would refer to

all Godzilla movies made from *Godzilla vs. Biollante* onward, but since *Godzilla vs. Biollante* operates as a direct sequel to *The Return of Godzilla*, which itself stands apart from the preceding films, *The Return of Godzilla* is generally "grandfathered in" to be considered the start of the Heisei Series.*

As the launch of a new era of Godzilla movies for a new era of Japanese life, *Godzilla vs. Biollante* self-consciously positions itself as a generational transition point. As the events of the film barrel towards their action-soaked climax, Colonel Kuroki (Masanabu Takashima) takes a much-deserved nap. As the chief military strategist against Godzilla, he has been obliged to concoct one contingency plan after another. The catastrophic loss of life and property damage is his personal responsibility. His colleague has just been killed in an effort to subdue Godzilla with yet one more last-ditch effort. (There have been so many "last ditch" tries by this point, the words have lost meaning.) The current plan is to use an experimental weather control system, never intended for any defense application, but any number of things could still go wrong. He's long ago left behind Plan B and is now on Plan M, or maybe R.

Doctors Shiragami and Kirishima remark on how much responsibility has been placed on such a young man. Shiragami notes to his younger colleague, "I guess it's time for my generation to move aside. From now on, it's up to you guys." Both onscreen and off, a torch was being passed.

There are passing callbacks to the heritage of Godzilla throughout *Godzilla vs. Biollante*: A few familiar Ifukube motifs have been dropped into Koichi Sugiyama's score, and there are appearances by Katsuhiko Sasaki (Goro Ibuki in *Godzilla vs. Megalon* and Ichinose in *Terror of Mechagodzilla*) in a small role as the Director of Science Technology, along with Akihiko Hirata's widow Yoshiko Kuga as secretary general of the Cabinet.[1] More in keeping with the idea of a generational torch pass-

---

*By the same token, the films made after Godzilla vs. Desotroyah tend to be "grandfathered-out" of the Heisei Series and considered as a separate cycle of "Millennium" films.*

ing, the actor playing Kuroki, Masanabu Takashima, is the son of Tadao Takashima, onetime star of *King Kong vs. Godzilla*.[2]

The incoming creative team, though, is less interested in paying homage to the past than they are in forcefully establishing a new generation Godzilla. Not since Yoshimitsu Banno hijacked the franchise for a personal tour through his own tripped-out psyche has the style of a Godzilla film been so confidently rewritten by a singular personality. Writer-director Kazuki Omori aggressively reboots the series, to the extent that his approach would dominate even after his departure, guiding it to the new millennium. From here on out, the films would pit Godzilla against both monsters and the military, with the JSDF's special anti–Godzilla team relying on a variety of experimental "mecha" machines and the aid of psychic girl Miki Saegusa (Megumi Odaka). The military officials would watch the battles unfold on a big screen, while in the field the commandos would find their strategies constantly backfiring. Time and again, the human heroes of these films would find their experiences with Godzilla challenging what they once believed: Godzilla as a teaching moment.

On paper, the idea behind the film beggars belief. *Godzilla fights a giant mutant flower!* For anyone who comes to this film with visions of seventies-style campiness in their head, there is a surprise in store. *Godzilla vs. Biollante* is not only played straight, it is pitched so seriously as to verge into the pretentious. This is Godzilla in the aftermath of *The Submersion of Japan*, where earnestness was a given. It is also in the style of "magic realism," an approach to fantasy that attempts to derive logical outcomes from an outlandish premise. *If* Godzilla existed, what then?

Like the Shinichi Sekizawa–authored screenplays of yore, the monster battles arise from human conflicts, of which this film has a seemingly limitless supply. The new technology imperils both the international balance of military power and the international balance of commerce. The two scientists at the heart of the tale are the pivot points for struggles between Japan, America, and the fictional country of Saradia in the Middle East — yet the two men are also pitted against each other, not to mention facing internal crises of conscience of their own. There is so much conflict spilling over every interpersonal interaction, it is no wonder it takes two mutated leviathans pummeling each other to sort it all out.

As in the original 1954 *Godzilla*, there is a brilliant scientist who has the unique ability to create a new super-weapon that will supplant nuclear bombs. This then poses the moral dilemma: The new weapon will put Japan ahead of the two former superpowers and likely incite significant international tension. At the same time, the new weapon is essential to defend Japan from Godzilla. Ultimately, the scientist does implement the weapon against Godzilla, but dies, taking the dangerous secret with him.

Viewed in closer detail, though, important differences between the 1954 and 1989 handling of this theme illustrate a generational change in attitude towards Japan's position in the world. While the first Godzilla series exhibited an optimism born out of Ishiro Honda's political beliefs, the new series reflected a modern, morally complex sensibility.

Scientists and reporters, the usual heroes of the first series of Godzilla movies, always sought the truth. This pursuit of truth differed from the values of, for example, politicians, who would gladly ignore inconvenient facts, or spin information to manipulate public opinion. Honda believed that a duty to truth for its own sake was stronger than nationalistic or political allegiances. He saw scientists as being able to unite across cultural, political, and national boundaries in the face of horrific threats to mankind. In the Godzilla series and in Toho's other science fiction films, Honda posited scientists as the salvation of a planet riddled with petty nationalistic conflicts.[3]

The new Godzilla series did not idealize science in this way. In *Godzilla vs. Biollante*, Shiragami goads Kirishima, saying, "So science is just another host of politicians." Notably, Kirishima finally decides against attending the Massachusetts Institute of Technology, a decision that partly reflects the negative portrayal of

Americans in the movie as a whole, but also addresses the issue of science-for-hire as well. MIT's reputation as a world-class science institute has much to do with the prominent positions its graduates obtain in research labs funded by large corporations. If Kirishima feels compromised working at a lab funded by the Okochi Foundation, he is unlikely to find anything in the United States that does not similarly compromise his integrity. Scientists like Kirishima do not research simply to improve the world's wealth of knowledge; their work is used to improve the wealth of their employers; science is a business. Unlike Honda's utopian vision, *Godzilla vs. Biollante* presents scientists who are manipulated by large companies and governments, contracted to produce weapons and monsters. When international politics demand it, the scientists are even forced to turn over the fruits of their research to terrorists.

Dr. Serizawa personally confronted the dilemma of his weapon: He had to resolve the moral issues at stake. Dr. Shiragami, however, feels little such conflict. He resents being forced to work with the Godzilla cells because he blames them for his daughter's murder, but he never grapples with the larger question of what anti-nuclear bacteria (ANB) will do to the international balance of power. Instead, Kirishima is the one most animated by that issue, and he spends much of his screen time arguing loudly against his own research. Okochi and Shiragami remain steadfastly indifferent to what Kirishima sees as a troubling issue.

This indicates a major shift in the series from a cautionary, anti-nationalistic attitude towards a more assertive nationalism. Honda was consistent in depicting his heroes as those who placed global brotherhood and the common good over patriotism. This was itself in keeping with the zeitgeist. In the fifties and early sixties, patriotism was something of a dirty word in Japanese pop culture. The seventies witness a slow shift away from this anti-patriotic attitude. In Godzilla movies, the trend towards extraterrestrial menaces allowed the positive depiction of the Japanese Self-Defense Forces acting independently of the rest of the world in

the defense of Japan against its enemies. In *Godzilla vs. Biollante*, this resurgent patriotism no longer hides behind a veil. The real-life JSDF would actively collaborate throughout the second series, providing personnel and equipment for such positive on-screen promotion.[4] By 1989, nationalism was no longer a bad thing. Okochi even makes a powerful and persuasive argument for an assertive Japanese military: "Japan has suffered devastation brought by nuclear bombers, and now there's Godzilla. It's only right we should have a weapon that can protect us from our enemies."

Pointedly, those "enemies" include American corporations. All of the film's English-speaking characters are villains. The film depicts America as jealous of its position and willing to resort to terrorist violence to protect its power.

While the science presented in the film is undeniably a crazy quilt of sci-fi conceits (genetically engineered freaks, ghosts, psychic children, flying tanks), it was born of the minds of scientifically literate creators who sought to bring some real-world realism into the mix.

The first member of the new creative team introduced himself to Tomoyuki Tanaka in a rather impertinent way. A brash young upstart named Kazuki Omori approached the venerable producer to berate him for letting the Godzilla brand deteriorate. Omori was a licensed physician who at the time worked for Watanabe Productions, the company that had represented the Peanuts when Toho cast them as Mothra's priestesses. Omori had grown up enthralled by Honda's films, especially *Atragon* and *The Mysterians*, but now considered them guilty pleasures. In his mind, the kind of action-soaked spectacle that Hollywood turned out in things like the James Bond series put Toho's monster movies to shame, and he felt that if Japanese films were ever going to seriously compete with American imports they needed to develop some of the same style. *The Return of Godzilla* struck Omori as a retrograde production, something still stuck in the ruts of past successes and unwilling or unable to break new ground. "We could make a better movie than this," Omori chided him.[5]

It was hard to argue with him. The commercial success of *The Return of Godzilla* had been strong enough to warrant a sequel, but not so strong as to make that happen very quickly. Prerelease publicity for *The Return of Godzilla* boasted that the comeback would earn twice as much as it ultimately did, and while the American release may have brought New World back from the brink of bankruptcy, it did little for Toho's coffers.[6]After Tanaka announced *Godzilla 2* in 1985, he almost immediately got cold feet. The commercial failure of Paramount's 1986 *King Kong Lives* suggested that the market was not really ready for monster movies. He changed his mind back again when *Little Shop of Horrors* opened to strong ticket sales later the same year.[7] Although the similarity between Biollante and *Little Shop*'s Audrey II is unmistakable, Tanaka says it was unintentional.

Rather than commission a script — and risk remaining stuck in his comfortable rut — Tanaka held a story contest, open to the public, to contribute suggestions for *Godzilla 2*. He had successfully used similar contests in 1975 and 1983.[8] In late 1985, a panel of renowned authors, cartoonists, and science fiction specialists selected five finalists out of 5,025 entries. To let Omori prove that he was more than just a blowhard, Tanaka handed the five finalist entries over to him to pick a winner. It did not take Omori long to choose "Godzilla vs. Biollante" by Shinichiro Kobayashi.

Kobayashi, a dentist, had also worked as a screenwriter for the *Return of Ultraman* and was a longtime fan of the *kaiju eiga*. He wanted to enter the *Godzilla 2* story contest, but expected to be too busy with a doctors' conference. When the conference ended, and with only two days left before the contest deadline, Kobayashi took a chance. He was pleasantly surprised to find his hastily written idea selected by Omori. Kobayashi had based his story on how he might feel if his six-month-old daughter were to die. Wanting to give her immortality, he started thinking about the competing promises and fears connected with genetic engineering. He combined this with a visual image he found intriguing, Godzilla consumed by a flower, and thus was Biollante born.

By January of 1986, Omori was turning Kobayashi's ideas into a workable screenplay. Using his background in biological science, Omori researched biotechnology and botany. He finished a draft by the summer, and continued to revise it off and on until 1989. Over those three years, Toho wanted to prove their new director on other projects before giving him the reins of their most expensive and taxing project. Omori directed three films for Toho before the approval came to put *Godzilla vs. Biollante* into production.

In 1988, Koichi Kawakita ascended to head of Toho's special effects department. Kawakita has lurked in the background of this story for some time now, having worked under Tsuburaya as far back as 1962's *King Kong vs. Godzilla*. In the intervening years, he also directed special effects for Tsuburaya Productions' *Ultraman Ace*, *Ultraman Taro* and *Ultraman 80*, as well as Toho's *Zone Fighter* television series. Beginning in 1976, Kawakita began working on complicated miniature effects for a number of war dramas, and directed special effects for Kohji Hashimoto's *Sayonara Jupiter*. He also directed a documentary of the making of *The Return of Godzilla*.

In 1988 he took over the special effects unit from Teruyoshi Nakano, and quickly distanced himself from the previous regime by displaying his talent for optical effects and creative usage of the camera. Kawakita's work on the 1989 science fiction film *Gunhed* especially signaled his arrival as a creative force. *Gunhed* was a tacky *Terminator*-style thriller about a dystopian future in which human renegades battle superpowered robots. What the film lacked in creativity, or for that matter popularity, it made up for with relentless images of a fully realized fantasy world dominated by machines and ray beams — the very things Kawakita would obsess over in his tenure on Godzilla. Tanaka recognized a renaissance in the special effects department, and felt fully confident placing the Godzilla series in Kawakita's hands. Ironically, *Gunhed* had in fact been based on a *Godzilla 2* story contest entry in which Godzilla confronts a supercomputer.[9]

With Kawakita as director of special effects, *Godzilla vs. Biollante* was announced in May 1989 for a December 1989 release date.[10] Over the years of waiting, Omori had embellished Kobayashi's story considerably. Omori has since said that directing Godzilla was his second choice of career, his true dream being directing a James Bond film. With that in mind, Omori included as much Bond-inspired touches in this picture as possible. Secret agents from several countries battle each other with gadgets, stunts, and chases; a standout sequence finds our heroes facing down a ticking doomsday clock. He took a reporter heroine from Kobayashi's outline and developed her into Miki Saegusa, psychic child prodigy.

With her uncanny ability to predict Godzilla's actions, Miki brings to mind little Ken Yanno from *Godzilla vs. Hedorah*. It is but one of several striking parallels between the two films. Like *Hedorah* before it, *Godzilla vs. Biollante* is unusual in its graphic depiction of human death. During the story, Biollante metamorphoses through several different body forms. As assistant director of special effects on *Godzilla vs. Hedorah*, Kawakita had taken a shine to the idea of an evolving monster. It should also be noted that designers from the animated series *Macross* were involved in the early planning stages of *Biollante*, and they carried over some of the same notions of monster transformations from one project to the next. From 1989 onwards, Godzilla and his opponents would undergo continual metamorphosis, as Kawakita believed this provided an identifying point of consistency for the series.[11]

*Macross*'s Studio Nue submitted designs for Super X2 that gave the flying tank similar transformative abilities. Their proposed Super X2 would have been able to shift its shape from a jet fighter to a tank-like "Markalite" (the laser tanks from 1957's *The Mysterians*) to a submarine. Although Kawakita rejected these ideas as impractical for his budget, he did advocate strongly for the use of metamorphosis in Biollante herself.

When Toho gave *Godzilla vs. Biollante* the official go-ahead in May of 1989, Kawakita selected Studio OX as his design team based on their work with him on *Gunhed*. For Biollante's initial appearance in the lake, Studio OX set out to fashion a fragile, somewhat feminine, and ambiguously threatening creature. Traditional suitmation techniques, though, put certain restrictions on the design. For Biollante's second appearance, Kawakita asked Studio OX to create a creature that was at once plant and animal, that seemed like a natural development of the rose-monster, and that exhibited characteristics of Godzilla's genes. This proved difficult. When the final, insanely complicated prop was delivered to the set, Kawakita's crew reportedly gasped, "Are we really going to do *that*?"[12]

Since Godzilla was an established character design, Kawakita could begin work on the Godzilla effects while Biollante was still on the drawing board. Seeking inspiration, Kawakita visited the zoo (much as Haruo Nakajima had in 1954). After watching the behavior of crocodiles, Kawakita began to think of redesigning Godzilla completely as a more authentic dinosaur. Tanaka rejected the idea, telling Kawakita in no uncertain terms, "Damn it, he's a monster!"[13]

Kawakita had worked with Godzilla performer Kenpachiro Satsuma many years earlier when they both served Teruyoshi Nakano on *Godzilla vs. Hedorah*. The two men were eager to take this opportunity to establish their own way of working, independent of Nakano.

Satsuma, already a veteran monster actor, felt that his 1984 Godzilla performance had been too much an imitation of what Haruo Nakajima had already established. "In 1984," Satsuma explained in an interview, "I had my first chance to play Godzilla, but I was so overwhelmed by the physical demands of the job that I could only think of the Nakajima Godzilla. However, by the time I felt I could finally succeed, the film was over! So this time I am determined to continue from the point I left in 1984 and make a Satsuma Godzilla."[14]

Satsuma's goal was to abstain from Nakajima's anthropomorphic characterization and portray Godzilla as a realistic animal. Satsuma particularly wanted to avoid human movements, such as those that would normally be used to keep his balance inside the heavy rubber suit, and emphasize small details like finger movements to express emotions.

The new Godzilla suit was designed to assist Satsuma in achieving a lifelike performance. Noboyuki Yasamaru, who had created the 1984 Godzilla costume, built the new one specifically around Satsuma's measurements, producing what Satsuma considered the most comfortable monster suit he ever wore. The 242-pound rubber suit sported a lower center of gravity than previous Godzilla costumes, and the large, muscular thighs gave Satsuma greater mobility. A second, lighter costume (176 pounds) was built for use in the outdoor tank, since it would soak up water and become heavier during shooting.

The new costume also featured a much smaller head with enhanced reptilian features. The eyes were changed to eliminate the whites around the pupil, a feature that (although part of earlier Godzilla designs) is only present in humans. At the suggestion of story author and dentist Shinichiro Kobayashi, the mouth contained multiple rows of teeth, like a shark.

Kawakita also commissioned four robot models of the upper half of Godzilla that, like Nakano's "cybot," would be used for close-up work. Unlike the cybot, these models were cast from the same mold as the suits, so that they would perfectly match the footage of Satsuma in the full suit. The cable-controlled robot models gave Godzilla considerable expressive power, with intricate eye movements, an articulated tongue, and other realistic motions. Coupled with Satsuma's studied portrayal of Godzilla as a true animal, a new and distinctive Godzilla came to life. With only minor variations, this would be the Godzilla design and personality used throughout the coming decade.[15]

Throughout the filming of the special effects, Kawakita employed varying scales for the miniatures in order to create forced perspective effects. Kawakita said, "It is not important that things look realistic, only that they film realistically." Although to the observer on the set, the wildly inconsistent scales of the miniatures looked bizarre, every set had been carefully designed for the camera. Kawakita distinguished himself from his predecessors by filming a staggering number of different angles. In some sequences, he never used the same camera position for more than one shot. This taxed the resources of his team, but produced sequences of high drama and visual excitement. Kawakita also shot many images he later discarded, unwilling to use any shot that did not fully satisfy him.

In addition to his remarkable number of camera set-ups, Kawakita also shot many complicated effects "live," reducing his reliance on optical effects. Bulbs were built into Godzilla's back fins so that they could light up on the set, rather than require optical animation. (Faulty wiring of the bulbs gave Satsuma a painful electric shock the first time they were turned on.) In Godzilla's battles with the military, real explosives were used in the same shot as Satsuma and the models. Because of the extensive pyrotechnics on the set, Satsuma wore protective goggles under the suit to protect his eyes in case of an accident. Miniature helicopters fired real missiles at Satsuma, cameras were mounted on cranes to provide point-of-view shots of helicopters approaching the monster, and footage of the real JSDF was spliced in to enhance the realism.

Although Kawakita strove to accomplish as many practical effects as possible on set, his optical unit produced nearly perfect mattes, something Nakano had never achieved. In one breathtaking shot, Godzilla appears in the ocean by the helicopter platform with actress Megumi Odaka as Miki Saegusa. This shot is so expertly done that the illusion of Godzilla as a real, giant animal is completely convincing (helped considerably by Satsuma's animalistic movements). Another startling composite occurs when Biollante is first discovered. The camera pans from the actors at the lake to the model stage with the suitmation rose–Biollante. Special effects cinematographer Katsuhiro Kato was especially proud of this seamless matte, in part because it represented the first Japanese usage of an 8-perf camera to film the two elements. Japanese cameras were historically too unstable for successful 8-perf filming, resulting in a jittery split between the composited elements. Kato's success with this shot was a first for Japanese cinematography.[16]

Godzilla's ray received more sophisticated treatment by Kawakita's optical animators than had been the case under Nakano. Kawakita used Godzilla's ray more extensively than in previous films; for the rest of the Heisei series, battles between monsters more frequently involved exchanging energy beams than anthropomorphic wrestling. In fact, it became increasingly rare for opposing monsters to have much direct physical contact with one another. Kawakita explained, "There are two reasons. One is the fact that it would be almost impossible for the monsters to wrestle with one another because of their tremendous size and weight. The other is my feeling that the monsters seem too human when they wrestle with each other."[17]

When the first form of Biollante was finally ready for filming, the crew had to contend with a complicated array of vines operated by overhead wires. The trunk of the monster rose housed actor Masao Takegami, who sat on a platform just above water level and operated the subtle motions of the rosebud.[18] Although he would later call the scene his best work, Satsuma found the filming of his battle with Biollante very difficult[19]:

> It was really tough to act with Biollante because I must perform all the battle's physical action...
> [T]he vines give no tension themselves since they just hang from wires, so I must act as if they are powerful in order for Biollante to really come alive. Usually, when I act inside the costume, I try to operate at about 70 percent of my full strength — if I use 100 percent effort, I will tire easily and not be able to continue for much time. But sometimes the director would insist that I react much more violently, so Biollante would look alive, so I had to use 100 percent effort. Also, since the enemy is moved only by wires, for me the battle is really with the wire technicians, and getting the timing just right between us was extremely difficult.[20]

The second incarnation of Biollante posed almost insurmountable problems for the special effects crew. The enormous, unwieldy network of vines took many hours to rig up on the set, and required thirty-two individual wires to control. Satsuma and Takegami could not see each other as they enacted their battle. Perhaps the worst aspect of the ten-day shoot was Biollante's acid sap, which the creature vomited onto Godzilla. The sap made permanent stains on anything it touched, but limited visibility inside the suit made it so that Takegami was unable to aim Biollante's mouth. To protect the cameras from wildly misfiring sap, the crew wrapped them in plastic bags.

In addition to traditional suitmation techniques, Kawakita also commissioned some stop-motion and traditional cell animation. None of this material was included in the final cut, as Kawakita was unconvinced that it could be effectively cut into the live-action footage. The special effects team did however take advantage of computer graphics. Computer animation had become the new craze in special effects worldwide, and had received much attention in Japan. Rather than try to animate the monsters digitally, Kawakita presented computer-generated images as themselves. The video game–like visuals made a striking, innovative impression.

In all, Kawakita spent about $3 million on the effects footage, just under half of the picture's total production budget. His work earned compliments from his peers in the United States; American special effects artist Richard Edlund and others praised Kawakita's accomplishments.

While Kawakita worked on the effects footage, Omori directed the live action from the final draft of his screenplay. Like his special effects director, he demonstrated a strong visual sense, and kept the human drama fast-paced. A fast pace was essential, given the extreme complexity of his screenplay.

Japanese films as a whole, not just Godzilla movies, involve large ensemble casts. In American films, a single protagonist usually drives the plot, with all major plot points deriving directly from the actions of that hero. By contrast, Japanese films often have secondary characters drive the plot as much as the protagonists. Kazuki Omori's writing takes this trend even farther, with provocative and politically charged subplots interconnecting around multiple "hero" figures. Kirishima, Asuka, Shiragami, Gondo, and Kuroki all deserve to be called the hero of the film, while very minor characters like Mr. Okochi and the Saradian president raise some of the most interesting issues.

Despite writing a densely plotted, issues-laden script, Omori failed to elicit effective performances from the cast. Both Koji Takahashi (Shiragami) and Kunihiko Mitamura (Kirishima) are bland. Yasuko Sawaguchi, the weakest link in *Return of Godzilla*'s cast, plays little more than a cameo here as Erica. Yoshiko Tanaka, as Asuka, does what she can with her inadequately written role. Although Megumi Odaka as Miki Saegusa would reprise her role in the next five installments, she also suffers from an underdefined character.

The best performances come from Masanobu Takashima as Colonel Kuroki and Toru Minegishi as Gondo. Twenty-three-year-old Takashima had already made his reputation as a popular comedian, and his natural charm and sense of timing serves him well in his role. He inhabits the character well, and the audience feels great respect for such a young man taking on such an awesome responsibility. He makes several costly miscalculations in dealing with Godzilla, but he keeps trying, with a relentlessness not unlike that of his foe. Minegishi also brings a comic sensibility to his role, and gives an appealing sarcastic quality to Gondo. His character resembles Dum-Dum Dugan, Godzilla's cigar-chomping nemesis from the Marvel comic books.

Although Tanaka insisted on including a few of Akira Ifukube's famous themes in the soundtrack, Koichi Sugiyama composed the rest of the score. Omori wanted a distinctive new sound for this new generation Godzilla, and so rejected returning to *Return of Godzilla* composer Reijiro Koruko. Tanaka wanted Hiroshi Miyagawa, who had scored the *Space Cruiser Yamato* animated television series, but Miyagawa had prior commitments. (He would later collaborate with Ifukube on 1992's *Godzilla and Mothra*.) Instead Omori approached Sugiyama,

who had written the music for the *Dragonquest* Nintendo video game.[21]

Sugiyama's score was orchestrated and recorded by David Howell, conducting the Kansai Philharmonic. Strangely, Howell never saw any of the film, nor any of the design work, and adapted Sugiyama's written score to incorporate Howell's own imaginings of what the movie might look like. The result was a soundtrack that often undercut the drama, at times sounding like a Bugs Bunny cartoon. Although Sugiyama's haunting and effective theme for Biollante herself conveyed beauty and mystery, the rest of the score did not help the film. Ifukube's themes stirred the emotions in ways more appropriate to the style of the film, and Tomoyuki Tanaka made sure that Ifukube himself scored the next three films.

Omori's and Kawakita's working methods did have some significant drawbacks. Omori rewrote the script continually from 1986 through production, changing it even as he filmed. Meanwhile, Kawakita discarded any effects footage with which he was dissatisfied. As a result, important plot details ended up discarded as a by-product of the process. Given Omori's already complicated story and ambiguous character motivation, such losses made the film harder to follow and left some character motivations muddled.

*Godzilla vs. Biollante* did not receive much promotion, especially compared to the previous film. Much of the promotion centered around Osaka, the city Godzilla destroys during the climax. Toho turned only a small profit on the picture. Tanaka received the approval for *Godzilla 3*, slated for a December 1990 release, but it was also decided to return to familiar, marketable monsters for Godzilla's opponents.[22]

Toho would produce both *Godzilla 3* and *Godzilla 4* before *Godzilla vs. Biollante* appeared in North America. Despite New World's success with *Godzilla 1985*, the American film industry did not see the new Godzilla film as a worthwhile risk. *Godzilla 1985* had benefited from an extensive amount of free publicity. From the thirtieth anniversary to Perry Mason to the Dr Pepper campaign, New World found ways to promote their release on someone else's bill. In the end, though, New World only made a profit in video release, and the profit was small compared to their expenses. Furthermore, Toho had pointed to *Godzilla*'s Japanese box office success as proof that it would do well in international release. *Godzilla vs. Biollante* performed much poorer at the Japanese box office than *Godzilla*, suggesting, by the same logic, that its American audience would be similarly smaller. Since any distributor that picked up *Biollante* would be faced with more advertising costs than *Godzilla 1985*, but a smaller audience, simple economics argued against the deal.

Adding to Toho's woes, the international film industry was undergoing the effects of a worldwide recession. The 1990 Cannes market, one of the largest and most important markets for the buying and selling of international distribution rights for feature films, left most attendees frustrated. "It's the worst I've seen in the five years I've been here," reported Toho representative Takiya Kazawa. The video market, which had boosted revenues through much of the 1980s, had disintegrated, forcing many independent producers out of business and crippling the typical film vendor at Cannes.

*Godzilla vs. Biollante*, like most films in 1990, were left without buyers.[23] The slump continued into 1991. Toho sales representative Kiyoto Takaya complained, "Every year it's getting worse, but this year [1991] it's a catastrophe."[24]

In the end, Miramax and HBO picked up *Biollante* for home video release in late 1992; the arrangement earned Toho little for their efforts. Miramax/HBO released *Biollante* with minimal expense, but much respect. Omori's film is flabby in places, and one can easily imagine that an Americanized version could have tightened it up with no loss to the story, and trimmed some of the dodgier effects to make Kawakita's already impressive work shine even better. No such thing was done. For the first time in America, the home video version was a widescreen presentation of the uncut international edition. The video box's package art made no effort to emphasize the obviously exploitable absurdity of Godzilla battling a giant flower, and in general kept a serious tone, the least intrusive Americanization imaginable. It was also the last Godzilla film to appear officially in the United States until almost the end of the millennium.

# Chapter 31

# Godzilla vs. King Ghidorah

## GOJIRA VS. KINGU GHIDORAH
## (GODZILLA AGAINST KING GHIDORAH)

*I nearly died on Lagos Island. The dinosaur saved me. The prosperity I built is being destroyed by the same dinosaur. How ironic!*

— Shindo

Japanese version: 103 minutes, Released December 4, 1991
Color, Widescreen
Produced by Shogo Tomiyama; executive producer Tomoyuki Tanaka; associate producer Tomiya Ban; directed by and screenplay by Kazuki Omori; music by Akira Ifukube; cinematography by Yoshinoru Sakiguchi; art direction by Ken Sakai; edited by Michiko Ikeda; special effects by Koichi Kawakita; special effects assistant director Kenji Suzuki; special effects art direction by Tetsuzo Osawa; special effects cinematography by Kenichi Eguchi and Toshimitsu Oneda
Starring Anna Nakagawa (Emmy), Megumi Odaka (Miki Saegusa), Kenji Sahara (Prime Minister), Isao Toyohara (Terasawa), Katsuhiko Sasaki (Prof. Mazaki), Kiwako Harada (Chiaki Morimura), Tokuma Nishioka (Takehito Fujio), Shoji Kobayashi (Security Chief Ruzo Dobashi), Yoshio Tsuchiya (Yasuaki Shindo), Richard Berger (Grenchiko), Chuck Wilson (Wilson), Robert Scott Field (M11)
GODZILLA portrayed by Kenpachiro Satsuma; GODZILLASAURUS portrayed by Wataru Fukuda; KING GHIDORAH portrayed by Hurricane Ryu

Writer Terasawa believes he has discovered the origin of Godzilla: A garrison of Japanese troops stationed on Lagos Island in 1944 made a last stand against the oncoming American forces. A dinosaur, improbably surviving on the island after millions of years, turned back the American invaders and saved the doomed soldiers — one of whom, Yosuaki Shindo, went on to become a primary architect of Japan's postwar economic prosperity. Terasawa believes that Shindo's "savior" was irradiated by the 1954 H-bomb tests and mutated into the Godzilla of today.

A time machine appears in Tokyo bearing visitors from the future who have a copy of Terasawa's not-yet-written best-seller with them! The time travelers claim to have come from a future where Japan was destroyed by Godzilla, and offer a solution: They will go back to 1944 and move the dinosaur so that the H-bomb blast has no effect.

Their mission is seemingly a success — Godzilla ceases to exist — but then the travelers reveal their true purpose. They are actually terrorists from a world where Japan is culturally and economically dominant, and have come back in time not to save Japan but to subjugate it. They secretly left behind genetically engineered creatures on Lagos in place of the dinosaur, so the atomic tests that once created Godzilla have instead given birth to the terrifying three-headed dragon Ghidorah.

The travelers unleash Ghidorah's destructive fury on the helpless nation — but their plan goes wrong. The dinosaur they moved to the ocean floor has consumed a couple of nuclear submarines and mutated into a monster even bigger and more ferocious than the original Godzilla. This new Godzilla will handily save Japan from Ghidorah — but what will save Japan from Godzilla?

Nineteen sixty-two marked the 60th anniversary of Toho Studios. Thirty years previously, the company had feted its birthday with a splashy blockbuster called *King Kong vs. Godzilla*, one of the biggest commercial hits in its long history. In honor of the occasion, Toho wanted to see if lightning could be made to strike twice.

The *Godzilla vs. Biollante* team returned: Shogo Tomiyama produced (with Tomoyuki Tanaka in an executive advisory role), Kazuki Omori wrote and directed, Koichi Kawakita supervised the effects. Some familiar faces from the past were revived, too: The new film fea-

179

tured the first Godzilla soundtrack composed by Akira Ifukube since 1975, the return of Kenji Sahara and Yoshio Tsuchiya (along with Megumi Odaka, Godzilla's recurring costar throughout the 1990s), and the first appearance of King Ghidorah since 1972.

Omori was hoping to revive Mothra and, believing that he was on the cusp of a monster movie renaissance, had been developing a script for *Mothra vs. Bagan* since 1990. The monster Bagan, based on a Chinese dragon, had been mooted in an unproduced script by Akira Murao in 1980. Some of Murao's ideas eventually became part of *The Return of Godzilla*, but Bagan would never make it to the screen. Notably, Murao's proposed 1980 version of Bagan metamorphoses through three distinct incarnations, sporting shape-shifting abilities that would later become a consistent monster trademark under Koichi Kawakita.[1]

*Mothra vs. Bagan* never got past the planning stages. The story involved the god Bagan, fated to defend the Earth from any force that threatened the environment, aroused by global warming and determined to eliminate the environment's greatest enemy: humanity. This in turn revives Mothra, the god of peace, who confronts Bagan in humanity's defense.[2] With a story that sprawled across the globe, the film promised to be an expensive production. Toho reluctantly began to acknowledge that although the new Godzilla series brought in profits, none of their other science fiction films were commercial successes. Furthermore, Toho saw Mothra as a uniquely Japanese monster, and one that would be hard to market overseas.*

*Godzilla 3* had originally been announced for a December 1990 release, but several factors intervened to disrupt this schedule. Following brain surgery, Tanaka began to show signs of his advanced age, and sharply curtailed his involvement with Godzilla. As he reverted to executive producer, Shogo Tomiyama took over as producer. Tomiyama would produce the subsequent four sequels, with Tanaka providing advice as he saw fit.[3]

More to the point, *Godzilla vs. Biollante* had not been even as popular as *The Return of Godzilla*, attributable in no small measure to the meager promotion Toho afforded the sequel. However, Tomiyama also felt that the film had been too sophisticated for children, and the new monster was not a sufficiently threatening one. He still wanted to pursue adult audiences with politically charged, topical scripts, but Tomiyama wished to bring back some of the fantasy of the older series in order to tempt child audiences as well. Instead of using one of the *Godzilla 2* story entrants, then, Kazuki Omori wrote a new story using Godzilla's most popular adversary, King Ghidorah.[4]

For his part, Omori blamed the lackluster box office performance of *Godzilla vs. Biollante* on the competition from Hollywood import *Back to the Future Part II*— and took from it the conclusion that audiences wanted time travel stories![5] While Omori paid tribute to his American inspirations with such details as a time travel control panel seemingly borrowed directly from Michael J. Fox's souped-up DeLorean and a cyborg copied from James Cameron's *Terminator 2*, he failed to cohere a sensible approach to time travel that functioned as anything other than a narrative non sequitur.

The time travelers move the dinosaur from Lagos Island, supposedly preventing it from becoming Godzilla, but then return to a 1992 where Godzilla has merely *disappeared*, not been erased from history. Miki Saegusa still works for the Godzilla Countermeasures Unit of the JSDF, and Terasawa's publisher still intends to go ahead with his book on Godzilla. When a new Godzilla appears, everyone's first reaction isn't "What's that?"; instead they compare its size and ferocity with the one they remember, from a time now undone.

Omori's script does not even follow its own rules. The time travelers explain that they cannot bring Shindo with them on their mission because a younger Shindo is already on Lagos, and it is impossible for two versions of the same person to coexist in the same time; one of the Shindos would vanish. However, Godzilla

---

*Omori's idea of launching a Mothra series did take off a few years later, with different creators at the helm.

dunks the almost dead King Ghidorah into the Sea of Okohsk in 1992, where it stays for two hundred years. Anna Nakagawa's character Emmy retrieves it in 2204 and turns it into the cyborg Mecha-Ghidorah, which is then sent back to 1992. Godzilla smashes it apart, and it too falls into the Sea of Okohsk. Consequently, Ghidorah and a future version of Ghidorah co-exist in the same sea at the same time, in clear violation of the law Omori established.

For that matter, the whole premise is pretty shaky. If you have a time machine, a teleport, and an indestructible robot, you already have all the tools you need to subdue Japan without having to rely on the unpredictable behavior of giant monsters.

If you are looking for logical storytelling and narrative realism, though, the world of Japanese monster movies is probably the wrong place to go hunting. Despite its shortcomings, illogic, and overpopulated cast, *Godzilla vs. King Ghidorah* is crammed full of ideas, richly visualized innovations, a genuine spirit of fun, and some of the most complex emotional manipulation ever to grace the series.

Taking inspiration from one of his favorite *tokusatsu* classics, *The Mysterians* (and by extension, its *Godzilla*-styled remake *Invasion of Astro-Monster*), Omori presents technologically advanced visitors who come to Japan with friendly words and generous offers. They offer to solve Japan's Godzilla problem, but there are hidden strings only revealed once the bargain is made. As before, the obvious implication is that Japan needs to remain ambivalent towards outsiders.

This time, though, those outsiders are not aliens from space wearing shiny jumpsuits, they are Westerners with names that unambiguously connote American and Russian origin. Their mission is to punish Japan for its economic success.

Viewers at the time would not escape the connection to real-world debates over "Japan, Inc." References to Japan buying entire continents merely exaggerate existing fears about the Japanese economic powerhouse. By the early 1990s, many American commentators were already suggesting that although the Allies were the military victors of the Second World War, Japan had staged a successful economic victory. Omori plainly makes this connection by depicting the architect of Japan's postwar economic prosperity as a commander of the Imperial Army in the war. Shindo loses the battle in 1944, but wins it five decades later.

The American press took one look at the Godzillasaurus trampling G.I.s in the Pacific and concluded the film was anti–American. In many ways, this contributed to Toho's difficulty in finding an American distributor. Nineteen ninety saw much anti–Japanese sentiment aired in the American press and the filmmaking community. After Sony bought Columbia Pictures and Matsuhita Electric Industrial Co. purchased MCA/Universal, the *Washington Times* editorialized:

> Lock the doors and hide the family silver. Here come the Japanese. First they want to make low-cost, high-quality cars to transport us. Then they want to build lots of plants to employ us. Now they want to make movies to entertain us. And that's going too far, say the critics. "Will Japan end up buying it all?" wondered *USA Today* in a front-page article this week…
>
> Some critics say the real problem is cultural. The Japanese are, well, different, and who knows what they'll do to our movies, force us to watch those old Godzilla films or something. Concerns about such cultural "differences" may help explain why nobody so much as peeped when an Italian financier swallowed up MGM–UA Communication for $1.3 billion earlier this month.[6]

*Godzilla vs. King Ghidorah* dramatized these fears perhaps too directly.

However, Omori's script displays a more complex attitude, one that indicts Japan as well. The real hero of the movie is Emmy, whose attitude towards Japan is deeply ambivalent. Terasawa stands around a lot while Emmy keeps the story moving, a reversal of the gender roles from the original series. Emmy engineers the birth of King Ghidorah because she truly believes Japan needed to be stopped. She is all for using Ghidorah as a blackmail threat to get Japan to obey, and only rebels against Grenchiko and Wilson when they unleash the monster without bothering with an ultimatum first. Like Miss Namikawa breaking from her Xian masters, Emmy switches sides—but only because she objects to their tactics, not their underlying motivation.

While Omori elevates a character critical of Japan's economic domination, he also criticizes the character who most represents that domination. Shindo has his office inside Tokyo City Hall in the Shinjuku district. Many Japanese people hate the 48-story-tall City Hall building, seeing it as an ugly symbol of Japan's wealth.[7] Godzilla destroys this symbolic building, and with it its symbolic tenant. Godzilla, who in the film plays alternating roles of hero and villain, tears City Hall down as he deliberately murders the man who led Japan's economic revival. Omori's script does not depict Japan's prosperity as good, nor does he depict it as evil.

What the situation needs is balance. Godzilla and Shindo represent an unlimited expression of Japanese might, which if left unchecked creates global problems. The film advocates for the containment of such forces.

Emmy, acting out of her principles, participates in a scheme that devastates Japan. When her conscience tells her that what she thought were noble motives have produced monsters (literally), she tries to set things right. Shindo begins on the side of military conquest, and transforms into a prominent businessman. He owns a nuclear submarine, which appalls the government, but his submarine provides the spark that brings Godzilla back to save Japan. Godzilla returns as a savior only to almost instantly revert to a destructive terror, without actually changing his behavior at all. Ghidorah, too, transforms from cute and cuddly "Dorats" into a horrific destroyer and then into a superhero.

Omori produces a wonderfully intricate climax, in which Emmy battles Godzilla from inside Mecha-Ghidorah. For audiences to sympathize with Ghidorah, in any form, already asks a lot. Mecha-Ghidorah looks terrifying, and Godzilla has already earned much audience sympathy throughout the film. When Godzilla survives, and destroys the cyborg, the audience has reason to be relieved and disturbed all at once.

Similarly, Godzilla's encounter with Shindo

at City Hall is a standout, rich with ambivalence. Yoshio Tsuchiya, one of the finest and most eccentric performers on Toho's lot, enacted the potentially risible moment with great dignity. Omori recalls the scene with deserved pride:

> The most important scene in the movie is where a tear comes to Godzilla's eyes when he's facing this human. And I think there's very few who could play the role opposite a [crying] Godzilla, and Tsuchiya's one of them who could do it.... When we brought this to him and said, "We'd like you to do this role," he said, "I've been waiting my whole life for this role." So I personally think we found the right actor, and we have Godzilla crying in the face of this human being, and I think of all the movies in the Godzilla series, this has to be the best scene, in my personal opinion.[8]

Another especially striking moment involves a Japanese camera crew that sneaks past the evacuation checkpoints in order to shoot footage live from Shinjuku as Godzilla and Mecha-Ghidorah in battle. With bravado, the reporter announces, "I'm Japan's Peter Arnett!" Like his real-life counterparts covering the Gulf War for CNN, the reporter and his cameraman find the most dangerous spot to get the most dramatic pictures. While they film through the window of a hotel room, Godzilla falls backwards at them, his back plates crashing through the glass and searing the building in two.

Kawakita had clearly come into his own by now, and demonstrates confidence in his work. The miniatures, pyrotechnics, mattes, and optical animation all show improvement over the already strong work done on *Biollante*.

Noboyuki Yasamaru repaired and reused the 1989 Godzilla suit. The revamped King Ghidorah and Mecha-Ghidorah variant show off wireworks techniques greatly improved since the sixties. The "Godzillasaurus" seen on Lagos Island gave the special effects team a chance to visualize Godzilla as a more paleontologically accurate dinosaur, in look and posture. Consequently, Kawakita's team also made a sly commentary on efforts to redesign Godzilla as a dinosaur: In Toho's world, after being mutated by the hydrogen bomb, Godzilla gains an upright, human-like posture.

Using the logic that *this* Godzilla was mutated by more powerful modern nuclear weaponry than the 1954 H-bomb test, Kawakita was able to officially increase Godzilla's size to 100 meters. Omori implies that Godzilla is an inevitable result of a human society that has covered the world with nuclear pollution. No matter where the dinosaur was teleported, Godzilla was fated to appear. In a further jab at humanity's hubris, the attempt to eliminate Godzilla has completely backfired. Emmy tells Terasawa that the Anti-Nuclear Energy Bacteria had in fact subdued Godzilla, and if they had left well enough alone, Godzilla would never be heard from again. Instead, they end up with a Godzilla that is 125 percent larger, more powerful, and impossible to defeat. In subsequent films, further attempts to battle Godzilla would continue to make the monster stronger.

Having learned their lesson from *Biollante*, Toho made sure to heavily promote the return of Godzilla's most popular adversary. In response, some 3.5 million Japanese viewers attended *Godzilla 3*, an audience base almost as strong as the 1984 *Godzilla*.[9] The economic slump that had contributed to Toho's difficulties in finding an American distributor for *Godzilla vs. Biollante* continued. Although *Godzilla vs. King Ghidorah* appeared in dubbed form on video in the United Kingdom, no American distributor showed interest at the time. (It would arrive on video in America only in 1998, associated with the publicity push for the Hollywood *Godzilla*.) When Shogo Tomiyama placed *Godzilla 4* on the schedule for a 1992 release, he found himself courting a Japanese audience only.

# Chapter 32

# Godzilla and Mothra: The Battle for Earth
## GOJIRA VS. MOSURA (GODZILLA AGAINST MOTHRA)

*Boy, what a day! Godzilla's at large once again!*

— Minamino

Japanese version: 102 minutes, Released December 12, 1992
Color, Widescreen
Produced by Shogo Tomiyama; executive producer Tomoyuki Tanaka; directed by Takao Okawara; screenplay by Kazuki Omori; music by Akira Ifukube, Yuji Koseki and Hiroshi Miyagawa; cinematography by Yoshinoru Sakiguchi; special effects by Koichi Kawakita; special effects art direction by Tetsuzo Osawa; special effects cinematography by Kenichi Eguchi
Starring Tetsuya Bessho (Fujita Tezuka), Satomi Kobayashi (Masako Tezuka), Akira Takarada (Environmental Planning Board Chief Joji Minamino), Keiko Imamura and Sayaka Osawa (The Cosmos), Shoji Kobayashi (Security Chief Ruzo Dobashi), Takehiro Murata (Marutomo Corporation Executive Andoh), Makoto Otake (Marutomo CEO Tomokane), Megumi Odaka (Miki Saegusa), Shinya Owada (Ship Captain), Saburo Shineda (Professor Fukazawa), Shiori Yonezana (Midori Tezuka)
GODZILLA portrayed by Kenpachiro Satsuma; BATTRA portrayed by Hurricane Ryu

*Millennia ago, Earth's ecology was held in balance by two great forces. Battra protected the planet from all enemies. But when Battra felt compelled to destroy human life to safeguard the world from their scientific interference, Mothra emerged to subdue Battra and restore peace. For thousands of years, these creatures have slumbered, drifted into myth, and been forgotten.*

*One afternoon, a meteorite plunges to the Earth and sets off a cycle of calamities. The explosion unearths Mothra's enormous egg on Infant Island, attracting the attention of the Marutomo Corporation, itself responsible for the callous destruction of the environment in favor of fast profits. With the reluctant help of adventurer Fujita and his good-hearted ex-wife Masako, Marutomo representative Andoh has the egg crated up and prepared for shipment back to the mainland.*

*This arouses the interest of Godzilla, revived from*

*his battle with King Ghidorah by the aftershocks of the meteor strike. Godzilla attacks the egg en route, releasing Mothra. Seeking to reclaim some secondary prize for their trouble, Andoh and Matsumoto firm members kidnap Mothra's priestesses and hope to use them as advertising gimmicks.*

*These shenanigans only serve to convince Battra that mankind has once again become an unacceptable nuisance, and so that giant beast slouches towards Tokyo to put an end to things.*

*The monsters converge, with the fate of the planet in balance.*

*Godzilla 4* offered the most monster-soaked spectacle of the Heisei era cycle, and a return to the kind of family-oriented fantasy that had marked the original series. This new trend brought both good and bad: On a commercial level, *Godzilla and Mothra: The Battle For Earth* attracted the best audience for the series since 1962, while on a creative level, it displayed less artistry and care than its immediate predecessors. Continuing with his ill-advised obsession with remaking Hollywood hits, Omori (this time serving only as screenwriter) opens the picture with a clumsily staged "homage" to Indiana Jones. It is, sad to say, merely the first of several Indiana Jones–ish scenes dominating the film's first act.

In adapting the unused ideas for *Mothra vs. Bagan* into a Godzilla film, screenwriter Kazuki Omori did little more than tack a few scenes with Godzilla into what otherwise remains a film about Mothra and Battra (whose narrative role and behavior match what was to have been Bagan's). The producers clearly felt it important to include Godzilla for marketing reasons, yet Godzilla was not well integrated into the story.

Although Omori's previous scripts confused many viewers with mutable character motivations and dense plots, they also displayed political and moral complexity. Omori's screenplay for *Godzilla vs. Mothra* lacks that sophistication, and the film suffers for it. The script handles the controversial issue of environmentalism in a clumsy, self-defeating manner. Omori evidently wants to indict modern human society for offenses done to nature. From Masuka's disgusted response at the Marutomo development site ("We humans did this. Someday all of Earth will be like this") to Minamino's litany of environmental damage ("We humans are still cutting down trees, destroying our forest without thinking of the consequences"), the script is packed with dialogue that reeks of "author's message." However, the dire events that occur during the film result primarily from the meteorite's impact, a natural disaster that can hardly be blamed on human civilization. Minamino says, "The meteorite may have pulled the trigger but we humans are the ones who built the gun." The film, though, neglects to show much of mankind's environmental abuse. While *Godzilla vs. Hedorah* spent considerable screen time showing oil spills, smog, sludge, and pollution, *Godzilla and Mothra* simply assumes the audience's sympathy already lies with the environmentalists. In fact, every character except Mr. Tomokane agrees on ecological issues. This one-sided presentation makes the film feel like propaganda.

In his previous scripts, Omori created complex characters who could be sympathetic while representing viewpoints that the storyline condemned. Mr. Okochi of *Godzilla vs. Biollante* makes a persuasive and compelling argument supporting corporate-funded genetic engineering. Mr. Shindo of *Godzilla vs. King Ghidorah* embodies a postwar economic prosperity that the film treats with ambivalence. In sharp contrast, Mr. Tomokane of *Godzilla and Mothra* is a paper tiger, an obvious and unsympathetic villain. The benefits and advantages of real estate development never get a fair hearing.

In fact, Toho had prospered as a movie studio in large part due to their real estate holdings, and audiences watched *Godzilla and Mothra* in theaters that had once been forests. The movie itself makes no comment on such potentially positive aspects of modern society. What makes environmental concerns so controversial in the real world is that good, nobly motivated people can disagree on how best to balance the social benefits of development with the desire to maintain unspoiled nature.

Oddly, though, the cartoonish villain Tomokane never receives his comeuppance. Andoh warns the sneering, wiry bad guy that the monsters will destroy his office building, setting audience expectations for a replay of Godzilla's destruction of Happy Enterprises from *Mothra vs. Godzilla* (so much else from that film has been revamped for use here). In fact, no such thing occurs. Tomokane survives to make trouble for future citizens of Tokyo, and the monsters never directly punish the only human character to exhibit anti-environmental attitudes. To the extent that Omori's writing does ascribe human blame for the world's woes, it also lets the culprit get away with it.

Omori handles the characters of Fujita and Masuka much better. Masuka is one of the series' best written heroines, with actress Satomi Kobayashi providing some of the best female acting since the glory days of the early sixties. She comes off as intelligent, brave, and strong, a much more rounded and realistic depiction of a woman than usual.

As her immature ex-husband Fujita, Tetsuya Bessho makes for a very different kind of hero. Far from the dashing, brave reporters and scientists of earlier films, Fujita is a man who still has a lot to learn. In his review of *Godzilla and Mothra*, critic Tim Lucas notes that Fujita is "an adventurer who plunders the ancient holdings of foreign countries while evading child support payments—in other words, depleting the reserves of the past while investing nothing in his own future."[1] In one scene, he and Masuka compare his growth with the metamorphosis of Mothra, making the metaphor obvious. In interviews promoting the film, Omori admitted that he felt Fujita's personal metamorphosis formed the emotional core of the story.[2]

Megumi Odaka continues in the role of Miki

Saegusa, although she has next to nothing to do. Even more superfluous to the action, Shoji Kobayashi reprises his role as Security Chief Ruzo Dobashi. A familiar face from the television series *Ultraman* and *Kamen Rider*, Kobayashi makes funny faces and little else.[3] Both he and Miki Saegusa are still part of the Special Godzilla Unit, control of which passes from governmental agency to governmental agency as the series continues. In *The Return of Godzilla*, the unit seemed to be a hastily arranged outgrowth of the Japanese Self-Defense Force. By 1989, the "Disaster Research G-Room" was a coordinated effort between the JSDF and the National Land Agency. Control of the "Special Godzilla Unit" was ambiguous in 1991, but by 1992 the group became part of the Environmental Planning Bureau (EPB).

It is nice to see Akira Takarada back again, after all these years, even if his face-lifted visage is not fully recognizable. As chief of the EPB, his scenes are brief, but his presence invites warm memories of the Toho classics of the fifties and sixties. Unfortunately, the new series has allowed the narrative device of the "master control room" to become a cliché. In all of the Heisei Godzilla outings, characters sit in such a control room and watch the movie unfold on a giant television screen. This time, however, there is no Super X or Mecha-Ghidorah to control, no commando unit with hand-held rocket launchers, no artificial lightning grid, no time machine — in short, nothing for Chief Minamino to oversee. He stands around, watching the big screen and making grave pronouncements, rubbernecking at the apocalypse.

Producer Shogo Tomiyama also intended to bring back Frankie Sakai, who played "Bulldog" Tsinchan in 1961's *Mothra*, but scheduling conflicts prevented this.[4] A familiar face did, however, appear behind the scenes. While working on Akira Kurosawa's latest film *Madadayo*, Ishiro Honda visited the set to see his legacy still thriving. Shortly thereafter, Honda passed away.[5]

Keiko Imamura and Sayaka Osawa play the new priestesses, now called the Cosmos. Although not real twins, the two women do bear an uncanny resemblance to one another. Takao Okawara claimed that directing the Cosmos' scenes was his most demanding task, since they had to mimic each other without looking at each other.[6] Kawakita's effects team improved their mattes, allowing the Cosmos to interact with full-size characters more believably than ever before.

Believability, though, is a fragile and elusive commodity. Throughout Toho's *kaiju eiga*, rarely does a character scoff at the notion that a giant monster might exist. Instead, monsters seem to be an accepted fact of life. Most of Toho's monsters have been presented as part of Earth's natural history, and its mythology. Since Godzilla, Anguirus, Rodan, King Kong, Ebirah, Manda, Megalon, and King Seesar are shown as natives of Earth, there is no reason not to accept them as real.

The revised histories of the monsters for the new series undid some of that unspoken reasoning. Mothra remains a god to her people, but those people are no longer depicted as human. Since the new Mothra does not hail from Earth, and her mythology has not been seen by human eyes for 12,000 years, the movie's characters really ought to be shocked to learn of her existence. This author had the opportunity to ask director Takao Okawara about this seeming contradiction, and his frank reply was, "It's a monster movie, so of course it has monsters in it."

By making Mothra and the Cosmos extraterrestrials, Omori also tampers with the powerful moral lessons of the original Mothra films. Shinichi Sekizawa's Mothra ruled a civilization that had suffered repeated injustices inflicted by the Japanese. Having exploited, abused, and insulted Mothra and her people time and again, the Japanese found themselves trapped in situations where they had no alternative but to ask Mothra's people for help. The characters then had to humbly beg forgiveness for the crimes committed by their society. Rather than gloat in their tormentors' agony, Mothra selflessly placed herself in danger to fight for the Japanese, an act of great compassion. Omori's Mothra also sacrifices herself for another civilization's sake, but the moral dimensions have lessened. While Mothra and the Cosmos may not owe mankind anything, and their sacrifices may indeed seem profound, the 1992 Mothra need not overcome an explicit reason to desire revenge on humanity.

For those who worry about Mothra's gender, the film does little to affirmatively establish an answer, but offers circumstantial evidence for Mothra being female. Godzilla's previous two opponents were female: Biollante included the spirit of Dr. Shiragami's daughter Erica as a fundamental part of its soul, and the time traveler Emmy played an integral role in the creation and operation of King Ghidorah and Mecha-Ghidorah. It seems logical to assume that this entry continues the trend.

Furthermore, unlike Sekizawa's Mothra films, this one presents the Cosmos as Mothra's *only* people. The telepathic link between the girls and their protector, as well as their ability to fuse with Mothra's body, portray the Cosmos as being part of Mothra, further suggesting Mothra's feminine qualities. Omori spoke in interviews of Mothra's "maternal instincts,"[7] while director Takao Okawara spoke of the creature as "a very feminine monster."[8]

Tomoyuki Tanaka and Shogo Tomiyama originally planned to follow-up *Godzilla vs. King Ghidorah* with *Ghidorah's Counterattack*, but a poll revealed that Mothra was the most popular monster among women. Ghidorah and Mechagodzilla were the most popular among men, but women comprised the largest segment of the Japanese movie-going audience. The theatrical success of Godzilla movies depended on appealing to women.[9]

Although Omori had both written and directed the previous two Godzilla films, for *Godzilla and Mothra*, Shogo Tomiyama sought a new director. Thus enters Takao Okawara onto the scene; he would play a prominent role in the development of the franchise for years to come. Okawara was a few years older than Omori, and had worked his way patiently through the Toho studio system. He had served as assistant director on such genre landmarks as *The Submersion of Japan* and *The Last Days of Planet Earth*, and alongside Honda on Akira Kurosawa's *Kagemusha* in 1980. After finishing

A.D. duties on *The Return of Godzilla*, he had been given the chance to direct his own picture. While *Supergirl Reiko* was not commercially successful, the man had earned his stripes.[10]

Recognizing *Godzilla and Mothra* as "a lighthearted film,"[11] Okawara was keen to emphasize both the screenplay's comedy and the action. He rewrote the script to introduce Battra earlier in hopes of quickening the pace.[12]

Omori's first revamped version of the Bagan character was "Badora," a Bad Mothra. As this name sounded disharmonious in Japanese, it was changed to Battra, for Battle Mothra.[13] Koichi Kawakita gave both monsters distinct life phases, in keeping with his commitment to monster metamorphoses. At one point, Kawakita planned to kill Mothra and later revive it as Mechamothra, a dragonfly-like cyborg.[14] This idea was dropped, making *Godzilla and Mothra* the sole Heisei series entry not to include a "mecha" monster or contraption.

Kawakita gave both Mothra and Battra the ability to fire energy beams. In the final conflict in Yokohama, the monsters fight one another with little other than blasts of glowing beams. Although Kawakita believed monster wrestling looked inappropriately anthropomorphic, Eiji Tsuburaya created a battle between Godzilla and Mothra in 1964 that realistically portrayed a mortal conflict between animals without relying on animated rays. Mothra's defense of her egg against the giant reptile in 1964 was a dramatic and believable sequence. Kawakita's uninspired staging of the three-way monster battle does not compare favorably.

Kawakita did, though, take pains to create little details that he felt would enhance the quality of the effects. He filmed some of Godzilla's underwater scenes through a large, specially built aquarium so that fish would be seen swimming between the camera and the monster. Kawakita shot stunning sunset scenes at Toho's massive outdoor pool, where much of the series effects had been filmed since Tsuburaya commissioned its construction in 1960.[15]

Kawakita also found use for cable-controlled Godzilla body parts of varying scales as well as a new costume that reduced and flattened

Godzilla's head, adding a yellowish tint to the eyes and emphasizing the fangs.[16] For the new series films, Kawakita's team had standardized Godzilla's look to the extent that changes from suit to suit were so subtle as to be noticeable only to the most eagle-eyed observer. This consistent look for Godzilla, coupled with continuing characters and interlocking storylines, maintains a marked continuity within the Heisei series.

Early in the production schedule on Kawakita's effects, the previous 1991 suit vanished from the Toho lot. It was needed for some stunt work for which the new suit was not intended; the loss threatened to hold up production. During the urgent search for the 100-pound rubber costume, Toho staffers joked with each other, "Is Godzilla at your house?"[17] The search received international publicity, even making the news in America:

> Tri-state citizens, beware! Godzilla is on the loose. Unbelievably, someone has stolen the rubber Godzilla model from a Japanese special effects department in Tokyo. The model was made for a new Godzilla movie coming out in Japan. Now, the theft won't affect the film's premiere, I'm sure you're glad to hear that, I know Jerry's relieved. But the thirteen-foot high-tech model is worth 39 thousand bucks and the Japanese have a real "yen" for their favorite movie star, they want him back. Has anyone checked with King Kong?[18]

Ultimately, an older woman was terrified to spot the monster costume on the shore of Lake Okutama outside Tokyo. By now the suit was in a sorry state, requiring significant repairs. The special effects crew had actually been somewhat relieved that it had been stolen, since it spared them the job of repairing it. Although the studio was happy to get the expensive prop back, Kawakita's team reportedly responded with a disgruntled, "Ugh. That thing's back!"[19]

In addition to reusing costumes, *Godzilla and Mothra* borrows the hoary cliché of monsters falling into the sea. The same ending capped the previous *Godzilla vs. King Ghidorah*, as well as *King Kong vs. Godzilla, Mothra vs. Godzilla, Godzilla vs. the Sea Monster, Godzilla vs. Mechagodzilla*, and others. In fact, a more elaborate and less derivative ending had been planned. As Battra hauled Godzilla out to sea,

Mothra was to spin her glowing symbol over the water's surface first to mark what the Cosmos call "a point which emanates a special force that will neutralize Godzilla — a submerged area which used to be part of our land." Godzilla kills Battra (as happens in the finished movie) and the two plunge into the glowing water down to the ruins of Mothra's sunken city. The Stonehenge-like structures, which form the shape of Mothra's icon, explode in a burst of energy that engulfs and traps Godzilla. The planned sequence got so far as to be storyboarded by design artist Hurricane Ryu (who also played Battra in the film), but perhaps for reasons of cost, the ideas were dropped.[20]

Evidently in an ecologically aware recycling mood, Toho reused sound effects along with plot devices. The mid-sixties high-pitched Godzilla roar replaced the deep, grumbling roar used since *Return of Godzilla*. Battra's roar was nothing more than the sound created for Rodan in 1956.

Akira Ifukube, however, composed some new music for the soundtrack. The score relies on his classic themes for Godzilla and Mothra, certainly, but also introduces a new theme for the new monster, Battra. Hiroshi Miyagawa, who had been Tomoyuki Tanaka's first choice for scoring *Godzilla vs. Biollante*,[21] assisted Ifukube in preparing the musical soundtrack.[22] Their soundtrack also highlights the famous 1960s Mothra songs, reorchestrated for a new age. The songs carry so much nostalgic and narrative connotations that they evoke even stronger emotional reactions from the audience in 1992 than they had thirty years earlier.

With Battra saving Mothra from a falling Ferris wheel and Mothra flying off into outer space, *Godzilla and Mothra* lacks the even the cod-realism of *Biollante* and *King Ghidorah*. The first Godzilla film since *Godzilla vs. Megalon* to include a small child as one of the principal characters, *Godzilla and Mothra* explicitly targets the children who had been turned off by the high-mindedness of the recent productions. The decision proved worthwhile, and 1992 saw the biggest audience and largest revenue for any Godzilla film since 1962's *King Kong vs. Godzilla*.

Higher ticket prices in 1992 meant that while *King Kong vs. Godzilla* still held the all-time attendance record with over 12 million viewers, *Godzilla and Mothra*'s handsome count of 4.2 million ticket buyers brought Toho the highest box office gross of any Godzilla film, 2.22 billion yen. This remarkable commercial success occurred despite the fierce competition provided by Steven Spielberg's *Jurassic Park*, which was Japan's top-grossing film for the year, with 8.3 billion yen in box office grosses.[23] In fact, when viewed in the larger context of the Japanese film industry in 1992, *Godzilla and Mothra*'s success becomes even more impressive.

The Japanese film industry had been in a state of steady decline since 1958, the year cinema attendance peaked at 1.3 billion tickets. The most calamitous drop had been in the seventies, but while the bleeding had been staunched the patient was still in critical condition. By the early 1990s, attendance had dwindled to 143.5 million, an 87 percent drop from the 1958 peak.[24] The number of theaters in Japan also plunged from a 1960 peak of 7,457 to a 1992 low of 1,744.[25]

Japan's recession in the 1990s helped fuel that decline. As the yen continued to appreciate, exports of Japanese films to foreign countries fell 40 percent. Video sales dropped, and Hollywood income from the Japanese market decreased by 2.5 percent. NikkatsuCorp., Japan's oldest studio, declared debts of $500 million and went into bankruptcy proceedings in 1993.[26]

Critics said the struggling domestic Japanese film industry was at its "nadir, starving for good scripts, stifling creativity with miserly production budgets and churning out a lot of trashy movies that rarely make much money." British film critic Alan Booth wrote, "In all honesty, I think that a weekly review of Japanese films is an unnecessarily promiscuous use of recycled rain forest timber." Even the revered Japanese film critic Kazuko Komori concurred: "Why is it that contemporary Japan is so advanced economically, but has so few serious movies to show the world its culture? I see a lot of foreign films, so when I review a Japanese production I've got to lower my standards drastically."[27]

Japanese viewers evidently agreed with the critics, and went overwhelmingly to foreign films. Japan in the early 1990s still stood as the world's second largest film market, with box office grosses for 1992 totaling 152 billion yen. Consequently, foreign producers, especially those in Hollywood, rushed to compete in Japan. Foreign films accounted for 60 percent of the films released in 1992, 55 percent of the theatrical income,[28] and 59 percent of the video business. United International Pictures, a distribution conglomerate that handles international releases by Paramount, Universal, and MGM/Pathe, claimed that 17 percent of their total income for 1991 came from the Japanese market.[29]

Despite such intense competition from Hollywood, the numbers also tell a different story: Japan remains one of the few markets in the world where the domestic film industry shares nearly equal footing with Hollywood. American films have become the norm around the globe, but in Japan, Hollywood has not yet captured much more than half of the market.

This has much to do with the fact that Japan's studios maintain a vertically integrated monopoly. Between them, Toho and Shochiku Studios control virtually all of Japan's theaters. They thereby control what movies play in Japan, as well as when and where. Toho and Shochiku pick which movies they want to play in their theaters, and those theaters have no choice but to agree to the company's decisions. Even independently owned theaters find dealing with the two major studios inevitable; Hollywood will not deal with independent theaters directly for fear of offending Toho or Shochiku. As of 1991, the Japanese studios had reserved a third of the nation's theaters exclusively for Japanese-made productions. When American movies open in Japan, they can appear in either a Toho- or a Shochiku-operated circuit, but not both. So even popular American features can be shown in only about 60 theaters in all of Japan, which puts a limit on the ability of American companies to dominate the market.[30]

This monopolistic power wielded by Toho and its sister studios can be partly blamed for the decline of Japanese cinema. Since the Japanese film market is the world's second largest, and since domestic productions are relieved from having to fully compete with foreign films for audiences, the Japanese film industry has evolved into a very insular one. Japanese filmmakers can still succeed while catering exclusively to domestic tastes. Director Juzo Itami (*Tampopo*, *A Taxing Woman*) says, "Japanese directors are only interested in looking at Japan from the inside, making movies only Japanese can possibly understand."[31] By contrast, the small domestic market in Hong Kong forces filmmakers to seek global appeal, which results in international commercial success.[32]

Kazuki Omori rejected the traditionally slow place of Japanese films, claiming that domestic features were "not interesting enough." He also felt that studios did little to rein in self-absorbed directors. "The things that a director finds interesting are simply conveyed to the audience without any filters."[33]

Omori and Okawara saw *Godzilla and Mothra* as their chance to turn the tide somewhat. In the slump of the nineties, long-running series like Toho's Godzilla and Shochiku's comedic Tora-san series (which neared its twenty-fifth year with its forty-fifth installment) had guaranteed audiences. However, Godzilla's latest effort would not only pit the series against the industry's overall decline, but a gargantuan foe from America as well. The release of *Jurassic Park* had many commentators expecting the expensive special effects extravaganza to do record-breaking business, predictions that indeed came true. Steven Spielberg's *E.T.: The Extraterrestrial* had set the box office

record a decade earlier, earning $142 million in film rentals. With *Jurassic Park* opening across 237 theaters on July 17, 1993, United International Pictures expected the dinosaur film to eventually bring in $82 million, putting *Jurassic Park* as number two on the list.[34]

In the final count, *Jurassic Park* did not quite make it that far, but at $75.6 million, it did not miss by much.[35] Spielberg's enormously popular film had gone head-to-head with the Japanese-made *REX, A Dinosaur Story*. *REX* hailed from director Haruki Kadokawa, one of Japan's most independent of independent producers. To describe Kadokawa: Imagine a combination of Lex Luthor, Donald Trump, and Richard Branson — and then imagine he ran a major publishing empire. Kadokawa's power gave him access to enough money and connections to compete with the Japanese studios. Hoping to capitalize on the dinosaur craze created by *Godzilla and Mothra* and *Jurassic Park*, he quickly churned out *REX*. The film proved remarkably popular, and stole a fair chunk of Spielberg's audience. In a surprising turn of events, the police arrested Kadokawa for cocaine use and drug trafficking. In a country where drug crimes are harshly treated, the scandal ruined his career. *REX* lost considerable public support.[36]

Despite its competition, *Godzilla and Mothra* became the highest grossing domestic feature for 1993, the only time a Godzilla film has achieved this honor. It beat *REX* by a mere 20 million yen, but lost to *Jurassic Park* and four other American films. *Godzilla and Mothra* took its place as one of the all-time box office hits in Japan, after fifteen other domestic features and thirty-three foreign ones. Its success guaranteed that there would be a *Godzilla 5*.

## Chapter 33

# Godzilla vs. the Gryphon
## (GODZILLA IN AMERICA, PART THREE)

*It's exciting that TriStar is committed to spending lots of money; I think that's a good sign.
I've heard people talk about an $80 million budget...*
*They're looking at state-of-the-art effects, digital effects, and have that be part of the draw,
part of what distinguishes this movie from all of the other Godzilla films."*
— Terry Rossio, screenwriter[1]

Americans have long considered the Hollywood film industry to be the best in the world. That perceived superiority has little to do with storytelling; ideas, being intangible and therefore free, are as accessible to producers around the globe as they are to Hollywood's moguls. What Hollywood can claim a monopoly on, though, is access to the money and resources to produce technically excellent motion pictures. With more money and time at their fingertips than their predecessors and their competitors, special effects companies like Industrial Light and Magic and the outfits that grew in their wake set a new standard for visual effects that few could match.

America's perceived superiority in the field of science fiction and fantasy films, then, came from technical expertise more than anything else. The independent producers who had inspired this new emphasis on special effects rankled at the new generation's priorities. Samuel Z. Arkoff, former head of AIP, remarked:

[I]t was the idea that was important in those days. Now, along come these new state-of-the-art special effects.... So what we have is that we're getting pictures where the special effects outweigh and out-proportion the rest of the piece.... [T]hey're losing something that's very important: the interest of the audience in the movie's characters and their identification with the people in trouble...

Today you're supposed to be awed — or over-awed — by the special effects. Well, I'm telling you that there's a limit beyond which the special effects just aren't going to take

anybody. And I think most young people today have seen just about all the special effects they care to.[2]

It was perhaps inevitable that Hollywood would eventually set their sights on making an American *Godzilla* with state-of-the-art special effects. Godzilla's influence on the new generation of Hollywood filmmakers was extensive. When Martin Scorsese played Vincent Van Gogh in Kurosawa's *Dreams* (1990), he sat down with Ishiro Honda and told him how he spent his youth watching Godzilla films and now wanted to buy fresh prints from Toho for his film library.[3] Tim Allen, star of ABC-TV's *Home Improvement*, wrote to a fellow Mothra fan, "Mothra rules!"[4] Director Tim Burton wanted to grow up to be the actor in the Godzilla suit.[5] Steven Spielberg acknowledged his appreciation of Toho's famed monster not only in interviews, but also by including Godzilla and Rodan frequently in his cartoon series *Animaniacs*.[6]

Indeed, Hollywood had already considered an American Godzilla production in 1983 — considered, and then rejected. After Hollywood passed, believing Godzilla to have too small a potential audience, the new series of Godzilla films took off in Japan to considerable commercial success — isolated almost entirely inside Asia. In particular, *Godzilla and Mothra* had performed remarkably well at the box office in Japan. In the wake of *Jurassic Park*, a dinosaur craze had erupted in the United States that boosted rentals of older Godzilla movies.[7] Hollywood realized that Godzilla's popularity was perhaps more robust than they first thought.

In 1992, Henry G. Saperstein brokered a deal between Toho and a (now-defunct) division of Columbia Pictures known as TriStar to make an American Godzilla movie. In initial discussions, TriStar proposed a budget of $40 million (five times what *Godzilla and Mothra* cost), of which Toho would receive $1 million in addition to a share of the profits. Toho retained veto power over Godzilla's design, but not the script or cast. TriStar and Toho finalized the deal in early 1993, making TriStar one of Hollywood's most active buyers. TriStar announced the film for a Christmas 1993 release.[8]

Meanwhile, ILM created their version of Godzilla for a television commercial for Nike shoes. The ad showed Godzilla and basketball star Charles Barkley competing one-on-one across downtown Tokyo. Filmed in the summer of 1992, the commercial gave the American special effects community their first real opportunity to show how they would tackle the problem. ILM's Clint Goldman admitted, "If we didn't do this spot, I would never hear the end of it from the Creature and Model Departments." He chose to film the effects using much the same suitmation techniques as Toho: "The idea was that we would show a modern look, but not with total 'ILM realism,' [or else] it just wouldn't be true to the subject matter."

Jeff Mann, head of the Creature Department, based the costume design on Koichi Kawakita's 1990s Godzilla. The actual construction of the foam rubber costume used techniques pioneered by Jim Henson for his suitmation-style full-size Muppets. Four puppeteers operated radio control devices imbedded in the head to generate Godzilla's various facial expressions. Unlike Toho's one-piece suit, the ILM costume was made of many pieces and therefore had many seams to hide. The foam rubber of ILM's suit was much lighter than Toho's rubber one, and while it was less durable, it was also much more flexible and less exhausting to wear.

Multiple layers of complex, overlapping optical mattes allowed the ILM team to create a full city out of a handful of buildings (props originally used in *Ghostbusters*), a technique that Kawakita's team could not employ due to the limited ability of Japanese cameras to produce good mattes.[9]

TriStar did not wish to pursue suitmation, and instead set their sights on creating their Godzilla using vastly more expensive computer animation techniques.

TriStar began their search for a director, and for a time rumors circulated that Alex Cox was their likely choice. The speculation appears to have been triggered by Cox's open letter to Toho asking permission to direct "one of your GODZILLA films":

> GODZILLA is one of the most important icons of the post–atomic age. Perhaps she is the most important. I assume Godzilla is a she, given that she has produced at least one son. And perhaps this has something to do with her great popularity: who could not love a giant, angry, fire-breathing dinosaur who was also a *mother*?
>
> Humorous, frightening, protective, endlessly destructive and totally self-absorbed. Godzilla is the perfect metaphor for our human species. Godzilla has sometimes been described as the Atomic Bomb, but she is also, surely, the men who made it. She has endless potential for destruction, and a personality — unlike the sluggish Mothra, or the single-minded Ghidorah. Without wishing disrespect to the actors, Godzilla is always the most human character in her films.
>
> In the film which I would like to make about Godzilla, I would like to return to her past — to the time when she and her tribe of nomadic, predatory dinosaurs ruled the Earth.
>
> Show their life — their pack-unity, their communication half by speech half by telepathy and a group mind — it is the late Cretaceous Period, and there is a second, bright sun in the sky — a Giant Comet on collision course with earth!
>
> The IMPACT of the meteorite in what is now the Pacific Ocean causes earthquakes, fires, freak storms. A huge Dust Cloud covers the sky. Godzilla and her tribe flee across the burning prarie...
>
> Cut to Godzilla waking from her dream. She sleeps, hunched up, giant spined tail — wrapped around her the ruins of a vast, levelled city. Lightning and wrecked power cables flicker. Godzilla is alone.[10]

Despite rumors that Cox was indeed TriStar's choice, in fact producer Cary Woods sought a more high-profile director. The rumor mill now placed Tim Burton on Woods' short list.

The Christmas 1993 date came and went without progress. In 1994, TriStar asked the screenwriting team of Terry Rossio and Ted Elliott (*Aladdin*, 1992) to submit a screenplay. By this point, TriStar management had undergone a shakeup, and producer Woods departed the company, leaving *Godzilla* without an official producer.[11]

Although Rossio and Elliott's ideas had not yet been green-lighted, they had already successfully competed against Tim Burton and the writing team of John and Jim Thomas (*Predator*, 1987). Rossio boasted, "We've tried our best to turn in a really smart script. Which isn't to say there might not be some humor, but we wanted to do a science fiction film that has Godzilla in it."[12]

Rossio and Elliott pitched their idea to TriStar and subsequently prepared a preliminary screenplay:

> The State Department calls in Dr. Jill Llewellyn to investigate a mysterious occurrence. A nuclear accident at sea has uncovered a dinosaur encased in some kind of amniotic fluid. Reviving, it kills her husband before escaping into the Arctic sea. Meanwhile, a meteorite lands in Utah. The meteorite turns out to be a living alien creature that fuses with a colony of bats to become a giant, hybrid bat-creature.
>
> An author, Aaron Vaught, working on a book called *The Waking Dragon*, names the newly discovered dinosaur Godzilla after a legendary Japanese basilisk. A security agent named Pike recruits Aaron into the St. George Project. Jill Llewellyn is already part of the St. George Project, hoping to kill Godzilla as revenge for what it did to her husband. Jill and the others investigate what appears to be an alien structure uncovered in the Arctic near where Godzilla was found. Jill suspects the amniotic fluid was an "atomic tranquilizer," preserving Godzilla through the ages.
>
> The bat-thing wreaks havoc on a murderous spree in Utah. Godzilla reappears, headed for San Francisco. Pike launches an all-out attack on Godzilla, but conventional weapons prove useless. Jill uses the amniotic fluid to temporarily tranquilize Godzilla for transportation to the St. George Project's New York headquarters.
>
> One Project member has come into contact with alien technology at the structure in the Arctic. This transforms him into one of the aliens. Through the transformed man, the aliens tell Jill that the probe that crashed in Utah is a "doomsday beast" that creates hybrid bodies for itself out of the genetic material of the life on whatever planet it attacks. Godzilla, apparently, was designed as a defense against the alien monster.
>
> Indeed, the alien monster has cobbled together bits of bats, lions, cows, and other odds and ends to create the Gryphon, a creature out of myth. The Gryphon heads towards upstate New York to attack the neutralized Godzilla. Godzilla does not stay neutralized for long, escaping from the amniotic fluid into the river. The Gryphon and Godzilla meet in New York City, battling at the World Trade Center. A tank of amniotic fluid is still strapped to Godzilla, weakening him and preventing him from using his ray. Pike does not understand that Godzilla is on his side, and wants to finish Godzilla off. His colleagues realize the Gryphon is a far worse monster, and blast the tank off Godzilla's back, unleashing his full power. Godzilla kills the Gryphon in the ensuing conflict, and the humans decide not to attack Godzilla any more; he may be needed to fight for them again.[13]

Rossio and Elliott's story, although full of exciting action, discards much of what made Godzilla movies distinctive. No longer the mutated result of atomic testing, Godzilla also lost any allegorical or symbolic dimension. Rossio and Elliott's Godzilla is not a curse on mankind's hubris, but a savior planted by an ancient civilization—not unlike Mothra in *Godzilla and Mothra*.

Of course, even Toho's Godzilla played the role of a heroic good guy, but the creature's symbolic importance still lingered under the surface. In films like *Godzilla vs. Hedorah* and *Godzilla vs. King Ghidorah*, this dual role of savior and curse gave the character a quirky ambiguity. Rossio and Elliott's *Godzilla* simply establishes that the creature has a mission to save the Earth, and leaves it at that.

Fumio Tanaka, associate producer of *The Re-*

*turn of Godzilla*, once said of Godzilla that he is "a vengeful god. There is no protection against him, no predicting his comings and goings, no human standards for understanding him."[14] In Rossio and Elliott's script, humans come to understand him fairly well, accurately predict his actions, and successfully subdue him. Tomoyuki Tanaka said, "From the beginning [Godzilla] has symbolized nature's revenge on mankind."[15] However, in Rossio and Elliott's script, both Godzilla and the Gryphon exist completely independent of mankind, exempting mankind from any responsibility. In their story, there are no lessons to be learned. As if to add insult to injury, TriStar's initial creature design even abandoned the familiar silhouette of the character, opting instead for a dinosaurian look borrowed from *Jurassic Park*.

Rossio admitted in an interview that he was not a fan of the series, and perhaps his lack of understanding of Toho's *kaiju eiga* prevented him from writing something more recognizably within that idiom. For the casual American viewer, Godzilla movies are Grade-Z drive-in flicks, whose only appeal derives from the scenes of monster-inflicted destruction. Most American filmgoers would scoff at the notion that Godzilla movies also dramatize major cultural issues, spin historical allegories, and engage in a variety of subtexts.

Hollywood saw Godzilla as so closely linked with schlock that the only way they could avoid that stigma was to discard anything connected to the original Godzilla. However, they still hoped to cash in on the monster's popularity. TriStar wanted it both ways. Rossio admitted, "The studio thinking is: What if you could do *Jurassic Park* with a highly recognized 'name' monster? You could have those incredible effects where you actually believe this thing was really stomping through a city and combine it with the worldwide name recognition of Godzilla."[16]

Toho produced the 1954 *Godzilla* during a period of intense fear about radiation and nuclear war, a fear rooted in the events of the time. Although Japan's perspective on the issue was indisputably heightened by the bombing of Hiroshima and Nagasaki nine years earlier,

the fear pervaded American culture as well. Over time, the issue passed to the back burner, and other concerns took center stage both in the public consciousness and in the Godzilla series as well. In the mid–1990s, after the end of the Cold War, the threat of a nuclear holocaust weighed less heavily on Americans and Japanese than it had at any point in the previous half century. The TriStar script avoids the nuclear issue in large part because the fear of genetic engineering had become a much more pointed one for the audience, making for a more topical drama.

To turn a well-worn phrase on its head: If it doesn't look like a duck, and doesn't quack like a duck, then why do you persist in calling it a duck?

Responding to news of TriStar's efforts, Koichi Kawakita said, "Godzilla has many overseas fans, but there's probably a big gap between their perception of him and ours. They know him primarily from his sixties and seventies films, where he's this lovable, comical figure. They really don't know the changes we've made in him in the later movies."[17]

Kawakita, however, did not believe the cultural gap was necessarily a drawback: "Godzilla is so thoroughly Japanese, I'm looking forward to seeing how Americans handle him."[18] For the most part, Kawakita's fellow filmmakers at Toho expressed support for TriStar's project. Teruyoshi Nakano said, "I am pleased because a new approach will be taken."[19] "I'm looking forward to seeing it," said Jun Fukuda, pointing to the extraordinary expense of special effects. "I think that Godzilla films must be produced by Americans."[20] Akira Kubo, star of *Son of Godzilla* and *Destroy All Monsters*, noted diplomatically, "I'm glad that a Godzilla film is going to be produced in the United States. I certainly would accept an offer to be in the movie."[22] Perhaps the lone voice of dissent came from Kenshou Yamashita, director of 1994's *Godzilla vs. Space Godzilla*: "Godzilla was created by radiation from a hydrogen bomb. He no longer would be Godzilla if TriStar were to change this."[23]

Toho Studios put their official stamp of approval on TriStar's project. On the eve of the late 1992 deal, Toho representative Takashi Nakagawa announced, "It's great news for all Godzilla fans."[24] From the start, Toho expected to discontinue the Japanese series as soon as TriStar's film got underway. Gradually, it became clear that the American Godzilla would miss the projected December 1993 release date, and so TriStar pushed the date back to Christmas 1994. Expecting to hand over the reins to their American counterparts, Toho entered production on what they assumed would be the last of the Japanese series.[25] As *Godzilla 5*'s Christmas 1993 release grew closer, Tomoyuki Tanaka and Shogo Tomiyama realized that TriStar was going to miss their 1994 date, too. Plans for *Godzilla 6* began, with Tanaka and Tomiyama breathlessly announcing the fortieth anniversary film as the last of the line.

Theatrical trailers in Japan advertised not only *Godzilla 6*, but TriStar's film too. The brief commercial promised "Dynamic Hollywood Film-Making" and "Ground-Breaking Special Effects."[26] By the time *Godzilla 6* opened, TriStar had at last settled on a director, two years after signing the deal with Toho. TriStar selected Jan de Bont, a former cinematographer who had scored a major box office hit with his first feature, *Speed*, starring Keanu Reeves. Toho flew de Bont out to Japan for a promotional tour, greeting him with a human-sized model of Godzilla with a sign reading, "I know you're going to make me a Hollywood *monstar*."[27]

The choice of de Bont had a number of expensive consequences for TriStar. In 1992, the initial discussion with Toho targeted a $40 million budget. De Bont, however, bargained for a $4 million fee simply for his own services, and insisted on a production budget of $130 million. At the time, the average studio production cost $30 million, and Toho had just spent a record $12 million on *Godzilla 6*. TriStar refused to authorize a budget of more than $100 million.

The budget arguments revolved around special effects. After years of deriding Japanese-made monster movies for using men in rubber suits, a certain degree of American pride was at stake. The only other aspect of Japanese *kaiju*

*eiga* to have received as much ridicule in the West as suitmation was the dubbing, and Rossio and Elliott's screenplay's only nod to Toho's original series is a snide joke about badly dubbed Japanese movies. Americans simply could not shoot a big-budget, high-profile monster movie with a man in a rubber suit without looking a little foolish.

In the wake of *Jurassic Park*, digital animation stood as the obvious alternative. Unfortunately, computer animation makes Harryhausen-style stop-motion animation seem a bargain by comparison. The computer effects consumed approximately $50 million worth of TriStar's projected $100 million budget, almost three times the amount spent on effects for *Jurassic Park*.

Ironically, the astronomical expenses of such effects techniques put the entire project in jeopardy. Having based its decisions on the argument that technical sophistication and production values mean more to audiences than storytelling or other narrative qualities, Hollywood backed itself into a corner. The name "Godzilla" had international appeal and could guarantee a sizable audience, but in order to avoid any B-movie stigma associated with that name, an American-made Godzilla movie would cost so much to make that it would be a terrible investment risk.

Rossio and Elliott's script had little emotional or psychological depth, but plenty of sprawling action. Between them, Godzilla and the Gryphon were to decimate a Japanese fishing village, the town of Traveler, Utah, Seattle, San Francisco, upstate New York and Manhattan. How much these effects would cost provided the major sticking point between de Bont and TriStar's management.

By December 1994, Robert Fried had replaced Woods as producer, and set a new release date for Memorial Day 1996. Fried proudly boasted that Godzilla and the Gryphon would be "virtually 100 percent computer animated." Fried sent a camera crew to Brookings, Oregon, to shoot test footage, with the intention of editing them into a theatrical trailer to run in the summer of 1995.[28] The crew constructed a set for a Japanese fishing village at

Lone Ranch Beach in September, with filming slated to commence in November.[29]

The camera crew returned empty-handed, however, when de Bont quit the project in early 1994. Unable to resolve the budget controversy with TriStar's management, he refused to participate further. TriStar paid him his full $4 million fee and released him from the contract. TriStar spokesperson Ed Russell tried to minimize the bad publicity by claiming the test filming was actually canceled due to bad weather. Meanwhile, Toho rejected TriStar's proposed Godzilla design, complaining it differed too greatly from the established image. Rumors that the special effects company and the screenwriters had also left the project only added to TriStar's woes.[30]

By spring of 1995, TriStar answered press queries by saying, "We're no longer involved with [Godzilla]."[31]

# Chapter 34

# *Godzilla vs. Mechagodzilla II**
## GOJIRA VS. MEKAGOJIRA
## (GODZILLA AGAINST MECHAGODZILLA)

*Since being unearthed, the egg's been straining its ears looking for its mother. Now it's found it. Ms. Gojo, it's you!*

— Professor Omae

Japanese version: 107 minutes, Released December 11, 1993

Color, Widescreen

Produced by Shogo Tomiyama; executive producer Tomoyuki Tanaka; directed by Takao Okawara; screenplay by Wataru Mimura; music by Akira Ifukube; cinematography by Yoshinoru Sakiguchi; special effects by Koichi Kawakita; special effects art direction by Tetsuzo Osawa; special effects cinematography by Kenichi Eguchi

Starring Masahiro Takashima (Kazuma Aoki), Ryoko Sano (Azusa Gojo), Megumi Odaka (Miki Saegusa), Yusuke Kawazu (Professor Omae), Tadao Takashima (Psyonics Institute Chief Hosono), Kenji Sahara (UNGCC Director Segawa), Akira Nakao (G-Force Commander Aso), Koichi Ueda (G-Force Commander Iwao Hyodo), Leo Mengetti (Dr. Asimov), Daijiro Harada (G-Force Capt. Takya Sasaki), Sherry Sweeney (G-Force Lt. Catherine Berger), Ichirota Miyagawa (G-Force Lt. Jun Sonezaki), Yoshi Osawa (G-Force Engineer Hiroshi Imai)

GODZILLA portrayed by Kenpachiro Satsuma; BABY GODZILLA portrayed by Hurricane Ryu; MECHAGODZILLA portrayed by Wataru Fukuda

*In 1992, following the events of Godzilla vs. King Ghidorah, the United Nations forms the Godzilla Countermeasures Center (UNGCC) so that the combined forces of the world can collaborate on the Godzilla problem. The UNGCC examines the wrecked remains of Mecha-Ghidorah and adapts the 23rd century cyber-technology to create the "ultimate battle machine."*

*Luckily it is ready just in time when Japan discovers a host of monsters: A paleontological expedition turns up a living pteranodon (Rodan) and what is believed to be a Rodan egg. The egg hatches to reveal a baby Godzillasaurus — with a telepathic link to the adult Godzilla, no less.*

*Hoping to use biological insights gleaned from the study of the baby Godzilla to develop an even more powerful weapon against the marauding titan, G-Force sends Mechagodzilla into battle. But with both Godzilla and Rodan feeling protectively paternal instincts towards the creature in G-Force's care, the battle is set to become much more daunting than planned.*

Nineteen ninety-three was a year of transition for Godzilla. The deal with TriStar promised to give the monster a larger audience than ever before. Toho recognized that the American film would bring in better profits than their own Godzilla movies, and in order not to compete with themselves, the Japanese series would come to an end. That year also saw the passing of Ishiro Honda. Although Honda had initially resisted Tomoyuki Tanaka's efforts to create a second series of Godzilla movies, that attitude had softened over time. In a gesture of goodwill to the new generation of Godzilla-makers, Honda visited the new series' set on several occasions in the early 1990s.[1] However, he showed no desire to take an active role in the new series, as he was happily involved in the "new series" of Akira Kurosawa movies. After completing the shooting of Kurosawa's *Madadayo*, Honda died at the age of 81. Some Japanese film crit-

---

*To distinguish this 1993 film from the 1973 film of identical title, Toho has added the number II to the English title; the designation is otherwise meaningless and does not appear on the Japanese title.

ics even wrote that Honda took Kurosawa's career with him when he died.[2] Certainly the *kaiju eiga* owed Honda its existence and international popularity.

*Godzilla 5* was to have been the final installment in the series, and coming as it did in the wake of Honda's death, it served as a tribute to the series' creator. *Godzilla 5* at once pays homage to the previous films in a more obvious and direct fashion than before, while also covering new ground with confidence and flair.

Having already revived King Ghidorah and Mothra, it was only natural for producers Tanaka and Shogo Tomiyama to turn next to Mechagodzilla. Koichi Kawakita had already showed an obsession with "Mecha," from the Super X machines to Mecha-Ghidorah and the proposed Mechamothra (not to mention his work on *Gunhed*, which got him the Godzilla job in the first place). Mechagodzilla had also provided the menace in Godzilla's twentieth anniversary outing. As the series neared its fortieth anniversary, the return of Mechagodzilla made for something of an apt bookend.

Not content to resurrect one of their most popular creations, the operating philosophy of *Godzilla vs. Mechagodzilla II* is "More!" For the price of one admission, they serve up Godzilla, Baby Godzilla, Mechagodzilla, *and* Rodan.

Rodan made a welcome return, but the reintroduction of a baby Godzilla, whether called Minilla or not, brought back many unfortunate memories. Tanaka had championed Minilla in the late 1960s as a way for the series to explore new territory and adapt its approach to a changing audience.[3] Although director Takao Okawara argued against it, the producers wanted to bring Minilla back, updated for a new generation.[4]

Part of the decision reflected the demographics of the marketplace. The primary audience for theatrical motion pictures in Japan is women (men comprise the majority of the video rental audience).[5] Consequently, the Godzilla series could only remain viable in the 1990s if the traditionally male-oriented movies learned how to target women as well. Resurrecting the son of Godzilla gave Toho a chance to court the same female audience that supported *REX, A Dinosaur Story*. Although not as successful as *Godzilla and Mothra*, *Godzilla vs. Mechagodzilla* nevertheless proved a savvy commercial move.

The Baby Godzilla provides the emotional core of the movie. "Baby" not only brought women in to see the movie, but also gave the filmmakers a device with which to create a moral ambiguity. Godzilla remains a destructive and horrifying monster, but Baby draws audience sympathy away from G-Force's plan to defeat Godzilla. In one striking scene, Miki Saegusa openly objects, almost mutinies. Her reasons clearly have to do with the baby Godzilla: Commander Aso calls the creature a "Godzillasaurus," she calls it "Baby." She has become emotionally attached to the baby Godzilla, something which has also happened to the other heroes, Azusa Gojo and Kazuma Aoki. Shortly later, Miki tells Gojo and Aoki, "Until now, I believed fighting Godzilla was a contribution to mankind. But now those feelings are gone."

Sandwiched between Miki's pronouncements of doubt comes a scene that firmly establishes the fundamental contradiction of the movie's attitude towards Godzilla:

> GOJO: Baby lives on this Earth, same as you or me. Baby is not our property or pet!
> UNGCC DIRECTOR: Ms. Gojo, our main priority is releasing the world from Godzilla's menace. That's this center's reason for being.

Although the heroes no longer have their hearts in fighting Godzilla, and begin to acknowledge that Godzilla has as much right to live as they do, Godzilla has not changed commensurately. Godzilla shows no respect for mankind's right to live. As a result, the audience is forced to sympathize with the very forces that threaten to destroy human civilization. Gojo says, "The dinosaurs ruled for a hundred million years. We've only been around for twenty thousand. It isn't strange to think their time will come again." Unfortunately for mankind, Godzilla does not seem inclined to wait.

Akira Ifukube's masterful score helps ally audience sympathy with Baby, and by extension with Godzilla, too. Miki's announcement that she no longer wants to fight Godzilla receives an elegiac musical accompaniment. Music also plays a role in the story, with the vines around Baby's egg singing a psychic song intended to help the creature mature into a Godzilla. This somber chorus underpins the scene in which Miki and Gojo "give Baby back" to Godzilla.

Gojo's apology that she could not protect Baby begs the question, "Protect him from whom?" Neither of the two "real" monsters ever threatened him, and in fact both Godzilla and Rodan seemed willing to sacrifice themselves to rescue the child. She must mean that she could not protect him from humans, a sentiment echoing Dr. Shiragami's remark in *Godzilla vs. Biollante* that men are the real monsters. In other words, humanity is its own worst enemy. From the Russian missiles in *Return of Godzilla* to the terrorists from *Godzilla vs. Biollante* to the futuristic terrorists from *Godzilla vs. King Ghidorah* to the irresponsible developers of *Godzilla and Mothra* to G-Force in this film, humans have created their own greatest problems. Furthermore, every effort to destroy Godzilla ends up making the monster even harder to destroy. At best, the war against Godzilla is a Pyrrhic battle. At the end of *Godzilla vs. Mechagodzilla*, at least Miki is prepared to surrender.

The filmmakers deftly handle this ambivalent approach to the characters, with audience sympathy split between opposing sides. When Godzilla returns from the dead, having absorbed Rodan's life force, the monster rises up into a golden halo, with Ifukube's famous Godzilla March thundering on the soundtrack. It is a triumphant moment of catharsis, an epiphany, highlighted by Ifukube's superb music. Only in retrospect does the viewer realize that powerful climax represented a *defeat* for humanity.

At the time of *Godzilla vs. Mechagodzilla*'s release, publicity claimed that Ifukube had provided his final score, and had retired following this swan song (although this would ultimately prove untrue). The score is a remarkable achievement, arguably Ifukube's best, and became the subject of a promotional documentary.

Koichi Kawakita and his team also surpassed themselves. From the optical mattes to pyrotechnics to computer animation, everything shows perfectionist care. *Godzilla vs. Mechagodzilla* also benefits from a wider variety of camera angles, some of them quite inventive.

Many of the special effects scenes pay visual tribute to famous scenes from the series' history. Rodan attacks Godzilla in homage to *Ghidrah, The Three-Headed Monster*, Godzilla destroys an oil refinery in a tip of the hat to *Mothra vs. Godzilla*, and many of Mechagodzilla's scenes recall moments from the two 1970s Mechagodzilla movies. Kawakita also stages some remarkable scenes that earn their own place alongside those classic moments from the past. Having endured criticism for his emphasis on energy rays, Kawakita this time stages violent physical fights between his monsters. The confrontation between Godzilla and Rodan on Andonoa Island is one of the series' most believable and exciting monster battles.

The opening title sequence, showing the development of Mechagodzilla, conspicuously avoids duplicating a famous shot. In both of the previous Mechagodzilla movies, Teruyoshi Nakano copied a shot originally created by Eiji Tsuburaya for *King Kong Escapes*, in which the human scientists at work on the giant robot march along the ground while the cyborg towers upright above them. The advantage of such a shot came in the straight line available for a matte along the robot's feet. Kawakita shows his Mechagodzilla prone, with people swarming all around it. The effect is a thoroughly convincing depiction of an enormous robot.

For Rodan, Kawakita used a variety of marionettes and hand puppets, rather than a man in a suit. In some scenes, Kawakita operated the hand-puppet used for close-ups.[6]

Baby Godzilla was a standard suitmation monster, performed by Hurricane Ryu, who had previously played King Ghidorah and Battra. One aspect of the Baby Godzilla costume deserves a mention: Baby has three toes. The Godzilla costumes used in the two 1950s films had four toes, but beginning with *King Kong vs. Godzilla*, the suits were made with only three. Not until *Return of Godzilla*, with Toho attempting to recreate the original Godzilla in every respect, did the fourth toe reappear on the costume, where it has since stayed. The "evil" Godzilla of the 1950s and the second series has four toes, while Godzilla's depiction as a comical figure and a "good guy" is associated with three toes.[7] While discussion of such trivia may seem hopelessly obsessive — perhaps even the definition of *otaku*— these are the things that keep Toho's lawyers awake at night: Contract negotiations with TriStar included a deal-breaking stipulation mandating four toes on the monster.

Wataru Fukuda played Mechagodzilla, inside a suit that lacked the angularity of the 1970s Mechagodzilla but seemed more convincing in its design. The costume was made of multiple separate elements, like ILM's Godzilla suit, and had to be applied to Fukuda in pieces, like a suit of armor.[8] Kawakita originally planned for Mechagodzilla to split into two parts, a plane and a tank, rather like the morphing "mecha" seen in Japanese animated productions.[9] Ultimately, Kawakita abandoned that idea in favor of Garuda, a Super X derivative named for a Japanese mythical bird spirit.[10]

Garuda provided a thematic symmetry for the climax. The final metamorphoses of the two headliner monsters highlight the theme of "life versus artificial life." Garuda, a mechanical bird, fuses with the mechanical Godzilla to become SuperMechagodzilla, the ultimate in human technology. A living bird, Rodan, fuses with the living Godzilla to become an even more powerful Godzilla, which thoroughly trounces self-important mankind's creations. Humans cannot hope to build anything superior to what nature can create.

Aoki's personal flying machine, although never identified as a "Mecharodan" in the film, has clearly been modeled on Rodan's image. That the flying machine crashes ignominiously on its maiden flight serves as an apt precursor to the climactic failure of G-Force's technology on the battlefield.

Rodan's transformation into "Fire Rodan" seems poorly conceived, tacked on merely to fulfill the dictates of having every monster evolve. The greatest drama comes simply from having Rodan come to Baby's rescue. Having seen the powerfully protective instincts Baby evokes in Gojo and Miki, Commander Aso and the others at the United Nations Godzilla Countermeasures Center display arrogance and stupidity in not expecting similar emotions to be aroused in the two monsters who consider Baby to be "family."

In the sequence in which Godzilla looks for Baby in Kyoto, Kenpachiro Satsuma depicts Godzilla's confusion, sadness, and frustration with precise body language. Throughout the film, Satsuma gives an impressive performance in what stands as one of Godzilla's most extensive screen appearance since *Godzilla vs. Biollante*. Satsuma very much wanted to explore Godzilla's emotions:

> The full range of Godzilla's expression is rather limited ... roaring, battling, shooting the atomic breath, returning briefly to its home. So my wish is to express Godzilla's emotions in short scenes or in subtle ways ... I also think there is a need for good scripts and understandable direction, and making suits which can directly reflect Godzilla's emotional condition.[11]

Wataru Mimura's screenplay, which revels in the emotional life of its monster characters, gave Satsuma such an opportunity. Mimura attended the same screenwriting school as Yukiko Takayama (*Terror of Mechagodzilla*) and greatly admired the work of Shinichi Sekizawa.[12] He keeps his script simple and focused, unlike the sprawling and often confusing work of Kazuki Omori. Not only does he illuminate the emotions of the monsters, he also highlights the emotions of many of the human characters. Azusa Gojo interacts with Baby in a maternal and protective fashion. Her despair when she realizes that she has failed to keep her promise to Baby and must return "custody" to Godzilla stands out as one of the most poignant moments in the forty-year series. Miki Saegusa, little more than a narrative device in previous entries, finally comes into her own as a character, revealing her motivations and priorities forcefully in several key sequences.

Some of the human drama ended up on the

cutting room floor to keep the running time down. One deleted subplot involved Lt. Berger, the tough American woman on the G-Force team, played by Sherry Sweeney. In a scene removed from the final cut, Aoki learns that Berger is actually an android. A scene identifying her as a "replicant" appeared on the Toho laserdisc release along with other deleted scenes. As Robert Biondi noted in his review of the disc, "Specifically, a point to consider is [Sherry] Sweeney's line at the film's conclusion, 'Life against artificial life.' If Sweeney's character was still supposed to be an android when this scene was filmed, her comment would indeed have been ironic since she represents artificial life."[13]

In another deleted sequence, Baby exhibits hostility towards Miki. Baby knows she used her psychic abilities to combat Godzilla, and therefore considers her an enemy. She then enters Baby's cage to win the creature's trust. Most likely, the filmmakers rejected the sequence because the Baby effects were subpar.[14] Unfortunately, the loss of the scene robs the movie of an even greater depth to the already well-developed relationship between Miki and the monsters.

Given meatier roles with which to work, Takao Okawara coaxes more developed performances from his cast than in the previous film. Megumi Odaka clearly relishes the chance to flesh out Miki. As Gojo, Ryoko Sano performs convincingly alongside suitmation actor Hurricane Ryu in scenes that develop a mother-child relationship between human and monster. The star of the film, Masahiro Takashima, previously starred in *Gunhed*. He gives Aoki the kind of charming, gently comic qualities his father Tadao displayed in such films as *King Kong vs. Godzilla*. Fittingly, Tadao returns to the series to appear briefly with his son as the director of the Psyonics Institute. Kenji Sahara also appears, here as the UNGCC Director, making him the most seen of all of the Godzilla series' performers. The American cast members, Sherry Sweeney as the tough-as-nails Mechagodzilla co-pilot and Leo Mengetti as Mechagodzilla's creator, give more effective and believable performances than

Toho usually got from its Western (non-)actors. Keiko Imamura and Sayaka Osawa, the Cosmos from the previous film, appear as teachers at the Psyonics Institute. Takao Okawara thought it would be an amusing in-joke to have them speak in unison, like the Cosmos.

Eager to repeat the success of *Godzilla and Mothra*, Toho released *Godzilla vs. Mechagodzilla II* with a publicity blitz. Capitalizing on previously published announcements that *Godzilla vs. Mechagodzilla II* was to have been the final film of the series, Toho "leaked" rumors that Godzilla dies in the conclusion. Of course, something like that does occur in the film, which lent some substance to the rumor. The speculation helped generate interest in the movie, and as such was very effective, yet inexpensive, publicity.[15]

One of the more unusual promotional efforts involved the early morning children's television program *Adventure Godzilla-land*, which aired on Thursdays. The program featured Godzilla and Mechagodzilla as rival news anchors presenting clips from the movie as "news footage." In another segment, Godzilla hosts an exercise program to a bouncy "Be Like Godzilla" theme song. With Godzilla toys offered as prizes for various on-air contests, the show promoted the new movie and the Godzilla merchandising enterprise as well.[16]

One such merchandising effort was made shortly after the release of *Godzilla vs. Mechagodzilla II*, an amusement park simulation ride called "Monster Planet of Godzilla." The ride features Megumi Odaka playing not Miki Seagusa but a hostess of a spaceship that crashes on a planet where Godzilla, Rodan and Mothra live. A second ship sent to rescue the first causes a freak time distortion that sends the monsters to modern-day Tokyo. Koichi Kawakita produced the ride's 3-D visual effects, which were then set to Akira Ifukube's music. The ride opened at Sanrio Puroland (an amusement park outside Tokyo) in the fall of 1994, coinciding with the film's appearance on home video.[17]

*Godzilla 5* had not, in fact, laid Godzilla to rest, which meant that there would be a *Godzilla 6* to provide a true 40th anniversary celebration.

Chapter 35

# Godzilla vs. Space Godzilla

## GOJIRA VS. SUPEESU GOJIRA*
## (GODZILLA AGAINST SPACE GODZILLA)

*NASA wasn't able to come up with an explanation for what happened here. We can only speculate that it's some sort of huge monster.*

— NASA representative Reynolds

Japanese version: 108 minutes, Released December 10, 1994
Color, Widescreen
Produced by Shogo Tomiyama; executive producer Tomoyuki Tanaka; directed by Kenshou Yamashita; screenplay by Hiroshi Kashiwabara; music by Takayuki Hattori; Godzilla and Mothra themes by Akira Ifukube (prerecorded); song "Echoes of Love" by Date of Birth; cinematography by Masahiro Kishimoto; special effects by Koichi Kawakita; special effects cinematography by Kenichi Eguchi
Starring Megumi Odaka (Director Miki Saegusa), Kenji Sahara (UNGCC Director Takayuki Segawa), Jun Hashizume (Lt. Koji Shinjo), Zenkichi Yoneyama (Lt. Kiyoshi Sato), Akira Emoto (Major Akira Yuki), Yosuke Saito (Dr. Susumu Okubo), Towako Yoshikawa (Dr. Chinatsu Gondo), Akira Nakao (G-Force Commander Aso), Koichi Ueda (G-Force Commander Iwao Hyodo), Keiko Imamura and Sayaka Osawa (The Cosmos)
GODZILLA portrayed by Kenpachiro Satsuma; MOGERA portrayed by Wataru Fukuda; SPACE GODZILLA portrayed by Ryo Hariya; LITTLE GODZILLA portrayed by Little Frankie

*Unwilling to accept defeat, G-Force presses on in search of a defense against Godzilla. The M-Project involves the reconstruction of Mechagodzilla's wreckage into a new battle machine, MOGERA (Mobile Operation Godzilla Expert Robot Aero-Type) which can fly, burrow underground, fire an array of weapons, and separate into two sections.*

*Meanwhile, Dr. Okubo and Dr. Chinatsu Gondo (sister of Lt. Goro Gondo from Godzilla vs. Biollante) begin work on a competing strategy, the T-Project. They hope to implant a psychic receiver in the base of*

*Godzilla's brain in order to psychically control him and abort his destructive tendencies. Miki Saegusa, now the director of G-Force's Psychic Center, is morally opposed to the T-Project.*

*G-Force counts on being able to wear down Saegusa's reluctance, and sends Lt. Kiyo Sato and Lt. Koji Shinjo to Birth Island to set the stage for the T-Project's implementation. Birth Island is the home of Little Godzilla, now grown to 30 meters, and receives regular visits from the King of the Monsters himself.*

*The first trial run of the T-Project goes awry when the island is attacked by an enormous and violent creature from outer space, resembling a crystalline Godzilla. It imprisons Little Godzilla and defeats the adult Godzilla, before flying off to wreak havoc on the Japanese mainland. In the face of such a threat, G-Force has to reconsider its strategies. Yuki and his team will have to swallow their pride and join forces with Godzilla against the cosmic monster.*

One of the problems with maintaining a running line of continuity from film to film, much like a serialized television show, is that as time goes on, it boxes in the writers. By the time of *Godzilla vs. Space Godzilla*, the Heisei series had settled into its own familiar routines, perhaps more rut-like than any of the Showa cycle. Surprisingly, this latest entry in the franchise simultaneously obsesses over continuity and "inside-baseball" references, yet feels the freshest and most idiosyncratic of the lot.

Back again are all the familiar faces: Miki Saegusa, General Aso, Kenji Sahara's UNGCC Director, etc. Once again G-Force has built a giant cyborg, which they will watch from a

*The Japanese word for space is "uchu," but the Japanese title is not Gojira vs. Uchu Gojira. Instead the characters spell out a Japanized rendition of the English word "space."

202

giant screen. Little Godzilla is an explicit carryover from the previous film, as is Miki's growing recalcitrance. The enemy monster only exists because Godzilla cells were expelled into space in *Godzilla vs. Biollante* and *Godzilla and Mothra*; Mothra and the Cosmos reappear; and yet *again* there is a character bearing an angry grudge against Godzilla for having killed a friend or family member — and this time, that fallen loved one just happens to be Gondo, from *Godzilla vs. Biollante*, whose death is represented by actual clips from that previous film. As if in a nod even further back into the past, Little Godzilla spews radioactive bubbles in a scene evoking Minilla's smoke rings from *Son of Godzilla*.

For all these similarities and connections, though, *Space Godzilla* is a box of novelties as well, thanks to the arrival of some newcomers in the director's chair and behind the typewriter.

Director Kenshou Yamashita first made his name directing "teen idol" movies like *Nineteen* (rather like Jun Fukuda rising up from a background in Young Guy films). Although *Space Godzilla* put Yamashita in charge of a budget eight times as large as he was accustomed, he approached the project in a manner not dissimilar to his earlier "teen idol" movies. He brought with him screenwriter Hiroshi Kashiwabara, his writer on *Nineteen*, to put a new emphasis on characterization and romance. A writer for many of the animated *Lupin III* adventures, Kashiwabara was well established as a populist screenwriter with a feel for mass appeal.

Although *Space Godzilla*'s screenwriter and director were relative newcomers to the series, they had connections through *Terror of Mechagodzilla*. Screenwriter Hiroshi Kashiwabara attended the same screenwriting institute as *Terror of Mechagodzilla*'s author Yukiko Takayama. After studying directing under Kihachi Okamoto[1], Kenshou Yamashita served as chief assistant director under Ishiro Honda on *Terror of Mechagodzilla* as well.[2]

Together, Yamashita and Kashiwabara placed Miki Saegusa at center stage. Little more than a narrative device in the preceding films,

at last the poor girl is given something to do. Producer Shogo Tomiyama had been anxious to make more of her role, something he feared previous writers had been squandering. With Megumi Odaka turning twenty-three, it seemed natural to let the character finally mature into a young woman.[3]

Some reviewers misleadingly reported that Saegusa falls in love. Although this is true, it is also equally true that Lt. Koji Shinjo (played by handsome leading man Jun Hashizume) falls in love with her. True to romance-movie formula, the two characters spend most of their screen time bickering. When men and women do not get along in movies, it can be taken as a sure sign that they are meant to fall in love with each other: Opposites attract.

Most of their arguments revolve around their attitudes towards Godzilla. Following her change of heart in *Godzilla vs. Mechagodzilla II*, Saegusa now sees Godzilla as a creature neither good nor bad, but deserving of respect as a living (albeit horrifyingly destructive) animal. For his part, Lt. Shinjo is an officer of G-Force and sworn to fight Godzilla. In the final scene, Saegusa has won over Shinjo to her way of thinking. Using telepathy, she even gets him literally to see things through her eyes. Shinjo now says, "He wasn't such a bad guy after all, Godzilla."

Likewise, Major Yuki has been softened by love. His hatred of Godzilla for killing Goro Gondo six years earlier drives him only so far. When Godzilla saves the world from Space Godzilla, Yuki finally decides the score has been settled. His relationship with Gondo's sister Chinatsu has been instrumental in this change of heart. As Yuki boards MOGERA for the final battle, she takes him aside and says, "You told me that you can only keep living because you have something that you can't give up on. I know what that something for me is." Although she never so much as tells him directly that she loves him, the implication is clear. His Clint Eastwood–like response is, "My lighter is out of gas. Would you refill it for me?" However, as MOGERA smolders in the ashes of Fukuoka, she returns the lighter to him and he asks her gently to show him around her home town.

Yuki previously claimed that hatred of Godzilla was all that kept him alive. For him to give up that vengeance means that, like Gondo, he has found something else to live for — her.

Both Koji and Yuki have changed their minds about Godzilla as a result of love. To emphasize how love has influenced this change of attitude, the final scene includes a fifth wheel, Kiyo. Without another's love, Kiyo's anger and violence has not been tempered by the experience. His colleagues now acknowledge respect for the King of Monsters, but Kiyo screams, "We'll have a rematch someday!"

The startling emphasis on romance forms a large part of the human drama, but other interpersonal relationships play a prominent role, too. Commander Aso holds strongly contradictory feelings towards Major Yuki. Reunited at UNGCC headquarters, Yuki scowls at Aso, "People change when they sit behind a desk all day, every day." Aso defends himself: "This kind of job makes everyone look old and worn-out." When he offers the leadership of MOGERA to Yuki, Aso grumbles, "I wish I could ask this of someone else." Akira Nakao reprises his role as Aso, and steals his few scenes. Akira Emoto gives an effective and understated performance as Yuki, ennobling a role that could easily have led to hammy overacting. Emoto's self-absorption and reticence make Yuki a fascinating screen presence.

Kenji Sahara returns as UNGCC director Segawa, last seen in Godzilla vs. Mechagodzilla II. His role provides little screen time, and less dialogue than the previous film, but fans were glad to see his familiar face anyway. Keiko Imamura and Sayaka Osawa also return, again as the Cosmos.

Megumi Odaka plays the starring role well, and her confidence on-screen begs the question of why Toho let her languish in a supporting role for four films before letting her shine. Co-star Jun Hashizume had been selected by Shogo Tomiyama for his prominence as a star of non–science fiction films. He seems somewhat at a loss in a new genre, but comes across charismatically enough.

Kashiwabara's screenplay provides the characters with a depth that had been sorely lacking.

Not only have the roles been written without reliance on stereotypes, but the cast plays against type as well; no one is quite what they seem. The human cast gives believable and compelling performances. Even the English-speaking characters are less embarrassing than in previous installments. The believability of the American characters results from how the lines are read, however, not the content of those lines. The NASA official who concludes that a space accident can only be attributed to "some sort of huge monster" is unlikely to get a gold star on his next job performance review.

The filmmakers evidently viewed Space Godzilla as an ecological statement, judging from the script. In promotional interviews, Kenpachiro Satsuma boasted, "What I am trying to express, just with my back as I walk away, is a warning against nuclear destruction."[4] In the closing moments of the film, Dr. Gondo announces gravely, "If we keep polluting space, I'm sure we'll face another Space Godzilla someday. This may have been a warning to the human race." Whereas the original Godzilla came into existence because mankind's nuclear pollution produced a mutated symbol of the nuclear age, Space Godzilla represents a different event. The "pollution" that created Space Godzilla was a piece of Godzilla himself, taken into space by another monster. Humankind played no direct role in Space Godzilla's creation. If any ecological lesson is to be learned from the film, then, it would seem that we should keep our giant monsters from leaving the planet.

Godzilla vs. Space Godzilla also harks back to 1964's Ghidrah, The Three-Headed Monster, with Godzilla gradually becoming a more sympathetic and heroic monster. In both films, Mothra acts an agent of this rehabilitation of Godzilla's image. In both films, Godzilla does not undergo a personality change, but rather seems the lesser of two evils, on the theory that the enemy of my enemy is my friend. G-Force only very reluctantly turns their attention away from Godzilla to fight Space Godzilla. Commander Aso gives a look of profound disappointment to UNGCC director Segawa after hearing that the "ultimate weapon against

Godzilla" will not be used against Godzilla after all, but will be sent into space to fight Space Godzilla. Old hatreds die hard.

That "ultimate weapon," MOGERA, also provides continuity to previous films. Beginning in 1944, three Dorats mutated into King Ghidorah, which was then converted into the cyborg Mecha-Ghidorah, which was later remade as Mechagodzilla, and now reborn as MOGERA. This mechanical marvel represents humanity's attempts at "artificial life," the hubris of which led to Japan's defeat in *Godzilla vs. Mechagodzilla II*. By contrast, Godzilla's life cycle always remains one step ahead. From a dinosaur on Lagos Island in 1944 to a 50-meter Godzilla to an 80-meter Godzilla to a 100-meter Godzilla to absorbing the life force of Rodan, Godzilla has consistently emerged from battles stronger than before. Human arrogance created him out of nuclear pollution, and with every attempt to get rid of this monstrous incarnation of poetic justice, the menace has worsened. "Real life" always beats "artificial life."

However, Godzilla's primary opponent in this film is not MOGERA, the latest creation of Japan's engineers, but a horrible version of himself. Kawakita had already shown a predilection for depicting "alternate Godzillas": Godzilla as a flower; Godzilla as a dinosaur; Godzilla as a baby; Godzilla as a robot. *Godzilla vs. Space Godzilla* is populated with alternate Godzillas, with both the baby and adult Godzillas and a reworked incarnation of Mechagodzilla facing a monster comprised of pieces of Biollante.

To highlight the dramatic first appearance of Godzilla, the soundtrack thunders with Akira Ifukube's famous musical motif. As director Kenshou Yamashita noted, "The members of the audience expect to hear Mr. Ifukube's music whenever they see a Godzilla movie."[5] However, despite such an acknowledgment, Ifukube did not score the film. Aside from the prerecorded Godzilla theme and a Mothra theme heard during the Cosmos' visit to Miki Saegusa, the score comes from newcomer Takayuki Hattori.

According to Yamashita, Ifukube was un-available due to a scheduling conflict.[6] Other sources suggest that Yamashita and Ifukube disagreed on the approach to the music, and Ifukube declined to participate.[7] Hattori's grandfather, Tadashi Hattori, had scored several of Akira Kurosawa's earliest films. The younger Hattori had earned a deserved reputation as a versatile composer.[8] However, his score is so markedly dissimilar to Ifukube's work that Ifukube's Godzilla theme seems out of place. Hattori's contemporary music recalls that of Masaru Sato, and helps place *Godzilla vs. Space Godzilla* in the same tradition as Sato-scored movies like *Godzilla vs. the Sea Monster* and *Son of Godzilla*.

Kenshou Yamashita one-ups Jun Fukuda with some clever action sequences that Fukuda would certainly have enjoyed. One highlight comes when a Mafia agent uses Miki strapped to a bed as a shield against G-Force's gunfire. The scene highlights Miki and Koji's developing relationship and puts the movie's heroine in extreme peril. Kazuki Omori aspired to that kind of dramatic action in *Godzilla vs. Biollante*, but was so focused on aping Hollywood films that he missed his own mark. Yamashita simply does his own thing, and the results are superior.

Koichi Kawakita responded to the new behind-the-scenes personnel by handling the effects for *Space Godzilla* in a markedly different fashion. Most notably, the monster scenes display wildly different angles and compositions. Confident in his improved mattes, Kawakita designs a few scenes solely to show off. In one, Yuki crawls through grass and weeds on Birth Island while Godzilla stomps alongside. Not only do the jagged and irregular edges of the leaves make for an extremely complicated matte line, but Kawakita also has the camera shudder with each of the monster's footsteps. It is an extremely difficult effect accomplished with precision. In another surprising and innovative shot, the camera both tracks over Godzilla and zooms past his head to Yuki running down the beach behind him. The combination of miniature photography and full-scale live action in moving shots seems elegant and effortless. Kawakita's cinematographer Kenichi

Euguchi coordinated his work well with Yamashita's photographer Masahiro Kishimoto.

The film's weakest effects occur during MOGERA's confrontation with Space Godzilla in outer space. The execution of the scene falls short, while the conception of the scene falls even shorter. Not even convincing special effects could redeem the idea that MOGERA managed to fly so far into space so quickly, endure a battle with the space monster, and still return safely to Earth promptly. The American film *Apollo 13*, released less than a year later, showed how treacherous even slight deviations from a planned space flight can be, and how maddeningly slow real space flight actually is.

Faced with an opponent too powerful to defeat in direct combat, Satsuma's Godzilla displays intelligence in devising a battle strategy. It is a testament to Satsuma's subtle characterization that Godzilla's display of wits does not depict an anthropomorphic intelligence, as had been the case with Haruo Nakajima, but remains animalistic and instinctive.

Satsuma had a prime opportunity to flesh out the emotions of his character in *Space Godzilla*, via the protective paternal relationship between Godzilla and Little Godzilla. Unfortunately, one such sequence ended up on the cutting room floor. Following the initial battle with Space Godzilla on Birth Island, Godzilla tries to free Little Godzilla from the crystals. Only reluctantly does he give up and retreat to the sea to recover. Kawakita deleted this scene.

In a cut scene from the end of the film, Godzilla's departure from Fukuoka originally involved Satsuma pausing. Satsuma explained:

> This is the kind of sequence which I feel there is a real need for ... Godzilla walking, stopping for a moment, and then continuing on again. But the directors ... have an image of Godzilla that he should constantly be in motion. But I think that just moving Godzilla is not enough. Sometimes pausing or holding an expression is necessary, but the matter of running time always leads to these kind of things being cut.[9]

Interestingly, Kawakita did not delete the footage of Godzilla struggling to free Little Godzilla because it was unconvincing, his usual reason for discarding special effects footage.

Instead, Kawakita found the footage "too serious."[10] The production team wanted *Space Godzilla* to be lighter than previous installments. From Hattori's contemporary musical score to Kashiwabara's lighthearted and silly humor in the script to the emphasis on romance, *Space Godzilla* broke with tradition.

In keeping with this lighter tone, Kawakita redesigned Baby Godzilla, now called Little Godzilla, to look cuter. Reportedly, Kawakita disliked the dinosaurian aspects of Baby Godzilla and changed the design to meet his own tastes.[11] With Little Godzilla's cuteness more to his liking, Kawakita tried to get Tomiyama's support for a separate project called *Little Godzilla's Underground Adventure*, a television special for children.[12] The appeal of the monster to children seems calculated, since Little Godzilla's gurgling noises are sound effects previously used in the children's movie *Daigoro vs. Goliath* (1972).[13]

Kawakita's MOGERA updates a monster design last seen in 1957, but not previously part of the Godzilla series. The original MOGERA appeared in Ishiro Honda's *The Mysterians*, as a giant robot employed in an alien attempt to conquer the Earth. Reviving the robot creature with a new history meant the film boasted a monster that was both "new" and "improved." Exactly why G-Force thinks rebuilding Mecha-Ghidorah/Mechagodzilla in a new shape will make it any more effective is a question beyond the scope of this book.

Suitmation actor Wataru Fukuda, last seen as Mechagodzilla, wore the three-piece MOGERA outfit.[14] Unlike *Mechagodzilla*, however, the film emphasizes the humans inside the machine and downplays the actions of the monster as seen from the outside.

The design of Space Godzilla included elements that suggested the monster's ostensible heritage, with tusks and a hissing roar that recalled Biollante. A *Space Godzilla* film had been tentatively announced by Toho in 1978, but like so many others never got produced.[15] In its own weird way, then, the eventual appearance of the monster made Space Godzilla, like MOGERA, simultaneously both a "returning" and a "new" monster.

These competing "new" and "returning" elements in the story, the monsters, and the production team all offered marketing hooks for Toho. *Godzilla vs. Space Godzilla* appeared in theaters forty years after the original, and as an anniversary film held a special importance to Toho's marketing department. The previous anniversary years had all marked milestones in the series' creative development. Expectations were high for 1994.

Since the film's release coincided with the tragic Kobe earthquake, and Space Godzilla attacks Kobe in the film, some feared that audiences would find the movie's monster-induced destruction too similar to real-life horrors. Indeed, the very premise of the *kaiju eiga* was to illustrate just such real-life horrors in a fictional setting. Fearing a Kobe-related backlash, Toho reduced ticket prices, a move that increased ticket sales during the film's last three weeks.[16]

Early ticket sales showed attendance lagging behind *Godzilla vs. Mechagodzilla II*. This by itself worried Toho little, since they never expected to beat the record set by *Godzilla and Mothra*. Furthermore, the greatest income from the Godzilla movies came not from ticket sales but from merchandising. The extensive line of *Space Godzilla*–related products virtually ensured high profits.[17] In any case, the previous anniversary films were not noted for their financial performance. The first series' biggest commercial hit came in 1962, not 1964, while the twentieth anniversary film made a modest sum, but not as much as *Godzilla vs. Gigan*. Godzilla's 1984 comeback performed only adequately, and Toho waited four years to produce a sequel. The anniversary films were notable as *creative* successes. The true test of *Space Godzilla*, then, would be the critical reaction.

Response to *Space Godzilla*, though, was mixed. Some disliked Hattori's score. Some disliked the emphasis on the human plot, while others found the monster plot too boring. Some disliked Little Godzilla in principle, and others disliked MOGERA and Space Godzilla in execution. Despite such negative reaction, there were viewers who responded positively. *Space Godzilla* was not universally panned, but neither was it universally supported.[18]

Back in 1992, *Godzilla and Mothra* performed so well at the box office (despite intense competition from *Jurassic Park*) that it caught TriStar's eye. Although *Jurassic Park* won in pure dollar terms, Godzilla's endurance in the face of such a competitor made the difference. The same dynamic worked against Godzilla in 1994. This time, Godzilla had the upper hand over its immediate competitor. As the much-ballyhooed, big-budget, internationally famed product of Japan's most prosperous movie studio, *Godzilla vs. Space Godzilla* made its profit tidily. In the shadows, though, a low-budget monster movie with almost nothing going for it won the admiration of fans and critics alike. Gamera had finally come of age.

Daiei first introduced Gamera in 1965. At a time when Toho's *kaiju eiga* were colorful and splashy, the *Gojira*-style black and white *Daikaiju Gamera* seemed like an anachronism. With the character of a friendly, fire-breathing giant monster turtle capable of jetting around like a flying saucer (or a Frisbee) with flames spewing impossibly out of its four leg holes, the Gamera series never sought realism. Aimed at a much younger audience than Toho's films, and produced with vastly smaller budgets, the Gamera series lumbered through a total of eight films between 1965 and 1980. During the 1970s, the Godzilla films began to exhibit characteristics evidently borrowed from the Gamera movies, but overall Daiei's series never achieved the same recognition as Toho's. In the 1980 *Gamera Super Monster*, comprised almost entirely of stock footage from previous adventures, Daiei ended the series.[19]

Ultimately, Daiei died off, too. Forced into bankruptcy, the once proud home of Akira Kurosawa's *Rashomon* closed its doors. Gamera lived on, but mostly as a joke. The original features had appeared in America courtesy of AIP, with titles designed to mimic the Godzilla features. In the 1980s, Sandy Frank reissued the films on video with new titles and new, inferior dubbing. *Mystery Science Theater 3000* on the Comedy Central cable network quickly took up the easily ridiculed Gamera as its mascot.

After reorganizing itself financially, Daiei

prepared to reenter the world of production. However, their work would be distributed through Toho. When the revamped Daiei announced a revamped Gamera for release in 1995, few monster fans expected anything special. *Gamera Daikaiju Kuchu Kessen* ("Gamera Giant Monster Midair Battle," officially *Gamera: Guardian of the Universe*) opened in the spring of 1995, marking the thirtieth anniversary of Gamera and the first film in fifteen years. Fans and critics alike had a buffet of humble pie to choke down.

Special effects director Shinji Higuchi had seen *Mystery Science Theater 3000* during a stay in Los Angeles: "While I was watching [Comedy Central], I saw someone say, 'Hey, I'm going to show you the funniest visual image that has ever been created on this planet!' It was Gamera doing a back flip from *Gamera vs. Guiron*. So, I learned that Americans also see the older Gamera films as comedies."[20]

Higuchi and director Shusuke Kaneko determined to distinguish the new Gamera from the notorious comedies of the past. The list of things going against them was daunting: a once-bankrupt studio struggling back to life, a movie franchise never regarded with high esteem, a monster so absurd as to almost *demand* laughter (really? a flying, jet-propelled, fire-breathing turtle that is friend of all children?). On top of that, Kaneko and Higuchi had less than half the budget of *Space Godzilla*, against which they would be competing head to head.

To summarize the situation: Young, untested filmmakers without the decades of institutional experience from which to draw set out to revive a ridiculous and ridiculed franchise with almost no money.

Like some kind of *kaiju* alchemists, Kaneko and Higuchi did the impossible. They took an anachronistic and moribund genre, whose commercial horizons were widely assumed to be constrained by inherent limitations of the form and the costs of special effects technology, and proved that there were new discoveries to be made.

Toho, and for that matter TriStar, had been operating under the assumption that the Godzilla series had maxed out its possible Japa-

nese audience and could only hope to maintain that level of popularity by steadily increasing the amount being spent — and the only way to break through that ceiling was to "go Hollywood" and spend even more. The inability of Toho to find a Western audience for the Heisei Godzilla movies was chalked up to cultural prejudices. Everybody took the existing situation for granted. And then came *Gamera*.

As an artistic achievement, it was astonishing. Characters have genuine emotional lives, personality quirks, and senses of humor — and events take place in what is recognizably the real world. This is not just to say that Higuchi's effects are convincing — which they are, more so than anything Kawakita did — but that they occur within a narrative context that seems real. The characters do not have access to things we do not either — no flying tanks or maser cannons. They have to make do with the limitations of the real world (except of course for the basic looniness of the premise, which is made all the more palatable by the realism with which it is treated).

Kaneko and Higuchi rewrote Gamera's mythology, but maintained the classic iconography. Things looked the same as before, but were given new explanations. Actually, *Gamera* borrows the structure of *Space Godzilla*, with a space monster intent on destroying Earth while the human military attempts to kill the "good" monster that could save the world — a plot structure that not only mirrored *Space Godzilla*, but also duplicated the plot of Rossio and Elliott's screenplay for the unmade TriStar *Godzilla*. The new Gamera was created especially for the purpose of defending the Earth from a doomsday monster foretold by legend. Like the proposed Gryphon, the new Gaos represents the product of alien genetic engineering.

In many ways, Daiei benefitted from the notorious reputation of Gamera. With the Gamera movies widely regarded as inferior and absurd, Daiei had no image to maintain, no legacy to preserve; they could recreate Gamera from scratch. In an ironic twist, the same fans who sharply criticized TriStar's proposed embellishments of the Godzilla myth warmly embraced the same ideas in Daiei's film. It was an audacious act for screenwriter Kazunori Ito to upstage Toho and TriStar's Godzilla projects by borrowing so many pages from their books.

Daiei's confidence was rewarded by audience reaction. Whereas the old Gamera was a cheap Godzilla imitator, the new Gamera proved to be solid competition. *Gamera* became a critical favorite, and remained in the top ten films for its first six weeks of release, shaming *Space Godzilla* by comparison.[21] Ultimately, *Gamera* grossed over $12 million in Japan.[22]

Although Toho had been unable to find American distribution for any of the Godzilla films following *Godzilla vs. Biollante*, *Gamera* received red carpet treatment in Dallas. A new AMC theater called The Grand showed a subtitled version as part of the inaugural ceremonies. *The Dallas Morning News* praised the movie highly, and singled out Higuchi's special effects for compliment.[23]

Other American critics agreed. *Variety* praised it as "an enjoyably cheesy and action-packed monster mash that zestily revives the Japanese megabeast tradition.... [D]espite its horrific countenance and plated shell, Gamera remains one of the most likable of all movie monsters."[24] Others noted that "the special effects are as realistic as anything in cinema."[25]

In dubbed form it started to play in England, and quickly appeared on DVD in America — even while the Heisei Godzillas remained unavailable. Daiei proudly announced two more Gamera sequels.[26] All of a sudden, Godzilla's dominance seemed shaky. Since returning in 1984, Godzilla had been almost synonymous with live-action Japanese science fiction films. Other, non–Godzilla efforts like *Sayonara Jupiter*, *Gunhed*, and *Yamato Takeru* failed at the box office while Godzilla films never lost money. Toho began to think it unwise to release any *kaiju eiga* without the Godzilla brand name, even though proposed projects like *Mothra vs. Bagan* still involved recognized and established monster characters. It was as if a curse had been placed on science fiction films without a Godzilla connection. *Gamera*'s surprising success revealed the fallacy of that, and showed that the *kaiju eiga* could exist without Godzilla. Indeed, it suggested that the future of the genre was not Godzilla's at all.

Toho sat up and took notice. After seeing *Gamera*, Koichi Kawakita demanded a last-minute rewrite on *Godzilla 7*. Producer Shogo Tomiyama made an even more drastic decision: that the time had come for the series to stop and regroup. For the time being, Tomiyama reasoned, the series was to end.

## Chapter 36

# Godzilla vs. Destoroyah*

## GOJIRA VS. DESUTOROIA
## (GODZILLA AGAINST DESTOROYAH)

*Yeah, right, the last one.*

— Henry Saperstein[1]

Japanese version: released December 9, 1995, 103 minutes

Color, Widescreen

Produced by Shogo Tomiyama; executive producer Tomoyuki Tanaka; directed by Takao Okawara; screenplay by Kazuki Omori; music by Akira Ifukube; cinematography by Masahiro Kishimoto and Yoshinori Sekiguchi; art direction by Takeshi Shimizu; edited by Chizuko Osada; special effects by Koichi Kawakita

Starring Momoko Kochi (Emiko Yamane), Megumi Odaka (Miki Saegusa), Yasufumi Hayashi (Kenichi Yamane), Yoko Ishino (Yukari Yamane), Tatsumi Takuro (Dr. Kensaku Ijuin), Masahiro Takashima (Lt. Kuroki), Sayaka Osawa (Meru Ozawa), Akira Nakao (Commander Aso), Ronald Hea (Professor Marvin), Takehiro Murata (Yukari's Editor), Sabura Shinoda (Professor Fukazawa), Koichi Ueda (Night Watchman at Aquarium)

GODZILLA portrayed by Kenpachiro Satsuma; GODZILLA JUNIOR portrayed by Hurricane Ryu, DESTOROYAH portrayed by Ryo Hariya

*In the early days of 1996, Japan hosts an international Godzilla Summit to discuss Godzilla's Hong Kong rampage, and why he now appears a fiery, glowing red. Perhaps due to overexertion in combat against Space Godzilla, the King of Monsters is now undergoing an uncontrollable nuclear reaction. The atomic furnace of his heart is racing towards a detonation — a cataclysm that threatens to engulf the Earth in an atomic blaze equivalent to the simultaneous explosions of the world's nuclear arsenal.*

*The theory that Godzilla is headed towards nuclear detonation comes from Kenichi Yamane, a Japanese college student living in America. The young man is the grandson of Dr. Yamane, the famed paleontologist who discovered Godzilla forty years ago.*

*Kenichi's sister Yukari, a network news anchor, has come to know Dr. Ijuin, a man who has continued Dr. Serizawa's research into micro-sizing oxygen. Dr. Ijuin believes that micro-oxygen could be used to stem the growing food shortage by causing animals and plants to grow abnormally large. Recognizing that his research is uncomfortably close to that which led to the Oxygen Destroyer in 1954, Ijuin persists in his studies because he feels the present food shortage distinguishes today's situation. To survive, mankind needs the benefits of micro-oxygen enough to warrant the risk.*

*The nature of that risk begins to manifest itself at a construction site on a landfill in Tokyo Bay. Fossils of Pre-Cambrian crustaceans have been revived and mutated by the effects of the Oxygen Destroyer in 1954 and now released into the world by the drilling. Mankind has yet again loosed upon itself the monstrous manifestation of its most diabolical weapons.*

*If Godzilla's internal temperature keeps rising at its current rate, in a matter of days he will undergo meltdown, burning a hole through the Earth and causing a China Syndrome. Hoping to use the mutated crab-like "Destroyers" as living embodiments of the Oxygen Destroyer against Godzilla is a last-ditch idea to avert the catastrophe — but getting the monsters to fight means sacrificing Tokyo, and this is one time where the cure could be worse than the disease.*

Toho was determined to renew the series following the perceived slump of *Godzilla vs. Space Godzilla*. In fact, although *Space Godzilla* officially marked the fortieth anniversary of the series, there is more in *Destoroyah* geared to a fortieth anniversary celebration. Momoko

*Although the English dubbing sure makes it sound like Godzilla's opponent is named "Destroyer," and some video copies have been sold under that title, the Japanese word is clearly written to have a different pronunciation, and the official English title is spelled in the awkward way seen here.

Kochi returns to reprise the character of Emiko Yamane, which she last played 41 years earlier in the original *Gojira*. Godzilla's opponent in his twenty-second starring vehicle is a monster born out of the chemical by-products of Dr. Serizawa's Oxygen Destroyer from the 1954 film. *Destoroyah* also brings back composer Akira Ifukube, director Takao Okawara and screenwriter Kazuki Omori.

The return of Omori of course meant another overwritten, overpopulated, heavily rhetorical screenplay. As with *Godzilla vs. Biollante* and *Godzilla vs. King Ghidorah*, Omori sets out a central moral quandary and then asks his characters to debate it — endlessly, even after their words no longer matter. The question of whether or not Serizawa's Oxygen Destroyer technology is too dangerous continues to obsess these people, even *after* it is revealed that the technology is overrunning the planet already anyway thanks to a malevolent swarm of mutant crustaceans capable of eliminating all human life.

*Destoroyah* does more than pay homage to the series' origins, it updates many elements, passing the torch to a new generation. Kazuki Omori depicts Emiko Yamane as so traumatized by the events of *Gojira* that she never married Ogata, and lives a lonely life haunted by nightmares. Her generation will never forget the events of 1954, easily interpreted as symbolic of the bombing of Hiroshima and Nagasaki. Emiko's generation still lives under the shadow of a war lost and a civilization crushed by the most horrible weapon ever used on humankind.

The next generation — Yamane's grandchildren — have grown up in a different world and are not plagued by those demons. Instead this new generation takes a proactive approach in trying (unsuccessfully) to exorcise those demons.

Interestingly, Yamane's grandchildren have pursued the archetypal careers of scientist and reporter. In the earlier films, these careers were linked as different routes towards the same end goal, namely the Truth. Here, scientists and reporters are at odds with each other, each distrusting the other's motives. Yuriko Yamane criticizes Dr. Ijuin for his hubris in revisiting Serizawa's terrible discovery. Her brother Kenichi lobbies G-Force to adopt Serizawa and Ijuin's technology *as a weapon*. Ijuin takes pains to remind Yuriko that his scientific search for truth is the same as her journalistic one, but she does not see it that way.

In the earlier films, the ubiquitous reporter character usually worked as a print journalist. Even recent reporter heroes in *Return of Godzilla* and *Godzilla vs. King Ghidorah* earned a living writing their thoughts in the traditional fashion. Yuriko belongs to the modern era of journalism, where television cameras and microphones have replaced pen and pad. Whereas the print journalist hero of past films often tagged along throughout the action as the sole reporter character, Yuriko moves in a mob of other TV reporters. These reporters throng together with lights and cameras, clogging the path for emergency vehicles and getting in the way at every disaster. They shout their questions in a cacophony, from which nothing reasoned or thoughtful could ever emerge.

The new view of scientists is not so major an update, though, since the Godzilla series abandoned early on the Serizawa-style "mad" scientist working alone in a basement lab. The newer series, especially in films like *Biollante*, had already developed a more complex take on science, recognizing its merits while also cautioning against its dangers.

This younger generation of Kenichi's lacks a sense of historical perspective. He is a brash young man, without the conscience of the older generation. For Ijuin, Emiko, and even Miki, Godzilla and the Oxygen Destroyer mean something. They are more than just monsters and objects of technology; they are emblems of a traumatic past. The Oxygen Destroyer carries such symbolic importance that no one dares say its name. The film is a third over before anyone breaks that taboo, and then it is Kenichi who shouts the name, against Miki's objections.

Notably, Kenichi has been studying at an American university. Being an expatriate no doubt has contributed to his outsider's perspective on Godzilla and the Oxygen Destroyer.

Meru Ozawa is another character connected to the United States. Her narrative role seems at first glance to be the same as Miki's. Both are young psychic girls employed by G-Force, and the inclusion of another such character could be seen as nothing more than stealing screen time away from the series' human star, Miki Saegusa. However, Meru makes a point of talking about her experiences developing her psychic skills in America. Like Kenichi, she not only brings the new generation's perspective to the Godzilla Summit, she brings an *American* perspective.

Production on *Godzilla vs. Destoroyah* took place in the summer of 1995, the fiftieth anniversary of the bombings of Hiroshima and Nagasaki. Historians and pundits on both sides of the Pacific reviewed the motives for the bombings. In the United States, the Smithsonian Institute became embroiled in controversy over a planned exhibit of the *Enola Gay* bomber. The exhibit would have questioned the official U.S. justification for the bombings: that despite the horror of the atomic bombs' effects, it produced less suffering and fewer casualties than if we had let Japan continue its war-mongering. Some modern historians suggested that Japan was already withering toward defeat, and the bombings were unnecessary from a military standpoint. This viewpoint threatened the older generation of American war veterans, who saw the bombings as their salvation from continued warfare.[2]

It is no coincidence that the arguments made on behalf of using the Oxygen Destroyer against Godzilla in *Destoroyah* parallel the arguments made in the U.S. on behalf of using nuclear bombs on Japan. In both arguments, the awful consequences of the weapon are downplayed as a lesser human cost than if the enemy continues unchecked. In both cases, the end result is a Japanese city devastated by nuclear carnage. It is also no coincidence that the argument echoing American justifications for Hiroshima and Nagasaki comes from the mouths of Meru and Kenichi, the two characters for whom screenwriter Kazuki Omori established American roots.

For that matter, the American roots of

Kenichi and Meru also carry connotations of Japan's film industry. Toho was poised to hand over the reins of the Godzilla series to TriStar and Hollywood; the death of Godzilla in *Destoroyah* meant an end to the Japanese series, but opened the field for a new American series to begin. As the generation of Emiko Yamane and Miki Saegusa pass the torch to their younger successors, they symbolically passed the series over to "American" hands as well.

Likewise, Godzilla's attack on Hong Kong in the beginning of the film has more to do with the symbolism of the film industry than it does international relations. Despite its status as the world's second biggest film market (after North America), Japan's film industry still slumped in the doldrums. By contrast, little Hong Kong had earned its rank as the world's second biggest film exporter (also after North America). While Toho remained unable to market the newer Godzilla movies in America, Hong Kong enjoyed a Renaissance of cinema with films by Jackie Chan, Tsui Hark, John Woo, and Ringo Lam earning praise and profits in America and around the world. Godzilla's attack on Hong Kong carried a little vicious wish-fulfillment for the makers of Godzilla movies.

The setting of the denouement also invokes symbolic meanings that have nothing to do with politics or the bombing of Hiroshima and Nagasaki: symbolic meanings that would be very obscure to Western audiences. Destoroyah appears at Tokyo's seaside development district, which had been planned as the site of the 1996 World City Expo. Omori's original script staged Godzilla's last battle with Destoroyah at the Expo, but Tokyo's Governor Yukio Aoshima canceled the event, calling it a waste of taxpayer money. This left the waterfront subcenter in the lurch, as few companies stepped forward to rent office space there. The Tokyo metropolitan government found that the new Yurikamome public transit system linking the seaside area with the city was idling, bereft of riders.

In the past, municipalities had lobbied Toho to stage Godzilla's exploits in their towns. Major companies took pride in seeing their billboards and neon signs trashed by the likes of Godzilla, Mothra, and King Ghidorah as a kind of prestigious publicity. So when the Expo was canceled, the city pressured Toho executives to stage *Destoroyah* at the site anyway. From an American standpoint, this kind of publicity seems bizarre: Yukari calls the area "troubled" on screen; a swarm of Destoroyahs infest the empty, unrented buildings; Destoroyah drops Junior to his death on top of the complex; and Godzilla dies in a fiery meltdown there — none of which seems like a positive corporate image to project. Nonetheless, the district saw the film as a much-needed publicity boost, and staged a Godzilla film festival to promote the release of *Godzilla vs. Destoroyah*.[3]

Ultimately, though, the focus of the final Godzilla movie is not real estate or film-industry in-jokes or even an allegorical discussion of the fiftieth anniversary of the atomic bombing of Japan. What brought in the almost-record-breaking four million viewers[4] to *Godzilla vs. Destoroyah* was the spectacle of Godzilla's death.

In 1993, Toho had leaked rumors that Godzilla perished in the climax of *Godzilla vs. Mechagodzilla II*. Although the earliest draft of the screenplay included such a death scene, and the finished film included something of the sort, Tomoyuki Tanaka dropped Godzilla's death from the story.[5] Toho cultivated the rumors, though, knowing that the public interest would only help the movie's revenues. *Godzilla vs. Destoroyah* sought to cash in on the windfall that would result from those rumors proving to be true.

To kill off such a famed (and profitable) character with the dignity befitting the moment required a sense of grandeur to Godzilla's opponent. For a time, Shogo Tomiyami pursued the rights to King Kong in order to stage a remake of the wildly successful 1962 film. Recognizing that such a deal would be too expensive for Toho's coffers, an alternative was kicked around that Godzilla's next opponent would be Mechakong, Mechagodzilla's forerunner from the 1967 *King Kong Escapes*. The new 1995 Mechakong would inject G-Force agents into Godzilla's bloodstream, in homage to the 1966 American science fiction classic *Fantastic Voyage*. While the giant mechanical monster did battle with Godzilla on a gargantuan scale, these G-Force soldiers would do battle from within, while experiencing what Koichi Kawakita called "many different strange worlds inside Godzilla." Even that altered image of Kong would have been prohibitively expensive.[6]

Another proposal pitted Godzilla against himself. In the mooted *Godzilla vs. Godzilla*, the filmmakers would have finally gone the distance with the idea they had already been toying with, after pitting Godzilla against a succession of near–Godzilla creatures (Biollante, Mechagodzilla, Space Godzilla). In this script, Godzilla's ghost returns from 1954 to do battle with his modern successor. This idea, too, would ultimately be abandoned.[7]

Tomiyama thought the return of the Oxygen Destroyer proved a satisfactory substitution, providing a marketable link with the early films. The Oxygen Destroyer represented something else, too: the only weapon that ever defeated Godzilla. In fact, the Oxygen Destroyer *killed* Godzilla, so its return invoked notions of Godzilla's impending death.

This startling news caught the eye of the American press, which gave the new film an unprecedented level of stateside publicity. Since none of the most recent films had appeared officially in America, promotion of the series had been minimal, largely confined to the fan press. News of Godzilla's death, however, warranted blurbs in *Time* and *Newsweek*. *The New York Times* gave it front page treatment on its "Sunday Week in Review" section. James Steingold's article "National Ids: Does Japan Still Need Its Scary Monster?" suggested that Godzilla's death represented a sea change in Japanese culture. The social and political situations Godzilla represented over the years had changed, and his usefulness as a metaphor had ended.[8]

However, Steingold argues from the vantage point of an American, for whom the ghosts of World War II have by and large been put to rest. Indeed, Japanese culture has moved on since the war, and a new generation now has come of age; for them, the War exists in history books but not in memory. Godzilla's power as an evocative symbol of the war and its aftermath has not diminished over time; instead that symbolism has evolved with the culture. In *Godzilla vs. Destoroyah*, Toho's filmmakers masterfully manipulate that symbolism to depict the same changes in Japanese society that Steingold describes.

This is not a generational issue: Miki is about the same age as Meru and Kenichi, but Miki holds Godzilla and Destoroyah in a reverence that her co-stars do not. Their attitude is influenced by their expatriate American connections.

It must be very hard for Americans to fully understand the significance of the Hiroshima bombings to the Japanese. The closest parallel in American history of that lasting fissure in the national psyche resulting from a military defeat would be the Vietnam War. Americans still have not healed those wounds, and perhaps it is presumptuous to expect that the Japanese would be any different. In a way, the endurance of Godzilla's popularity suggests that those wounds have not healed at all. For some reason, Japanese popular culture still feels the need to discuss these issues in the coded context of giant monsters.

Helping fuel rumors of the end of the series, Kawakita announced on the eve of *Destoroyah*'s release that he was retiring from the post of special effects director to work as a consultant for the Bandai toy company (which markets Godzilla toys in Japan).[9]

Reporting on the "death" of Godzilla, many sources from *The Daily Telegraph*[10] to CNN[11] to the Reuters News Service[12] emphasized the pending TriStar film to show that Godzilla's franchise was merely moving west. Shogo Tomiyama saw the transfer to Hollywood as a natural stage in the series' life: "When Godzilla dies at the end of the first movie, a Japanese professor says there might be more than one Godzilla. This time even though he dies, the one who comes back for TriStar could be a different Godzilla."[13]

The hype surrounding the monster's demise brought record-setting crowds.[14] Three days after the movie's opening, the studio received 10,000 protest letters demanding the monster be revived.[15] Tomiyama acceded, "As long as Godzilla is a star, he could make a comeback."[16]

The decision to end the series and kill off what Henry Saperstein called the "golden goose" may indeed be little more than a cynical promotional move to get press attention and bring in viewers.[17] This has certainly been the result. However, Toho claims that they had simply "run out of ideas."[18]

The slump in the Japanese film industry also argues for at least a hiatus in the series' production. Although all of the second series sequels have been profitable for Toho, the greatest Godzilla income has come from licensed merchandising. Each of the films has cost Toho approximately $10 million and subsequently returned $30 million in proceeds. By contrast, each film has generated some $150 million in merchandising revenue.[19] This merchandising industry can support itself without a new film every year, drastically reducing Toho's cash outlays without drastically cutting their income.

It is the great contradiction of the series that over forty years and two dozen movies, it has seen such artistry and depth in what is first and foremost a commercial enterprise. Critics and fans alike make a mistake when they attempt to separate the two. The commercial motives of the series do not invalidate the artistry of its makers or the sophistication of its subtexts. Likewise, the skill of its makers and their artistic aims do not change the fact that the series exists solely to make Toho money.

Godzilla is at once a pop culture icon and a profit-making industry. It is poetic justice that this indomitable movie monster, a product of commercial economic forces, should rise up out of the sea to demolish the very symbols of modern democratic capitalism.

## Part Five

# The Godzilla Millennium (1998–2005)

The advent of the much-delayed American revision of *Godzilla* proved to be a pivotal moment in the history of the franchise. Intended to inaugurate a new cycle of Hollywood films, it was greeted by impressive box office numbers but widespread disappointment. However, the publicity attending the blockbuster raised the profile of the Japanese cycle, and triggered a revitalized series of films from Toho that each very consciously answered back to their American cousin.

# Chapter 37

# Godzilla vs. Godzilla

## (GODZILLA IN AMERICA, PART FOUR)

*We basically had set a goal for ourselves of giving birth to the whole Godzilla legend again. We wanted to distance ourselves from the other films and, at the same time, pay homage to the original.*

— Dean Devlin, producer of *Godzilla*[1]

*They could have put any name on the film besides* Godzilla *and it probably would have done just as well at the box office, and they could have owned it outright without having to pay any licensing fees to Toho.*

— Doug Moench, writer for Marvel Comics' *Godzilla*[2]

On Memorial Day weekend 1998, TriStar Pictures released the long-gestating American version of *Godzilla*. This motion picture is now widely regarded as a flop — a punchline to a joke at its makers' expense. Exactly why this is the case, though, deserves some careful discussion.

As a commercial effort, *Godzilla* would seem to be an unqualified success. It opened on an unprecedented 7363 screens across the country, with what was at the time the third-highest opening-weekend box office gross in history.[3] It remained the number one movie for two consecutive weeks, and ultimately tallied nearly $400 million in worldwide sales. It was the seventh highest grossing motion picture of the year. To put those numbers into perspective, consider the fact that this one film earned more than the entire Heisei series added together, and then tripled.

Prior to the opening of *Godzilla*, TriStar publicists had boasted about even more ambitious expectations. While these figures remained elusive, that alone says little. Most big American films of that year underperformed expectations (indeed, this is true of most years). It is the job of studio publicists to make unreasonable predictions, as a means of generating "news." Nearly all of the Toho Heisei era Godzilla films also underperformed studio

expectations. $400 million remains a staggering achievement, and should not be belittled.

In terms of cinematic accomplishment, it was widely understood in the lead-up to 1998 that the primary benchmark by which to judge an American adaptation of *Godzilla* would be its special effects. Indeed, it was the battle over exactly how much to spend on those effects that had derailed the Jan de Bont project. On these grounds, again *Godzilla* appears to triumph. Whatever else one may say, its visual effects are both extensive and photorealistic. The creature genuinely seems to trample its way through what appears to be the real Manhattan.

In what way then was *Godzilla* a failure?

An analysis of the film's content will follow in the next chapter. First it is appropriate to examine how a series of carefully thought-out and seemingly reasonable creative decisions, one after the other, accrued to lead this project into a public relations disaster.

Each of Toho's Heisei-era Godzilla features was manufactured at a cost of one billion yen. As the actual buying power of the yen changed, and the exchange rate of yen to dollars fluctuated, the apparent cost of the films as measured in dollars crept slowly upward over the decade, rising from around $10 million to just over $12 million. The films generally returned $18 million in Japanese ticket sales. Again, however,

217

the numbers are potentially deceptive. The highest attendance for any of the cycle was 1992's *Godzilla and Mothra*, with audiences receding over the subsequent years. The box office tallies do not reflect this fact because ticket prices were jacked up to compensate.

To sift out some sense from these numbers: At best, Toho had nestled itself into a comfortable rut whereby they could reliably turn $12 million into $18 million every year or so. But this was not a perpetual motion machine, and as the years progressed, the money needed to put in at one end gradually rose higher, while the returns out the other end gradually sank lower. It was a functional business model, but not one destined to last forever.

Meanwhile, the revived Gamera series not only ate into their market share, but suggested an alternate path: Toho distributed the Gamera films themselves. Not only were the Gamera movies more profitable than the Godzilla ones (they didn't make as much, but they cost a lot less), Toho was the one making the profit.

Not since 1984 had a Godzilla film been given access to a mass American audience. Making Godzilla movies that were sober in tone and classy in appearance was not enough to break into the American market; the essential problem faced by any Japanese film regardless of genre was its Japanese-ness. Americans wanted to see English-language films with familiar stars—and, as it happened, Japanese audiences had the same preference. Toho's Godzilla films were competing against Hollywood imports even in Japan, even in theaters owned and operated by Toho.

If Toho could license Godzilla to a Hollywood company, it would solve all of these problems: The American-made production would reach the vast audience denied Toho's homegrown works, and still reap huge rewards among Japanese viewers. Toho could continue to license merchandising rights, which had always been the juiciest part of the pie, while shouldering virtually none of the risk.

This then was the position Toho was in

throughout the 1990s—increasingly desirous of handing the franchise over to an American partner. But while Toho may have been a motivated seller, to use real estate terminology, it was a buyer's market.

Up to this point, this book has taken the American film industry as a given, a powerhouse whose global dominance could be taken for granted in discussing the local challenges faced by the Japanese industry. However, to understand what forces drove the TriStar production, it is now necessary to fill in some of those details so far elided:

At the time the Showa Godzilla series was winding down, even fairly modest metropolitan areas in the United States boasted dozens of one-screen theaters catering to different tastes and audiences, with films coming from an array of distributors both major and minor. But after an intense period of consolidation, by the 1990s this was no longer the case. At the time that Henry G. Saperstein began brokering the deal between TriStar and Toho, on average any given movie theater screen in the United States was showing one of that week's top five highest grossing pictures. Put another way, the marketplace only made room for a handful of top performing titles at a time, and most films that did not meet those expectations would be likely replaced by the next week's cycle of incoming new releases.

Once upon a time a movie had several weeks to prove itself, and good word-of-mouth from happy patrons could encourage others to give it a chance over time. By the mid–1990s, good word-of-mouth was only valuable to films that had already established themselves right from the start. The first two weeks were critical, the first week more so, and the opening weekend was the most vital.* The pressure to get viewers into the theater on opening night, one way or another, was thus substantially higher than the pressure to make that initial experience especially satisfying. It is possible to make too much of this, to draw the cynical conclusion that Hollywood had no interest in making good

---

*There are of course exceptions to this rule, the slow-simmering success of Napoleon Dynamite being an obvious example. But I offer up this rubric as a baseline to show the typical expectations for a studio release.

movies. This is going too far. However, it is the case that a good movie that does not inspire a lot of pre-release buzz is generally of less value to Hollywood than a mediocre one with strong buzz.

Spending money on advance publicity is one way to build those opening weekend grosses, but is a fairly inefficient approach. Ideally, the marketing department would want to spend money only in support of pre-existing attributes of the film. For example, popular movie stars with enormous marquee value can help "open" a picture — but their services cost money. The least expensive way to enhance the pre-release allure of a film is to tap into an existing audience familiarity. Sequels, remakes, renditions of novels (or comic books), films whose titles are popular songs, adaptations of popular TV shows — or, for that matter, unpopular TV shows...

The brand name "Godzilla" was by itself the most valuable item Toho had to offer an American partner. It was also, paradoxically, the least valuable. Therein lay the problem.

Any American producer would be attracted by the vast pre-existing name recognition that came with the word "Godzilla." That word, though, conjured up for most Americans a host of negative connotations: cheesy special effects, bad dubbing, drive-in movie camp and anachronistic matinee-stylings. Most Americans may not even have seen a Godzilla movie at all, or if so, chances are it was *Godzilla vs. Megalon*. People knew what the word suggested — and it was not positive.

An American-made *Godzilla* could exploit the name recognition best if it somehow managed to avoid what that named signified.

The dedicated Godzilla aficionado reading this may balk at such a statement. Remember, though, that by 1998 there had been no fewer than six opportunities for an American distributor to acquire a new Godzilla movie with everything that brand name implies — and even in the unlikely event that such a buyer had chosen to pay full face value of its manufacturing costs for such a privilege, any one of those films could be had for less than 1/20th of what TriStar would spend to make its own. It would have

been a bargain — but only if it could be profitably sold, which is why this never happened. American movie companies do not make their decisions blindly, they follow the dictates of cold research and number-crunching. The audience of dedicated Godzilla fans in America, the ones who would have preferred a stateside release of a Heisei cycle Godzilla film over an American version, were not numerous enough to merit much attention. Toho's goal was to get an American Godzilla of *mass* appeal, one that would draw in those crowds their existing films did not reach — and for that they needed a Godzilla movie tailor-made to appeal to people who didn't like Godzilla movies.

As it happened, there was a solid example of this very sort of thing to turn to for inspiration. Since 1939, *Batman* had thrilled millions as a comic book superhero, but the comic medium had contracted over the years to a smaller niche of hardcore enthusiasts, while mass audiences associated the name "Batman" with images of the campy 1960s TV series starring Adam West. Tim Burton's 1989 movie successfully broke free of those camp connotations by aggressively reconfiguring the iconography. The movie created a new vision of Batman, one that defied the traditions of the comic books in some ways but appealed to mass audiences.

According to rumor mills, Burton had been considered as director for an American *Godzilla*, and it is tempting to fantasize about what Burton would have done. His goofball sensibility and idiosyncratic vision, combined with his fanboy love of the character, would have made a potent mix — but this was not to be. Nevertheless, Burton's *Batman* would stand as the model for the entire *Godzilla* enterprise: a case study in how to rescue a franchise tainted by the shadow of camp.

Flash back to 1993, in the aftermath of *Godzilla and Mothra*'s box office success in Japan. Cary Woods and Rob Fried had convinced Toho that a big-budget American *Godzilla* was in Toho's best interests — but these two producers then found themselves unable to sell the idea to a Hollywood studio. Even Columbia, the eventual home of the project, initially said no. According to Woods, "Their response was, they felt it had the potential for camp." With much chin-wagging, Woods and Fried convinced Peter Guber at Sony to say yes (Sony did not yet own Columbia). Guber's first act was to offer the project to the team of Roland Emmerich and Dean Devlin — who turned it down flat, because of what they called "the cheese factor."[4]

Having been rejected by Emmerich and Devlin, *Godzilla* came to the desk of Jan de Bont. He planned to maintain the familiar iconography of Godzilla, and the traditional monster vs. monster set-up, with a revised explanation of how such things came to be — basically, the same approach successfully taken by the makers of the new Gamera films. "I believe, if you do a Godzilla film, you have to have a second monster," said De Bont, "because you can't make Godzilla the bad guy."[5]

This was the decision that ultimately destroyed that version of the project. De Bont's determination to have not one CGI monster but two gave TriStar accountants apoplexy. Special effects films almost always go over-budget, so when De Bont said he planned to spend somewhere in the $130–145 million range (reports varied), the studio calculated he would actually spend closer to $200 million.[6] This at a time when three blockbusters with budgets above $100 million had all tanked: *Batman and Robin*, *Starship Troopers*, *The Postman*. Warner Brothers announced in May of 1998 a complete institutional pullback on event movies; most other studios had already unofficially done the same. Columbia/TriStar was groaning under the weight of a $3 billion debt, and so taking on an expensive event movie with a budget anywhere near the $200 million range was simply not an option. De Bont was removed from the project, and once again the studio asked Emmerich and Devlin to take it over.

The irony, visible only in hindsight, is that De Bont had secured a deal with Industrial Light and Magic to supply effects for *Godzilla* at a fixed fee. The highest reported budget figure for the De Bont version, $145 million, may have been high, but the special effects costs contractually should not have overrun that, whereas the Devlin and Emmerich *Godzilla* did in the end cost $200 million.[7] This was not evident, though, in May of 1996 when Emmerich and Devlin finally agreed to take on *Godzilla*, which was then budgeted to cost no more than $90 million.[8]

There is another irony in that TriStar took the project away from a man who seemed to very much want it, to instead force it upon a team who were never anything other than reluctant. But Emmerich and Devlin's hesitancy was its own weird form of qualification for the job. If the fear was that the audience would have some inherent resistance to the campiness associated with the name, then putting the project in the hands of people who shared those fears was a good thing. If Emmerich and Devlin could overcome their own resistance, they were well on the way to selling their new Godzilla to a potentially indifferent public as well.

"It's a very old theme, it makes for good movies, but lately nobody has done it," Emmerich explained. "And I've always been a believer that if nobody's seen it for a long time, the technology and the way movies stories are told have changed so much that you can take an old story and make it feel fresh and new."[9]

This was the philosophy behind *Independence Day* — to revitalize the 1950s style of alien invasion pictures with contemporary effects for an audience that had lost its familiarity with the source. While Emmerich's remarks imply he was unaware that Toho was in fact still making Godzilla movies — even as he was speaking — this is of little matter. Those films were not released in the U.S. and therefore might as well not exist, and certainly his intended audience would be unfamiliar with them. For all intents and purposes, the Godzilla movie paradigm would be as much an old throwback as *Independence Day*'s precursors.

*Independence Day* had not yet been released as of the time TriStar signed its makers to handle Godzilla. The extraordinary popular success of *Independence Day* was still just wishful thinking. Devlin and Emmerich were however busy with the heavy promotional push for the anticipated blockbuster, and saw *Godzilla* as yet another daunting task piled on top of an already tiring workload — and perhaps this feeling informed what happened next.

While the story has been repeated ad nauseum, exactly what transpired is unclear. Director Roland Emmerich, producer Dean Devlin, and special effects supervisor Volker Engel have all told the same story, with the same details, at every opportunity — a suspiciously consistent account whose self-serving nature leads one to suspect that it has been cleaned up for public consumption. However, even taking this possibly apocryphal tale at face value reveals some telling truths.

Emmerich and Devlin called on Patrick Tatopoulos, their creature designer from *Independence Day*, to design their new Godzilla. He was given a very specific remit: "It had to be scary and it had to be huge," Emmerich told him. "It could not be a dinosaur and while, to a degree, it had to have some aspects of the original Godzilla it had to be reconstructed and reinvigorate the initial concept Toho had of the creature back in 1954."[10]

"Roland told me to go crazy with it and not be a slave to the original design," Tatopoulos remembers. "The old Godzilla is what it is, cartoon eyes and all. The new Godzilla has the same spirit, but it inhabits a different form. The old Godzilla was a lumbering beast, whereas this would be a sleek and agile animal — Godzilla after fitness training."[11]

Tatopoulos reworked the design so extensively, little more than a vague hint of the Toho creature remains in what is essentially a new monster. The filmmakers felt that making an extreme break with the past was not only necessary, but perhaps in its own way respectful: "If someone asks you, 'Can you paint this same scene that Rembrandt painted, and just give it some interesting flavor,' if you're going to try to make the Rembrandt better, you're going to fail," Tatopoulos explained. "If you forget his technique and try to do your own, you have a chance to succeed."[12]

Tatopoulos built a model of his creature, which Devlin and Emmerich brought to Japan for a strategy meeting with Toho. At first, the model was draped in a cloth, to conceal it until the dramatic reveal — a dry run, actually, for the marketing strategy Devlin would take with the film itself. Throughout the meeting, Devlin reports, the Toho executives were anxious to see under the cloth. When at last he pulled it away and unveiled the creature, a deadly silence fell across the room.

Toho had stipulated in their license agreement such nit-picking design specifics as that Godzilla must have three rows of dorsal fins, four toes on each foot.[13] To them, Godzilla was a corporate symbol as much as Mickey Mouse is for Disney. Tatopoulos' design flagrantly defied both the letter and the spirit of Toho's expectations.

According to Devlin, Toho's representatives were struck speechless. Two minutes of silence elapsed, before one of the Japanese businessmen said, "It's so different that we don't want to comment on it. Could you come back tomorrow?" The next day, the filmmakers returned, and were greeted with, "We love your idea. Go do it."[14]

This, then, was the moment where everything changed — and where, in most respects, it all started to go wrong. The full repercussions of this decision will be explored below, but first it is important to understand *why* this happened.

In 1960, TV producer Sydney Newman was developing *The Avengers*, and wanted actor Patrick Macnee for the lead role of secret agent John Steed. Macnee was reluctant to take the job, but rather than refuse outright, he chose instead to demand an absurdly high salary, assuming that would be the equivalent of turning the job down. Instead, Newman agreed to Macnee's fee, and the actor went on to play the defining role of his career.[15] A similar impulse drove the TriStar team's bold move. Devlin and Emmerich were well aware that Jan de Bont had been obliged to constantly negotiate with Toho, whose micromanaging and interference was something to be avoided if possible. With their aggressive and confrontational redesign, Devlin and Emmerich intended to force the issue right away. Either Toho would balk, and the filmmakers could walk away from the project with a face-saving claim of having given it an honest try, or Toho would capitulate, and the filmmakers would have declared their independence.[16]

Devlin and Emmerich had the upper hand, whether they realized it or not. The protracted development process of the American *Godzilla* was doing Toho few favors. They did enjoy the continued license fee from TriStar, but what they really wanted was the actual movie. Perhaps fearing that a fight over the redesign would derail the project after it had once again been delicately re-established, Toho did indeed capitulate. By this point, *Independence Day* had opened to outstanding business, and Toho perhaps felt that these two men had proven their ability to read the American public's tastes. If they said this was the right way to present Godzilla to an American audience, then perhaps they deserved the benefit of the doubt.

Having gotten permission to revamp Godzilla almost completely, Devlin and Emmerich immediately suppressed the new design, opting for a blanket of secrecy. Then, they made a point of drawing attention to this blanket of secrecy. On May 9, 1997, Devlin posted the following statement to the official Godzilla.com message board: "Our Godzilla will be completely original in look, actions, and style. You will not be disappointed with our creature."[17]

Some fans would find those two statements in contradiction, but such people were not the intended audience for Devlin's remarks. Somewhat cynically, but quite accurately as it turned out, the dedicated fanbase of American Godzilla enthusiasts would pay to see the movie no matter what. In fact, some fans went more than once, all the while complaining about how much they hated it.* That audience had been judged too small to court. Devlin wanted to appeal to a larger body of viewers who were at best indifferent and at worst hostile to the existing associations around Godzilla.

This book has covered an array of differing Godzilla movies, some funny and some serious, some technically sophisticated and some slapdash, some visionary and some risible. But they all share more in common with each other than they differ, and the most salient common feature is that they are, at heart, about a giant monster trashing a city. In the end, whatever else TriStar's *Godzilla* would be, it would be about a giant monster trashing a city.

In telling the world that his Godzilla was to be different, and that nobody would be allowed to see it until the movie came out, Devlin signaled that the new film was to be on this one basic level unpredictable. If you for some reason never enjoyed a Godzilla movie before, that did not mean you would not enjoy this one — because this one was to be different. If this Godzilla were reasonably similar to previous versions, there would be little point in keeping it secret — there would not be enough of a secret to keep. By making the secret a central focus of the publicity campaign, Devlin assured viewers that he was consciously bucking tradition, and giving the press something to guess about that might create some pre-release attention.

What Devlin did not anticipate was that Toho's habit of micromanagement and interference was not merely directed against their licensing partners, but against their own fanbase as well. American fans had been carrying the torch for Godzilla for years, building a domestic audience for the Heisei series and for Japanese imports like toys. This was done through an underground network of fanzines, vanity press books, and conventions — all of which Toho tried to suppress or extinguish. Over the years, the American fan community had developed an ingrained habit of mind as outsiders defending the Godzilla faith against its own creators, accustomed to being disrespected and ignored. Devlin's public statements tended to incite a fan community already predisposed to be antagonistic. By the summer of 1997, Devlin was already defending himself and his film from an increasingly hostile fan press. "Please stop listening to rumors!" he posted to the Godzilla.com site.[18]

---

*G-Fan *Number 33, published May-June of 1998, features no less than one hundred short reviews, nearly all of them angry, from fans as well as numerous longer reviews from featured writers. The entire issue is an exhaustive testament to how much Godzilla fans hated the film, and how many of them went and paid to see it anyway.*

Another unfortunate consequence of the secretive design was the pressure it put on TriStar's various merchandising licensors. The studio partnered with over 250 separate companies to sell items such as tie-in books, toys, soundtrack albums, T-shirts, and other gee-gaws. Taco Bell was the largest partner, having paid the studio $60 million for the rights to link their ad campaign with *Godzilla*'s. However, no merchandise was allowed to hit store shelves prior to the film's opening, so as to save the monster's appearance for the theatrical debut. As has been discussed above, even as a successful film its theatrical run might be limited to weeks, and if it did not live up to expectations those weeks might be few. Compressing merchandise sales into the same timeframe as the actual film's release inevitably reduced profits, and forced the merchandisers to bear an unusual level of risk.[19]

Theater owners too were asked to shoulder a substantial level of risk to support the unconventional marketing. Parent company Sony strong-armed theaters into giving the distributor a higher share of the box office. Typically, a theater pays 60 percent of its ticket revenues back to the distributor during the first week. Sony President Jeff Blake asked theaters to send back a staggering 80 percent of *Godzilla*'s opening week grosses in the most competitive markets—and 90 percent in smaller cities. National Association of Theater Owners President Bill Kartozian noted, "Clearly what Sony is asking would break through above historic norms."

The problem was not just the exorbitant 80 percent (or 90 percent) front week demand. It was certainly unpleasant, but not nearly as ruinous as the studio's insistence on a 70 percent "floor," industry terminology for a minimum guarantee.

As *Hollywood Reporter* journalist Kirk Honeycutt explains, assume a theater in an ordinary American city obliged to split 90/10, and that *Godzilla* earns a nice round figure of $10,000 for the week at that location. The theater management deducts their operating expenses (the "house nut") from that figure, and applies the 90/10 percentage to the remaining amount. A typical "house nut" would be around $3,000,

leaving $7,000. The theater gets to keep 10 percent, or $700, and returns the rest to Sony. But, the 70 percent floor is applied to the total gross, before any deductions, meaning the theater is actually contractually obliged to pay $7,000 back to the studio, not the $6300 calculated under the 90/10 terms. In such a situation, the theater would merely break even. In order to see a profit, given a 70 percent floor and $3,000 operating expenses, they would have to receive more than $10,000 per screen.[20]

Sony however opted to open *Godzilla* on a record-setting number of screens. This meant that the total audience would be distributed more thinly across the many venues, reducing the per-screen intake. The inevitable result: Even if *Godzilla* did well in overall box office performance, the odds were that most theaters would lose money by showing it.

These negotiations did not occur in a vacuum. Whereas most distributors lay out blanket terms with all of their exhibitors, Paramount chooses to negotiate separate terms with each theater individually. And they do this, strangely enough, after the fact. The idea is to slide the scale with respect to how any given movie actually performs for that given venue. If a movie does especially well, the theater must pay more to Paramount—and if the movie tanks, the theater gets to keep a higher percentage of the smaller kitty. In the main, it is a fair enough system. Nineteen ninety-eight was not a normal year, however. *Titanic*, the biggest hit in American movie history, had come out the previous year, and Paramount was still working out with its exhibitors exactly how to divide up the proceeds. Paramount distribution executive Wayne Lewellen realized that the precedent-setting *Godzilla* terms had fundamentally changed the situation between distributors and exhibitors—and he held off on *Titanic* negotiations while waiting to see how *Godzilla* played itself out. His goal was to leverage Sony's new tactics to force theaters to give up higher percentages of the *Titanic* revenue. Sony's hardball strategy had the potential to affect massive swaths of the distribution marketplace far beyond its own immediate consequences.[21]

The entire film industry began to step aside to make room for Sony's anticipated block-buster. Other studios moved the release dates of their pictures to avoid a direct head-to-head confrontation on *Godzilla*'s opening day. Inside the studio, confidence was not as strong. The previous year, it had been assumed that *Godzilla* would be among a pack of expensive blockbusters and equally overhyped event movies—but an industry-wide retrenchment had pulled back from such fare, leaving *Godzilla* not only the most expensive movie of 1998, but largely alone in its category.[22] The lack of competition was worrying.

"When *Independence Day* came out," explained Devlin, more presciently than he knew, "the three big movies that summer were supposed to be *Twister, Mission: Impossible,* and *The Hunchback of Notre Dame*—which was great as far as we were concerned. Now it's almost a no-winner. We could make a movie that makes $300 million worldwide and people would say it's a letdown."[23]

A screening for Sony's staff convinced the publicity department that they had a turkey on their hands, and that in order to recoup losses they would need to focus all efforts on that first week, that first weekend, that first night, that first screening. Their solution was to run more ads—spending over $50 million on ads all told, two million went to a single trailer broadcast during the *Seinfeld* finale.

"You don't suddenly back off when you know it's not there," an anonymous source inside Sony told *Newsweek*. "You can't overhype an exploitation movie."[24]

For their money, Sony was buying unconventionally brief ads. Avoiding shots of the monster forced the trailers to run shorter than usual. "Not seeing Godzilla has become a real positive for us," said Dana Precious, Columbia/TriStar's senior vice-president for creative advertising. The words, in hindsight, seem all too apt.[25]

A week before the movie was set to open, market research showed weak "want to see" levels.[26] Disaster was on the horizon.

"It's not campy, it's not a farce," *Godzilla* star Matthew Broderick told *Newsweek* on the eve of the release. To its production team, this was the most important detail—the primary goal of the entire $200 million endeavor. The obsession with the perceived campiness of traditional Godzilla pushed Devlin and Emmerich down a self-destructive road. Their implacable determination to set their *Godzilla* apart from its predecessors meant that as it opened on Memorial Day 1998, they had deliberately alienated the core audience of potential viewers for whom the name Godzilla had the most meaning. They had made enemies of their merchandising partners, and all but destroyed the good will of theaters. They had sparked hostile press coverage of what was perceived as their bullying attitude. They were unrolling a bloated hulk of a blockbuster in a filmgoing environment that had largely abandoned such things (at least temporarily). And they had spent more of TriStar's money getting to this point than the studio had wanted to put into a seemingly more promising project by Jan de Bont, which had formerly enjoyed more support from fans and Toho alike.

*Godzilla* arrived, a public relations catastrophe like no other.

# Chapter 38

# *Godzilla*

*Ladies and gentlemen, we New Yorkers like to believe we've seen it all. What you're going to see right now will shock you beyond belief. This is footage we have that indicates there is a dinosaur loose in Manhattan.*

— Charles Caiman

U.S. version: Released May 19, 1998, 139 minutes
Color, Widescreen
Produced by Dean Devlin; executive producers Roland Emmerich, Ute Emmerich, and William Fay; directed by Roland Emmerich; screenplay by Dean Devlin and Roland Emmerich; story by Ted Elliott and Terry Rossio; music by David Arnold; cinematography by Ueli Steiger; art direction by Oliver Schloo, William Ladd Skinner, and Robert Woodruff; editing by Peter Amundson and David Siegel; special effects by Volker Engel
Starring Matthew Broderick (Nick Tatopoulos), Jean Reno (Philippe Roache), Maria Pitillo (Audrey Timmonds), Hank Azaria (Victor "Animal" Palotti), Kevin Dunn (Col. Hicks), Michael Lerner (Mayor Ebert), Harry Shearer (Charles Caiman), Vicki Lewis (Elsie Chapman), Doug Savant (Sgt. O'Neal), Malcolm Danare (Dr. Craven), Arabella Field (Lucy Palotti), Lorry Goldman (Gene), Christian Aubert (Jean-Luc), Philippe Bergeron (Jean-Claude), Francois Giroday (Jean-Philippe), Frank Bruynbroek (Jean-Pierre)

*French nuclear tests in the Pacific give rise to a new organism, mutated by radiological exposure. The behemoth trashes everything in its path as it makes its way to New York, an island of metal and glass where it intends to lay its eggs. A team of researchers led by biologist Nick Tatopoulos is engaged by the military, under the command of Colonel Hicks. Their efforts to subdue the creature lay waste to the city while doing little to stop it.*

*French secret service agent Phillipe Roache is meanwhile working secretly alongside the military's efforts on his own plan to stop Godzilla, hoping to prevent the monster's damage from being traced back to his own country's actions. Roache and Tatopoulos find the monster's nest, as hundreds of little Godzillas hatch. If the military might of the United States cannot stop even one Godzilla, what chance does anyone have if hundreds spill out across the country?*

Godzilla fans hate this movie.

When they speak of it at all, it is with words of anger and vitriol. They call it *Fraudzilla*, or more charitably, *Deanzilla*—but never *Godzilla*. At best, they call it *GINO*, for *Godzilla In Name Only*. They nitpick every plot hole or production gaffe; they berate the abilities of the cast using words that would make their mothers cry.

Most reasonable observers would find these critiques apply at least as well to any of the preceding Toho versions—and to some extent, that is the point. Having defended their peculiar passion against the ridicule and condescension of others for so long engendered a powerful sense of turnabout being fair play: Every criticism leveled fairly or not against traditional Godzilla would be turned back on Hollywood's version.

The antipathy with which the community of dedicated Godzilla enthusiasts met the TriStar film while still lovingly embracing the Japanese originals is ultimately less a reaction to any particular attribute of the films in themselves and more a cineaste's version of tribal loyalty. Think of the historic rivalry between the Boston Red Sox and the New York Yankees: Outsiders see two evenly matched athletic organizations doing the same things in the same ways for the same reasons. Insiders feel the pull of passions and hatred beyond rational analysis.

The biggest complain stems from the name *Godzilla* itself—a perceived misappropriation of the name to dishonestly advertise a film with little relationship to its Japanese precursors.

Remove that issue, and in fact some of the most hostile critics of *Godzilla* seem willing to enjoy it on its own terms were it shown under an alternate title, such as *Attack of the Killer Iguana*.

Much of the production team from *Independence Day* was ported over, including effects supervisor Volker Engel and monster designer Patrick Tatopoulos, and the CGI teams at Centropolis Effects, Sony Imageworks, Digiscope and Vision Art, as well as production designer Olive Scholl, costume designer Joseph Porro, cinematographer Ueli Steiger, and composer David Arnold. Arnold was a John Barry protégé and multiple award-winning soundtrack composer whose grand score for Godzilla, like so many Ifukube scores over the years, is better than the film it supports.

For the first reel or two, *Godzilla* follows the pattern laid down by its 1954 namesake. A nuclear test in the South Pacific predicates a mysterious attack on a Japanese fishing vessel. Attacks of ships continue as anxious officials lead an expedition to investigate the wreckage of an island, where the scientist hero stands in the middle of an irradiated footprint. He does not pluck a trilobite from the mud, but he might as well have. The source of these images is clear.

There is some filmic justice in the fact that *Godzilla* then proceeds to borrow from *The Beast from 20,000 Fathoms*—the American revision of *Godzilla* returning to the source material that in turn inspired the Japanese *Godzilla*. As in *Beast*, the enormous critter is drawn by reproductive instinct to nest in Manhattan, where the army desperately tries to contain it. Several shots from Godzilla's initial foray into the city faithfully duplicate memorable moments from *Beast*. So far, no one can accuse the filmmakers of not doing their homework.

Previous attempts to initiate an American rendition of Godzilla had reconfigured the monster's origin: He would merely be a dinosaur, or perhaps a superhero genetically engineered by an advanced civilization. Given the opportunity to reboot the Gamera franchise, Shusuke Kaneko chose the "genetically engineered freak" route, leaving the old "radioactive mutant" explanation on the dustbin of history.

That *Godzilla*'s makers reinstated the nuclear origins of the monster for their film is something of a pleasant surprise.

This author owns a print of a government-issued public safety film from 1954, the year of *Godzilla*, in which agents from the Department of Health, Education, and Welfare set out to demonstrate how to protect the American public from nuclear fallout. These poor saps, dressed in ordinary everyday clothes, stand in the foreground as a mushroom cloud rises in the Nevada desert behind them. Off they trudge into the test blast zone to brush radiation off of household objects and foodstuffs using whisk brooms and damp cloths. In an environment of such shocking ignorance about the effects of radiation on living tissue, sci-fi stories about atomic tests turning animals into giant monsters can be forgiven. As a metaphor for the effect of American nuclear technology on Japan, the 1954 *Godzilla* need not even pass that forgiving test of plausibility, for the symbolism is in itself enough. For a *contemporary* monster movie to wholeheartedly embrace this throwback idea (as opposed to radiation merely killing the exposed animal, or giving it cancer) is a sign that Devlin and Emmerich meant what they said about respecting their source material.

In order to maintain this backstory and yet still set the film in the modern world, some tweaking was required. The United States has dramatically scaled back its nuclear testing—and as of this writing has not tested a nuclear device since 1992. French nuclear testing in Polynesia in 1996 was the right sort of event in the right place at the right time, and caused such a wave of international controversy that referencing it allowed the movie to exploit topical events.

Whether it was intended by the filmmakers or not, using France as the film's nuclear bugbear was an effective way to translate one of the 1954 film's underlying themes. As was discussed earlier in this book, the original *Godzilla* functioned as something of a Frankenstein movie without a Dr. Frankenstein. The Japanese are punished for scientific hubris that was not theirs, damned for the sins of others. TriStar's *Godzilla* too finds its American characters victimized by the nuclear arrogance of another, supposedly friendly, nation.

The film's heroes, all the familiar archetypes of Godzilladom, are portrayed with unusual vulnerability. Reporter, scientist, army guy — the gang's all here, but clouded by self-doubt and naïveté. Doug Savant plays the stammering Sergeant O'Neal with none of the blustery machismo one would customarily expect from such a role. Maria Pitillo, an inexperienced ingénue whose limitations were cruelly exposed by the movie, is at least cast in a role as awkward and fragile as the actress herself: aspiring journalist Aubrey, lacking the hardness of spirit demanded by her chosen profession. Finally, the film's scientist hero wraps Yamane, Serizawa, and Ogata into one young man. Nick Tatopoulos is named in honor of creature designer Patrick Tatopoulos and played with the easy charm of the ever-likable Matthew Broderick, whose part was written expressly for him.[1]

The only leading character to show unwavering self-confidence and surety of purpose is Jean Reno's French secret agent Philippe Roache. It is yet another quirky and endearing touch by the filmmakers to have made their action hero a Frenchman — not the typical go-to choice for macho man stature.

Of all the character choices, though, the adaptations made to Godzilla himself are the most significant and consequential. Having decided that the American movie-going public would accept a nuclear test causing a reptile egg to hatch a mutant as big as a skyscraper, Emmerich and Devlin decided to stop there. The "God" part of "Godzilla" would be omitted from this version.

This Godzilla is an animal. Although very strong, and remarkably resistant to military firepower, this Godzilla survives the army's assault by wit and speed rather than brute strength — and so, when outwitted and outrun, he would fall. Although fan outrage forced the last-minute inclusion of a pair of ambiguous shots where the creature appears to ignite fires with his breath, this Godzilla does not have any death ray, arguably the most iconic trademark of Toho's monster.

Gone is the mystery. One young man, armed only with his intuition and some supplies purchased at a corner drug store, manages to understand everything of importance about this unique creature within days of its discovery. Even at mankind's darkest hour we are to take for granted our ability to comprehend what we face. The film expects us to be in awe of Godzilla's size — the central aspect of the entire marketing campaign — but nothing else. None of the original's implacable "why me?" pointlessness has been maintained.

The filmmakers' studied insistence on looking only to the 1954 original for inspiration, purposefully ignoring the nearly two dozen sequels, was born of the desire to avoid any suggestion of "camp." That choice also meant they were working from the only model in which mankind did successfully defeat Godzilla. By ignoring the sequels, they missed a common characteristic possibly even more defining than the atomic death breath: the idea that Godzilla cannot ever be defeated. Having loosed this symbol of nuclear devastation, we cannot put him back.

If Godzilla merely symbolizes the negative side effects of nuclear testing, the risk of something going wrong, then we can reassure ourselves that whatever lessons needed learning, we have learned. We stopped testing nuclear weapons a while back, and if any mutants show up as unintended consequences, then all we need do is contain them and everything will be okay (Jean Reno even speaks dialogue to this effect in the film).

However, the undying Godzilla of the sequels represents something else: the enduring presence of nuclear weapons. Instead of a story about a nuclear bomb test in the past, it becomes a story about the world after that — the world we actually live in. The Cold War is over, the Soviet Union gone, yet the planet is still covered with enough nukes to obliterate all life many times over. New nations continue to join the nuclear fraternity, and many of the newest pledges are crazier and less stable than the rival superpowers who set the whole thing in motion. It has all gotten out of hand, and we cannot turn it back. Godzilla, at least in his Japanese iteration, served as a handy symbol with which to dramatize this condition.

Shots of a giant monster tearing apart Manhattan landmarks as a terrorized populace flees were images conceived in innocence. The events of September 11, 2001, would come to lend new, previously unintended significance to such visions, but it would be up to future filmmakers to exploit the connection in movies such as *Cloverfield*. In the summer of 1998, *Godzilla* was still comfortably just the stuff of popcorn movies.

Devlin and Emmerich's fear of camp did not mean they exorcised all humor from their picture. Oddly, given the impressive comic chops and comedy background of many in the cast, the film does not take advantage of that latent talent. Instead what comic relief there is has been relegated to the margins, for example the characters of Mayor Ebert and his political aide Gene, clearly intended to remind viewers of the famed movie reviewers Roger Ebert and Gene Siskel. The real-life Siskel and Ebert had given negative reviews to *Independence Day*, and in a petty act of revenge, Devlin and Emmerich made sport of them with this clumsy and insular joke.* Mayor Ebert is depicted as a cynical, self-important grandstander solely concerned with how the crisis inconveniences voters so close to his re-election. Tragic events of the too-near future would show how real-life New Yorkers warmly rewarded a leader who guided the city through catastrophe, but this film is content with its lazy stereotype.

*Godzilla*'s greatest failing is not the redesigned monster. *Godzilla* disappoints because as a piece of cinematic storytelling, it is so tame. It never tries to be more than a functionally entertaining collage of familiar tropes and shorthand stereotypes. Godzilla fans — and this author most decidedly counts himself in this camp — habitually gloss over the little deficiencies and missteps of any given Godzilla flick, to focus on the most enjoyable aspects instead. We forgive ludicrous nonsense-science, underdeveloped characters, overwritten melodrama, awkward dubbing, visible wires, wrinkles in the rubber suits of monsters — we forgive these because we love the whole, and such glitches are never grievous enough to disrupt the pleasure we take in all that is right. We got good at loving Godzilla warts and all ... but never stopped longing for one without the warts. It was not unreasonable to expect that a major Hollywood studio with twenty times as much money at play and all the institutional resources of a team accustomed to manufacturing crowd-pleasing blockbusters would have the ability to finally make a Godzilla movie that needed no excuse.

TriStar's team spent all that money, made all that bombastic noise, pushed around licensing partners and exhibitors like a playground bully, and yet delivered a film of flaws and limited ambition. A film with warts.

*Godzilla*'s flaws may not have been any greater than any committed by Toho before. That they were there at all, though, was unforgivable.

A year before *Godzilla* came out, Godzilla.com reported that Devlin was in talks with Toho regarding not just one but two sequels. TriStar's license gave them access to any or all of Godzilla's classic opponents, and allegedly Ghidorah and Mothra were at the top of the short list of future American opponents. The site also reported the possible red herring of Gamera as a possible enemy monster. (As the distributor of the new Gamera movies, Toho did at least have some commercial stake in the character and may well have been able to work out a deal if Devlin had been seriously interested.)

Devlin claims that, had a sequel gone forward, more traditionally Godzilloid traits like the atomic breath would have been added over time, as the character evolved through the mooted trilogy. This was said to J.D. Lees, opposition leader, in an interview that resembled nothing so much as the cross-examination of a hostile witness, so this may merely have been said as something to placate his critics.[2] How-

*It has been alleged that they also cast a J.D. Lees lookalike as the first New Yorker killed by Godzilla, in retaliation for his role in organizing and publicizing fan opposition to the film prior to its release. I have no firsthand knowledge that this is true, but all I can say is the guy really does look a lot like Lees.

ever, there is some circumstantial evidence that TriStar's Godzilla would regain his death ray, and it appeared on the small screen.

September 12, 1998, saw the closest thing Devlin's *Godzilla* would have to a sequel: a Saturday morning cartoon spin-off airing on Fox affiliates. Sony's animation division was used to creating cartoon tie-ins for tentpole films. *Jumanji, Men in Black,* and *Ghostbusters* had all been converted into kidvid fare to help squeeze some excess money out of the relevant properties. Executive producer Jeff Kline and series producer-director Audu Paden were tasked with *Godzilla: The Animated Series* even while the feature itself was in production. With the animators denied access to any image of Godzilla, they were forced to use placeholders in early storyboards and animatics while waiting for the curtain of secrecy to lift. While they had limited access to information about the new Godzilla, these creators were all fans of the Toho series—and inevitably Paudu and artist Keith Aiken let in many Toho-esque features that had been consciously removed from the live-action version. The TV Godzilla walks upright, behaves with an anthropomorphic Haruo Nakajima–style swagger, beats the crap out of other monsters—and spits atomic fire![3]

The series adopted a format not dissimilar to the Hanna-Barbera show. The giant monster is allied with a research team exploring mysterious phenomena from a boat. Nick Tatopoulos (voiced by Ian Zeiring) brings his humane and Godzilla-friendly expertise to H.E.A.T. (Humanitarian Ecological Analysis Team).

The animated *Godzilla* was unexpectedly successful, especially for a kidvid spinoff to a much-maligned movie. It helped boost the reputation of the tarnished blockbuster. Had a sequel been made, it likely would have been closer in spirit to the cartoon than the 1998 film.

As late as 1999, plans for *Godzilla 2* still seemed viable. This remained the case even as Toho announced that they were reviving the Japanese cycle with the planned 2000 release of *Godzilla Millennium.* Devlin said that parallel Godzillas had always been part of the plan and that it was never his intention to replace the Japanese films: "That's why we're very pleased about [*Godzilla Millennium*]. That was always the dream. For instance, if you look at the sales of Godzilla merchandise, and I'm talking about Classic Godzilla merchandise, it's quadrupled since our *Godzilla* has come out."[4]

Not only did TriStar's *Godzilla* substantially raise interest in Classic Godzilla memorabilia and DVDs, it also brought about a change in how the press approached the classic series. As the press took to excoriating the 1998 film, they inevitably compared it — unfavorably — to the Japanese versions, and turned to "experts" to serve as talking heads to help make the point. Naturally enough, they drew their experts from the leagues of fans and film historians who had spent the 1990s championing the series. For years these voices had been suppressed, forced to express themselves in fanzines and vanity press publications, but suddenly the likes of Steve Ryfle, Ed Godziszewski, Stuart Galbraith, J.D. Lees, and others (including myself) were called out from the fan underground to speak on the radio, on TV, in magazines and newspapers. From there it was a short jump to providing audio commentaries on official DVD releases and publishing mainstream books.

Almost overnight, the critical consensus on Godzilla movies was overhauled to correspond with what fans had been saying all along.

Whatever else *Godzilla* did, it did this.

# Chapter 39

# *Godzilla 2000*

## GOJIRA NI-SEN MIRENIAMU (GODZILLA MILLENNIUM)

*Boy, that's ironic. It woke up after sixty million years, and then Godzilla destroyed it the very next day.*

—Yuki

**Japanese version: 107 minutes, Released December 11, 1999**
**U.S. theatrical version (Columbia): 99 minutes, Released August 18, 2000, MPAA rating: PG**
**Color, Widescreen**
**Produced by Shogo Tomiyama; U.S. Version produced by Michael Schlesinger; directed by Takao Okawara; screenplay by Hiroshi Kashiwabara and Wataru Mimura; music by Takayuki Hattori; cinematography by Katsuhiro Kato; art direction by Takeshi Shimizu; edited by Yoshiyuki Okuhara; special effects by Kenji Suzuki**
**Starring Takehiro Murata (Shinoda), Hiroshi Abe (Katagiri), Naomi Nishida (Yuki), Mayu Suzuki (Io Shinoda), Shiro Sano (Miyasaka), Koichi Ueda (Army Official)**
**GODZILLA portrayed by Tsutomu Kitagawa; ORGA portrayed by Makoto Ito**

*The ambitious Katagiri and the introspective Shinoda, once university friends and colleagues, are now working at cross purposes. Shinoda runs the Godzilla Prediction Network, a scrappy independent organization dedicated to studying, and perhaps one day containing, Japan's greatest threat. Katagiri runs the Crisis Control Intelligence Agency, a governmental bureau determined to eradicate that threat.*

*As Godzilla rampages across the country, destroying power plants and nuclear facilities, Katagiri's CCI secretly harvests a prehistoric meteorite discovered under the sea. Its unusual properties promise an alternate source of energy. The rock turns out to be a crashed alien spacecraft, which soon reveals decidedly hostile intentions.*

*As the dire events bring Shinoda and Katagiri into the final test of their tense relationship, Godzilla too will face his otherworldly rival, to battle for the fate of Japan.*

Toho had assumed that the reason the last decade's worth of Godzilla movies had languished without an American distributor was the fault of inherent properties of the films themselves—special effects below Hollywood's standards, or the limitations of dubbing. In other words, the only way to feasibly break into the American market was to hand the enterprise over to an American producer. This was done, and left egg on nearly everyone's faces. TriStar's *Godzilla* did all the things an American Godzilla was expected to do, except connect with audiences. The public response was consistent on one surprising point: People *liked* the Saturday matinee aesthetic they associated with Godzilla, and missed the man in the suit.

Devlin and Emmerich had been so determined to avoid any stigma of the old drive-in Godzilla that it never occurred to anyone to actually research that and find out whether the camp quotient was that big a deal. It turned out audiences were nostalgic for the very attributes the TriStar production deliberately removed.

It was a liberating revelation.

Not two months after *Godzilla* opened in Japan, Shogo Tomiyama called in some of the stalwarts of the latter-day Heisei-era film cycle to plot a return to first principles. From this would emerge *Godzilla 2000*, as atavistic as anything Toho had manufactured. It is unabashed in reveling in men in rubber suits pummeling each other, and was put together by more or less the same creative forces that had been doing this for years. Yet, somehow, it is unexpectedly fresh, and the most *fun* Godzilla movie in two or three decades.

The X factor, the variable that explains why *Godzilla 2000* is superior to its Heisei-era precursors, is simple enough to pinpoint: It is TriStar's *Godzilla*.

*Godzilla 2000* is self-consciously a reply to that film, an exercise in prideful one-upsmanship. The filmmakers compile a litany of images cribbed directly from the previous film: Godzilla introduced in fragmentary views of isolated body parts, a man nearly killed by a falling structure that luckily only pins him down, objects catapulted with Godzilla's approaching footsteps, a shot of Godzilla swimming towards the camera, a shot of a scientist standing in a giant footprint, Godzilla's landfall announced by a bulge in the water as his dorsal fins begin to break the surface tension, a sequence in which Godzilla chases a car through a tunnel — and a story built around an aspiring journalist and her Godzillologist boyfriend.

For all that the film begs, borrows, or steals from the American *Godzilla*, *Godzilla 2000* also takes great pains to draw attention to its retrograde characteristics. A military officer, played by recurring series character actor Koichi Ueda, declaims, "As we know from experience, when Godzilla is attacked he advances instead of retreats," stopping short of adding, "*unlike that other Godzilla.*" In the Japanese poster art, producer Tomiyama inserted an almost subliminal image of the Japan islands into the texture of Godzilla's skin in a visual message that he says "clearly defines this as a Godzilla movie made in Japan."[2]

In the summer of 1999, with the *Godzilla 2000* production team on a ten-week, $12 million shoot, Tomiyama and the rest of the creative team appeared on a Japanese talk show to promote the upcoming picture. Tomiyama explained that the project was conceived as a direct consequence from the TriStar *Godzilla*: "Actually, we had no plans for another Godzilla film until the year 2005. [The change of heart] came about, I will admit, because now TriStar's *Godzilla* is Godzilla. We had a feeling that after seeing TriStar's film, we couldn't keep [the Japanese Godzilla] silent until 2005."[3]

Meanwhile, plans for a putative Godzilla 2 were still on track back at TriStar, with Devlin and Emmerich set to oversee it. As the press got wind of *Godzilla 2000*, though, it was inevitably presented as a rebuke to the TriStar picture, a cinematic equivalent to a glove slap across the face. Anxious to defuse the idea that the new film was somehow intended as an insult, Toho issued a formal statement:

> We at Toho are deeply dismayed by a recent article in the press announcing our plans to bring back a version of Godzilla because that story did not represent our feelings in spirit or in fact on several points. We are deeply gratified by the worldwide box office success of TriStar's *Godzilla* and since it was always our intention to bring back the classic Godzilla, we appreciate the support our partners at Sony and Centropolis* have given us to achieve our goal. Currently we enthusiastically support the highly successful Godzilla animated series and Sony's sequel to the film. We hope that this will put to rest any misinterpretations resulting from previous statements.[4]

Devlin, too, took to the press to squelch rumors that there was any institutional discord between the two companies: "Our hope was always that Godzilla and the associated creatures in Japan would continue."[5]

Tomiyama envisioned a trilogy, rebooted anew without connection to any existing continuity.[6] After the obsession with internal continuity that dominated the preceding decade, the clean break is refreshing.

Tomiyama later explained his ambitions for the Millennium franchise:

> We wanted to do something different from the TriStar film. We wanted to try something new, but not something too different from the past Godzilla movies that we produced. Three things must not change: ... First, Godzilla was born or created by nuclear testing. Because of nuclear testing, something was created that man could not kill. That was the image we wanted to keep. Second, he would stand on his two feet like he always has, and that his fins would sparkle as he emitted his atomic ray. Third, the character would be created by a man in a suit, smashing miniature buildings.[7]

*\*Centropolis was the name of Dean Devlin's production company.*

Beyond that, everything was on the table.

The most conspicuous change in personnel on the new movie was special effects supervisor Kenji Suzuki, inheriting Koichi Kawakita's former position. Suzuki had served as chief assistant director under Kawakita on several films beginning with *Godzilla vs. King Ghidorah*. Where his mentor had focused on miniatures and optical effects, Suzuki broke ranks to try a bold new approach. Using digital compositing techniques and computer-assisted animation, Suzuki's Godzilla rampages through real cityscapes.

The first step was designing the new Millennium Godzilla. Veteran suitmaker Shinichi Wakasa sat down with Suzuki, Tomiyama, and director Takao Okwara to discuss ideas. Wakasa explained:

> I used their opinions and my own, and brought them all together to come up with the final design. There were also a lot of people who brought me their opinions without my even asking! But for those, I hardly listened to them at all. But even listening to just those three was very difficult! They all had different opinions ... "make the head smaller, make the fins larger, make the tail longer," that kind of thing.[8]

Taking over from Kenpachiro Satsuma inside the suit, stuntman Tsutomo Kitagawa said he felt like he "was carrying two adults on my back! I was dead tired after walking just a few steps. When we started filming, they put an air tube in the suit from the area of the feet, which made breathing a little easier, but they had to take it away for the actual takes. Playing Godzilla is not for somebody who's claustrophobic!"[9]

For the first time in the history of the series, the Godzilla suit was not painted black or gray, but was actually painted green, to finally conform with the public's widespread and longstanding belief that it had always been so.

Suzuki had Kitagawa stomp around on a raised platform while a remote-controlled camera skittered around him, to create the feeling of enormous height. Kitagawa performed many of his scenes against a green background, from which he was composited into live action backdrops, along with CGI-animated army

hardware.[10] Toho outsourced the computer animation to twelve different companies, who variously tackled the monster shots, animated tanks, and wire removal.[11]

One month after filming Godzilla's raid on the Tokaimura nuclear facility, a genuine accident occurred at the site. The deadly uranium leak not only terrified the public and inflamed environmental protestors, it reminded the nation that just two years earlier the very same nuclear plant had been the site of the worst nuclear accident in Japanese history. Takao Okumura worried about including the scene, for fears of exploiting such a recent tragedy, but decided in the end that the film was not exploiting the event so much as using the fantasy of Godzilla as a metaphor for the continuing nuclear crisis in Japan.[12]

While Suzuki's clever innovations squeezed the most onscreen value out of his limited budget ($12 million being the most then spent by Toho on any Godzilla film, but still a meager fraction of TriStar's budget), the strength of *Godzilla 2000* is its human dimension. Not since the sixties had the series so fully realized its characters as interesting, quirky personalities worth spending an hour or two with.

Screenwriters Wataru Mimura and Hiroshi Kashiwabara returned to two fundamentals of Godzilla storytelling that served the Heisei cycle so well. The first is the essential triangulation of conflict: Godzilla vs. monster vs. JSDF vs. Godzilla. Arranging the opponents in a three-pronged pattern enables Godzilla himself to be at once menace and hero—or, as Mimura put it, "scary, strong, and very cool." Kashiwabara said it more succinctly: "charming."[13]

The second well-heeled fundamental is the idea that Godzilla's monster foe is some variant derived from Godzilla himself. An old favorite, the Godzilla cells make a return appearance, with the alien creature sampling Godzilla's self-regenerative DNA to form a body that, as the film unfolds, increasingly resembles Godzilla.

Five years earlier, this stuff seemed stale. Now it is served up in the context of high-spirited fun — and, yes, camp — that invigorates the whole show. In *Godzilla vs. King Ghidorah*, the monster tore down a building around a human antagonist in a moment of tear-jerking pathos and overweening earnestness. A similar scene caps *Godzilla 2000*: Having vanquished the alien threat, Godzilla swaggers up to the high rise where Katagiri has been watching the action. He fixes the CCI chief in his steely reptilian gaze, and menacingly stabs his enormous claws into the skydeck as a warning of what is to come. Katagiri returns the stare and accepts his fate, screaming in some absurd admiration, "Godzilla!"

Over-the-top it may be, but this is what makes it so eminently watchable. It had been decades since a Godzilla film embraced its inner silly, and it was long overdue.

Helping such moments tremendously is the casting. As Kitagawa, Hiroshi Abe gives the series its most singularly weird villain since Yoshio Tsuchiya. Abe is an unusual leading man who built his stardom on the brilliantly wacky (and wackily brilliant) TV series *Trick* (2000–2006). One part George Clooney and two parts Steve Carell, Abe is a strangely handsome and debonair figure with a self-deprecating sense of slapstick and unctuous charm, capped by a memorable pair of eyes.

As his opposite number Shinoda, Godzilla veteran Takehiro Murata gives perhaps his best performance in the series. Murata had previously appeared as Andoh in *Godzilla and Mothra* and Yukari's editor in *Godzilla vs. Destoroyah*, and would return for cameos in both *Giant Monsters All-Out Attack* and *Godzilla x Mechagodzilla*.

Naomi Nishida, as reporter heroine Yuki, was an ex-fashion model recently crowned Best New Actress by the Japanese Oscars. She had some experience playing to special effects in Toho's popular *School Ghost Story* series.

Shiro Sano was a cult movie favorite and a fan of Godzilla, familiar to genre buffs for his roles in *Violent Cop* (1989), *Evil Dead Trap 2* (1991), and *The Mystery of Rampo* (alongside Hiroshi Abe, as it happened, 1994). In the years to come, he would meet *Princess Blade* (2001), suffer Masayuki Ochiai's *Infection* (2004), and fight Takashi Miike's *Great Yokai War* (2005). Sano returned to the Millennium Godzilla cycle

for *Giant Monsters All-Out Attack* and *Godzilla Final Wars*.

With the Heisei Godzilla series newly released in America on DVD from Columbia/ TriStar, it was initially assumed that *Godzilla 2000* would follow suit. When Columbia executive Jeff Blake attended the Japanese premiere, he was struck by long lines and enthusiastic crowds. As he watched the film, he realized that they had a crowd-pleasing piece of entertainment on their hands with a built-in audience and a favorable moment inadvertently nurtured by the response to the American *Godzilla*. Columbia could send this out theatrically, making it the first Godzilla film theatrically released in America in fifteen years. First, however, like those theatrical releases of the past, it would need some tweaking for American consumption.[14]

Historically such steps were taken by American distributors to retroactively conform the storytelling to stateside expectations. Political subtexts were twisted, Western actors shoved into scenes, and other such tamperings. In the case of *Godzilla 2000*, this is not the case. Here, the point of the Americanization was to correct deficiencies in production technique.

The story begins when Michael Schlesinger, Sony's vice-president of Repertory Sales and Acquisitions, was shown Toho's English-dubbed "international" print of the film. Schlesinger is a film historian and cult movie buff of catholic tastes, naturally inclined to respect the Japanese originals on their own terms and disinclined to waste Sony's money. Comparing the international print of *Godzilla 2000* to the English-translated screenplay, he noticed discrepancies—chunks of narrative and character detail unaccountably missing from the existing English dialogue. To rectify this, the dubbing would have to be rewritten and re-recorded. Doing so would provide the opportunity to correct other problems with the Japanese soundtrack. "There were numerous scenes of Godzilla walking where no footsteps were heard, for example," Schlesinger explained, "There were many scenes that had no foley or background — mostly interiors — where all you heard were the voices of the principals."[15]

As Schlesinger and his team wrote the new dialogue, he decided to prioritize storytelling and entertainment value over raw technical precision. "Our philosophy was basically, if it starts and stops at the same point, and no talking over obvious pauses, then we were pretty much in the zone." It was an approach different from that taken on the sixties-era dubbing jobs, but one that greatly simplified the process—even if the process was still far from simple. "It was especially difficult because so many lines had long, long pauses in them. For example, Miyasaka's final speech has three." They continued to refine the dialogue even as they were on the dubbing stage, adjusting lines with the voice actors to fine-tune their synchronization. However, as Schlesinger noted, given a choice between a line-reading that was of superior performance versus one more in synch with the onscreen lips, he chose performance every time.[16]

Working with editor Mike Mahoney, sound designer Darren Paskal, and composer J. Peter Robinson, Schlesinger trimmed the film to a tighter 99 minutes. Although a few story points were reordered along the way, the reduced running time was accomplished without major deletions or alterations. In most cases, Sony's editors pruned transitions and small moments here and there.

As the film's American debut approached, Jeff Blake said he would be satisfied if *Godzilla 2000* returned $5 million on its opening weekend. The actual figures came back closer to $4.6 million, a little under his prediction but not disappointingly so.[17] It was a modest critical and popular success. Toho was so pleased with the improvements made by Schlesinger's team, they used that version for all territories where *Godzilla 2000* had not yet played, and (subtitled back into Japanese!) released it in Japan as well.[18]

To the outside observer, it may well have looked as if Godzilla was at last triumphant.

# Chapter 40

# Godzilla x. Megaguirus

## Gojira Tai Megagirasu: G Shometsu Sakusen
## (Godzilla vs. Megaguirus: G Annihilation Strategy)

*Why do you need to be fit when we're going to make Godzilla disappear up his own butthole?*
— Kudo

Japanese version: 106 minutes, Released December 16, 2000
Color, Widescreen
Produced by Shogo Tomiyama; directed by Masaaki Tezuka; screenplay by Hiroshi Kashiwabara and Wataru Mimura; music by Michiru Oshima; cinematography by Masahiro Kishimoto; art direction by Yukiharu Seshimo; edited by Shinichi Fushima; special effects by Kenji Suzuki
Starring Misato Tanaka (Major Kiriko Tsujimori), Shosuke Tanihara (Hajime Kudo), Masato Ibu (Motohiko Sugiura), Yuriko Hoshi (Yoshino Yoshizawa), Masanobu Katsumura (Niikura), Mansaku Ikeuchi (Mima), Makiya Yamaguchi (Hosono), Tetsuo Yamashita (Okumura), Toshiyuki Nagashima (Miyagawa), Kazuko Katou (Kaoru), Hiroyuki Suzuki (Kaoru's Son), Koichi Ueda (Government Official), Wataru Mimura (Military Officer), Hiroshi Kashiwabara (Military Officer)
GODZILLA portrayed by Tsutomu Kitagawa; MEGAGUIRUS portrayed by Minoru Watanabe

*In 1954, an enormous beast rose from the ashes of atomic tests to lay waste to Japan. It was a living embodiment of the worst terrors of nuclear technology. Twelve years later, a rebuilt Japan unveils its own nuclear reactor — and the monster Godzilla reappears to destroy it. Speculating that Godzilla is attracted to nuclear energy, the Japanese struggle to develop a new energy source capable of meeting the needs of its growing population. In 1996, they establish a revolutionary plasma core, burning clean energy — only to watch in despair and horror as once again Godzilla arrives to punish them for their ambitions.*

*The plasma reactor was shuttered, but continued research into plasma technology yielded a possible solution to the problem. Code-named "Dimension Tide," the weapon fires isolated, short-lived, and targeted black holes from a satellite. Aim the thing at Godzilla, and Japan could be rid of him once and for all. A test*
of the Dimension Tide produces an unexpected side effect: a rip in the fabric of time that allows a prehistoric insect to pass into the present day. The Meganulon reproduces, and its swarm begins to eat human beings. The bugs also jam the Dimension Tide's targeting mechanism, leaving Japan vulnerable to Godzilla's onslaught — provoked by the reactivation of the plasma engines.

*Monsters large and small converge as the scientists responsible for the Dimension Tide race the clock to get their weapon online.*

The morning after the party revealed the cold, sobering reality. The American release of *Godzilla 2000* was an anomaly. Western audiences had warmed to the film much like one might welcome an old pal at a high school reunion, but there was no long-term future in the friendship.

Inside Sony, the growing consensus was that *Godzilla 2000*'s performance would have been much better with a different marketing campaign — one that targeted not just children, but a broader mass audience. The possibility existed to try again, and Sony adopted a wait-and-see policy for the Millennium sequels, evaluating each one individually for possible theatrical release. Toho was accustomed to making Godzilla films on a yearly cycle, yet there was little room for an annual Godzilla picture to fit into the crowded and competitive American marketplace. *Godzilla 2000* benefited from a "perfect storm" of external factors: the lingering aftertaste of the TriStar film, the novelty of seeing Classic Godzilla on the big screen all over again, and positive critical response — none of which were likely to be repeated. A mass American release was nothing Toho could take for granted.[1]

Which meant that the ongoing Godzilla cycle would be built, as ever, with the Japanese market as the primary — if not the exclusive — target. The Japanese audience had been rather cool towards *Godzilla 2000*, and without the bonus provided by the Americanized version, the film would have lost Toho money. If Toho was to continue making Godzilla pictures, they would need to cost less and there would need to be creative changes.[2]

Shogo Tomiyama therefore decided not to follow his earlier ideas about a trilogy following the *Godzilla 2000* setup and instead announced that each new film would be a stand-alone project with its own private continuity. Each would reboot the franchise, striking out in new directions and exploring experimental new approaches. Or, to put it another way, they planned to keep changing things until they found the approach that worked best.

Screenwriters Hiroshi Kashiwabara and Wataru Mimura were back, but director Takeo Okawara was not. In his place came enthusiastic greenhorn Masaaki Tezuka, former assistant director on *Godzilla vs. Mechagodzilla II*. Special effects supervisor Kenji Suzuki was back, but the lower budget shows in his miniature work.

In many ways, Kashiwabara and Mimura recycled their *Godzilla vs. Space Godzilla* script with new monsters. The result is disappointing. In *Godzilla 2000*, the two writers crafted interesting characters and a story that wrapped human and monster conflicts together, in a throwback to Shinichi Sekizawa's storytelling style. This time around, the writers look back instead to the nineties pattern of an institutional response to Godzilla that unintentionally unleashes worse monsters. As with the dullest Heisei series scripts, the human characters are just ciphers, narrative pawns moved around to keep the monster action going. Aside from the age-old "I want to study Godzilla"/"I want to kill Godzilla" debate, there is no character development whatsoever. Many characters are introduced by name and then given nothing more to say or do.

The male hero is a wacky young inventor, heir to the mantle previously served by Tadeo Takashima in *King Kong vs. Godzilla*, Akira Kubo in *Invasion of Astro-Monster*, and Eisei Amamato in *All Monsters Attack*.

When the G-Graspers team take to the flying Griffon to attack Godzilla, it is G-Force in the Super X all over again but with new names. Misato Tanaka's character Major Tsujinori harbors a personal grudge against Godzilla for the death of someone she cared for, which puts her in company with similar figures from *The Return of Godzilla*, *Godzilla vs. Biollante*, *Godzilla vs. Space Godzilla*, and *Godzilla vs. Desotroyah*— but with no new spin added to the idea.

Thirty years after starring in *Ghidrah, The Three-Headed Monster*, the lovely Yuriko Hoshi returns as this film's special guest star. Hoshi plays Miss Yoshizawa, the scientist responsible for creating the new weapon. Yoshizawa also lost a loved one to Godzilla in a previous attack, by the way, which accounts for nearly all of the characterization applied to her. Hoshi is a fine actress who once stole entire movies from casts full of Toho stalwarts, and she still looks fantastic. It is a shame this film offers her so little worthy of her.

Akira Ifukube's music had become so much an integral aspect of the Godzilla mythos that it was by now corporate policy to include his "Enter Godzilla" fanfare somewhere in every film, regardless of the composer of record. Even before Ifukube's passing in 2006, it was clear to the studio that a new generation of musical talent needed to be cultivated, but finding the right musician to back Godzilla was a tall order. Whoever it was would need to simultaneously bring a fresh musical voice while still meeting the very high standards of expectations set by Ifukube's legendary tracks.

Michiru Oshima was a graduate of the National College of Music with extensive experience composing for television, video games, and theatrical features. Toho's music producer Togo Kitahara sat her down with some DVDs of past glories to review the assignment. "Needless to say," Oshima recalled, "it is understood that Ifukube's music has become the preconception of the image of monster music." Oshima then did the unlikely, and delivered an iconic score that had all the epic authority of Ifukube's soundtracks but was also distinctive and original. More than any other composer attached to the series in its long run, she provided a musical accompaniment to the on-screen mayhem that was both worthy of Ifukube and unlike his approach.[3]

In composing the theme for the Meganulon bugs, Oshima took inspiration from Alfred Hitchcock's *The Birds*. "The string instruments emulated a bird's crying voice," she said (probably mixing her memory of the string-heavy score to Hitchcock's *Psycho* with the music-less soundtrack for *The Birds*).[4] Ironically, the resulting theme sounds remarkably like an uncredited library cue added by UPA to the American cut of *War of the Gargantuas*.

The movie has isolated moments of clever invention, including a fun sequence as Misato Tanaka rides Godzilla's dorsal plates like a mechanical bull. It is interesting to note that director Tezuka resisted this sequence as an instance of too-pulpy action movie histrionics, but acquiesced to pressure from Tomiyama.[5]

Special effects supervisor Kenji Suzuki continued to innovate, although with variable results. Officially the film was reported to have cost the same one billion yen as was budgeted for the other Heisei and Millennium series films, but the filmmakers themselves reported a lower, more restrictive budget — which may explain the lower quality miniatures on display. Nevertheless, budget woes or no, Suzuki nicely stages a battle between a suitmation Godzilla and an army of CGI-rendered insects.

Suitmation actor Tsutomu Kitagawa was pleased that the special effects team saw fit to build him a new Godzilla suit. The *Godzilla 2000* costume had been made somewhat generically, whereas this revised version was custom-tailored to Kitagawa's physique. "This year it was fairly enjoyable to move," Kitagawa explained. "On the supervisor's instructions, the suit was fitted to my form. Last year was frantic, this year I had a little room."[6]

With that extra room, Kitagawa lets his past as a Japanese TV superhero show through. His fight scene with the full-size Megaguirus of the title might as well have been filmed in 1973.

Despite bright spots, pacing problems and a lack of narrative thrust plague the film, preventing its pieces from cohering into an entertaining whole. Where *Godzilla 2000* was cheerfully retrograde, *Godzilla x Megaguirus* is a wan recitation of familiar ideas.

Audiences were unimpressed, and *Megaguirus* was overwhelmed at the box office by its most obvious competitor, Disney's *Dinosaur*. *Godzilla x Megaguirus* sold a paltry 1.35 million tickets, far below *Godzilla 2000* and the lowest attendance figures of the Godzilla series yet.[7]

As the year drew to a close, there was no plan on the books for a 2002 Godzilla...

## Chapter 41

# *Godzilla, Mothra, and King Ghidorah: Giant Monsters All-Out Attack*

## GOJIRA, MOSURA, KINGU GHIDORAH: DAIKAIJU SOKOGEKI

*This animal represents the collective will to survive of many thousands of people. This animal contains the restless souls of the countless people who perished during the terrible battles that took place during the Pacific conflict.*

— Isayama

Japanese version: 105 minutes, Released December 15, 2001

Color, Widescreen

Produced by Hideyuki Honma; executive producer Shogo Tomiyama; directed by Shusuke Kaneko; screenplay by Shusuke Kaneko, Keiichi Hasegawa and Masahiro Yokotani; music by Ko Otani; cinematography by Masahiro Kishimoto; art direction by Toshio Miike and Isao Takahashi; edited by Isao Tomita; special effects by Makoto Kamiya

Starring Chiharu Niiyama (Yuri Tachibana), Ryudo Uzaki (General Taizo Tachibana), Masahiro Kobayashi (Teruaki Takeda), Shiro Sano (Haruki Kodokura), Eisei Amamoto (Hirotoshi Isayama), Takashi Nishina (Aki Maruo), Kaho Minami (Capt. Kumi Emori), Shinya Owada (Lt. General Katsumasa Mikumo), Kunio Murai (Masato Hinogaki), Hiroyuki Watanabe (Yutaka Hirose), Shingo Katsurayama (Tokihiko Kobayakawa), Toshikazu Fukawa (Miyashita), Koichi Kawakita, Masaaki Tezuka (Military Officers)

GODZILLA portrayed by Mizuho Yoshida; KING GHIDORAH portrayed by Akira Ohashi; BARAGON portrayed by Rie Ota

*For a nation defeated in World War II and whose Self-Defense Forces have never seen conflict since, Godzilla's attack in 1954 marked an important moment in Japanese history: a singular instance of military heroism. Nearly fifty years after the JSDF beat back Godzilla, General Tachibana warily tallies the signs that the monster is returning, and that Japan's days of peace are numbered.*

*His daughter Yuri is a hack reporter for BS Digital Q, a tabloid TV show exploiting urban legends. She learns of an ancient prophecy regarding three legendary "Guardian Monsters," and evidence that indeed the creatures Baragon, Mothra, and King Ghidorah are stirring, readying to protect Japan from Godzilla's return.*

*It begs the question, "Why Japan?" Why of all the places in the world would monsters congregate there? Yuri meets a man with the answer: A mysterious prophet explains that Godzilla has absorbed the life forces of all those killed in the Pacific during World War II. Countless angry souls who suffered and died from Japanese aggression, as well as Japanese soldiers whose patriotism is something their country would now like to forget, are using Godzilla as a force of supernatural revenge. Godzilla is literally the specter of war, and his rage and power will surely overwhelm Japan.*

*Godzilla destroys everything in his path — obliterating hospitals and schools as well as vaporizing even the JSDF's most advanced weapons. The only hope lies with the Guardian Monsters — but Godzilla dispatches Baragon, Mothra, and Ghidorah in turn.*

*In Japan's darkest hour, will an old solider facing the demon of war find his own moment of heroism?*

One story, two outcomes:

Shusuke Kaneko approached Shogo Tomiyama in 1992 to ask for a job directing the next Godzilla movie. Tomiyama gave the kid the "thanks but no thanks" brush-off. Ten years later, Tomiyama came to Kaneko, asking him to take over the next Godzilla movie. Kaneko, unsurprisingly, agreed, and the result was the gloriously inventive, if awkwardly titled, *Godzilla, Mothra, King Ghidorah: Giant Monsters All-Out Attack.*[1]

The difference between the two conversations, and the reason that the second one was a mirror image of the first, was *Gamera.*

In 1995, as previously discussed, Kaneko directed a great monster movie. Then in 1996 he made an excellent one, and in 1999 a superlative one. The Gamera trilogy made Kaneko a virtual brand name in *kaiju eiga* revitalization.

Kaneko grew up thrilling to the cinema of Ishiro Honda. Any aspirations he may have had towards following in Honda's footsteps, though, were scotched when the Japanese film business collapsed. He opted for a safer career choice, and studied to become an elementary schoolteacher. On a whim, Kaneko took an entrance exam to Nikkatsu Studios, and was stunned when he was one of only two applicants out of three hundred to be accepted. Suddenly, Kaneko was in the film business after all.[2]

However, he was at Nikkatsu in the 1980s, which meant he was working on softcore sex films. Nikkatsu called them "roman pornos," for "romance pornography." It was a seedy way to pay the bills, perhaps, but a vital proving ground for the next generation of talent who in the new millennium would rebuild the Japanese film business.[3]

Kaneko continued to nurse fantasies of one day making his own monster movie. When *Godzilla vs. King Ghidorah* opened in 1992, he lobbied, unsuccessfully, for the chance. Tomiyama chose Takao Okawara instead. Now a freelancer, Kaneko went to Hollywood with screenwriting partner Kazunori Ito to create one of the segments of Brian Yuzna's anthology horror opus *Necronomicon* (1993). As Daiei started planning the revival of its Gamera series, Kaneko was determined not to let another opportunity slip past. He lobbied again, unrelentingly, until he won his career-making chance.[4]

Working with less than half the budgets given to Godzilla movies, and expected to rehabilitate the derelict wreck of a monster franchise laughingstock, Kaneko and his team did the impossible, and outdid themselves with each subsequent attempt.

Kaneko brought a distinctive three-pronged strategy to his monster movies. The first characteristic "Kaneko touch" was his constant and consistent subversion of genre conventions. By way of an example, the climactic monster confrontation of *Gamera 3* does not actually occur in the movie. *Gamera 3* builds to a final battle between the giant turtle and a horde of almost invincible Gyaos mutants, but ends with that battle just about to begin—and its outcome very much in doubt. (Not for nothing is the Japanese title *Gamera 3: Incomplete Struggle*.)

Secondly, Kaneko's monster films carefully establish characterization for nearly every person who appears on screen, no matter how small the role. Compared to the growing reliance of recent monster films on distinguishing characters by nothing more than clothing and name, Kaneko's films employ a Sekizawa-worthy wit to underpin their horror with humanity and comic relief.

Lastly, Kaneko is not shy about rewriting the histories of his monsters. He maintains their recognized iconic appearances, but discards their established origins. To Kaneko, such a move was an essential acknowledgment that the old monster origins were anachronisms:

> Nowadays, I think monsters cannot exist in science fiction. That's because now science has advanced and the audience knows so much more about science. Back in the 1960s, a fifty-meter monster could have been in science fiction; we really did not know if it was impossible. But now everyone knows a fifty-meter monster can't exist if you think in scientific terms.... So now what we do is, because everyone still wants to see a fifty-meter monster, we actually create a fantasy movie which has the atmosphere or mood of a science fiction movie with fifty-meter monsters.... Look at what happens in *Megaguirus*, which tries to be science fiction. It doesn't work, it can't be explained by science. So the only way to explain things is in a fantasy realm.[5]

In other words, a Kaneko *kaiju eiga* establishes a fantastical premise but, having done so, proceeds from there with logic and emotional realism. A case in point: *Godzilla x Megaguirus* includes a sequence in which the G-Grasper Unit consults a scientific advisor straight out of *Gigantis the Fire Monster*. Professor Exposition has at his fingertips the complete life cycle and behavioral profile of an insect species that has been extinct for millions of years. By contrast, *Giant Monsters All-Out*

*Attack* repeatedly cuts back to its military and political decision-makers squabbling in a wood-paneled room. There is no giant screen showing perfect bird's eye views of the monsters, no paleontologists with all of the answers. Instead, they have to rely on sketchy, confused, and sometimes contradictory reports from the field. Only fairly late in the movie does one soldier suggest, to the derision of his superiors, that military communication could be simplified if they assigned *names* to the different monsters.

Speaking of monster names, there is a clever jab at TriStar's *Godzilla* early in the picture. Tachibana lectures a group of cadets about the possible omens of Godzilla's return, including the 1998 destruction of New York. A cadet asks, "The New York attack was Godzilla, right?" A second cadet answers, to the delight of the audience, "That's what all the American experts claim. But our guys here have some doubts."

However, kidding aside, the genre film from 1998 with the biggest impact on the future of Godzilla was not TriStar's movie, but a low budget Japanese ghost story called *Ringu*.

Throughout the 1990s, a group of young filmmakers and budding artists toiling in the margins of the Japanese film business began experimenting with a novel approach to horror movies. Combining modern technology, urban legends, and ancient folklore, they gradually refined a new kind of horror movie that emphasized suspense and atmosphere, and packed an enormous dramatic punch.

When director Hideo Nakata and screenwriter Hiroshi Takahashi collaborated on *Ringu*, it was merely another in a string of similar low-budget ghost stories—but in it they struck the perfect balance of constituent parts to achieve monumental popularity. *Ringu* became the most commercially successful horror film in Japanese history and one of the biggest horror movies of all time anywhere.[6] It kicked the burgeoning J-Horror subgenre into overdrive. J-Horror films were cheap to make, they had unprecedented appeal to female audiences, and they sold well internationally.

The economics of Godzilla suddenly looked very poor by comparison. In 2001, Toho spent $10 million on *Godzilla x Megaguirus* only to lose money on the bid. The same year, Toho released Kiyoshi Kurosawa's *Pulse* to enormous international critical and commercial success, but with a fraction of the upfront investment. In the years to come, the growing popularity of inexpensive J-Horrors would completely unseat Godzilla as Toho's genre staple.

*Giant Monsters All-Out Attack* is a Godzilla movie for the J-Horror age. In it, Kaneko directly addresses an obvious question: Why do monsters attack Japan, and only Japan? The fantasy mythology he invents to answer that question turns Godzilla into something akin to *Ringu*'s Sadako. Like her, or other vengeful ghosts in the J-Horror world, Godzilla is an avenging force from the afterlife come to punish everyone for the long-ago sins of the few.

To this end, Kaneko plays up the horror like never before. This Godzilla, with his dead, milky-white eyes, *kills people*. Each time, just before he does, Kaneko invites us to care about the victims. Here's a teenage girl in a hospital bed, cowering in terror, praying for her life, heaving a sigh of relief ... and here is her hospital erased in a flash, a mushroom cloud billowing into the sky.

Throughout the picture, various characters make light of the monsters, only then to die. A young woman poses for a tourist photo against the picturesque backdrop of an oncoming Baragon—and is killed. A news helicopter hovers over the monster bout, offering color commentary as if at a sporting event—and is blown to bits. In a direct homage to TriStar's film, a group of fishermen on a wharf are the first witnesses—and first victims—of Godzilla's landfall. The message is clear. Those expecting light-hearted fun are in the wrong movie.

Originally, Kaneko's script called for Baragon, Anguirus, and Varan to be the three Guardian Monsters. Kaneko wanted them to seem earthy and animalistic, creatures of the ground, without special powers. Facing the dismal box office showing of *Megaguirus*, however, Toho felt an urgent need to shore up the commercial appeal with their biggest draws—Mothra and Ghidorah.[7] Kaneko understood the logic and agreed, but the change meant that for the first time

Ghidorah would be portrayed as a heroic monster. Ghidorah was also designed uncharacteristically small, to allow Godzilla to be the dominating figure. Suitmation actor Akira Ohashi played Ghidorah, using his arms inside the heads like puppets. While Mothra was realized using a variety of CGI and puppet techniques, Baragon was played by the first female suitmation performer, Rie Ota.

The Millennium Godzilla design otherwise used throughout the new series was for this outing abandoned in favor of a grim and monstrous suit built by Fuyuki Shinada of Bishop Studios. It was the largest Godzilla costume yet made, and for the only time in the Millennium series the man inside it was not Tsutomu Kitagawa. Instead, Mizuho Yoshida, *Gamera 2*'s Legion performer, took the role.[8]

Other nods to the Gamera series are seeded through the film. The most noticeable would be the basic premise of the Guardian Monsters. The idea that giant monsters are relics of a past civilization, left behind to guard against some future threat, is the same idea underscoring *Gamera 3*. Musician Ko Otani, Kaneko's composer for the Gamera cycle, wrote a dark, driving score more reminiscent of a horror film than the usual Godzilla soundtrack.

Several *Gamera 3* cast members appear in *Giant Monsters All-Out Attack*, including Yukijiro Hotaro (*Gamera*'s Mr. Osako) as the man who discovers Ghidorah's frozen body. Ai Maeda, the star *of Gamera 3*, appears with her sister Aki in a cameo.

Returning to Godzilladom after 33 years was Eisei Amamoto. The man who once played Dr. Who in *King Kong Escapes* and toy inventor Imami in *All Monsters Attack* had been on Kaneko's mind for years, and the filmmaker was thrilled to get to work with the veteran actor. The role of the mysterious prophet was written especially for Amamoto. Kaneko joked, "He is just like a monster. Godzilla, Baragon, King Ghidorah, Mothra, and Amamoto."[9]

Chiharu Niiyama was the youngest actress to take a leading role in a Godzilla film. Kaneko first saw her as a teenage star on a daytime drama and followed her career. "I have been paying attention to her since her debut because

she is very beautiful," he said.[10] Kaneko hoped he could snag her at what he called "the balance moment," that critical instant of transition from pop idol to serious actress. She had a background in J-Horror as well, having played in the TV series adaptation of *Ringu* (1999), and later in Takashi Shimizu's *Ju-On 2* (2003).

As her father, Kaneko cast Ryudo Uzaki — an untrained non-professional actor chosen perversely because he did *not* look like a military man. Ever keen to undermine audience expectations, Kaneko felt that Uzaki's atypical appearance would deny his climactic kamizake-like actions any unwanted right-wing taint.[11]

Shiro Sano, last seen as *Godzilla 2000*'s Miyazaki, plays the editor of *BS Digital Q*. During production, Sano and Chiharu Niiyama watched *King Kong vs. Godzilla* as a sort of mood-setter. Niiyama started giggling at the miniature trucks, and Sano immediately called her on it. "Don't laugh," he told her. "It would have been easier and cheaper for Tsuburaya to have gone to a construction site and filmed ordinary trucks lugging dirt than to have built a sprawling miniature set like this. Realism is not the point. It's about style — it's about mood. There's integrity in the way Tsuburaya and his people worked."[12]

The latest person to serve in the position pioneered by Eiji Tsuburaya all those years ago was Makoto Kamiya. It almost did not happen. Seeking to maintain authorial control over the entire process, Kaneko initially planned to supervise both the live action and the special effects units himself. He had storyboarded the effects sequences and begun work, when the crushing pressures of Toho's tight deadlines forced him to reconsider. Kamiya stepped in to supervise the work, from Kaneko's plans.[13]

In the final frames of *Giant Monsters All-Out Attack*, Kamiya lingers on a shot of Godzilla's still-beating heart at the bottom of the sea. Akira Ifukube's "Enter Godzilla" march swells, the credits roll, and the viewer presumes that a sequel is anticipated. In point of fact, while both previous Millennium Godzilla entries similarly capped off with a sort of "to be continued" tease, no sequels were ever planned.

Tomiyama had embarked on the Millennium cycle with the plan to make but three films, and after the debacle of *Megaguirus* had been willing to call it off there. Kaneko's pitch for *Giant Monsters All-Out Attack* sounded exciting, and Tomiyama trusted the young auteur to deliver — but as the film wrapped, no continuations were expected. Relations between Kaneko and Tomiyama had been strained, with the director's artistic instincts often at odds with Tomiyama's commercial imperatives.

*Giant Monsters All-Out Attack* was released as the second part of a double bill with *Hamtaro*, a theatrical version of the popular kid's cartoon about a chubby hamster. Toho's thinking was to bolster the possibly weak commercial prospects of another Godzilla picture with one of their most reliable properties, and with any luck expose a new generation of children to Godzilla at the same time. The strategy worked. *Giant Monsters All-Out Attack* sold 2.4 million tickets, and made back double its production costs. Market researchers for Toho took notice that most of *Hamtaro*'s child crowd stuck around for Godzilla.[14]

Sony was impressed by Kamiya's superior effects work and the film's adult tone. A nationwide theatrical release was seriously mooted. Although Sony and Toho were unable to agree on terms, and the picture was eventually distributed instead on DVD, Sony did acquire prints for repertory screenings.[15]

It was a strong enough revival to persuade Toho that there was life left in Godzilla yet.

# Chapter 42

# Godzilla Against Mechagodzilla

## GOJIRA TAI MEKAGOJIRA

*Godzilla put a curse on Japan. Ever since it first appeared, it seems we keep being invaded by these giant monsters.*

— Igarashi

Japanese version: 88 minutes, Released December 14, 2002

Color, Widescreen

Produced by Shogo Tomiyama; directed by Masaaki Tezuka; screenplay by Wataru Mimura; music by Michiru Oshima; cinematography by Masahiro Kishimoto; art direction by Yukiharu Seshita; edited by Shinichi Fushima; special effects by Yuichi Kikuchi

Starring Yumiko Shaku (Akane Yashiro), Shin Takuma (Tokumitsu Yuhara), Kana Onodera (Sara Yuhara), Kumi Mizuno (Prime Minister Machiko Tsuge), Akira Nakao (Prime Minister Hayato Igarashi), Takeo Nakahara (JSDF Chief Hitoyanagi), Koichi Ueda (Dobashi), Koh Takasugi (Lt. Togashi), Yosuke Tomoi (Lt. Hamaya), Junichi Mizuno (Lt. Sekine), Yoshikazu Kanou (Hishinuma), Akira Shirai (Shinji Akamatsu), Midori Hagio (Kaoru Yamada), Naomasa Rokudaira (Goro Kanno), Misato Tanaka (Nurse), Hideki Matsui (Himself), Ko Takasugi (Hayama), Kenji Suzuki, Masaaki Tezuka (Maser Operators)

GODZILLA portrayed by Tsutomu Kitagawa; MECHAGODZILLA portrayed by Hirofumi Ishigaki

*Japan is besieged by monsters. First Godzilla in 1954, then Mothra, then the Gargantuas. The Self-Defense Forces struggle to keep pace with their monster opponents, but the return of Godzilla after 45 years shows how useless even the most advanced weapons can be. In the heat of battle, Maser Cannon operator Akane fumbles, then watches helplessly as the monster kills her commanding officer and fellow combatants.*

*The Japanese government assembles an elite team of scientists to build a new superweapon — a remote-controlled mechanical duplicate of Godzilla. Using the salvaged remains of the 1954 Godzilla, the creators of Mechagodzilla give it a DNA-based computer brain, capable of instantaneous reflexes in hand-to-hand combat against the enormous monster.*

*Akane, seeking redemption for her past failure and revenge against Godzilla, is assigned to pilot Mechagodzilla, nicknamed Kiryu. On its maiden outing, however, the sound of Godzilla's roar reawakens some deep instinct in Mechagodzilla's bones. It goes berserk, attacking Japan with all the fury of the living Godzilla.*

*There is no Plan B, no other option for defeating Godzilla. Somehow, Kiryu must be stopped, repaired, and sent back into battle against an opponent whose godlike power is matched only by its mindless destruction.*

Godzilla movies, and the multitude of Japanese giants that flower in their shadow, trade in images of metropolitan destruction. For your ticket price (or DVD purchase), you can be assured of seeing buildings toppled, treasured landmarks reduced to rubble, and panicked citizens herded into evacuation.

Once, when all of this started, such images carried deep cultural resonance. The very first Godzilla movie in 1954 presented itself as a science fiction film, but what it *looked* like wasn't fiction at all. Audiences of that time were shown pictures that looked like the real-world horror of the firebombings of Tokyo, the atomic bombings of Hiroshima and Nagasaki, the H-bomb tests on the Bikini islands.

The Millennium Godzilla cycle has that first film very much in mind. Overt references abound, clips from it are shown, famous scenes from it are recreated. But the meaning of those images has been blanched by time. New generations have come of age knowing only peace and prosperity. The horror of the past has receded into memory, the province only of history books.

A promotional film for *Godzilla Against Mechagodzilla* was shown on Japanese TV masquerading as a documentary about those traumatic incidents (with such historical experts as Shogo Tomiyama on hand to explain the cultural significance of the Lucky Dragon incident). Masaaki Tezuka's daughter saw the show and told her father afterwards that maybe if other people saw it, they might better understand what his movie *Godzilla Against Mechagodzilla* was all about. In other words, it took a puffball piece of tabloid history to explain to a young Japanese what happened in the not-so-distant past, by way of promoting a piece of pulpy SF entertainment.[1]

While the specific reference points that inspired the imagery of Godzilla may have grown dusty with time, by 2002 the world had witnessed the recent terror attacks on New York and Washington. The events of September 11, 2001, involved the destruction of but two buildings and damage to a third; no mass evacuation of either city was attempted. Nevertheless, the economic, environmental, and cultural consequences of that day left lasting scars on the nation — not to mention the almost unfathomable loss of life.

I trust the reader will forgive a brief intrusion of the personal into this discussion: I lived just outside Washington when the attacks took place and the Pentagon was hit. I lived in a neighborhood largely populated by military personnel and military contractors; several of my neighbors were in the Pentagon when it happened. My wife worked downtown but, by a quirk, happened not to be in the city at the time. Had she been in her office, she would probably have been unable to get home that day. Even without a formal evacuation, the limited departure of masses of people all at once clogged the city's bridges and thruways. Many people abandoned their cars, while others were more or less trapped in the city until the chaos subsided.

I can no longer watch the imagery of a Godzilla movie with the innocence I once had. To evacuate a city of millions so orderly, so swiftly, as depicted in these movies is laughable. If the destruction of two buildings could

choke the air of New York so thoroughly, how could entire cities be crushed by monsters without leaving behind a loss of life and permanent ecological damage the likes of which these movies never show?

It was estimated that the damage to New York fictionally caused by the TriStar Godzilla would have been on the order of $10.5 billion — compared to $7.7 billion of damage actually caused by Hurricane Andrew.[2] If monsters really existed, and they did the things these movies show, the consequences would be the stuff of awe. The movies lost sight of such consequences, and were happier playing innocently with the imagery of horror.

Ironically, the only Millennium cycle film to *feel* like a post–9/11 production is none of those actually made after 9/11, but the one made just before it. Shusuke Kaneko recognized that his audience had lost the connection between the roots of Godzilla imagery and its original cultural context, and so reassigned that context onto something new. Kaneko understood that images have meanings. He emphasized the effects of monster actions and played to the horror — and found himself on the wrong side of Toho corporate policy for doing so.

Godzilla movies were family-oriented adventure films released at the holidays and aimed at children. With the studio deciding to pair Godzilla movies with Hamtaro animes, it was not the time to start showing innocent people vaporized in atomic blasts. *Giant Monsters All-Out Attack* outperformed both of its predecessors in box office returns, but Kaneko was not asked back. Instead, Tomiyama turned once again to Masaaki Tezuka, the man behind the worst Godzilla box office showing since the days of *Megalon*.

Tezuka was a graduate of the Nihon University of Art and a fan of *kaiju eiga* since childhood. He had worked as an assistant director for many years, most significantly alongside legendary filmmaker Kon Ichikawa. Tezuka's A.D. credits cover a range of important Japanese genre films, including *Virus* (1980), *Sayonara Jupiter* (1984), *The Burmese Harp* (1985), *47 Ronin* (1994), *Mothra 2* (1997) and *Mothra 3* (1998). While his *Godzilla x Megaguirus* was a commercial flop, Shogo Tomiyama saw in the man a reliable workhorse with a solid background, a promising creative outlook, an infectious enthusiasm for the genre, and a good nature. It also helped that Tezuka was a loyal company man without a difficult ego. When Kaneko took over for *Giant Monsters All-Out Attack*, Tezuka made the self-deprecating move of voluntarily demoting himself to second unit director on the picture. Thus, he stayed on board, stayed in Tomiyama's sight, and learned from Kaneko. Tomiyama could see that Tezuka was a reliable and humble man, newly seasoned and ready to improve.[3]

Tomiyama planned to have Tezuka helm a trilogy. The three interconnected films would develop a single story arc about how the JSDF built Mechagodzilla from the bones of the original Godzilla, saw it go out of control, and attempted to tame it. The third part of the trilogy would find Godzilla facing down a clone of himself: *Godzilla vs. Godzilla*. This had been the original storyline for the finale to the Heisei series. Tomiyama decided in 1995 that after *Space Godzilla*, having another clone of Godzilla was too similar, so he mothballed the story and had writer Kazuki Omori adapt some of the themes into what became *Godzilla vs. Destoroyah* instead. Now he was planning to return to that idea, with *Godzilla vs. Godzilla* to be the epic 50th anniversary celebration.[4]

As Tezuka began working with writer Wataru Mimura to develop the first of the trilogy, *Godzilla Against Mechagodzilla*, Tomiyama rejected some of their ideas as too extreme for the family audience he wanted to court. Tezuka thought about killing off the heroine at the end, and concluding the film with a wounded Godzilla filling the sea with blood as he swam away. "I want to make a film so intense it makes people cry," Tezuka declared. Tomiyama shook his head, adamant that a holiday picture was to be light fantasy only — no death, no blood.[5]

Tezuka once commented that *Mechagodzilla* could almost be seen as a sequel to *Godzilla x Megaguirus*. Indeed, it is all but a remake. As in *Megaguirus*, it opens with a scene in which a female JSDF officer watches her commanding officer killed by Godzilla, and her thirst for revenge becomes her primary characterization for the rest of the film. As in *Megauirus*, she strikes up a flirty relationship with a scientist who is aggressively recruited by the military because his particular specialty is needed for the development of a new anti–Godzilla weapon. As in *Megaguirus*, the person who initiates the program to develop that weapon is a woman played by a famous cast member of the sixties Godzilla cycle. As in *Megaguirus*, there is a G-Force–like organization (this time called the Anti-Megalosaurus Force) and a Super X–like ship (the AC-3). As in *Megaguirus*, the first combat use of the weapon backfires terribly, making the situation significantly worse. As in *Megaguirus*, the decision-makers sit back in a comfy control room watching the action on a big screen, as if playing a video game. Misato Tanaka even has a cameo as a nurse.

Michiru Oshima felt that her *Megaguirus* score had been overwhelmed by the sound effects, and so for this film she sought a bigger, brassier sound. That search took her to Russia, where Moscow's International Symphony Orchestra recorded her score. "Godzilla's bass sound is extremely important," Oshima explained. "The brass instruments also have a special importance. My thinking was that Russia's spacious studio is necessary for the brass sound. There is a significant difference in the tone quality between twenty people and sixty people performing."[6]

Oshima's score is wonderful and lush. She had by now proven herself as the worthy successor to the musical throne, and *Godzilla Against Mechagodzilla* has the distinction of being the first Godzilla movie since 1984 not to include even a single Ifukube cue.

In an effort to help imbue Mechagodzilla with some personality, an important detail for a film about the giant robot's resistance to its human controllers, this Mechagodzilla is given the nickname Kiryu, which means "mechanical dragon." Few of the human characters have as much personality assigned to them: Widower Tokumitsu Yuhara (played by Shin Takuma) romances the embittered Akane Yashiro (Yumiko Shaku) while worrying how his daughter Sara (Kana Onodera) will accept her new mommy. The actors do their best with some melodramatic material, but there is no genuine humanity here. The characters are mopey, repressed people who only ever talk about Godzilla.

In an acknowledgment that the series was openly courting younger viewers, child actress Onodera stars as Sara. In one scene, she is seen with some of her classmates, one of whom prominently holds a pet hamster. *Hamtaro* fans in the audience probably cheered. Toho had assumed that the stronger ticket sales of *Giant Monsters All-Out Attack* was attributable to the *Hamtaro* feature on the top half of the double bill. Again paired with a *Hamtaro*, *Godzilla Against Mechagodzilla* pulled a weak 1.7 million attendees. On a budget of 1 billion yen (about $8.5 million), it made 1.91 billion yen back (about $16 million).[7]

Across the world, America was so shaken by the terrorist attacks that some in the media wondered if the kind of shoot-'em-up action films for which Hollywood was known were now dead forever. Eventually, Hollywood found its way back to mindless violence, but only slowly — and only by working through how such images resonated with people who had seen the real thing.

Other monster movie makers sought out ways to make monster movies reengineered for the new political realities: Films like *The Host* (2006) and *Cloverfield* (2007) were as adroit as the original 1954 *Godzilla* in converting real-world horror into cathartic screen entertainment. Meanwhile, J-Horror thrillers like *Suicide Club* (2002), *Noriko's Dinner Table* (2005), and *MPD Psycho* (2005) reworked the Aum Shinrikyo terrorist attacks of 1995 into powerful works of fictional drama.

Toho had a chance to revitalize their flagship franchise as something relevant for a post–9/11 world — and had they done so, they may well have come up with something brilliant, or maybe something stupid or tasteless. They never tried. Instead, *Godzilla Against Mechagodzilla* lopes pointlessly along, never less than competent or more than derivative, contentedly wandering into total cultural irrelevance.

# Chapter 43

# Godzilla: Tokyo S.O.S.
## GOJIRA X MOSURA X MEKAGOJIRA: TOKYO S.O.S.

*Prepare yourself for the final battle!*

— Igarashi

Japanese version: 91 minutes, Released December 13, 2003
Color, Widescreen
Produced by Shogo Tomiyama and Kazunari Yamanaka; directed by Masaaki Tezuka; screenplay by Masaaki Tezuka and Masahiro Yokotani; music by Michiru Oshima; cinematography by Yoshinori Sekiguchi; art direction by Yukiharu Seshita; edited by Shinichi Fushima; special effects by Eiichi Asada
Starring Noburo Kaneko (Yoshito Chujo), Miho Yoshioka (Azusa Kisaragi), Mitsuki Koga (Kyosuke Akiba), Hiroshi Koizumi (Dr. Chujo), Akira Nakao (Prime Minister Hayato Igarashi), Takeo Nakahara (JSDF Chief Hitoyanagi), Koichi Ueda (Dobashi), Masami Nagasawa, Chihiro Otsuka (Mothra's Fairies)
GODZILLA portrayed by Tsutomu Kitagawa; MECHAGODZILLA portrayed by Motokuni Nakagawa

*A year has passed since the battle between Godzilla and Mechagodzilla, and little has changed. Japan still lies in ruins, the giant robot Godzilla is still mothballed and awaiting repairs, and Godzilla is still wounded from the fight. But, fight on they will, summoning the last reserves of energy for the war ahead...*

*Except one thing has changed: Mothra has returned. Mothra's fairies seek out Dr. Chujo, the man who helped them back in 1961, entrusting him with an urgent message. Mankind must let Mechagodzilla die, must allow the soul of the 1954 Godzilla within it to return to peace. If this happens, Mothra will protect Japan from Godzilla. If not, all bets are off.*

*It is too much to ask for Japan to unilaterally disarm in the face such an enemy. As Godzilla comes ashore again, they have no choice but to put the partially repaired Mechagodzilla out to stop it. Mothra enters the fray, too, prepared to put her life on the line to restore the natural balance of things.*

In evaluating a picture like the 1961 *Mothra*, it is important to take cultural context into account. That is to say, rather than compare its special effects techniques, storytelling style, or thematic concerns against contemporary films, these attributes should instead be evaluated against other science fiction films, or other Japanese movies, of the early sixties. Godzilla enthusiasts are quick to make this point whenever they feel their beloved films being unfairly attacked or ridiculed. However, the thing of it is, this works the other way, too. *Tokyo S.O.S.* should not be merely compared against other Godzilla movies, but against the state of genre cinema of 2003 — by which this film comes up wanting.

Ironically for a picture that purports to lecture against digging up the bones of the dead, *Tokyo S.O.S.* is a Frankenstein work stitched together from the repurposed fragments of other, older, films. This time it is the corpse of 1961's *Mothra* that is exhumed, reanimated, and thrust back into service. Hiroshi Koizumi even reprises his role as anthropologist Dr. Chujo. Throughout the picture, the various characters endlessly recite the events of the 1961 film, a constant and unfavorable reminder of glory days past.

The Mothra films of the sixties deftly concocted ethical conundrums wrapped in the stuff of light fantasy. *Tokyo S.O.S.* initially sets up a dilemma worthy of that heritage. Mothra's priestesses put forward an ultimatum. If Japan dismantles Mechagodzilla, then Mothra promises to protect Japan against other monster attacks. If Japan insists on keeping Mechagodzilla as a weapon, then it may have to face Mothra's wrath. Accepting Mothra's terms means taking at face value the word of a giant monster, one which quite recently attacked Japan. Rejecting Mothra's offer means placing all the nation's hopes in a single, unreliable and inferior weapons system.

No great effort is required to see this as a metaphor for Japan's relationship with America: a former foe turned friend, conditioning the change in relations on Japan's demilitarization. Such issues would have been much in the news at the time of the film: As the United States sought allies for its planned invasion of Iraq, it pressured Japan to provide troops. When Japan declined, it was excoriated in the American press for failing to stand by its ally. Japan for its part coolly noted that they were *bound* to refuse, by the terms of the Constitution that the Americans had written for them.

Having established this promising political subtext, the filmmakers almost immediately abandon it. No further mention of Mothra's ultimatum is ever made. Mothra steadfastly defends Japan against Godzilla even as the JSDF defiantly trundles Mechagodzilla into battle. The moral dilemmas shuffle off the geopolitical stage, replaced by personal ones, and concentrating on the character of Yoshito Chujo.

As played by Noboru Kaneko (no relation to Shusuke), Yoshito is a ball of fit. He has firsthand knowledge of Mothra's warning and a family loyalty to Dr. Chujo's anti–Mechagodzilla stance, yet at the same time is the proud chief mechanic responsible for keeping the giant robot in operation — and he's a fannish enthusiast of military hardware to boot. He is relentlessly bullied by Mechagodzilla pilot Akiba (Mitsuki Koga) while secretly harboring a crush on Akiba's co-pilot Azusa (Miho Yoshioka). Azusa however also teases poor Yoshito, for not showing enough sexual aggression in pursuing her! The young man in torn in every possible direction at once, doomed at every decision to betray some aspect of his nature in favor of some other aspect of his nature. He can't win for losing.

*Tokyo S.O.S.* should resolve by bringing Yoshito's inner conflicts and the raging monster war to a simultaneous head, each part solving the other and vice versa. This it does — perfunc-

torily. Noboru Kaneko need not overexert himself because for all the dramatic conflict bound up in his role, almost none of it is openly expressed. Yoshito winds up inside Mechagodzilla during the climactic battle, but this is the same thing that happened to the heroine of the previous year's film. While the new movie updates it with more action and stuntwork, the sense of *déjà vu* is tough to escape.

This is a movie in which terse ejaculations take the place of actual dialogue. A sampling of key lines from various characters: "Chujo!" "Mothra!" "Fire at will!" "Good luck!" "Mechagodzilla!" and so on.

Masaaki Tezuka wrote the screenplay, with the assistance of Masahiro Yokotani, but is as indebted to Mimura's story ruts as Mimura was. The film *looks* handsome. First-time special effects supervisor Eiichi Asada acquits himself nicely. Michiru Oshima provides yet another thrilling score, again deemed strong enough to stand alone without Ifukube's "Enter Godzilla" march. These things are all true — yet they ought to be almost beside the point. After fifty years, Toho can be assumed to have perfected the process of manufacturing craftsmanslike monster movies. A high standard of production values should be expected, but are not in themselves a reason to recommend a film — any more than one would rate it a sign of a good restaurant that the waiters brought the food you ordered, on time and at the right temperature.

*Tokyo S.O.S.* sold a paltry 1.1 million tickets. That's as many people as suffer from shingles in the United States. It was a new low for a cycle in decline. Not even the co-feature *Hamtaro: Ham Ham Grand Prix* could save the ship from sinking.[1] The post-credits coda lingers on a cache of Godzilla cells frozen and ready to be cloned for use in *Godzilla x Godzilla*. Making that film would surely be folly. As the saying goes, the definition of madness of doing the same thing over and over again and expecting a different result.

With the historic fiftieth anniversary of Godzilla just around the corner, though, could Toho really let Godzilla go idle?

# Chapter 44

# *Godzilla Final Wars*
## *Gojira: Fainaru Uozu*

*You mean we'll go to the South Pole, straight through the enemy, wake up Godzilla, bring him here and make him fight the monsters—meanwhile, one way or another, we'll annihilate the Xilians, then we'll go back to the South Pole and lock up Godzilla again?*

—Major Komuro

*Yes.*

—Captain Gordon

Japanese version: 125 minutes, Released December 4, 2004

Color, Widescreen

Produced by Shogo Tomiyama; directed by Ryuhei Kitamura; screenplay by Ryuhei Kitamura and Isao Kiriyama from a story by Wataru Mimura and Shogo Tomiyama; music by Keith Emerson, Nobuhiko Morino, and Daisuke Yano; cinematography by Takumi Furuya; art direction by Deborah Riley; edited by Shuichi Kakesu; special effects by Eiichi Asada

Starring Masahiro Matsuoka (Ozaki), Rei Kikukawa (Otonashi), Kazuki Kitamura (Controller of Planet X), Don Frye (Captain Gordon), Akira Takarada (U.N. Secretary General Daigo), Kumi Mizuno (Akiko Namakawa), Kenji Sahara (Jinguji), Masami Nagasawa, Chihiro Otsuka (Mothra's Fairies), Kane Kosugi (Kazama), Maki Mizuno (Newscaster Anna Otonashi), Masakatsu Funaki (Kumasaka), Masato Eve (Xilian General)

GODZILLA portrayed by Tsutomu Kitagawa; KING SEESAR and MONSTER X portrayed by Motokuni Nakagawa; RODAN and MINILLA portrayed by Naoko Kamio; ANGUIRUS, EBIRAH, and KAISER GHIDORAH portrayed by Toshihiro Ogura; GIGAN and HEDORAH portrayed by Kazuhiro Yoshida

*Faced with the challenge of confronting periodic attacks by giant monsters, the nations of the world have cultivated an elite squad of human mutants whose abilities give them a unique edge in handling unusual threats. Years ago, this force achieved its greatest success by entombing Godzilla in ice at the South Pole.*

*Sudden, simultaneous attacks on major world cities by giant monsters seem to portend a terrible new age—but just as suddenly the monsters vanish, apparently* vanquished by the arrival of space aliens from Planet X.

*The Xilians promise peace, and are quickly embraced as friends and allies, until they reveal their true mission: to subjugate humanity and control the world. The Xilians unleash the monsters, and overnight, civilization is destroyed and the human population decimated. A rogue team of mutants led by Captain Gordon heads out on a suicidally insane mission to free Godzilla. To do so certainly spells the doom of the world, but if the world is doomed anyway, at least Godzilla can ruin the Xilians' triumph.*

The experience of watching *Godzilla Final Wars* is relatively simple to describe. Imagine some eight year olds, hopped up on sugar and childish aggression, playing the *Godzilla Unleashed* video game while rock music plays at full volume from a nearby boombox. Further analysis of the content of the film would be beside the point. There is nothing significant in the plot of *Final Wars* that has not already been discussed in this book (in the chapters on *Invasion of Astro-Monster* and *Destroy All Monsters*). This movie is not *about* anything; the story is merely a framework upon which artist Ryuhei Kitamura has draped a succession of high-octane and mostly absurd scenes of monster antics and sci-fi action.

If the point of the whole Godzilla genre has been to sell images of monsters fighting, then *Final Wars* embraces this concept most fully. Present and accounted for are: Godzilla, Mothra, Rodan, Gigan, Manda, Anguirus, King

Seesar, Kamakurus, Kumonga, Ebirah, Hedo-rah, Minilla, King Ghidorah, and the TriStar version of Godzilla! Other icons of Toho's golden age of *tokusatsu* films join the party — the "mysterious star" Gorath and *Atragon*'s flying battleship Gotengo.

The previous Millennium series films saw fit to tip their hats to the 1954 *Gojira* and then pretend to ignore all other sequels; this was the philosophy behind TriStar's film, too. *Final Wars* throws a big bear hug around the entire history of Godzilla, from the sublime to the ridiculous. Here are crazy clips from *Space Amoeba*, here are Masaru Sato music cues from *Son of Godzilla*, here are the most maligned Godzilla costars from Minilla to King Seesar! It is as if the whole fifty-year history of Toho special effects spectaculars was tossed into a blender and served up as a fever dream. Where Masaaki Tezuka turned up his nose at some of Shogo Tomiyama's pulpier suggestions, Kitamura packs in as much over-the-top nonsense as possible, and then maintains a delirious pace throughout.

Every shot counts. In past entries, impatient filmgoers sometimes had to bide their time through the human scenes awaiting the next bit of monster mayhem. In this picture, the human plot is a crazy quilt of wireworks, CGI, and kung fu action. Godzilla movies are no strangers to Hollywood ripoffs — especially whenever Kazuki Omori was involved. What sets *Final Wars* apart in this regard is that all of its *Matrix*-derived material displays such sheer showmanship. This stuff holds it own against the original without seeming like an embarrassing also-ran, and gives the film a relentless take-no-prisoners pace.

To that end, Toho gave Kitamura ¥2 billion (roughly $19,500,000). It was the biggest budget for a Japanese-made monster movie in history; it was twice as much as they had been spending on these films and more than any of them were making back in ticket sales.[1]

Why Toho did that is the story worth pursuing. While analyzing the *content* of *Final Wars* may be an exercise in futility, analyzing the film's place in the history of the franchise is fascinating. What this movie means to viewers depends very much on whom you ask.

Until now, this book has divided Godzilla audiences in two. Japanese and American viewers come from markedly different social contexts, with different film industrial infrastructures evolving on separate paths to cater to those respective markets. Thus we have seen Godzilla movies come in two forms. The first include pictures like *Gojira/Godzilla, King of the Monsters!, Godzilla Raids Again/Gigantis the Fire Monster, The Return of Godzilla/Godzilla 1985* and *Godzilla Millennium/Godzilla 2000.* Such movies were substantially reworked by American distributors so that audiences on the two sides of the Pacific actually thrilled to distinguishably different versions. Then there have been those like *Son of Godzilla* and *Tokyo S.O.S.* that were not reworked, but released instead to smaller stateside audiences directly to TV, drive-ins, or home video. It has been possible to track the relative divergence of American and Japanese tastes by observing the distribution strategies applied to these pop cultural products.

It is a critical rubric whose relevance has been steadily eroding. What was demonstrably true in the fifties was by the new millennium no longer the case.

In 2005, domestic ticket sales for Hollywood films totaled $9 billion; those same pictures drew $12 billion overseas. It had come to the point where Hollywood could not survive without the foreign market; indeed, the foreign market was the *primary* audience. Japan was the largest foreign market, and the whole of Asia collectively accounted for the vast majority of overseas sales. Movies that lost money in America could become blockbuster hits based on the proceeds from places like Japan and South Korea. Increasingly, certain movies were being made solely because of their likely appeal to Asian audiences. Any film studio executive who did not think first of what Asians wanted to see, was not doing their job.[2]

Inevitably, the style of American films gradually became Asianified. Where once American producers felt a need to efface the Asian connection in certain films, it had now become an asset to flaunt Asian attributes. Hollywood headhunted stars like Jackie Chan, Jet Li, and

Chow Yun Fat. Movies like Quentin Tarantino's *Kill Bill* cycle and TV series like *Lost* and *Heroes* proudly displayed scenes in Japanese and Korean, with subtitles.* When Hollywood remade the J-Horror hit *The Ring*, the American version slavishly maintained the style and tone of the original — and then hired Japanese filmmaker Hideo Nakata to shoot the sequel. For the remake of *The Grudge*, Japanese director Takashi Shimizu was allowed to take his American cast back to Tokyo with him to shoot a largely scene-for-scene remake of his own movie, with extended Japanese-language sequences. For the Americanized revamp of the Thai horror film *Shutter*, Japanese director Masayuki Ochiai was brought in — and he proceeded to take an American cast back to Japan for a *Grudge*-like approach. In other words, the Americanization of *Shutter* was its Japanization.

While Hollywood appropriated Japanese filmmakers and techniques to try to capture ever more of the Japanese market, the Japanese film business retrenched in an effort to hold on to what little they had. The better they got at narrowcasting and risk avoidance, the harder it became to do anything but.

Toho could turn out a couple of decades' worth of carbon copies of *The Submersion of Japan* because there was no institutional structure counteracting that impulse. The endless repetition of past successes was a predictable and reliable method of turning movie investments into profit, with none of the crazy risk — or enormous blockbuster success— that the unruly Hollywood approach promised.

At the dawn of the 21st century, the Japanese film world was especially poor at nurturing visionary artists with their fingers on the pulse of popular tastes. Occasionally bright young men and women would emerge from the system, but overall the Japanese studios were fearful of the kind of risk that attended such creativity. Instead, places like Toho got very good at nurturing the likes of Masaaki Tezuka —

loyal company men who followed orders. The Tezukas of the world were competent showmen, predictable and reliable. They were also patient, to undergo the lengthy process of understudying and apprenticeship that the Toho system demanded.

From the age of sixteen, Ryuhei Kitamura knew that he wanted to make movies. He also knew that his conception of what this meant was at odds with remaining in Japan. So he dropped out of high school and left the country, enrolling in a school for the visual arts in Sydney, Australia.

Kitamura's influences were largely Australian: George Miller, Russel Mulcahy, Peter Weir. His heroes were outlaws like Sam Raimi and John Carpenter —filmmakers whose DIY ethic and independent spirit had no analog in the Japanese system.

Still, he tried. After graduating from film school and making a few wildly anarchic amateur films to hone his craft, Kitamura dutifully made the rounds of the various Japanese studios and production houses, pitching his ideas for a new breed of action movie. Kitamura loved movies. More to the point, he loved big, loud, action-packed entertainment movies. He loved a kind of movie that Japan had long ago abandoned, but which — imported from the West — dominated the Japanese market. Kitamura wanted to steal that market back. Yet there was nothing this insubordinate youngster could say to the old moneymen to change their minds.

Taking inspiration from Sam Raimi, Kitamura realized he did not need to take their "no" for an answer. He put up his own money, alongside that raised from a network of like-minded friends and investors, to produce his first professional feature. *Versus* (2000) is a lunatic endeavor mixing Quentin Tarantino–style action with zombies, swordplay, and vicious humor. It was a worldwide cult sensation. It was also a startling upset in the traditional ways of doing business. As Kitamura explains:

---

*There is an additional irony in the fact that Kill Bill's Uma Thurman, Heroes' Masi Oka, and Lost's Daniel Dae Kim do not speak anything other than English, and learned their dialogue phonetically. The subtitled sequences are not an accommodation for a particular non–English-speaking performer, but a deliberate aesthetic choice in itself.*

A lot of Japanese producers and directors like to work in [a] low-risk way. They shoot on low budgets and for the straight-to-video market. You can get a little money, but it doesn't go anywhere. There are too many people around who think that way. I had to do something different, something that no other director would think of. No other director would risk their life to make a movie, but that's what I did. I called everybody, my family, my friends, my ex-girlfriends, producers. We called everybody to raise money. Every day we were shooting in the mountains and as soon as we finished we would start making calls, because we didn't have any money for the next day.[3]

On the strength of *Versus*, Kitamura was hired to direct the hotly anticipated theatrical adaptation of the popular manga *Azumi* in 2003. Almost overnight he went from a nobody to big business. Producers who once snubbed him now called to ingratiate themselves. Even more tantalizingly, Hollywood was calling. Kitamura began to pack his bags to move to Los Angeles for his debut as Hollywood's next big thing when Shogo Tomiyama called and asked him to take over Godzilla.

"Who can resist that?" Kitamura noted. "Only the chosen ones get to direct those films. It's going to be a special one, because it's the fiftieth anniversary and it will be the last Godzilla movie. It will be the last and the biggest."[4]

In calling Ryuhei Kitamura, poster boy for the anarchic world of independent cinema, Toho, Japan's most conservative movie studio, was making a Hail Mary pass. The Millennium series had deteriorated too soon, and the decision to proceed with a fiftieth anniversary film at all was more a sign of sentimentality than logic. Tomiyama told the Associated Press, "We have done all we can to showcase Godzilla, including using computer graphics technology. And yet we haven't attracted new fans. So we will make the fiftieth anniversary film something special, a best-of-the-best, and then end it for now."[5]

To make a best-of-all-possible-Godzilla, Toho was prepared to cede control to an outsider artist with a record of rebellion. That is, cede control up to a point.

In early discussions, Kitamura floated a handful of suggestions, all of which Tomiyama rejected. Kitamura's natural instincts leaned towards darker, grittier approaches more aligned with American horror movies than the family-oriented fantasy Toho demanded.

It was a battle over tone. Kitamura felt the reason for hiring him in the first place was to substantially redirect the rudderless enterprise:

Shogo knew he was missing something, and decided to bring me in. We had a first meeting and I just spoke my mind. I was really honest and told him what I thought about the Godzilla movies. I hadn't been to the theaters in ten years. I'd seen the more recent Godzilla films on TV and didn't like them. I mean, the last three or four Godzilla movies have been shown in the theaters together with kids' animation. Why would anyone want to go see a Godzilla movies if it is being shown alongside a little mouse cartoon? It seemed like the company was only making Godzilla movies for kids and the diehard Godzilla fans, not for the general audience.[6]

For his part, Tomiyama felt that aiming the pictures at children was essential to the long-term health of the property:

Up to now, the people who created the original Godzilla — Mr. Tanaka, Mr. Honda, and Mr. Tsuburaya — they created it for the children of that time. So those children had a Godzilla that would continue with them until they became adults, uncles, grandfathers, old people. So what we want to try to find now is what the children of these days will like. If we can manage that, Godzilla will have another long run.[7]

Seeking compromise, Tomiyama presented Kitamura with an eight-page synopsis describing the "aliens attack Earth" scenario the studio favored. The outline called for eight monsters to be resurrected from the franchise's history. Kitamura scoffed, "We should go for a new record!"[8]

Tomiyama, Kitamura, and special effects director Eiichi Asada assembled a collection of Godzilla action figures and started to array them on a desk as they argued who should make the cut. Like a bunch of fanboys making an amateur video, they kept picking figures out of the box and putting them back in, until they had assembled their dream cast. "This film is going to be like an Ultimate Championship Fight," Kitamura decided.[9]

That would be Asada's job. Kitamura had the vision for the project as a whole, but lacked prior experience in the *kaiju eiga* and its peculiarities. He and Asada came together with mutual trust and respect, knowing they had each other's backs. Asada was a fan of Kitamura's; Kitamura counted 1974's *Godzilla vs. Mechagodzilla* as his favorite of the series, and noted with admiration that Asada had been assistant director on that film. Together, they set out to do Godzilla proud.[10]

Asada got a workout. No corners were cut, and the movie is packed with more effects than almost any previous entry. Kitamura manipulates a varied color palette and aggressive editing pattern to keep the audiences on the edges of their seats (all tricks and techniques Kitamura displayed in *Versus*). It is vulgar, violent, and loud — and immensely entertaining.

Of all the Godzilla movies made in Japan, *Godzilla Final Wars* is the most Western in its aesthetic sensibilities — a fact signaled right from the opening titles. Kitamura brought in Kyle Cooper, the artist behind the striking title sequences of *Se7en* and *Dawn of the Dead*, to design the credits. Cooper arranged blazing English letters intercut with a barrage of clips from past films set to a thunderous track by Keith Emerson, of the rock band Emerson, Lake and Palmer. These men were not, you will note, Japanese.

Aside from a scattering of cues from Ifukube and Sato offered up as tributes, Emerson's score is a wall of noise unlike anything before it. One could parse the different approaches by the various composers — Ifukube vs. Sato, David Arnold vs. Michiru Oshima — but Emerson plays an entirely different game. This is a rock album illustrated by exploding cities and giant monsters, punctuated by punk tracks by Sum 41 and Zebrahead.

It was the only Toho film to include footage shot outside of Asia. Location shooting in Sydney (and brief second unit filming in New York) help to give a feeling of global scale to the proceedings.

As always, familiar faces pop up. Kumi Mizuno and Akira Takarada play significant supporting roles, as does *tokusatsu* regular Masatu Eve. Masahiro Matsuoka does his best Keanu Reeves impression, while Kazuki Kitamura (no relation) plays the Xilian leader like some kind of angry toddler having a temper fit. The scene-stealing star of the show, though, is Don Frye as Captain Gordon. Frye is not even technically an actor — he is a professional wrestler with a huge Asian fan base. He is built like a human Godzilla and speaks with a voice of gravel and stale cigarettes. Few men have the screen presence to deliver a line like, "There's two things you don't know about the Earth: one is me, and the other is Godzilla." Frye has the rare authority to compare himself to Godzilla and get away with it.

Traditionally, Toho premiered its annual Godzilla pictures at the Tokyo International Film Festival each November. In keeping with the momentous nature of the fiftieth anniversary, and Kitamura's westward-looking aesthetics, *Godzilla Final Wars* received its world premiere at the fabled Chinese Theater in Los Angeles on November 29, 2004. It was the culmination of a series of celebrations that also saw Godzilla honored with a star on the Hollywood Walk of Fame. An actor in a Godzilla suit greeted fans, while Shogo Tomiyama was on hand to serve as the monster's handler and interpreter. "Godzilla cannot speak English," Tomiyama explained. The American audience at the premiere thrilled to the picture, and the press coverage was warm and positive.[11] The staff at Sony that had been responsible for *Godzilla 2000* were eager to take *Godzilla Final Wars* around on a full theatrical run. However, an impasse over Toho's monetary demands kept the film on DVD, with isolated repertory screenings.[12]

When *Godzilla Final Wars* opened in Japan in December, the enthusiasm of the moment quickly waned. Just the year before, *Tokyo S.O.S.* had chalked up $10,724,345 in ticket sales over six weeks, and in so doing earned a record as the series' poorest performer to date. *Godzilla Final Wars* made just $9,133,840 in five weeks before dropping off the top ten and into oblivion. It had earned back less than half its cost.

*Howl's Moving Castle* was the movie sensation of the year, breaking records with a historic $160 million take. Less spectacularly, but just as damning, 2003 also saw Toho release Takashi Miike's *One Missed Call*, a pedestrian J-Horror that was neither Miike's best work nor the best example of its genre. Yet *One Missed Call* brought in $13.5 million at the box office — substantially more than *Final Wars* — and only cost $1.7 million to make.[13]

The days of the big-budget, special effects–driven spectacular seemed over. On October 13, two months before *Godzilla Final Wars* opened, Toho demolished the Big Pool. If Godzilla movies or anything like them were to be made ever again, they would belong to the new technologies of film production. Godzilla did reappear, as a CGI-rendered creature, in a sequence in 2007's *Always 2*. Shinji Higuchi, the special effects director on the 1990s Gamera revivals, directed the 2006 remake of *Submersion of Japan*, using CGI techniques exclusively to render onscreen the havoc that, back in 1973, Teruysohi Nakano created with miniatures. CGI monsters rampaged in films like *The Host* (2006) and *Cloverfield* (2007) — neither of which were big-budget tentpoles like TriStar's 1998 *Godzilla* but which used similar digital animation to create innovative and moving thrillers. The era of Tsuburaya's technique was over.

Although the Japanese box office of *Final Wars* was an embarrassing piffle, and an American theatrical release was scuttled due to contract disputes, there are other ways to quantify a film's success. The enormous profits reaped by TriStar's 1998 *Godzilla* are a case study establishing that box office proceeds are a poor marker for whether an audience actually enjoyed the movie. The reverse can also be true: A box office flop may have been embraced more deeply by its audience than numbers can easily show.

One way to measure such a thing is critical response — although Godzilla movies have never been critical darlings. Perhaps a more direct gauge would be the response of the target audience: *G-Fan*, the monthly magazine of or-

ganized American Godzilla fandom, publishes an annual reader's poll in which the popularity of individual films are ranked. According to this poll, *Godzilla Final Wars* regularly finishes in the bottom third, above only the most maligned entries of the destitute seventies.[14]

While such poll results seem to bear out the dismal box office figures as a sign that *Final Wars* missed its target, it is worth remembering here that Ryuhei Kitamura felt it his mission to reach a broader mass audience, beyond that of the hardcore fan. There are signs that Kitamura succeeded in this. Internet Movie Database users' rank *Final Wars* the same 6.7 out of 10 as all of the Millennium series entries. Amazon's sales put *Final Wars* as the second most popular Godzilla DVD of all, after the 1954 original — and ninth overall for science fiction DVDs (and this as of May 2009, four years after the disc's release). The online DVD rental service Netflix ranks *Final Wars* as the second most rented Godzilla disc, after TriStar's film.[15]

It is impossible to quantify how often audiences sit down to rewatch the DVDs they own. It is this author's personal experience that of all the Godzilla DVDs and laserdiscs collected over the years, *Godzilla Final Wars* is the most watched of them all, and enjoyed repeatedly by a new generation of fans. My son and his friends from school make Godzilla costumes, shoot Godzilla home videos on their camcorders, collect and play with Godzilla action figures, attend Godzilla conventions, and choose whenever possible to watch this film over all of the others.

It is a curious coincidence that on three separate occasions, Toho felt that the Godzilla franchise was overreaching and underperforming, but rather than let it end, they — each time — tried to do something special, only to be defeated at the box office. *Godzilla vs. Mechagodzilla* in 1974 was followed by the box office disappointment of *Terror of Mechagodzilla*; *Godzilla vs. Space Godzilla* nearly spelled the end until *Godzilla vs. Destoroyah* fell even flatter; *Tokyo S.O.S.* led to *Final Wars*. Each time, the studio let the property cool on a back burner until the time was right to start up again.

Toho had never said that *Godzilla Final Wars* was to be the last one ever, merely the last one for the present. "The choices for kids are more varied now and they are watching the cuter monsters, like the ones from *Pokemon*," Tomiyama told the *Washington Post*. "If Godzilla does come back, it will be in the hands of another generation of movie directors."[16]

That, or an older generation. As of this writing, *Godzilla vs. Hedorah*'s director Yoshimitsu Banno has licensed the rights from Toho to produce a new Godzilla film from an original story of his own. Banno has for years been working with partners like Robert Holden to make 3D IMAX pictures for various museums and expos, and he devised a plan to produce *Godzilla 3D*.[17] According to pre-production information circulated in the spring of 2009, Banno hopes to make the film with Eiichi Asada handling the effects. Whether this project materialized remains to be seen, but it shows that life is in the franchise yet.

# Epilogue

Memories of childhood become so clouded by the passing of time that recalling minute details, for example the precise chronology of half-remembered events, becomes futile. However, to the extent that I can remember my childhood, I count *Godzilla vs. the Bionic Monster* as the first motion picture I independently asked to see. I had seen newspaper and television ads, and desperately wanted to see Godzilla battle his mechanical duplicate. I had, in fact, never before seen a Godzilla film, but his robot double was something I could not miss. My parents eventually gave in, against their better judgment, and hauled me off to the drive-in. By the time the Azumi prophetess revived King Seesar with her sacred song, my parents and my little brother were sound asleep. I had not really followed the story, but my six-year-old self took immense delight in the sprawling destruction and havoc wreaked by these giant monsters.

In subsequent years, I caught showings of *Godzilla, King of the Monsters!*, *Rodan*, *King Kong vs. Godzilla*, *Monster Zero*, and *Godzilla's Revenge* on television. At that time, video recorders were not yet a common household item. In order to satisfy my fandom for all manner of horror and science fiction films, of which Godzilla movies were but a part, I could not collect the movies themselves. Instead, I had to read books on the subject. Through such books, packed with lurid photos of movie monsters and plot descriptions, I vicariously saw many movies. These books also taught me that some movies are "good" and some are "bad." I relied on these authors to give me my monster movie fix, and so I was in no small part indebted to them. If the authors wanted me to praise *King Kong* and ridicule *Godzilla*, then I would obey.

On a conscious level I bought into the attitude that Godzilla movies were silly and of lesser quality than American productions. On a deeper emotional level, though, that entranced six-year-old at the drive-in still stood in awe of Godzilla, and still looked up to the monster as a hero, a role model. As I matured, Godzilla remained a familiar spirit, scribbled in the margins of school notes, repeatedly invoked in conversation.

On my eighteenth birthday, I received a videotape of *Godzilla vs. Mechagodzilla*, the very movie I had seen at the drive-in twelve years earlier. The true epiphany, however, came on the eve of my wedding five years later. I discovered a magazine called *Cult Movies*, with a cover that depicted Godzilla blasting a city skyline with his atomic breath. I chose that magazine as my reading material for the beach on my honeymoon. That issue included some eye-opening information: Toho was *still* making Godzilla movies. The monster I had grown up with lived on, and David Milner's article reported that these new films had hi-tech special effects and intelligent scripts.

So I looked at the cinematic history of my hero with fresh eyes. Instead of letting others make up my mind for me, I watched the films myself. I discovered that not only did the newest films live up to the reputation of being smart and well-made, *but the old ones did, too.* I discovered that I had been duped, that I had been cheated all these years of something that brought me pleasure. I wrote this book to share my discoveries. Perhaps someone like me will find this book as they step forward into adulthood, and they too can reach back into their youth and connect the two with Godzilla.

That hope may seem absurdly pompous and pretentious. Yet over the years, Godzilla has been many things to many people. The enduring international commercial success of

Godzilla owes much to the versatility of the character, and the ingenuity of the various men and women who have remade that character to suit new audiences and new times.

Tim Burton once said that he wanted to grow up to be the actor inside the Godzilla suit. It is not a glamorous job, though. During his tenure on the job, Kenpachiro Satsuma suffered oxygen deprivation, nearly drowned, concussed his head during one stunt fall, almost burned his eyes, and endured painful electrical shocks. The costumes were so heavy that he would grind his teeth while moving about in them, causing dental problems. Years of wearing the suit, however, immunized Satsuma against pain killers, so he underwent dental treatment without anesthetic. The steel wire reinforcements in the Godzilla suit wore through the rubber and tore into his legs, leaving them lacerated and bloody. The pyrotechnic staff once neglected to remove the staples used to adhere explosive charges to the costume, and the staples fell inside where they penetrated Satsuma's knees. Nevertheless, Satsuma endures, survives, and continues. His indomitable qualities made him the perfect choice for the role of a character that has lived for millions of years, survived volcanoes, nuclear explosions, all weapons known to humankind and quite a few completely fictional ones to boot. Godzilla has withstood every attack alone and friendless, yet he survives.

His fans around the world can only hope to endure life's challenges with a small part of that endurance and determination.

Godzilla lives.

# Chapter Notes

## Introduction

1. William Chapman, "Kurosawa's Comeback: A Samurai Spectacular," *The Washington Post*, April 20, 1980.
2. Interview with Kimi Honda (Ishiro Honda's widow), *Cult Movies* #16, 1995, p. 52.
3. Bailey, "Your City Could Be Next," *Asiaweek*, December 21–28, 1994.

## Chapter 1

1. John Burgess, "Godzilla Rises Again," *The Washington Post*, December 19, 1984.
2. Jeff Rovin, *Fabulous Fantasy Films* (Cranbury, NJ: A.S. Barnes, 1977), p. 120.
3. Bill Warren, *Keep Watching the Skies! Volume 1: 1950–1957* (Jefferson, NC: McFarland, 1982), p. 103.
4. Warren, *Vol. 1*, p. xiv.
5. August Ragone, *Eiji Tsuburaya: Master of Monsters* (San Francisco, CA: Chronicle Books, 2007), p. 23.
6. Ragone, *Eiji Tsuburaya*, p. 22–27.
7. Guy Tucker, remarks as panelist, G-Con '95, Radisson Hotel, Arlington Heights, Chicago, IL, August 18, 1995 [hereinafter: Tucker, August 18, 1995].
8. Stuart Galbraith IV, *Japanese Science Fiction, Fantasy and Horror Films* (Jefferson NC: McFarland, 1994), p. 9.
9. Ed Godziszewski, "The Making of *Godzilla*," *G-Fan* #12, November-December 1994, p. 34.
10. Ibid.
11. Warren, *Vol. 1*, p. xiii.
12. Godziszewski, "The Making of *Godzilla*," p. 34–35.
13. Interview with Randy Stradley and Bob Eggleton, "Dark Horse G," *G-Fan* #17, September-October 1995, p. 42.
14. Godziszewski, "The Making of *Godzilla*," p. 35.
15. Steve Ryfle, Ed Godziszewski and Keith Aiken, commentary track on *Gojira* DVD, BFI, 2004 [hereinafter: Ryfle et al. commentary, *Gojira*].
16. John Roberto, "In Memory of Ishiro Honda," *G-Fan* #12, November-December 1994 [hereinafter: Roberto, "In Memory"], p. 45.
17. Akiko Ono, "Memories of Godzilla," *G-Fan* #12, p. 48.
18. Galbraith, *Japanese Science Fiction*, p. 9–10.
19. Guy Tucker, "The Films of Ishiro Honda," *G-Fan* #14, March-April 1995, p. 60.
20. James Kirkup, "Obituary: Ishiro Honda," *The Independent*, March 3, 1993.
21. Tucker, August 18, 1995.
22. Interview with Ishiro Honda, *G-Fan* #12, p. 46.
23. Steve Ryfle and Ed Godziszewski, "Designing Godzilla," DVD extra on *Gojira*, BFI, 2004.
24. Godziszewski, "The Making of *Godzilla*," p. 35–36.
25. Ono, "Memories of Godzilla," p. 48.
26. Ryfle et al. commentary, *Gojira*.

27. Ed Godziszewski, *The Illustrated Encyclopedia of Godzilla* (Steinbach, Canada: Ed Godziszewski, 1996) [hereinafter: Godziszewski, *The Illustrated Encyclopedia of Godzilla*], p. 102.
28. Galbraith, *Japanese Science Fiction*, p. 12.
29. Ryfle et al. commentary, *Gojira*.
30. Steve Ryfle, *Japan's Favorite Mon-Star: The Unauthorized Biography of the Big G* (Toronto: ECW Press, 1998) [hereinafter: Ryfle, *Japan's Favorite Mon-Star*], p. 97.
31. Galbraith, *Japanese Science Fiction*, p. 11–12.
32. Godziszewski, *The Illustrated Encyclopedia of Godzilla*, p. 130.
33. Steve Ryfle and Ed Godziszewski, "Designing Godzilla," DVD extra on *Gojira*, BFI, 2004.
34. Michiko Imamura, Ed Godziszewski and Kuni Kakikawa, "Godzilla Speaks! A Conversation with Haruo Nakajima," *G-Fan* #22, July-August, 1996, p. 48.
35. Ono, "Memories of Godzilla," p. 48.
36. August Ragone, letter to the editor, *G-Fan* #14, p. 11.
37. Godziszewski, "The Making of *Godzilla*," p. 38.
38. Ryfle et al. commentary, *Gojira*.
39. Godziszewski, "The Making of *Godzilla*," p. 37–38.
40. Ibid., p. 37, 39.
41. Steve Ryfle and Ed Godziszewski, "Designing Godzilla," DVD extra on *Gojira*, BFI, 2004.
42. William Tsutsui, *Godzilla on My Mind* (New York: Palgrave Macmillan, 2004), p. 22.
43. Godziszewski, "The Making of *Godzilla*," p. 39.
44. Ibid., p. 37.
45. Ibid., p. 39.
46. Bailey.
47. Godziszewski, *The Illustrated Encyclopedia of Godzilla*, p. 79.
48. Bailey.

## Chapter 2

1. Ryfle et al. commentary, *Gojira*.
2. John Rocco Roberto, "*Godzilla*: A Commentary," *G-Fan* #12 [hereinafter: Roberto, "Commentary"], p. 29.
3. Bill Goodmunson, "The Classical Works of Akira Ifukube," *Japanese Giants* #7 (December, 1985), p. 33.
4. Interview with Akira Ifukube, *G-Fan* #18, November-December 1995, p. 30.
5. Interview with Akira Ifukube, *G-Fan* #18, p. 30–32.
6. Ibid., p. 32–34.
7. Ibid., p. 30.
8. Godziszewski, "Akira Ifukube — A Profile," *G-Fan* #18 [hereinafter: Godziszewski, "Ifukube"] p. 38.
9. Damon Foster, "Live Action Mainly Non-Superhero Sci-Fi of Japan," *Oriental Cinema* #8 (December 1995) p. 22–23.
10. Godziszewski, *The Illustrated Encyclopedia of Godzilla*, p. 84.

11. Interview with Akira Ifukube, *G-Fan* #18, p. 30.
12. Roberto, "Commentary," p. 29.
13. Godziszewski, "Ifukube," p. 38–42.
14. Godziszewski, "The Making of *Godzilla*," p. 39.
15. Tucker, August 18, 1995.
16. Anthony Faiola, "Letter from Japan: Leaving a City Crushed," *The Washington Post*, December 21, 2004, p. C5.
17. Bailey.
18. Robert Biondi and John Rocco Roberto, "Godzilla in America, Part 2," *G-Fan* #11, September-October, 1994 [hereinafter: Biondi and Roberto, "Godzilla in America, Part 2"], p. 20.
19. Bailey.
20. Tsutsui, p. 37.
21. Bailey.

## Chapter 3

1. Interview with Ishiro Honda, *G-Fan* #12, p. 47.
2. Armand Vaquer, "Godzilla: Made in Hollywood," *G-Fan* #68 (Summer 2004) [hereinafter: Vaquer, "Made in Hollywood"], p. 22.
3. Dirk Lammers, "*Star Trek*'s Sulu maintains steady hand on career helm," *The Tampa Tribune*, November 17, 1994, Section: Baylife, p. 1.
4. Galbraith, *Japanese Science Fiction*, p. 17.
5. Kerry Segrave, *Foreign Films in America* (Jefferson NC: McFarland, 2004), p. 3–115.
6. Ibid., p. 142–47.
7. Tim Lucas, "Godzilla 40th Anniversary Special Box, Review," *Video Watchdog* Special Edition #2 (Cincinnati, OH: Tim and Donna Lucas, 1995–96), p. 66.
8. Vaquer, "Made in Hollywood," p. 22.
9. Galbraith, *Japanese Science Fiction*, p. 11.
10. Ibid., p. 347.
11. "Japanese Film Series Opens at Public Today," *The New York Times*, June 22, 1982 [hereinafter: "Japanese Film Series"].
12. *Godzilla, Koenig der Monster*, German DVD edition, Mawa Film & Medien, 2001.
13. Interview with Ishiro Honda, *G-Fan* #12, p. 46.

## Chapter 4

1. Bill Powell, "Who's Sorry Now?" *Newsweek* (July 24, 1995), p. 38–39.
2. David Halberstam, *The Fifties* (New York: Villard Books, 1993), p. 24–48, 330–54.
3. *The Japanese Fishermen*, a 1954 documentary made in England, included on the *Gojira* DVD, BFI, 2004.
4. Kirkup.

## Chapter 5

1. Bailey.
2. Galbraith, *Japanese Science Fiction*, p. 14.
3. Joseph L. Anderson and Donald Richie, *The Japanese Film* (Princeton, NJ: Princeton University Press, 1982), p. 500.
4. Ragone, *Eiji Tsuburaya*, p. 30, 44.
5. Interview with Jun Fukuda, *Cult Movies* #13, 1995, p. 52.
6. Steve Ryfle and Ed Godziszewski, commentary track, *Godzilla Raids Again*, Classic Media, 2005 [hereinafter: Ryfle et al. commentary, *Godzilla Raids Again*].
7. Foster, "In Godzilla We Trust," p. 4.
8. Bill Warren, *Keep Watching the Skies! Volume 2: 1958–1962* (Jefferson NC: McFarland, 1986), p. 106.
9. Robert Skotak, *Ib Melchior: Man of Imagination* (Baltimore: Midnight Marquee Press, 2000), p. 72–73.
10. Ryfle et al. commentary, *Godzilla Raids Again*.
11. Ibid.
12. Godziszewski, *The Illustrated Encyclopedia of Godzilla*, p. 92.
13. Galbraith, *Japanese Science Fiction*, p. 16–17.
14. Ryfle et al. commentary, *Godzilla Raids Again*.

## Chapter 6

1. Galbraith, *Japanese Science Fiction*, p. 25.
2. Richard Lloyd Parry, "The Year of Living Dangerously," *The Independent*, August 6, 1995, p. 4.
3. Galbraith, *Japanese Science Fiction*, p. 25–26.
4. Ono, "Memories of Godzilla," p. 48.
5. Galbraith, *Japanese Science Fiction*, p. 367.
6. Guy Tucker, *Age of the Gods* (Brooklyn, NY: Daikaiju Publishing, 1996) [hereinafter: Tucker, *Age of the Gods*], p. 142–43.
7. Warren, *Vol. 1*, p. 386.

## Chapter 7

1. Ragone, *Eiji Tsuburaya*, p. 55.
2. Tucker, *Age of the Gods*, p. 99.
3. Ibid., p. 102–03.
4. Ibid., p. 104.
5. Ragone, *Eiji Tsuburaya*, p. 55.
6. Galbraith, *Japanese Science Fiction*, p. 43.
7. Ragone, *Eiji Tsuburaya*, p. 55.
8. Tucker, *Age of the Gods*, p. 100–01.
9. Ibid., p. 165.
10. David Kalat, audio commentary on *Ghidrah, The Three-Headed Monster*, Classic Media, 2006 [hereinafter: Kalat commentary, *Ghidrah*].

## Chapter 8

1. Tucker, August 18, 1995.
2. Tucker, *Age of the Gods*, p. 127.
3. Steve Ryfle and Ed Godziszewski, audio commentary on *Mothra vs. Godzilla*, Classic Media, 2006 [hereinafter: Ryfle and Godziszewski commentary, *Mothra vs. Godzilla*].
4. August Ragone, "Toho's Fantasy Femme Fatales," *Kaiju Review* #8, p. 16.
5. Kalat commentary, *Ghidrah*.
6. Galbraith, *Japanese Science Fiction*, p. 71.
7. Diana Rowland, *Japanese Business Etiquette: A Practical Guide to Success with the Japanese* (New York: Warner, 1985), p. 5, 33–35.
8. J.D. Lees, "Trendmasters' Mothra Out," *G-Fan* #15, May-June 1995, p. 5.

## Chapter 9

1. Shapiro, p. 2.
2. Rovin, *Fabulous Fantasy Films*, p. 101–15.
3. Galbraith, *Japanese Science Fiction*, p. 77.
4. Stuart Galbraith IV, commentary to *Invasion of Astro-Monster*, Classic Media, 2006 [hereinafter: Galbraith commentary, *Invasion of Astro-Monster*].

5. Robert Biondi, *"Godzilla vs. Mechagodzilla*: The Filmbook," *G-Fan* #9, May, 1994, p. 19.

6. Interview with Teruyoshi Nakano, *Cult Movies* #12, 1994, p. 57.

7. August Ragone, "Toho vs. Universal International," *Video Watchdog* Special Edition #2, p. 76.

8. Bailey.

## Chapter 10

1. Foster, "In Godzilla We Trust," p. 3.

2. Ed Naha, *Horrors From Screen to Scream* (New York: Avon Books, 1975), p. 171.

3. Shapiro, p. 8.

4. Warren, *Vol. 2*, p. 259.

5. Rovin, *Fabulous Fantasy Films*, p. 107–08.

6. Warren, *Vol. 1*, p. 9.

7. Galbraith, *Japanese Science Fiction*, p. 9.

8. Interview with Teruyoshi Nakano, *Cult Movies* #12, p. 57.

9. Godziszewski, *"The Films of Eiji Tsuburaya*, book review," *G-Fan* #15, May-June, 1995, p. 58.

10. Interview with Henry Saperstein, *G-Fan* #15, p. 44.

11. Don Shay and Jody Duncan, *The Making of Jurassic Park* (New York: Ballantine Books, 1993), p. 15.

12. Interview with Henry Saperstein, *G-Fan* #15, p. 44.

13. Bailey.

14. Interview with Teruyoshi Nakano, *Cult Movies* #12, p. 57.

15. Godziszewski, "The Making of *Godzilla*," p. 38.

16. Jim Danforth, letter to the editor, *Wonder* #10 (Atlanta, GA: Spring 1995), p. 23.

17. Warren, *Vol. 2*, p. 329.

18. Interview with Koichi Kawakita, *Cult Movies* #14, 1995, p. 52.

## Chapter 11

1. Damon Foster, "In Godzilla We Trust," p. 4.

2. Steve Ryfle and Ed Godziszewski, audio commentary to *Mothra vs. Godzilla*, Classic Media, 2006 [hereinafter: Ryfle and Godziszewski commentary, *Mothra vs. Godzilla*].

3. Ibid.

4. Masataka Kosaka, *A History of Postwar Japan* (New York: Kodansha International, 1972), p. 200–09.

5. James L. McCain, *Japan: A Modern History* (New York: W.W. Norton, 2002), p. 520, 571–72.

6. Kalat commentary, *Ghidrah*.

7. Interview with Ishiro Honda, *G-Fan* #12, p. 46–47.

8. Ryfle and Godziszewski commentary, *Mothra vs. Godzilla*.

9. David Milner, "Selling Godzilla," *Cult Movies* #14 [hereinafter: Milner, "Selling Godzilla"], p. 52.

## Chapter 12

1. Ryfle, *Japan's Favorite Mon-Star*, p. 98.

2. Stuart Galbraith IV, personal correspondence with author, May 30, 2007.

3. Ryfle, *Japan's Favorite Mon-Star*, p. 127–28.

4. Stuart Galbraith IV, personal correspondence, April 19, 2006.

5. Ibid.

6. Godziszewski, *Illustrated Encyclopedia*, p. 145.

7. Ibid., p. 154–155.

8. Tucker, *Age of the Gods*, p. 174–75.

9. Ryfle, *Japan's Favorite Mon-Star*, p. 116.

10. Ibid., p. 116–17.

11. Tucker, *Age of the Gods*, p. 176.

12. Robert Biondi and John Rocco Roberto, "Godzilla in America, Part 3," *G-Fan* #13 [hereinafter: Biondi and Roberto, "Godzilla in America"], p. 14.

13. Frank Dello Stritto, "The British 'Ban' on Horror Films of 1937," *Cult Movies* #14, p. 23.

14. Janne Nolan, "When Three Heads Are Better Than … Three Heads," *Bulletin of the Atomic Scientists*, July-August 2000, p. 11.

## Chapter 13

1. William Theodore DeBary et al., *Sources of Japanese Tradition, Volume 2: 1600–2000* (New York: Columbia University Press, 2005), p. 1094.

2. Biondi and Roberto, "Godzilla in America, Part 3," p. 15.

3. Stuart Galbraith IV, commentary to *Invasion of Astro-Monster* DVD, Classic Media, 2006 [hereinafter: Galbraith commentary, *Astro-Monster*].

4. Interview with Henry Saperstein, *G-Fan* #15, p. 44.

5. Galbraith commentary, *Astro-Monster*.

6. Interview with Henry Saperstein, *G-Fan* #15, p. 44.

7. Interview with Akira Kubo, *Cult Movies* #15, 1995, p. 79–81.

8. Tucker, August 18, 1995.

9. Robert Brown, "Monster Zero," *Oriental Cinema* #4, p. 18.

10. Galbraith commentary, *Astro-Monster*.

11. Brown, p. 18.

12. Ibid., p. 18–19.

13. Tucker, August 18, 1995.

14. Interview with Henry Saperstein, *G-Fan* #15, p. 45–46.

15. Galbraith, *Japanese Science Fiction*, p. 118.

16. Biondi and Roberto, "Godzilla in America, Part 3," p. 15.

17. Galbraith, *Japanese Science Fiction*, p. 119.

18. Godziszewski, *The Illustrated Encyclopedia of Godzilla*, p. 83.

## Chapter 14

1. J.D. Lees, "Godzilla Tramples Opponents for Top Spot," *G-Fan* #8, March, 1994 [hereinafter: Lees, "Godzilla Tramples Opponents"], p. 3.

2. Stuart Galbraith, *Monsters Are Attacking Tokyo* (Venice, CA: Feral House, 1998), p. 84.

3. Kalat commentary, *Ghidrah*.

4. Tucker, *Age of the Gods*, p. 157.

5. Galbraith commentary, *Astro-Monster*.

6. Tucker, *Age of the Gods*, p. 138.

7. Ibid., p. 157, 193.

8. Ragone, *Eiji Tsuburaya*, p. 90, 94.

9. "Special announcement" Japanese trailer for *Frankenstein vs. Barugon, Frankenstein Conquers the World* DVD, Media Shock, 2007.

10. Ragone, *Eiji Tsuburaya*, p. 94–95.

11. Galbraith commentary, *Astro-Monster*.

12. Keith Aiken, "King Kong Cartoon Series Guide," scifijapan.com.

## Chapter 15

1. Tucker, *Age of the Gods*, p. 115–20, 157–62.
2. Interview with Fukuda, *Cult Movies* #13, 1995, p. 52.
3. Galbraith, *Japanese Science Fiction*, p. 155–57.
4. Ragone, *Eiji Tsuburaya*, p. 145.
5. Biondi and Roberto, "Godzilla in America, Part 4," p. 14, and J.D. Lees, "Visit to Monsterland," *G-Fan* Special Collection #1, 1994, p. 58.
6. Tucker, *Age of the Gods*, p. 190.
7. Biondi and Roberto, "Godzilla in America, Part 4," p. 14.
8. Ibid., p. 15.
9. Interview with Jun Fukuda, *Cult Movies* #13, p. 52–53.

## Chapter 16

1. John Tulloch and Henry Jenkins, *Science Fiction Audiences: Watching Doctor Who and Star Trek* (New York: Routledge, 1995), p. 213–27.
2. Tucker, *Age of the Gods*, p. 192.
3. Interview with Teruyoshi Nakano, *Cult Movies* #12, p. 56.
4. Galbraith, *Japanese Science Fiction*, p. 153.
5. Ibid., p. 152.
6. Biondi, "The Evolution of Godzilla," p. 28.
7. Galbraith, *Japanese Science Fiction*, p. 163.

## Chapter 17

1. Robert Biondi and John Rocco Roberto, "Godzilla in America, Part 5," *G-Fan* #15 [hereinafter: Biondi and Roberto, "Godzilla in America, Part 5"], p. 20.
2. Biondi and Roberto, "Godzilla in America, Part 5," p. 20.
3. Ibid., p. 21.
4. Milner, "Selling Godzilla," p. 52.
5. Lees, "Godzilla Calendar," p. 21.
6. Tucker, *Age of the Gods*, p. 171.

## Chapter 18

1. Tucker, *Age of the Gods*, p. 204.
2. Biondi and Roberto, "Godzilla in America, Part 5," p. 22.
3. Galbraith, *Japanese Science Fiction*, p. 184–85.
4. Rovin, *Science Fiction Films*, p. 142–43.
5. Ibid., p. 142–43.
6. Masataka Kosaka, *A History of Postwar Japan* (New York: Kodansha International, 1972), p. 250–51.
7. Biondi and Roberto, "Godzilla in America, Part 5," p. 23.
8. Guy Tucker, "*The Defilers*, review," *Cult Movies* #12, p. 10.
9. Biondi and Roberto, "Godzilla in America, Part 5," p. 21–22.
10. Tucker, *Age of the Gods*, p. 205.
11. Galbraith commentary, *Astro-Monster*.
12. Mike Bogue, "Deploy All Monsters," *Wonder* #10, p. 14.

## Chapter 19

1. Interview with Jun Fukuda, *Cult Movies* #13, p. 53.
2. Donald Richie, *A Hundred Years of Japanese Film* (Tokyo: Kodansha International, 2001), p. 177.

3. Tucker, *Age of the Gods*, p. 212.
4. Richie, p. 208–09.
5. Ibid., p. 208–12.
6. Tucker, *Age of the Gods*, p. 214.
7. Lees, "Godzilla Calendar," p. 21.
8. American Cinema: The Film School Generation, 20th Century–Fox, 1995.
9. Tucker, *Age of the Gods*, p. 206–07.
10. Interview with Jun Fukuda, *Cult Movies* #13, p. 53.
11. Ibid., p. 52.
12. Ibid, p. 52.

## Chapter 20

1. Tucker, *Age of the Gods*, p. 212.
2. Brett Homenick, "The Man Who Made Godzilla Fly," *G-Fan* #73, Fall 2005, p. 9.
3. Ibid., p. 9–12.
4. Ibid., p. 12.
5. Interview with Teruyoshi Nakano, *G-Fan* #27, May-June 1997, p. 22.
6. Foster, "Sci-Fi of Japan," p. 22.
7. Interview with Kenpachiro Satsuma, *G-Fan* #17, p. 23–27.
8. Robert Biondi and John Robert Roberto, "Godzilla in America, Part 6," *G-Fan* #16 [hereinafter: Biondi and Roberto, "Godzilla in America, Part 6"], p. 16.
9. Interview with Teruyoshi Nakano, *G-Fan* #27, May-June 1997, p. 23.
10. Lees, "Godzilla Calendar," p. 21.

## Chapter 21

1. Biondi and Roberto, "Godzilla in America, Part 6," p. 16.
2. Ibid.
3. Interview with Jun Fukuda, *Cult Movies* #13, p. 52.
4. Biondi and Roberto, "Godzilla in America, Part 6," p. 16.
5. Biondi, "The Evolution of Godzilla," p. 29.
6. Biondi and Roberto, "Godzilla in America, Part 6," p. 17–18.
7. Lees, "Godzilla Calendar," p. 21.

## Chapter 22

1. Michael Ross, "Godzilla lives!" United Press International, July 11, 1984 [hereinafter: Ross, "Godzilla lives"].
2. Ragone, *Eiji Tsuburaya*, p. 81–85.
3. John Rocco Roberto, "The Lost Godzilla Episodes," *G-Fan* #9 [hereinafter: Roberto, "Lost Episodes"], p. 42.
4. Ibid., p. 42–43.
5. Galbraith, *Japanese Science Fiction*, p. 225.
6. Ross, "Godzilla lives."
7. Ibid.
8. Biondi and Roberto, "Godzilla in America, Part 5," p. 20.
9. Roberto, "Lost Episodes," p. 43.
10. John Marshall, "*Johnny Sokko and His Flying Robot*, A Reflection and an Appreciation," *Cult Movies* #12, p. 72–73.
11. Kevin Grays, "Power Women," *Kaiju Review* #8, p. 32–39, 50–51, and Galbraith, *Japanese Science Fiction*, p. 376–81.

12. Teresa Watanabe, "Just Say It's the 'Power' Source; Pop Culture: For Two Decades, Toei Studios of Japan Has Churned Out Versions of Those Ubiquitous Power Rangers," *The Los Angeles Times*, March 9, 1995, p. E1.

13. Christopher Elam, "Japanese Superheroes (American Style)," *Kaiju Review* #8, p. 52–53.

14. Damon Foster, "*Ryusei Ningen Zone*, review," *Oriental Cinema* #4 [hereinafter, Foster, "*Ryusei Ningen Zone*"], p. 21.

15. Roberto, "Lost Episodes," p. 44.

16. Andre Dubois, panelist, G-Con '95, Radisson Hotel, Arlington Heights, Chicago, IL, August 19, 1995.

17. Biondi, "Lost Episodes," p. 44–46, and Foster, "*Ryusei Ningen Zone*," p. 21–24.

18. Interview with Jun Fukuda, *Cult Movies* #13, p. 53.

## Chapter 23

1. Tucker, *Age of the Gods*, p. 214.

2. Biondi and Roberto, "Godzilla in America, Part 6," p. 19.

3. Galbraith, *Japanese Science Fiction*, p. 213.

4. Ibid.

5. Ibid., p. 212.

6. Biondi and Roberto, "Godzilla in America, Part 6," p. 19.

7. Lees, "Godzilla Calendar," p. 20.

## Chapter 24

1. Tucker, *Age of the Gods*, p. 216.

2. Galbraith, *Japanese Science Fiction*, p. 230–31.

3. August Ragone, "*Godzilla vs. the Cosmic Monster*, review," *Oriental Cinema* #4, p. 16.

4. J.D. Lees, editor's response to letter, *G-Fan* #16, p. 12.

5. Robert Biondi and John Rocco Roberto, "Godzilla in America, Part 7," *G-Fan* #17 [hereinafter: Biondi and Roberto, "Godzilla in America, Part 7"], p. 16.

6. Biondi and Roberto, "Godzilla in America, Part 7," p. 17.

## Chapter 25

1. Tucker, *Age of the Gods*, p. 219–24.

2. Ibid., p. 225.

3. Ibid., p. 226.

4. Interview with Yukiko Takayama, *Cult Movies* #12, p. 59.

5. Tucker, *Age of the Gods*, p. 226.

6. Interview with Yukiko Takayama, *Cult Movies* #12, p. 59.

7. J.D. Lees, "*The Terror of Godzilla*: A Commentary," *G-Fan* #17, p. 21.

8. The history of *Terror of Mechagodzilla*'s various versions was complied from two sources: Shane Dallmann, "*Terror of Mechagodzilla*: A 'Cutting Room Floor' Report," *Video Watchdog* Special #2, 1995/96, p. 87–90, and Robert Biondi with John Rocco Roberto, "Godzilla in America Part 7: Mechagodzilla!" *G-Fan* #17, p. 15–20.

9. Godziszewski, *The Illustrated Encyclopedia of Godzilla*, p. 82.

10. Biondi, "The Evolution of Godzilla," p. 30.

11. Lees, "Godzilla Calendar," p. 21.

12. Bailey.

13. Tucker, *Age of the Gods*, p. 225.

14. Ibid., p. 233–34.

## Chapter 26

1. Ono, "Memories of Godzilla," p. 48.

## Chapter 27

1. Shapiro, p. 76.

2. *Godzilla, King of the Monsters* #10, written by Doug Moench and drawn by Herb Trimpe, Marvel Comics Group, New York, May 1978, p. 2.

3. J.D. Lees, "Godzilla in Comics (The Marvel Years)," *G-Fan* Special Collection #1, p. 8–11.

4. Vernon Scott, "*The Incredible Hulk*, he's big and he's back," United Press International, *Hollywood Reporter*, May 13, 1988.

5. Stan Lee, editor's response to letter, *Godzilla, King of the Monsters* #10, p. 18.

6. Lees, "Godzilla Calendar," p. 41.

7. Mark Evanier and Michael Swanigan, "Remembering Doug Wildey," *Toon Magazine*, Vol. 1, Number 8, Fall, 1995, p. 35–59.

8. Mattel Jones, "Amerigoji x2, Tales of Two Godzillas," *Kaiju Review* #8, p. 9.

9. Jones, p. 9–11.

10. Interview with Dave Stevens, *Cult Movies* #15, p. 56–59.

11. Shapiro, p. 74–76.

12. Peter Guttmacher, *Legendary Horror Films* (Friedman/Fairfax Publishers, New York, 1995), p. 56.

13. Tom Shales, "The Lizard of Flaws," *The Washington Post*, October 1, 1985 [hereinafter: Shales, "Lizard of Flaws"], and Rick Kogan, "Bad Effects, Bad Writing, Bad Godzilla!" *The Chicago Tribune*, September 20, 1985 [hereinafter: Kogan, "Bad Godzilla!"].

14. Wayne Walley, "Giant, rampaging reptile that laid golden egg is 30," *Advertising Age*, March 13, 1986.

15. Shapiro, p. 76.

## Chapter 28

1. Foster, "In Godzilla We Trust," p. 7.

2. Galbraith, *Japanese Science Fiction*, p. 268.

3. Carlson and Gross.

4. Burgess.

5. Rick Kogan, "It was a long time coming, but Godzilla, this is your life," *Chicago Tribune*, Sept. 15, 1985.

6. Tucker, *Age of the Gods*, p. 238.

7. Bailey.

8. Clyde Haberman, "After 9 Years, Godzilla Returns to the Screen," *The New York Times*, December 17, 1984.

9. Tucker, *Age of the Gods*, p. 238.

10. Bailey.

11. Peter Carlson from a report by Neil Gross, "The Return of Godzilla," *People Magazine*, January 14, 1985.

12. Michael Ross, "Godzilla Comes Home for Christmas," United Press International, December 17, 1984.

13. Ed Godziszewski, "*Godzilla*: Commentary," *Japanese Giants* #7 [hereinafter: Godziszewski, "*Godzilla 1985*"], p. 6.

14. Tucker, August 18, 1995.

15. Godziszewski, "*Godzilla 1985*," p. 6.

16. Ross, "Godzilla Comes Home."

17. Burgess.

18. Carlson and Gross.

19. Burgess.

20. Carlson and Gross.

21. Ibid.

22. Interview with Teruyoshi Nakano, *Cult Movies* #12, p. 57.

23. Godziszewski, *"Godzilla 1985,"* p. 8.

24. Ibid., p. 9.

25. Burgess.

26. Godziszewski, *"Godzilla 1985,"* p. 9.

27. Ibid., p. 10.

28. Ross, "Godzilla Comes Home."

29. Carlson and Gross.

30. Bailey.

## Chapter 29

1. Ross, "Godzilla Comes Home."

2. "Japan's Godzillas," *The Economist*, April 11, 1987.

3. Bruce Keppel, "New World Pictures to Acquire Marvel," *The Los Angeles Times*, November 21, 1986.

4. Peter Nulty and Robby Miller, "New World's Boffo B Movie Script," *Fortune*, February 17, 1986.

5. Jack Matthews, "Dr Pepper Bubbles Up to Godzilla," *The Los Angeles Times*, August 2, 1985.

6. Galbraith, *Japanese Science Fiction*, p. 349.

7. Walley.

8. Charles Leerhsen and Susan Katz with Barbara Burgower and David Lewis, "Going Gaga for Godzilla," *Newsweek*, July 28, 1986.

9. Joshua Hyatt, "Nice Girls Don't Explode," *Inc.*, May 1988.

10. Kogan, "This Is Your Life."

11. Tom Shales, "Raymond Burr, Back on Appeal," *The Washington Post*, May 23, 1986 [hereinafter: Shales, "Raymond Burr"].

12. Michael Hill, *"Perry Mason Returns* with Nostalgic Appeal," *The Washington Post*, December 1, 1985.

13. R.J. Kizer, letter to the editor, *Video Watchdog* #34, 1996, p. 78–80.

14. Brett Homenick, "Urban Renewal: The Americanization of Godzilla 1985," *G-Fan* #80, Summer 2007, p. 48.

15. Linda Seig, "Godzilla Returns, But with Political Overtones," Reuters, January 11, 1985 [hereinafter: Seig, "Godzilla Returns"].

16. Seig, "Godzilla Returns."

17. Anthony Enns, "The Mutated Flowers of Hiroshima," *Popular Culture Review*, Vol. 12, #2, Las Vegas: University of Nevada, August 2001, p. 41.

18. Kizer, p. 78–79.

19. Homenick, "Urban Renewal," p. 49.

20. Galbraith, *Japanese Science Fiction*, p. 269.

21. Nulty and Miller.

22. Shales, "Raymond Burr."

23. Walley.

24. Nulty and Miller.

25. Ibid.

26. Shales, "The Lizard of Flaws."

27. Hill.

28. Kogan, "Bad Godzilla."

29. Bruce Williamson, *"Godzilla 1985,"* *Playboy*, December, 1985.

30. *"Godzilla 1985,"* Cineman Movie Reviews, December 31, 1985.

31. Doug Mason, "Godzilla? Yup, break out the pasta," *The Chicago Tribune*, November 12, 1986.

32. "Japanese Film Series."

33. Tom Shales, "The Washington Post critics choose their favorite shows of the week," *The Washington Post*, October 3, 1982.

34. Ronald Grover and Keith Hammonds, "High Drama from the Folks Who Brought You *Godzilla '85,"*

*Business Week*, September 17, 1987, and Denise Gellene, "New World Pictures May Scrap Kenner-Parker Bid," *The Los Angeles Times*, July 29, 1987, and Bruce Keppel, "New World Pictures To Acquire Marvel," *The Los Angeles Times*, November 21, 1986.

35. Shales, "The Lizard of Flaws," and Kogan, "This Is Your Life," and Burgess.

36. Galbraith, *Japanese Science Fiction*, p. 270.

## Chapter 30

1. Godziszewski, *"Godzilla vs. Biollante,"* *Japanese Giants* #8, Spring, 1994 [hereinafter: Godziszewski, *"Biollante"*], p. 16.

2. Galbraith, *Japanese Science Fiction*, p. 77.

3. Interview with Honda, *G-Fan* #12, p. 47.

4. Bailey.

5. Brett Homenick, "The Man Who Revived Godzilla," *G-Fan* #78, Winter 2007, p. 34–36.

6. Haberman.

7. Tim Lucas, "Godzilla Regained: Toho's New Sequels," *Video Watchdog* Special #2 [hereinafter: Lucas, "Godzilla Regained"], p. 106.

8. Bailey.

9. Interview with Koichi Kawakita, *Cult Movies* #14, p. 51.

10. Godziszewski, *"Biollante,"* p. 18.

11. Interview with Koichi Kawakita, *Cult Movies* #14, p. 51.

12. Godziszewski, *"Biollante,"* p. 7–39.

13. Bailey.

14. Interview with Kenpachiro Satsuma, *Japanese Giants* #8, p. 20.

15. Godziszewski, *"Biollante,"* p. 18–19.

16. Ibid., p. 21–38.

17. Interview with Koichi Kawakita, *Cult Movies* #14, p. 51.

18. Godziszewski, *"Biollante,"* p. 21–38.

19. Interview with Kenpachiro Satsuma, *G-Fan* #17, p. 26.

20. Interview with Kenpachiro Satsuma, *Japanese Giants* #8, p. 20.

21. Godziszewski, *"Biollante,"* p. 29–39.

22. Ibid., p. 39.

23. Martin Kasindorf, "The report from Cannes," *Newsday*, May 21, 1990.

24. James Ulmer, "Japanese find MIFED lacking," *The Hollywood Reporter*, October 23, 1991.

## Chapter 31

1. Godziszewski, *The Illustrated Encyclopedia of Godzilla*, p. 169.

2. J.D. Lees, *"Mothra vs. Bagan,"* *G-Fan* Special Collection #1 [hereinafter: Lees, *"Mothra vs. Bagan"*], p. 30.

3. Tucker, August 18, 1995.

4. Godziszewski, *"Biollante,"* p. 39.

5. Brett Homenick, "The Man Who Revived Godzilla," *G-Fan* #78, Winter 2007, p. 35.

6. "Godzilla's Revenge," editorial, *The Washington Times*, November 30, 1990.

7. Jay Majer, "Toho's Monsters Speak Out," *Cult Movies* #7, 1993, p. 57.

8. Homenick, "The Man Who Revived Godzilla," p. 38–39.

9. Lees, "Godzilla Calendar," p. 21.

## Chapter 32

1. Lucas, "Godzilla Regained," p. 118.
2. Information compiled by Nawan Bailey and Koji Ichinomiya, "*Godzilla vs. Mothra* Biographical Sketches," *Cult Movies* #7 [hereinafter: Bailey and Ichinomiya, "Biographical Sketches"], p. 51.
3. David Milner, "*Godzilla vs. Mothra*: Godzilla lands in Hollywood a little sooner than expected," *Cult Movies* #7, p. 49.
4. Interview with Takao Okawara, *Cult Movies* #13, p. 54.
5. Lucas, "Godzilla Regained," p. 119.
6. Bailey and Ichinomiya, "Biographical Sketches," p. 51.
7. Ibid.
8. Interview with Takao Okawara, *Cult Movies* #13, p. 54.
9. Interview with Koichi Kawakita, *Cult Movies* #14, p. 51.
10. Interview with Takao Okawara, *Cult Movies* #13, p. 55.
11. Ibid., p. 54.
12. Bailey and Ichinomiya, "Biographical Sketches," p. 51.
13. Ibid.
14. Interview with Kenpachiro Satsuma, *Cult Movies* #12, p. 58.
15. Godziszewski, *The Illustrated Encyclopedia of Godzilla*, p. 79.
16. Biondi, "The Evolution of Godzilla," p. 32.
17. Anecdote related by Ed Godziszewski at G-Con '94, included in article by Robert Biondi, "The Evolution of Godzilla," p. 32.
18. Television news report included in Godzilla soundtrack compilation broadcast on *The Mouldy Fig*, with guest Godzilla expert Bill Worrell, WFHB 91.3 FM, Bloomington, Indiana, 6:00 pm, September 23, 1995.
19. Anecdote related by Ed Godziszewski at G-Con '94, included in article by Robert Biondi, "The Evolution of Godzilla," p. 32.
20. August Ragone, "The unused ending for *Godzilla vs. Mothra*," *G-Fan* #11, p. 41.
21. Godziszewski, "*Biollante*," p. 16.
22. Galbraith, *Japanese Science Fiction*, p. 354.
23. Lees, "Godzilla Tramples Opponents," p. 3.
24. Karl Schoenberger, "Japanese Film: The Sinking Sun," *The Los Angeles Times*, April 4, 1990.
25. Ushio. AUTHOR: WHO'S USHIO?
26. Frank Segers, "Hunt for Bright Spots After a Year of Struggle," *Variety*, September 27, 1993.
27. Schoenberger.
28. Ushio.
29. Michelle Magee, "Coming soon: another foreign film," *The Nikkei Weekly*, March 7, 1992.
30. Gale Eisenstodt, "A cozy Japanese near monopoly," *Forbes*, September 30, 1991.
31. Magee.
32. "Rex, Down," *The Economist*, July 24, 1993.
33. Ushio.
34. Segers.
35. Lees, "Godzilla Tramples Opponents," p. 3.
36. Segers.

## Chapter 33

1. Interview with Terry Rossio, *G-Fan* #9, p. 24.
2. Tom Weaver, *Interviews with B Science Fiction and Horror Movie Makers* (McFarland, Jefferson, NC, 1988), p. 21–22.
3. Interview with Ishiro Honda, *G-Fan* #12, p. 46.
4. Whit Fisher, letter to the editor, *G-Fan* #11, p. 12.
5. Bailey.
6. Appearances of Toho monsters on *Animaniacs* documented by John Rocco Roberto in "Godzilla Spotted on *Animaniacs*, Again!" *G-Fan* #8, and Roberto, "Godzilla Meets the Warner Brothers (and their sister, Dot)," *G-Fan* Special Collection #1, p. 31.
7. Bob Mondello, *All Things Considered*, broadcast on National Public Radio, July 5, 1993.
8. "On Screen," *The St. Petersburg Times*, December 20, 1992 [hereinafter: "On Screen"].
9. Godziszewski, "*Biollante*," p. 40–43.
10. Reprinted in *G-Fan* #11, p. 44. [NOTE: Letter as printed in *G-Fan* contains many spelling errors and misprints which have been corrected here, although grammatical errors and punctuation errors remain.]
11. J.D. Lees, "TriStar Godzilla lives!" *G-Fan* #9, p. 3.
12. Interview with Terry Rossio, *G-Fan* #9, p. 24.
13. Jones, p. 4–9.
14. Bailey.
15. Mason.
16. Interview with Terry Rossio, *G-Fan* #9, p. 24.
17. Bailey.
18. J.D. Lees, "Koichi Kawakita: Master of Monsters," *G-Fan* #8, p. 31.
19. Interview with Teruyoshi Nakano, *Cult Movies* #12, p. 57.
20. Interview with Jun Fukuda, *Cult Movies* #13, p. 53.
21. Interview with Akira Kubo, *Cult Movies* #15, p. 81.
22. Interview with Kenshou Yamashita, *Cult Movies* #14, p. 50.
23. "On Screen."
24. Galbraith, *Japanese Science Fiction*, p. 297.
25. Robert Biondi, "*Godzilla 6*: What's Next?" *G-Fan* #7 [hereinafter: Biondi, "What's Next?"], p. 40.
26. Bailey, emphasis added.
27. J.D. Lees, "TriStar Godzilla Details Revealed," *G-Fan* #12 [hereinafter: Lees, "Details Revealed"] p. 3.
28. J.D. Lees, "Godzilla back 'in development,'" *G-Fan* #14 [hereinafter: Lees, "Back in development"], p. 4.
29. Lees, "Back in development," p. 4, and Lees, "Details Revealed," p. 3.
30. Lees, "Back in development," p. 4.

## Chapter 34

1. Lucas, "Godzilla Regained," p. 104–29.
2. Roberto, "In Memory," p. 45.
3. Interview with Jun Fukuda, *Cult Movies* #13, p. 52.
4. Interview with Takao Okawara, *Cult Movies* #13, p. 54.
5. Magee.
6. Robert Biondi, "*Godzilla vs. Mechagodzilla*, CAV Box Set, review," *G-Fan* #14 [hereinafter: Biondi, "CAV Box Set"], p. 55.
7. Biondi, "The Evolution of Godzilla," p. 24–33.
8. Biondi, "CAV Box Set," p. 55.
9. J.D. Lees, "Designs on Mechagodzilla," *G-Fan* #8, p. 24.
10. Robert Biondi, "*Godzilla vs. Mechagodzilla*: A Filmbook," *G-Fan* #9, p. 5.
11. Interview with Kenpachiro Satsuma, *G-Fan* #17, p. 27.
12. Interview with Wataru Mimura, *Cult Movies* #16, p. 51.

13. Biondi, "CAV Box Set," p. 56.
14. Ibid.
15. Biondi, "What's Next?" p. 40.
16. J.D. Lees, "*Bouken Gojiland* for kids, and foreign Goji-lovers," *G-Fan* #8, p. 46.
17. Hiroshi Nakamura and Robert Biondi, "Visiting Monster Planet of Godzilla," *G-Fan* #13, p. 56–57.

## Chapter 35

1. Hikari Takeda, "The Otaku View '95," *G-Fan* #13, p. 5.
2. Interview with Kenshou Yamashita, *Cult Movies* #14, p. 50.
3. Ibid., p. 49.
4. "Dubious Achievement Awards," *Esquire*, Vol. 123 Number 1, January 1995, p. 35.
5. Interview with Kenshou Yamashita, *Cult Movies* #14, p. 49.
6. Ibid.
7. Tucker, August 18, 1995.
8. John Rocco Roberto, "*Godzilla vs. Space Godzilla*, soundtrack album, review," *G-Fan* #15, p. 57.
9. Interview with Kenpachiro Satsuma, *G-Fan* #17, p. 27
10. Interview with Kenshou Yamashita, *Cult Movies* #14, p. 49.
11. Ibid.
12. J.D. Lees, "*Space Godzilla* Doing Brisk Business," *G-Fan* #13 [hereinafter: Lees, "Brisk Business"], p. 3.
13. David Milner, "*Godzilla vs. Space Godzilla*, Toho provides a fresh look at Godzilla on his 40th birthday," *Cult Movies* #14, p. 48.
14. Interview with Kenpachiro Satsuma, *Cult Movies* #12, p. 58.
15. Foster, "In Godzilla We Trust," p. 7.
16. J.D. Lees, "*Godzilla 7* Plan Still Under Wraps," *G-Fan* #14 [hereinafter: Lees, "*Godzilla 7*"], p. 5.
17. Lees, "Brisk Business," p. 3.
18. J.D. Lees, "*Space Godzilla* draws mixed reviews," *G-Fan* #13, p. 5.
19. Galbraith, *Japanese Science Fiction* p. 300–13.
20. Interview with Shinji Higuchi, *Cult Movies* #15, p. 78.
21. Diane and Dan Reed, "Kaiju Buzz Notes," *Kaiju Review* #8, p. 3.
22. Todd McCarthy, "*Gamera: Guardian of the Universe*," *Variety*, September 4–10, 1995 [hereinafter: McCarthy, "*Gamera*"], p. 77.
23. Jon Lewis and Mike Keller, "*Gamera* hits Indonesia, Texas, Cannes," *G-Fan* #16, p. 7.
24. McCarthy, "*Gamera*," p. 77.
25. "Tokyo's mightiest turtle wages war in the air," *The Mainichi Daily News*, April 7, 1995, p. 9.
26. Lees, "*Godzilla 7*," p. 5.

## Chapter 36

1. James Steingold, "National Ids: Does Japan Still Need its Scary Monster?" *The New York Times*, July 23, 1995, Week in Review, p. 1.
2. Evan Thomas, "Why We Did It," *Newsweek*, July 24, 1995, p. 22–23.
3. Yomiuri Shimbun, "Godzilla promoting Tokyo waterfront development," *The Daily Yomiuri*, November 2, 1995, p. 3.
4. J.D. Lees, "Boffo Box Office," *G-Fan* #21, May–June 1996, p. 4.

5. Biondi, "What's Next?" p. 40.
6. Interview with Koichi Kawakita, *Cult Movies* #14, p. 51.
7. Interview with Takao Okawara, *Cult Movies* #18, 1996, p. 68.
8. Steingold, p. 1.
9. J.D. Lees, "Kawakita says 'Sayonara!,'" *G-Fan* #18, p. 7.
10. Robert Guest, "Monstrous protest as Godzilla is killed off," *The Daily Telegraph*, December 12, 1995, p. 15.
11. Bill Hemmer, anchor, and May Lee, correspondent, "Godzilla goes out with strong anti–nuclear message," CNN, 5:59 am EST, December 1, 1995.
12. Linda Seig, "Japan's Godzilla Faces Extinction — Maybe," The Reuters Asia-Pacific Business Report, December 8, 1995 [hereinafter: Seig, "Japan's Godzilla"].
13. Seig, "Japan's Godzilla."
14. "Godzilla Meets Final Fate," *The Sun–Sentinel* (Fort Lauderdale), December 10, 1995, p. 2A.
15. Guest, p. 15.
16. Seig, "Japan's Godzilla."
17. John Layman, "At 41, one of the biggest actors of our time is dead," *The San Diego Union-Tribune*, December 10, 1995, p. E1.
18. "A star is destroyed," *The Financial Times*, December 11, 1995, p. 19.
19. Panel discussion, August 19, 1995.

## Chapter 37

1. Anthony Timpone, editor, *Godzilla, The Official Movie Magazine*, Starlog Group, 1998 (hereinafter, *Official Movie Magazine*), p. 27.
2. Danny DeAngelo, "Godzilla in Comics," *G-Fan* #53, 2001, p. 28.
3. J.D. Lees, "Godzilla misses TriStar's target," *G-Fan* #33, May-June 1998, p. 5.
4. Chris Nashawaty, "Stomp the World I Want To Get Off," *Entertainment Weekly* #433, May 22, 1998 [hereinafter *Entertainment Weekly*], p. 26.
5. "Jan de Bont on Godzilla," interview, *G-Fan* #42, November-December 1999, p. 53.
6. *Entertainment Weekly*, p. 28.
7. "Jan de Bont on Godzilla," interview, p. 53.
8. *Entertainment Weekly*, p. 28.
9. *Official Movie Magazine*, p. 28.
10. Ibid., p. 25.
11. Kevin H. Martin, "The Sound and the Fury," *Cinefex* #74, July 1998, p. 86.
12. Interview with Patrick Tatopoulos, *G-Fan* #39, May-June 1999, p. 12.
13. Sam Stall, "Green Machine," *America West Airline Magazine*, May 1998, p. 103.
14. *Official Movie Magazine*, p. 25
15. Dave Rogers, *The Complete Avengers* (London, Boxtree Publishing, 1989), p. 12.
16. *Official Movie Magazine*, p. 25.
17. Clark Collis and John Patterson, "Nearly Godzilla," *The Face* #16, May 1998, p. 139.
18. Collis and Patterson, p. 139.
19. Corie Brown, "The Lizard Was a Turkey," *Newsweek*.
20. Kirk Honeycutt "Wide tracks of Godzilla on path to holiday mark," *The Hollywood Reporter*, April 15, 1998, p. 8–9.
21. Honeycutt, p. 8–9.
22. Sharon Waxman, "Endangered Species?" *The Washington Post*, May 19, 1998, p. D9.

23. *Entertainment Weekly*, p. 25.
24. Robert Brown, "Monster Zero," *Oriental Cinema* Issue #4, p. 18.
25. Honeycutt, p. 8
26. Waxman, p. D9.

## Chapter 38

1. *Official Movie Magazine*, p. 26.
2. Interview with Dean Devlin, *G-Fan* #39, May-June 1999, p. 12.
3. Bob Johnson, "Godzilla: The Series," *G-Fan* #44, March-April 2000, p. 9–11.
4. Interview with Dean Devlin, p. 12.

## Chapter 39

1. J.D. Lees, "Millennium Goji Revealed," *G-Fan* #40, July-August 1999 [hereinafter: "Millennium Goji Revealed"], p. 4.
2. "Millennium Goji Revealed," p. 51.
3. "New Toho Godzilla for '99," *G-Fan* #37, January-February 1999.
4. Dean Devlin interview, p. 12.
5. "Millennium Goji Revealed," p. 4.
6. Interview with Shogo Tomiyama, *G-Fan* #55, 2002, p. 17.
7. Interview with Shinichi Wakasa, *G-Fan* #53, 2001, p. 43–44.
8. J.D. Lees, "Godzilla 2000," *G-Fan* #46, July-August 2000 [hereinafter Godzilla 2000] p. 19.
9. Michael Szczepanski, "Making *Godzilla 2000*," *G-Fan* #51, 2001, p. 7.
10. Godzilla 2000, p. 18.
11. Godzilla 2000, p. 16.
12. Godzilla 2000, p. 17.
13. Bob Johnson, "Godzilla Wrangler," *G-Fan* #48, November-December 2000, p. 18.
14. Ibid., p. 19.
15. Ibid.
16. J.D. Lees, "*Godzilla 2000* Review," *G-Fan* #47, September-October 2000, p. 7.
17. "Godzilla Wrangler," p. 19.

## Chapter 40

1. Personal correspondence with senior staff at Sony.
2. Ed Godziszewski, "The Comeback Kaiju," *G-Fan* #49, 2001, p. 6.
3. Michael Szczepanski, "Stoking the Savage Beast," *G-Fan* #65, November-December 2003, p. 26.
4. Ibid., p. 6.
5. Conversation between Masaaki Tezuka and Wataru Mimura, transcribed at www.henshinonline.com/tezuka-mimura.html.
6. Michael Szczepanski, "Godzilla Inside Out," *G-Fan* #52, 2001, p. 10–11.
7. "The Comeback Kaiju," p. 12.

## Chapter 41

1. Interview with Shogo Tomiyama, *G-Fan* #55, 2002, p. 17.
2. www.shusuke-kaneko.com.
3. Steve Ryfle, "Guardian of Gamera's Universe," *G-Fan* #40, July-August 1999, p. 40.
4. www.shusuke-kaneko.com.

5. www.shusuke-kaneko.com.
6. For more information on the J-Horror genre and its history, consult my book *J-Horror: The Definitive Guide to The Ring, The Grudge, and Beyond* (New York: Vertical, 2007).
7. www.shusuke-kaneko.com.
8. J.D. Lees, "Happy 25th, Big Guy," *G-Fan* #55, p. 11–12.
9. www.shusuke-kaneko.com.
10. J.D. Lees, "GMK staff fresh, yet experienced," *G-Fan* #51, 2001, p. 5.
11. www.shusuke-kaneko.com.
12. Ragone, *Eiji Tsuburaya*, p. 183.
13. www.shusuke-kaneko.com.
14. "Happy 25th, Big Guy," p. 6, 15.
15. Personal correspondence with senior staff at Sony.

## Chapter 42

1. Conversation between Masaaki Tezuka and Wataru Mimura, transcribed at www.henshinonline.com/tezuka-mimura.html.
2. E! promotional video for TriStar's *Godzilla*, May 19, 1998.
3. Conversation between Masaaki Tezuka and Wataru Mimura transcribed at www.henshinonline.com/tezuka-mimura.html.
4. Ken Hulsey, from robojapan.blogspot.com/2008/05/Godzilla-x-mechagodzilla-2002toho.html.
5. Conversation between Masaaki Tezuka and Wataru Mimura transcribed at www.henshinonline/tezuka-mimura.html.
6. "Stoking the Savage Beast," p. 27.
7. www.tohokingdom.com.

## Chapter 43

1. www.tohokingdom.com.

## Chapter 44

1. J.D. Lees and Armand Vaquer, "The End of Godzilla," *G-Fan* #71, Spring 2005, p. 37.
2. David Kalat, *J-Horror: The Definitive Guide to The Ring, The Grudge, and Beyond*, Vertical Inc, 2007, p. 245–246.
3. Tom Mes, Interview with Ryuhei Kitamura, www.midnighteye.com, May 17, 2004.
4. Mes.
5. Kenji Hall, "Goodbye Godzilla," Associated Press, March 4, 2004.
6. Mark Schaefer, "Godzilla Stomps Into Los Angeles," www.pennyblood.com.
7. Interview with Shogo Tomiyama, p. 17.
8. Schaefer.
9. Ibid.
10. Ibid.
11. Armand Vaquer, "Godzilla Raids Again," *G-Fan* #71, Spring 2005, p. 5–7.
12. Personal correspondence with senior staff at Sony.
13. www.tohokingdom.com.
14. *G-Fan* #80, Summer 2007, p. 31.
15. www.imdb.com, www.amazon.com and www.netflix.com rankings were taken as of May 2009.
16. Anthony Faiola, "Leaving a City Crushed," *The Washington Post*, December 21, 2004, p. C-5.
17. "Banno announces 3D G-project," *G-Fan* #72, Summer 2005, p. 4.

# Bibliography

## Books

Anderson, Joseph L., and Donald Richie. *The Japanese Film* (Princeton, NJ: Princeton University Press, 1982).

DeBary, William Theodore, et al. *Sources of Japanese Tradition, Volume 2: 1600–2000* (New York: Columbia University Press, 2005).

Galbraith, Stuart, IV. *Japanese Science Fiction, Fantasy and Horror Films* (Jefferson NC: McFarland, 1994).

_____. *Monsters Are Attacking Tokyo* (Venice, CA: Feral House, 1998).

Godziszewski, Ed. *The Illustrated Encyclopedia of Godzilla* (Steinbach, Manitoba: Canada: Ed Godziszewski, 1996).

Guttmacher, Peter. *Legendary Horror Films* (New York: Friedman/Fairfax, 1995).

Halberstam, David. *The Fifties* (New York: Villard Books, 1993).

Kalat, David. *J-Horror: The Definitive Guide to The Ring, The Grudge, and Beyond* (New York: Vertical, 2007).

Kosaka, Masataka. *A History of Postwar Japan* (New York: Kodansha International, 1972).

McCain, James L. *Japan: A Modern History* (New York: W.W. Norton, 2002).

Naha, Ed. *Horrors from Screen to Scream* (New York: Avon Books, 1975).

Ragone, August. *Eiji Tsuburaya: Master of Monsters* (San Francisco: Chronicle Books, 2007).

Richie, Donald. *A Hundred Years of Japanese Film* (Tokyo: Kodansha International, 2001).

Rovin, Jeff. *Fabulous Fantasy Films* (Cranbury, NJ: A.S. Barnes, 1977).

Ryfle, Steve. *Japan's Favorite Mon-Star: The Unauthorized Biography of the Big G* (Toronto: ECW Press, 1998).

Segrave, Kerry. *Foreign Films in America* (Jefferson, NC: McFarland, 2004).

Skotak, Robert. *Ib Melchior: Man of Imagination* (Baltimore: Midnight Marquee Press, 2000).

Tsutsui, William. *Godzilla on My Mind* (New York: Palgrave Macmillan, 2004).

Tucker, Guy Mariner. *Age of the Gods* (Brooklyn: Daikaiju Publishing, 1996).

Warren, Bill. *Keep Watching the Skies! Volume 1: 1950–1957* (Jefferson, NC: McFarland, 1982).

_____. *Keep Watching the Skies! Volume 2: 1958–1962* (Jefferson, NC: McFarland, 1986).

Weaver, Tom. *Interviews with B Science Fiction and Horror Movie Makers* (Jefferson, NC: McFarland, 1988).

## Magazines

*Cinefantastique*: defunct, published by Frederick Clarke, Forest Park, Illinois.

*Cinefex*: quarterly, published by Don Shay, Riverside, California.

*Cult Movies*: defunct, published by Cult Movies, Hollywood, California.

*Entertainment Weekly*: weekly, published by Time, Inc., New York, New York.

*G-Fan*: quarterly, published by Daikaiju Enterprises Ltd., Steinbach, Manitoba, Canada.

*Japanese Giants*: defunct, published by Happy Enterprises, Chicago, Illinois.

*Oriental Cinema*: defunct, published by Damon Foster and Hugh Gallagher, Centralia, Illinois.

*Video Watchdog*: published by Tim and Donna Lucas, Cincinnati, Ohio.

## Interviews

de Bont, Jan: *G-Fan* no. 42.

Devlin, Dean: *G-Fan* no. 39.

Fukuda, Jun: *Cult Movies* no. 13.

Higuchi, Shinji: *Cult Movies* no. 15.

Honda, Ishiro: *G-Fan* no. 12.

Honda, Kimi: *Cult Movies* no. 16.

Ifukube, Akira: *G-Fan* no. 18.

Kawakita, Koichi: *Cult Movies* no. 14.

Kubo, Akira: *Cult Movies* no. 15.

Mimura, Wataru: *Cult Movies* no. 16.

Nakajima, Haruo: *G-Fan* no. 22.

Nakano, Teruyoshi: *Cult Movies* no. 12 and *G-Fan* no. 27.

Okawara, Takao: *Cult Movies* no. 13 and *Cult Movies* no. 18.

Ryuhei Kitamura, Ryuhei: www.midnighteye.com.

Saperstein, Henry: *G-Fan* no. 15.

Satsuma, Kenpachiro: *Cult Movies* no. 12, *G-Fan* no. 17 and *Japanese Giants* no. 8.

Stradley, Randy and Bob Eggleton: *G-Fan* no. 17.

Takayama, Yukiko: *Cult Movies* no. 12.

Tatopoulos, Patrick: *G-Fan* no. 39.

Tezuka, Masaaki, and Wataru Mimura: www.henshinonline/tezuka-mimura.html.

Tomiyama, Shogo: *G-Fan* no. 55.
Wakasa, Shinichi: *G-Fan* no. 53.
Yamashita, Kenshou: *Cult Movies* no. 14.


## News Articles

Bailey, Jim. "Your City Could Be Next." *Asiaweek*, December 21–28, 1994.

Brown, Robert. "Monster Zero." *Oriental Cinema*, Issue #4, p. 18 (n.d.).

Burgess, John. "Godzilla Rises Again." *The Washington Post*, December 19, 1984.

Carlson, Peter, from a report by Neil Gross. "The Return of Godzilla." *People Magazine*, January 14, 1985.

Chapman, William. "Kurosawa's Comeback: A Samurai Spectacular." *The Washington Post*, April 20, 1980.

Eisenstodt, Gale. "A cozy Japanese near monopoly." *Forbes*, September 30, 1991.

Faiola, Anthony. "Leaving a City Crushed." *The Washington Post*, December 21, 2004.

Gellene, Denise. "New World Pictures May Scrap Kenner-Parker Bid." *The Los Angeles Times*, July 29, 1987.

"Godzilla Meets Final Fate." *The Sun–Sentinel* (Fort Lauderdale), December 10, 1995.

"Godzilla's Revenge." Editorial, *The Washington Times*, November 30, 1990.

Grover, Ronald, and Keith Hammonds. "High Drama From the Folks Who Brought You *Godzilla '85*." *Business Week*, September 17, 1987.

Guest, Robert. "Monstrous protest as Godzilla is killed off." *The Daily Telegraph*, December 12, 1995.

Haberman, Clyde. "After 9 Years, Godzilla Returns to the Screen." *The New York Times*, December 17, 1984.

Hall, Kenji. "Goodbye Godzilla." Associated Press, March 4, 2004.

Hemmer, Bill, and May Lee. "Godzilla goes out with strong anti-nuclear message." CNN, December 1, 1995.

Hill, Michael. "*Perry Mason Returns* with Nostalgic Appeal." *The Washington Post*, December 1, 1985.

Honeycutt, Kirk. "Wide tracks of Godzilla on path to holiday mark." *The Hollywood Reporter*, April 15, 1998.

Hyatt, Joshua. "Nice Girls Don't Explode." *Inc.*, May 1988.

"Japanese Film Series Opens at Public Today." *The New York Times*, June 22, 1982.

"Japan's Godzillas." *The Economist*, April 11, 1987.

Kasindorf, Martin. "The report from Cannes." *Newsday*, May 21, 1990.

Keppel, Bruce. "New World Pictures To Acquire Marvel." *The Los Angeles Times*, November 21, 1986.

Kirkup, James. "Obituary: Ishiro Honda." *The Independent*, March 3, 1993.

Kogan, Rick. "Bad Effects, Bad Writing, Bad Godzilla!" *The Chicago Tribune*, September 20, 1985.

Kogan, Rick. "It was a long time coming, but Godzilla, this is your life." *The Chicago Tribune*, September 15, 1985.

Lammers, Dirk. "*Star Trek*'s Sulu maintains steady hand on career helm." *The Tampa Tribune*, November 17, 1994.

Layman, John. "At 41, one of the biggest actors of our time is dead." *The San Diego Union-Tribune*, December 10, 1995.

Leerhsen, Charles, and Susan Katz with Barbara Burgower and David Lewis. "Going Gaga for Godzilla." *Newsweek*, July 28, 1986.

Magee, Michael. "Coming soon: another foreign film." *The Nikkei Weekly*, March 7, 1992.

Mason, Doug. "Godzilla? Yup, break out the pasta." *The Chicago Tribune*, November 12, 1986.

Matthews, Jack. "Dr Pepper Bubbles Up to Godzilla." *The Los Angeles Times*, August 2, 1985.

McCarthy, Todd. "*Gamera: Guardian of the Universe*." *Variety*, September 4–10, 1995.

Nolan, Janne. "When Three Heads Are Better Than ... Three Heads." *Bulletin of the Atomic Scientists*, July/August 2000.

Nulty, Peter, and Robby Miller. "New World's Boffo B Movie Script." *Fortune*, February 17, 1986.

Parry, Richard Lloyd. "The Year of Living Dangerously." *The Independent*, August 6, 1995.

Powell, Bill. "Who's Sorry Now?" *Newsweek*, July 24, 1995.

"Rex, Down." *The Economist*, July 24, 1993.

Ross, Michael. "Godzilla Comes Home for Christmas." United Press International, December 17, 1984.

Schaefer, Mark. "Godzilla Stomps Into Los Angeles." www.pennyblood.com.

Schoenberger, Karl. "Japanese Film: The Sinking Sun." *The Los Angeles Times*, April 4, 1990.

Segers, Frank. "Hunt For Bright Spots After A Year of Struggle." *Variety*, September 27, 1993.

Seig, Linda. "Japan's Godzilla Faces Extinction-Maybe." *The Reuters Asia-Pacific Business Report*, December 8, 1995.

Shales, Tom. "The Lizard of Flaws." *The Washington Post*, October 1, 1985.

_____. "Raymond Burr, Back on Appeal." *The Washington Post*, May 23, 1986.

Shimbun, Yomiuri. "Godzilla promoting Tokyo waterfront development." *The Daily Yomiuri*, November 2, 1995.

"A Star Is Destroyed." *The Financial Times*, December 11, 1995.

Steingold, James. "National Ids: Does Japan Still Need its Scary Monster?" *The New York Times*, July 23, 1995, Week in Review.

Thomas, Evan. "Why We Did It." *Newsweek*, July 24, 1995.

"Tokyo's mightiest turtle wages war in the air." *The Mainichi Daily News*, April 7, 1995.

Ulmer, James. "Japanese find MIFED lacking." *The Hollywood Reporter*, October 23, 1991.

Walley, Wayne. "Giant, rampaging reptile that laid golden egg is 30." *Advertising Age*, March 13, 1986.

Watanabe, Teresa. "Just Say It's the 'Power' Source; Pop Culture: For Two Decades, Toei Studios of Japan Has Churned Out Versions of Those Ubiquitous Power Rangers." *The Los Angeles Times*, March 9, 1995.

Waxman, Sharon. "Endangered Species?" *The Washington Post*, May 19, 1998.

Williamson, Bruce. "*Godzilla 1985.*" *Playboy*, December, 1985.

# Index